The World Colored
Heavyweight Championship,
1876–1937

The World Colored Heavyweight Championship, 1876–1937

Mark Allen Baker

McFarland & Company, Inc., Publishers
Jefferson, North Carolina

ISBN (print) 978-1-4766-7765-1
ISBN (ebook) 978-1-4766-3987-1

LIBRARY OF CONGRESS AND BRITISH LIBRARY
CATALOGUING DATA ARE AVAILABLE

Library of Congress Control Number 2020031351

On the cover: George Godfrey (left) sparring
with Jack Johnson (Library of Congress)

Printed in the United States of America

McFarland & Company, Inc., Publishers
Box 611, Jefferson, North Carolina 28640
www.mcfarlandpub.com

To Richard and Debra Long—
Thank you for proving that those who are happiest
are those who do the most for others.

"The problem of the twentieth century is the problem of the color line."
—W.E.B. DuBois, *The Souls of Black Folk*

Table of Contents

Acknowledgments

"No person has the right to rain on your dreams."
—Martin Luther King, Jr.

Thankfully, I was never alone during the difficult task of writing this book. In my corner were many extraordinary individuals, many whose presence alone was a motivating factor.

Those who know me know of my proud association with the International Boxing Hall of Fame in Canastota, New York. My service has been particularly rewarding because of some incredible people: Edward Brophy, Jeffrey S. Brophy, Chris Bowers, Rachel Shaw, and Mike Delaney. Numerous other individuals, too many to mention, are volunteers who spend tireless hours servicing the needs of this non-profit organization. I would like to single out in particular the efforts of Jeffrey S. Brophy for his outstanding research and ongoing friendship.

This book would not have been possible without the assistance of the Library of Congress and their Digital Collections and Services staff. The George Grantham Bain photographs came to the institution with very little description, but tremendous potential. I am proud to display many of those images in this work. The Chronicling America website, too, was an invaluable source, providing access to information about historic newspapers and select digitized newspaper pages provided by the National Digital Newspaper Program (NDNP). The NDNP, a partnership between the National Endowment for the Humanities (NEH) and the Library of Congress (LC), is a long-term effort to develop an Internet-based, searchable database of U.S. newspapers with descriptive information and select digitization of historic pages.

To the hundreds who appear in the Bibliography, especially members of IBRO, and to all my fellow boxing historians, I am so very grateful to share this work with you.

Living in the historic state of Connecticut, I am fortunate to have a great support system. My gratitude to all of the independent bookstores in Connecticut for supporting local authors, especially Bank Square Books in Mystic. Also, my appreciation to Larry Dasilva (Nutmeg TV), Larry Rifkin (WATR), Ryan Kristafer & Teresa Dufour (CTSTYLE, on ABC 8), Wayne Norman (WILI-AM), Roger Zotti (The Resident, IBRO), Heidi Kurpiela, Kat Hughes, Randy Donahue (LWR Life), The Authors Guild, IBRO, USA Boxing News and the Connecticut Boxing Hall of Fame (John Laudati, John "Coach" Callas, and so many others) for their inspiration and contributions to my work. Also, thanks to friends, Dana Beck and Brian Brinkman, Ann and Mark Lepkowski, Jim Risley, and Steve Ike.

To my family: Marilyn Allen Baker; Aaron, Sharon and Elliott Baker; Elizabeth, Mark and Paisley Taylor; and Rebecca Baker, thank you for your love and support. My wonderful father-in-law, Richard Long, who has always been a second in my corner, continues to inspire me. Also to Dick and Debra Long for their love and wonderful hospitality. To the loving memory of Ford William Baker, James Buford Bird, Flavil Q. Van Dyke III, Deborah Jean Long, and David Arthur Mumper.

To my wife Alison, I will turn to Jane Austen and her classic Emma: "If I loved you less, I might be able to talk about it more."

Preface

Bused during the 1960s, while attending high school in Virginia Beach, Virginia, I met racism early in life and abhorred it. Egregious, sometimes violent incidents, involving ignorant and immature youngsters of every color, were a common occurrence. Like others, I had a difficult time understanding the purpose it served. Why would someone draw the color line?

As the author of many books about the fight game, including, *TITLE TOWN, USA*; *Boxing in Upstate New York*; *Battling Nelson: The Durable Dane*; *The Fighting Times of Abe Attell*; and *Between the Ropes at Madison Square Garden: The History of an Iconic Boxing Ring, 1925–2007*, I thought long and hard as to whether I should write about such a controversial issue. Using an obscure boxing title to monitor the evolution of a restriction—no, a racist and exclusionary excuse—based on differences of skin pigmentation presented more than its fair share of challenges. But as the only person to serve the International Boxing Hall of Fame as a historian, chairperson, sponsor, volunteer, and biographer, I believed it was part of my responsibility. Like others, I stand proud that the sport we love has come such a long way since the 19th century and made great progress against racism.

The color line was originally used in reference to the racial segregation that existed in the United States after the abolition of slavery. So how in the world did it end up in boxing? How long did the color line exist in pugilism? Did the sport eliminate the color line? Searching for answers, I found none. I discovered intriguing books on the periphery of the issue, but no single reference that got to the heart of the matter. There were no reliable sources for all of the details I sought. Using the fight game as my canvas, I immersed myself in the project for a year. Desiring a book that painted a picture of the color line, I needed an artist's tool. I chose to use a vague title bestowed during the segregated era of boxing, the World Colored Heavyweight Championship, as my paintbrush. It was the perfect choice. As a leverage mechanism or a tool to counter racism, it brought to my canvas the realism I was looking for. The classification embraced some of the finest pugilists the sport has ever known, refined the fight game, and elevated the Heavyweight Championship of the World into the most sought-after designation in all of sports.

This work traces the advent of the World Colored Heavyweight Championship through those individuals many historians believe held it, from Charles C. Smith in 1876 to Larry Gains in 1935–1937. The courage of remarkable athletes, each extraordinarily talented, and that of those around them polished many aspects—from training and conditioning even to ring strategy—of the fight game. Tracing their careers, despite incomplete and even contradictory accounts, wasn't always easy. But meeting all the fascinating individuals involved in the story made it worthwhile. The brief biographies will highlight the acquisition and disposition, as most historians view it, of the Colored title. The victor's name will always

1

appear first in the subheading that acknowledges a contest. Using this approach will typically give you two separate accounts of each likely major title exchange. The end of most chapters will also briefly note the evolution of the color line (during the pugilist's believed title reign), both in and occasionally out of the ring. Citations, timelines, and even significant events will accomplish this task. They will assist you in visualizing the physical setting in which the book's action is occurring. By comparing the achievements of these boxers to the statements or actions of others, you will be able to evaluate the erosion, if any, of the color line.

The Appendix includes three important elements: *A. Roster of Pool Fighters*; *B. World Colored Heavyweight Championship & Timeline*; *C. World Colored Heavyweight Champions & Associated Members of the International Boxing Hall of Fame*; followed by Chapter Notes, Bibliography, and Index. As Black fighters often fought each other, rather than providing redundant chapter information, I included a selection of useful biographies in *Roster of Pool Fighters*. As an informal title lends itself to disorganization and interpretation, *World Colored Heavyweight Championship & Timeline* acts as a practical tool—a starting point for your subjective analysis. Recognition, which includes an accepted official fight record for comparison purpose, is provided in *World Colored Heavyweight Champions & Associated Members of the International Boxing Hall of Fame*. The last three elements—Chapter Notes, Bibliography and Index—speak to definition.

This chronological work was built primarily on contemporaneous sources and where possible allows the fighters to speak for themselves. This will provide you the ability to judge, if you can, the validity of any claim. The World Colored Heavyweight Championship was a subjective designation. Therefore, the pieces don't always fit, and forcing them (which at one point or another you will attempt) doesn't help.

As an author, historian, and devotee of the sweet science, I am grateful for the opportunity to contribute such a work.

Introduction

"Nearly all men can stand adversity, but if you want to test a man's character, give him power," quipped President Abraham Lincoln. Certain positions in society are associated with power, or control if you will. A superiority can be based on many things, used in a variety of ways, and perceived differently. Since man has walked the earth, those with the greatest physical strength, often large and intimidating figures, lived to see another day. Perception, perhaps the most devious noun in the English language, led people to believe that the bigger the man, the greater his strength. Perception also led many to believe that the color of a man's skin must have something to do with it.

Heavyweight Championship of the World was one such position during the late 19th and early 20th centuries. Giants among mere mortals, those who held the boxing title were considered the most powerful men in the world. As the epitome of physical prowess, they commanded respect and got it.

Those who held the esteemed title, it soon became clear, became as popular as world leaders. Their names even appeared in history books alongside the greatest warriors of the past. Sociologists, in an attempt to digest the phenomenon, reflected on virtually every element of its attainment. To boil it down to a single factor, or force, was to simplify its existence. Having done that, they confirmed that the title was not solely one of personal achievement but of ethnic pride.

Pride, along with prestige and profit, quickly created a demand and thus placed the forefathers or benefactors of the championship into a preservation or defensive mode. The designation, at least in their minds, was an indication of racial superiority and a revenue source. They understood that to control the factors or the necessary steps for its attainment was to control the laurels itself. Paramount to the process was the protection of the title and its monopolization by a single race. That race was White. After all, to disrupt the natural order, so the benighted believed, would be cataclysmic. The process proved to be complex.

During the late 19th century and early 20th centuries, Black fighters with innate skill took whatever training and backing they could find. Opportunity, as limited as it was, was financially dependent, and many Black fighters were poor. To make a name for yourself, regardless of your race, you had to call out a popular or proven pugilist. You had to put yourself and a wager on the line. If the stake and challenger were acceptable, a battle could be arranged. The stake spoke for itself. Acceptable, as it would turn out, referred to a gladiator's complexion.

Title preservation meant the system could not be compromised. Athletic clubs, most of which acknowledged only White fighters, had to maintain that stance. A match between a proven Black gladiator and a popular White fighter, as they understood, could lead to the success of the former. Triumph could translate into newspaper coverage, improved economics (paydays), and increased social pressure to proceed with the process. Success also meant further options for Black fighters, such as improved management and training. And it could—this is where the fear factor crept into the equation—lead to an encounter with the Heavyweight Champion of the World. Granted, you could press the legality of a Black fighter meeting a White fighter, and some did, but that was complex. A simpler solution was: Draw the color line. No opportunity, no title.

Drawing the color line was the fail-safe solution should all other barriers of entry— my apologies for using an economic term used to describe the obstacles that prevent new competitors from entering a market—collapse. All the conditions surrounding the lucrative title's acquisition—from access to key venues and their resources to fighter management— needed to be safeguarded. Fair or unfair, conscious or not, that was the process. It was racist behavior, part of a discriminatory society, and it was wrong. The motivation behind the process was fear, and its cause was ignorance.

Prejudice relates to the attitudes and feelings—whether positive or negative, or even conscious or not—that people have about members of other groups. It is a preconceived opinion—how a White promoter might feel about a Black boxer for example.

Specific beliefs about a group, such as descriptions of what members of a particular group look like, how they behave, or their abilities, are stereotypes. The falsehood that all Black boxers had a yellow streak, or a tendency toward cowardice, was a common example. Stereotypes are acquired through thought, experience, and the senses—the result being a perception, sensation, notion, or intuition.

Dynamic, prejudice and stereotypes have evolved. Occasionally taking a leap forward or a step back, they haunt us like a former love interest. Both act to preserve the dominance of powerful groups, rather than to sustain a social equilibrium.

As no race need ever answer to another, alternatives were considered. The World Colored Heavyweight Championship was born, but it lacked substance, or organization you might say. However, as the level of talent increased, the assertions became tough to ignore. The emergence at the end of the 19th century of George Godfrey, who trained under the watchful eye of John B. Bailey, was the first real signal that change was inevitable. Peter Jackson, a talented, handsome, and distinguished gentleman from the Danish West Indies, was so impeccable that he elevated the image of the sport—he countered the racist perception of the colored boxer. Each subsequent holder of the World Colored Heavyweight Championship contributed to the erosion of the color line.

Not surprisingly, some champions had a greater impact. Upon crossing the color line and capturing the Heavyweight Championship of the World, Jack Johnson rocked the sport of boxing like no other. When he, of all people, drew the color line, nobody could believe it. (Please extract "Battling" Jim Johnson from the equation.) He, along with Sam McVey, Joe Jeannette, and Sam Langford, would establish themselves as the four most intimidating heavyweight fighters of their era. Their talent was beyond what any man, of any color, had yet seen. They were the four pillars of the World Colored Heavyweight Championship and, as such, capable of beating one another on any given day. Jack Johnson understood this and, since he was at the heavyweight summit, frankly, it was his kingdom.

But every champion after Johnson—Jess Willard (1915–1919), Jack Dempsey (1919– 1926), Gene Tunney (1926–1928), Max Schmeling (1930–1932), Jack Sharkey (1932–1933), Primo Carnera (1933–1934), and Max Baer (1934–1935), all of whom happened to be White—drew the color line. Dominant among these heavyweights was Jack Dempsey. If anyone could have dramatically altered racial history, it was "The Manassa Mauler." But he did not—multiple safeguards, such as Jack Kearns and Tex Rickard, would see to that. If anybody paid the price, it was Harry Wills. Since the mission wasn't accomplished, the World Colored Heavyweight Championship, without coordination, regulation, or fanfare, was resurrected.

The courage it took for Tommy Burns, a White man, to defend his title against Jack Johnson, a Black man, wasn't seen again until James J. Braddock. "The Cinderella Man" possessed, then lost, the golden slipper—the World Heavyweight Championship—to Joseph Louis Barrow. The talented Black pugilist crossed the color line on June 22, 1937. While some believe it was at this point that the color line was placed in the coffin, along with the World Colored Heavyweight Championship, the final spikes were not yet driven into the lid.

Joe Louis sealed the color line's casket with three more nails, or events if you will. First he avenged his loss to Max Schmeling on June 22, 1938. Then he knocked out John Henry Lewis on January 25, 1939—the second World Heavyweight Championship fight between two Black boxers. While Jack Johnson had a custom color line (he eventually defended the title with a 10-round draw against Battling Jim Johnson on December 19, 1913, in Paris, France), Joe Louis proved he did not. The final nail came when "The Brown Bomber" held the title for 12 years and defended it 25 times. Joe Louis became to every young child a noble figure, a hero who did what heroes were supposed to do.

The World Colored Heavyweight title can be viewed as three phases: Phase I—from inception to Jack Johnson capturing the Heavyweight Championship of the World (December 26, 1908); Phase II—from December 26, 1908, until September 7, 1915, the obscured title was exchanged between Sam McVey, Joe Jeannette, and Sam Langford; and Phase III—prompted by Jack Johnson's loss to Jess Willard on April 5, 1915, Harry Wills resurrected the World Colored Heavyweight Championship from obscurity by claiming it on September 7, 1915.

As a necessary vehicle to the substantive integration of the Heavyweight Championship of the World, the World Colored Heavyweight Championship played a critical role in the destruction of the color line. The entire sport of boxing owes a tremendous debt of gratitude to those who sought, or held, this designation and to those who assisted along the way. It was their courage, dedication, and persistence that added the prestige that was missing in the sweet science.

ONE

Clearing a Path

Where there has been man, there has been conflict. A clash of opposing wishes or needs commonly was reduced to a person's hands as a primary means of persuasion or an expedient option to overcoming a language barrier. The practice of fighting with fists dates to the third millennium BCE, or before the Christian era. Fighting evolved and became popular in Ancient Greece, before finding a stage at the Olympiad—about 880 BCE, Ancient Rome took it a step further by building impressive amphitheaters and exploiting conflict as a form of entertainment. Gladiators transformed their fists into lethal weapons with the use of the cestus, or leather strips fitted with blades or spikes—weaponry that added an interesting twist to a conflict. Death often marked the conclusion of a battle.

Proficient warriors, however, were soon considered valuable commodities. Alternatives, in the form of slaves, thieves or criminals, became an option. When the excessive brutality came to a pinnacle, such conduct was abolished. Nonetheless, fist fighting didn't disappear altogether but found safe havens in places like southern Europe. It was the Roman occupation (43 CE until 410 CE) that brought boxing to England.[1]

From the late 14th century onward, it became fashionable to wear protective garb or armor often complemented by weaponry, in particular a sword. The trend began in Spain before spreading to Italy and Germany. So accepted was the adornment that the sword became required by law in parts of central Europe. But it must also be noted that part of the reason for the law was the government's reliance on a primed and trained militia.

While the term boxing surfaced by the end of the 17th century, it wasn't until the reign of George I (1714–1727) that the sport grew in popularity.

Bare-knuckle Boxing

Bare-knuckle boxing was the original form of the fight game. Closely related to ancient combat, it involved two individuals fighting without padding or protection on their hands. As the form evolved, so too its obvious need for regulation.

The first bare-knuckle champion of England was James Figg, who claimed the title in 1719 and held it until his retirement.[2] The wide-shouldered, six-foot-tall Englishman possessed such a wealth of talent in the art "of the noble science of defense" that he started his own school (English School of Arms and Self-Defense Academy, 1719). Instruction on boxing, fencing, and quarterstaff (cudgel or hardwood pole) enabled Figg's London fighting academy to garner an impressive reputation. With the support of friends such as Charles Mordaunt, an English nobleman and military leader, along with painter and satirist William Hogarth, the fight academy attracted the aristocracy along with some of the finest warriors of the day, including Figg's appointed successor, George Taylor.[3]

Taking his art a step further, Figg established Figg's Amphitheatre in Oxford Road, one of several London arenas devoted to prizefighting events. It was at this venue that many elements of the game advanced, including everything from the ring to the artfulness of sparring. While his Amphitheatre was successful at attracting his upper class demographic, Figg also promoted the game's attraction to the working class. He took his exhibitions to places such as London's Southwark Fair. Impressing the layman with his skill set, he wasn't bashful about taking on all comers. As impressive as he was with his mitts, he was even better with a foil.

Figg's passing in 1734 eventually brought Taylor a challenge from Englishman John "Jack" Broughton. Trouncing Taylor, as he had done with claimants Tom Pipes and Bill Gretting, Broughton anchored himself as champion until 1750. As an adept defenseman, Broughton was the first person to codify a set of seven rules (Broughton's Rules) for all contests. This, along with his evolution of the padded glove, became his legacy.

Broughton also opened his own amphitheatre to stage boxing exhibitions. It catered to his elite friends who included the Duke of Cumberland. Nobility always took pride in their association with the current Champion of England and weren't hesitant about picking up a few extra pounds on a wager. Be that as it may, glory has always been fleeting, so when Broughton lost to Jack "The Knight of the Cleaver" Slack, his friends and businesses faded away. Such was the pattern for many English champions.

Notable subsequent heavyweight bare-knuckle champions included: Tom Johnson (Jackling), Benjamin "Big Ben" Brain, Daniel Mendoza, John "Gentleman" Jackson, James "Jem" Belcher, Henry "Hen" Pearce, John Gully, Tom Cribb, Jem "The Black Diamond" Ward, James "Deaf" Burke, Tom Hyer, John "Old Smoke" Morrissey, Tom Sayers, Joe Coburn, James "Jem" Mace, Tom Allen, Joe Goss, Paddy Ryan, and finally, John L. Sullivan.[4]

Slavery in America—The Advent

Slavery was practiced in the American colonies in the 17th and 18th century. Many Africans, against their will, were transported to a new land and sold. They performed exhaustive labor for their owners in trade for food and shelter. America's agrarian economy, and those who catered to it, benefited through the production of lucrative crops such as cotton and tobacco. For the slave, at the epicenter of this monetary system, nearly all freedom was restricted. To little surprise, many plantation owners who produced an abundance of profit-making harvests became wealthy. Wealth translated into power—much of it in the form of political dominance.

American slavery can be traced to Jamestown, Virginia, in 1619, when a Dutch ship brought African slaves to the shore of the British colony. It was expected that they would provide a more cost-effective alternative to the current form of indentured servants—many of which were poor Europeans. It was the Southern colonies that benefited most by the influx of millions of Black slaves imported during this period.

Bill Richmond—"The Black Terror"

Hugh Smithson, born on August 14, 1742, was the son of Sir Hugh Smithson and Lady Elizabeth Seymour, heiress of the House of Percy. As was customary, the youngster became Hugh Percy on his father's ennoblement and name change in 1750.

Following an Eton education, the young man joined the British Army in 1759 and was quickly made a captain. Accomplished and inspired, Hugh married Lady Anne Crichton-Stuart, daughter of Lord Bute, in 1764. Taking command of the 5th Foot in 1768, Percy prepared his regiment for what he assumed was an inevitable trip to America.[5]

In 1774, the 5th Regiment of Foot was ordered to Boston. It seems the American colonies were stirring up trouble against the mother country. As fate might have it, Percy led the relief column at the Battle of Lexington and Concord on April 19, 1775.[6] His strategic actions during a retreat saved the lives of his men, and indeed impressed his antagonists. Even if he didn't always see eye-to-eye with his superior, General William Howe, Percy was respected for his impeccable manners and tactical remarks. Following his noteworthy Revolutionary command during the Battle of Long Island and the assault on Fort Washington, he found his way back home.[7] The latter was one of the worst Patriot defeats of the war and a clear message to Howe that Percy was an extraordinary commander.

It was while stationed at the British stronghold of Staten Island that Percy noted an athletic and articulate Black slave by the name of Bill Richmond.[8] Born into the designation on August 5, 1763, in the tiny town of Cuckhold (later known as Richmond), Staten Island, New York, the lanky lad was the property of the Rev. Richard Charlton.[9] This is where the story becomes murky. One tale has the good Reverend fleeing to England once the war began, leaving his slaves essentially to fend for themselves, while another has Percy persuading the slave-owner to release the youngster in his care. Nevertheless, the teenager had impressed the British military leader.[10] Percy transported the youth, who was acting as his valet, to England.

Richmond entered the British education system and later accepted an apprenticeship as a cabinetmaker in Yorkshire. At this point, it was believed that he met his White wife, Mary Dunwick. As an educated Black man, married to a White woman in Georgian England, he caught many a British eye. Naturally, this prompted a fair share of churlish remarks. Adding to the visible contrast was Richmond's passion for bright-colored, gaudy clothes.[11] On occasion, this also led to conflict.

To the dismay of the bigoted fools who challenged Richmond, suffice it to say they were quickly put in their place. Adding insult to injury, the talented pugilist, with his passion for etiquette, often apologized for his retaliation. Of course, such behavior, combined with articulate speech, quickly quelled any reference to the stereotypical thug. At a time when racists viewed Blacks as intellectually inferior to Whites, Richmond was labeled a contradiction. In truth, he routinely found himself better educated than his contemporaries, regardless of color.

Whether it was his love of sport—England, a haven for boxing and horse racing during the early 19th century—his athletic prowess, prompting from his employer (Richmond was a personal valet to Lord Camelford) or simply a need to add to his income, Richmond turned to the sweet science. This was during an era when bare-knuckle boxing was a brutal sport. Having adequately defended himself numerous times in bootleg battles—his more noteworthy victories during the late 1700s were against George "Dockey" Moore, Paddy Green, and Frank Meyers (Myers)—was one thing, but choosing prizefighting as more than just an avocation was another.[12] This was especially true for someone as cultivated and mature as Richmond.

After an inauspicious start—he suffered an embarrassing loss to George Maddox at Wimbledon Commons in 1804—in the professional prize ring, Richmond scored victories over Youssop, the Jew, and Jack Holmes.[13] Success bred confidence, perhaps overly so. Richmond, aka "The Black Terror," turned his attention to the "Black Diamond," Tom Cribb. As a proficient pugilistic peer and former coal heaver, the British-born boxer's moniker was ideal. Roughly at the same stage of his career, Cribb was White and believed to be a British Navy veteran. Their battle, on October 8, 1805, took place in Hailsham, Sussex, England. Cribb, having defeated George Maddox during a lengthy—over two hours—event held at Wood Green in January 1805, was not the least bit intimidated by Richmond.[14] Not only was he taller and much heavier, he was also more polished. Cribb, 18 years younger than his antagonist, amused himself with Richmond for an estimated hour and a half before finally putting him away. As fate might have it, Cribb was a mere two years removed from the world title he would take from Jem Belcher. In defeat, Richmond, who had gained a level of notoriety seen by few Blacks in Georgian England, looked to life outside the ropes.[15]

Opening the "Horse and Dolphin" in St. Martin's Lane proved to bolster his popularity and his reputation; consequently, the establishment catered to London's Black community and naturally—based on location (near Five Courts)—to those interested in the sweet science.[16] In the 18th century, the area was also noted for the Academy founded by painter and satirist William Hogarth and as the home of cabinetmakers and "upholsterers."[17] So Richmond was in his element.

Wise before his time, Richmond also used his fame and winnings to open "Richmond's Rooms," a private boxing academy where Trafalgar Square and Nelson's Column stand today. Attracting city gentry, including Lord Byron, it quickly became the pulse of London's pugilistic scene. Richmond even used the forum to spot and enlist a stable of his own pugilists including Tom Molineaux, believed to be a freed American slave. It was Richmond who would train Molineaux for his pair of memorable bouts with Tom Cribb.

The freedom exerted by Richmond and Molineaux, a pair of noteworthy Black men, stood in stark contrast to the ethnic climate of the time. Slavery was a dynamic public issue. Supporters of the Slave Trade Act of 1807 believed it would result in the end of slavery and curb racial tension.[18] However, servitude remained legal in most of the British Empire until the Slavery Abolition Act of 1833.

In 1809, Richmond emerged and defeated five consecutive opponents including Isaac Wood, Jack Carter, and the aforementioned George Maddox. For years, Richmond, age 46, had wished to avenge his loss to Maddox, age 54. When an August opportunity to step inside a ring near Margate, England, presented itself, he took it. Although not favored, Richmond was no less determined. The fighting began in haste, Richmond being thrown through the ropes by the aggressive Maddox in the first round. Both courageous warriors lasted 52 rounds. Eventually an exhausted Maddox, bleeding profusely and unable to see, fell to the ground. Richmond had his revenge.

Three more battles, and three more victories, rounded out Richmond's record: Jack Power (1810), a popular London fighter; Jack Davis (1814), in a club tournament; and finally a 23-round skirmish against Tom Shelton (1815).[19] By this time, Richmond was well known and a favorite among the nobility and local gentry. When Frederick William III of Prussia visited London in 1814, Richmond was one of the individuals commissioned to spar in his company.

By the time of his death, on December 28, 1829, at the age of 66, Richmond was revered as not only one of the best heavyweights of his time but one of England's finest sportsmen. America's first contributor to pugilism was so accepted by the English Society and sporting circles that he was a welcome presence at the coronation celebrations of George IV.[20]

Slavery in America—The American Revolution

The economic policies of Great Britain—in particular taxing the American colonists—harbored resentment toward the fatherland. Colonists were exempted from participation in political decisions affecting their interests. When that indignation reached its pinnacle, rebellion became an option. The American Revolution, which took place essentially from 1775 until 1783, secured the colonists' independence from British rule. The colonists, or the White settlers if you will, simply wanted a voice or a say in their future.

America's founding fathers were committed to private property rights and principles of limited government, along with harmony. But the considerable investment of Southern founders in slave-based agriculture, combined with their deep-seated racial prejudice, posed additional obstacles to emancipation. While most of the Founding Fathers acknowledged that slavery violated the core American revolutionary ideal of liberty, the abolition of servitude was not an immediate consideration. While the prominent seven non-slaveholders—Oliver Ellsworth and Roger Sherman (Connecticut); John Adams, Samuel Adams, and Robert Treat Paine (Massachusetts); Thomas Paine (Pennsylvania), and Alexander Hamilton (New York)—had a powerful voice, they did not have the votes to overshadow the slaveholders amongst them. Those who held slaves at some point in time included: Button Gwinett (Georgia); Charles Carroll and Samuel Chase (Maryland); John Hancock (Massachusetts); John Jay (New York); Benjamin Franklin and Benjamin Rush (Pennsylvania); Charles Cotesworth Pinckney and Edward Rutledge (South Carolina); Pat-

"**Washington family. George, his Lady, & her two grandchildren by the name of Custis**"; a Black servant or slave is standing in the background on the right (Library of Congress, LC-USZ—4003).

rick Henry, Thomas Jefferson, Richard Henry Lee, James Madison, and George Washington (Virginia).

Speaking of Washington, when he was 11 years old, he inherited 10 slaves; by the time of his death, 317 slaves lived at Mount Vernon, including 123 owned by Washington, 41 leased from a neighbor, and an additional 153 "dower slaves."[21] Although accounts vary with regard to just how the "Father of His Country" handled Mount Vernon's enslaved population, certain was his use of harsh punishment when he deemed it necessary. Thus Mount Vernon's enslaved community was like others who welcomed the opportunity to escape servitude. During the American Revolution (1781), 17 members of the Mount Vernon enslaved population—14 men and three women—fled to the British warship HMS *Savage*, anchored in the Potomac off the shore of the plantation.[22] Washington, in his will, left directions for the eventual emancipation of his slaves after the passing of Martha Washington.[23] By law, however, he could not free the Custis dower slaves. Apparently supporting abolition in theory was one thing, practice another—slavery was subordinate to the birth of a nation.[24]

Using George Washington, an extraordinary man and perhaps the greatest leader of his generation, as an example, was proof of the complexity of the issue. During his presidency (1789–1797), he witnessed the South's transition from a tobacco-based economy to that of cotton, thanks to Eli Whitney's invention of the cotton gin. The evolution only proved the region's dependency on slave labor. It was a transition that the North didn't completely understand, as all of the northern states had abolished slavery between 1774 and 1804.

President John Adams wrote on January 24, 1801, "My opinion against it [slavery] has always been known…. I have always employed freemen both as Domisticks [*sic*] and Labourers, and never in my Life did I own a Slave."[25] At the time, Adams was under the impression that slavery was diminishing. It was not.

In 1808, President Thomas Jefferson saw the U.S. Congress outlaw the African slave trade. It was a complete failure. A "moral depravity" and a "hideous blot" was how Jefferson viewed slavery. It ran counter to the laws of nature that proclaimed that everyone had a right to personal freedom. These statements were made by the principal author of the Declaration of Independence, who enslaved more than 600 people during the course of his life.

James Madison (1809–1817

Mount Vernon Ladies' Association marker placed at the Slave Cemetery in Mount Vernon, Virginia, in 1929 (author's collection).

Presidential tenure), the "Father of the Constitution," proposed that a slave be counted as three-fifths of a person. It was a position that reflected the distorted ethical logic of slaveholders, of which he was one.

As the owner of an estimated 250 enslaved persons in his lifetime, James Monroe (1817–1825 Presidential tenure) never freed any of them. Describing slavery as "one of the evils still remaining, incident to our Colonial system," he, like most of his predecessors, was a contradiction.[26]

The American Revolution had succeeded in giving White colonists, previously excluded from participation in political decisions affecting their interests, a voice. They demanded the right and fought for it. Given the opportunity to preserve that right, they did so for themselves but not for all. By 1830, the slave population in the United States numbered more than two million, making the ratio of free to enslaved Americans approximately 5.5:1.[27]

Tom Molineaux

The origins of one of the most famous bare-knuckle fighters of all time, Tom Molineaux, also spelled Molyneaux, remain unclear to this day. Some believe he was be born into slavery on March 23, 1784, in Virginia, while others aren't certain of the conditions or location. If brought into this world on a Virginia tobacco plantation, as some speculate, it would be an origin he would never forget.[28]

One aspect was clear: He was born into a genetically gifted Black family. According to some sources, his father, Zachary Thomas Molineaux, who was one of four brothers and had four sons of his own, was well known locally as a scrapper even before the American Revolution. Historian Nat Fleischer, in his monumental book series *Black Dynamite*, was quick to establish the Molineaux kinsfolk as America's first family of bare-knuckle boxing. Thus Zachary Molineaux's race were founders of American pugilism.

During this time, bare-knuckle skirmishes were not formal, nor were they a prelude to an occupation, but rather good old-fashioned entertainment for slave-owners. Weekend wagers—often only a few dollars—on impromptu challenges were common. During this "my slave can whip your slave" period, plantation owners seeking a peculiar sense of recognition happily challenged their neighbors. If the wager included a wagon, horse, or even the services of the enslaved, then so be it.

As was tradition, the oppressed took the surname of their owner. The brothers Molineaux had the blessing of broad shoulders, thick necks, superb arm and leg development, not to mention the pugilistic wisdom of their father to enhance their maturation. Unfortunately, Tom's father passed, leaving the family to fill what gaps they could at their master's estate—at the time, Tom was only 14 years old.

So the story goes: Years later, Tom was promised his freedom—the exact moment of the offering uncertain—by Squire Molineaux, his wealthy owner, should he defeat in battle another Virginia slave possessed by a popular plantation owner. As a healthy wager was on the line, Squire Molineaux acquired the assistance of an English sailor in port, Patrick Davis, who had some ring skills that would translate well to the youngster. Tom was less than enthusiastic. But an additional purse solved that problem—he quickly honed his skills to an extraordinary level.[29] All that was needed was a few bloody rounds for Tom to pound his adversary into submission.

Free to leave, Tom Molineaux charted a course to London via New York City. This was a suggestion from Davis—the sailor had mentioned to his pupil that the capital of the United Kingdom had a lively boxing scene that paid well. Eventually landing a job as a deckhand aboard a vessel bound for England, Molineaux, who was illiterate, began his journey.[30] London, during the winter of 1809, could be an unforgiving place, yet the youngster persevered. Desperate, he proclaimed himself the "Champion of America"—what was there to lose? Eventually, word made it through the local sporting houses and taverns that a challenge, as ridiculous as it sounded to most, had been made and was directed to England's best fighter at the time, Tom Cribb.

The English boxer, in self-imposed retirement, considered the American's challenge an insult. Instead, he suggested a pupil of his, Jack Burrows, aka "Bristol Unknown," as a more suitable option. The fight took place on July 24, 1810, at Tothill Fields in Westminster. Standing five feet, nine inches in height and scaling at just about 200 pounds, Molineaux appeared crude and unpolished. In his corner, however, was Bill Richmond—no introduction needed.[31] The famed trainer was able to steer his pupil to a victory by suggesting short-arm jolts and powerful body punches. Cribb was livid at his man being defeated, but not furious enough to enter the ring himself. Since defeating Bill Richmond back in 1805, Cribb had defeated Jem Belcher, not once but twice, and was clearly the champion of England. Then, due to the lack of competition, he retired.

Molineaux, given the moniker "The Moor," next met "Tom Tough" Blake on August 21, 1810. The brisk battle, which lasted a mere eight rounds, garnered significant attention and ended in another victory for the American—a straight right sent Blake to dreamland. Cribb, who was watching from Blake's corner at the Castle Tavern at Epple Bay, pondered the inevitable. Since prizewinners don't come cheap, it took noted trainer Captain Robert Barclay to convince Cribb to rethink retirement.[32]

Molineaux finally got his wish and met the English champion on December 18, 1810, on Copphall Commons, near East Grimstead (about 30 miles outside of London). A torrential rain soaked everyone on hand to witness the mill, but it did little to curtail the excitement generated by the affair. At the end of 39 rounds, the American dropped from exhaustion and Cribb had avenged the losses of his understudies.[33] But the battle was marred by controversy: Between the 28th and 29th rounds, an unclear incident took place. Most accounts state that Tom Cribb was unable to come to scratch after 30 seconds, and therefore the fight should have ended. It did not.[34] Molineaux fell from exhaustion in the 39th round. Nonetheless, the Virginia slave, who had felt the muddy sod more than once, delivered a stunning performance that held everyone's attention. After the fight, Molineaux challenged his victor to a rematch.

Setting the Stage

Born on July 8, 1781, near Bristol, the birthplace of many a British pugilist, Thomas "Black Diamond" Cribb fought his first public battle at the age of 24. Unlike some of his predecessors, success did not come easy for the fighter. His victories had been arduous and his sole defeat a heartbreaking 52-round marathon.

The *Salt Lake Tribune* later recounted his journey:

Of modest, unassuming nature, Cribb had gradually won a following before he stepped into the championship. No fairer or cleaner fighter ever held the honor. He had kept his record without reproach. For the rest, he had attained his superiority by hard work and careful study of the science. No natural boxer, like Belcher, he had shown but mediocre ability at the start. He had been classed a "slow hitter," and never developed into a remarkably swift or agile pugilist. His best qualities in the ring were his excellent generalship, his knowledge of the game, his wonderfully sound wind and his rock-founded courage.[35]

Cribb had pondered retirement—he had nothing to prove following his second victory over Jem Belcher in 1809. There was no opponent standing in the wings, and absolutely no question that he was the Champion of England.

Cribb v. Molineaux, II

But, as the *Salt Lake Tribune* continued:

> When the ambitious defiance of the Negro was presented, however, he had yielded readily to the wishes of his friends [The situation would be replayed when Jeffries exited retirement to meet Johnson.] Cribb was called upon to uphold the supremacy of the race in the ring and gave over his private arrangement for a quiet life in retreat to respond to that call.[36]

The *Salt Lake Tribune* referenced an unnamed newspaper of the day: "Some persons feel alarmed at the bare idea that a Black man and a foreigner should seize the championship of England and decorate his sable brow with the hard-earned laurels of Cribb. He must, however, have his fair chance, though Tom swears that for the honor of old England he'll be damned if he will relinquish a single sprig except with his life."[37]

Molineaux, with his previous performance, deserved a rematch. Cribb understood this and did not despise his adversary. He was also well aware of the fact that a rematch would draw thousands. Cribb was correct. On the morning of September 28, 1811, at Thistleton Gap, in the parish of Wymondham, Leicestershire, throngs of fight fans were on the move. All were in search of a position near the 25-foot square erected in a large stubble field. Outside of the ring, a larger, roped area surrounded the stage to ensure positions for the more favored spectators—Lord Yarmouth, Sir Henry Smith, the Marquis of Queensberry, and Lord Pomfret found solace there. Just beyond them was an area for horsemen and their associated vehicles.

Cribb entered the ring at 12 o'clock and was seconded by former champion John Gully and "Joe" Ward. Molineaux followed, seconded by Bill Richmond and "Bill" Gibbons.[38] Both fighters stripped to breeches, stockings and pumps and awaited word from the umpires. Cribb, who had been trained by Captain Barclay, entered at 188 pounds on a frame that looked like it had been etched out of marble—all bone and muscle draped by firm skin.[39] Molineaux, at about 185 pounds, could not match the precise proportions of his adversary, but his intense arm development and deadly reach were clearly noticeable.

Both fighters familiarized themselves with their ground in Round One. Molineaux took Round Two. Swiftly the odds fell to 6 to 4 on Cribb—the American also scored first fall. By the third round, spectators were screaming for Cribb to make his mark on Molineaux. He did so by sending his opponent across the ring. However, Cribb's right eye was closing, and he was dropped for a second time. Molineaux, who was tiring quickly, seemed to be at an advantage up until the sixth round.

The tide appeared to turn in the sixth as an exhausted Molineaux endured some fierce body punches before being floored with a shot to the jaw. Molineaux fell again in the seventh. He attempted a brief rally in the eighth before being dropped another time. It was a Cribb left that fractured Molineaux's jaw in the ninth and set the stage for the closing act.

The *Salt Lake Tribune* noted:

Finally the courageous Negro came weaving to the center for the tenth round. He attempted to bore in, but fell from weakness. Cribb gave him another long interval, but Molineaux was too far-gone. His attendants carried him to the center for the 11th round, and he stood there for an instant, weaving and helpless, then fell before a blow was struck. The battle was accorded to Cribb amid thundering cheers, and the champion, as proof of his condition, danced a Scotch reel with Gully about the stage. The fight lasted 19 minutes, 10 seconds.[40]

The loss sent Tom Molineaux into a downward slide. His patience ran thin as his bar tabs grew thick—as did his waistline—and he lost all self-respect. In stark contrast to his disciplined mentor, it wasn't long before Bill Richmond broke all ties with his fighter. Speaking of broke, Richmond lost virtually everything he owned orchestrating the battle. Molineaux dabbled in wrestling a bit, took a fight and won against Richmond apprentice Jack Carter, fought a two-part battle against William Fuller that climaxed with his victory by a foul, and was defeated in his final fight by George Cooper in March of 1815. A shadow of what he once was, his reputation still preceded him. Just the thought of entering a ring against Molineaux was still a treat for a young boxer.

By the end of 1817, Molineaux was teaching boxing in Ireland. The country had a vibrant boxing scene that welcomed the fighter's exhibitions. The Irish slave trade was still quite active at the time, and Molineaux stood in antithesis to it—he conducted lessons for those who saw owning a slave as a status symbol.

Living day-to-day, the former fighter depended on the generosity of his friends for his existence. Although a spendthrift, he was generous to a fault. Tom Molineaux passed in the band room of the 77th Regiment, stationed at Galway, on August 4, 1818. His final resting place was a hilltop graveyard in Mervue, close to Galway City.

Courageous and talented, Molineaux has been recalled often by historians as a former slave and the first black man to fight for a championship.[41] He, along with Richmond, refused to allow the extreme racism, which afflicted both pugilism and society in general, to destroy their aspirations. If that meant relocation, even to a different continent, then so be it.

Slavery in America—Abolitionist Movement

The only thing worse than rebellion was what caused it, or so believed a youth born into slavery on the Eastern Shore of the Chesapeake Bay in Talbot County, Maryland. The exact date of his birth was undetermined, but many believed it was February 14, 1818. He was of mixed race, which likely included Native American on his mother's side, as well as African and European. It was his mother, Harriet Bailey, who gave him the name of Frederick Augustus Washington Bailey—later, after escaping to the North, he took the surname Douglass, having already dropped his two middle names.

Rebellions by the oppressed, common in history, did little to alter the slave labor system. Yet they were successful at raising an eyebrow, or even a gun, with White slaveholders. In August of 1831, a slave named Nat Turner led a revolt in Southampton County, Virginia. Traveling house to house, Turner's large group (estimated at 75) of freed slaves murdered every man, woman, and child they encountered that was White (estimated at 60). It took two days to suppress the rebellion but not before Turner's group succeeded in spreading terror and alarm among slaveholders. On November 5, 1831, Turner was tried for "conspiring to rebel and making insurrection," convicted, and condemned to death. He was hanged on November 11 in Jerusalem, Virginia, before his body was flayed, beheaded, and displayed. It sent a clear message to anyone considering another uprising that they might want to rethink their approach.[42]

The White-controlled press had a field day. They scorned abolitionists while pointing to the Black insurrection as a lack of discipline. The slave codes needed to be strengthened, and it must be done quickly in order to limit all the outside sources that could prompt another uprising. This while the increased repression of southern Blacks nauseated the North. The line was being drawn.

From the 1830s until the beginning of the American Civil War (1861–1865), the abolitionist movement gathered strength. Fueled by Black and White supporters—people like Frederick Douglass, William Lloyd Garrison, White founder of the radical newspaper *The Liberator*, and Harriet Beecher Stowe, a White author who published the bestselling antislavery novel *Uncle Tom's Cabin*—the faction remained undeterred from their mission.

The practice of assisting the escape of fugitive slaves from Southern plantations to the North became more formalized. Known as the Underground Railroad, it assisted anywhere from 40,000 to 100,000 slaves in reaching freedom. Southern animosity toward the process grew by leaps and bounds.

As the borders of the United States grew, so did the antipathy. Each expansion, or application for statehood, prompted controversial legislation. For example, Missouri was admitted to the Union as a slave state, Maine as a free state, and all western territories north of Missouri's southern border were to be free soil. The Missouri Compromise was just that, designed to maintain a delicate balance between slave and free states. But, as most wondered, for how long?

The process continued with the territories won during the Mexican-American War (1846–1848) and the Kansas-Nebraska Act (1854)—the latter contributing to the failure of the Whig Party and the advent of the Republican Party. The abolitionist bonfire had never burned brighter. A mere two more major incidents, and it would be out of control.

In March 1857, the United Sates Supreme Court effectively repealed the Missouri Compromise with the Dred Scott decision. The case involved a slave who sued for his freedom on the grounds that his master had taken him into free territory—this entitled him to emancipation. The court decided that no black, free or slave, could claim U.S. citizenship, and therefore blacks were unable to petition the court for their freedom. All territories, as the court saw it, were open to slavery. The abolitionists were furious.

Over two years later, October 16 thru 18, 1859, an armed band of abolitionists, led by John Brown, took control of the military arsenal at Harpers Ferry

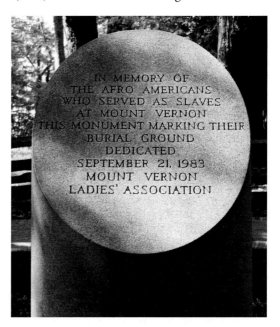

Close-up of the 1983 Mount Vernon Ladies' Association Burial Ground Monument at the Slave Cemetery in Mount Vernon, Virginia (author's collection).

Distant view of the 1983 Mount Vernon Ladies' Association Burial Ground Monument at the Slave Cemetery at Mount Vernon (author's collection).

(formerly Virginia and now West Virginia). The motive was simple, at least in Brown's eyes, to establish an independent stronghold of freed slaves. The Connecticut-born White leader was captured during the raid, convicted of treason, and hanged on December 2, 1859. As fate would have it, the U.S. Marines who restored order and captured Brown were Colonel Robert Edward Lee and Lieutenant James Ewell Brown "Jeb" Stuart.

The United States was on the brink of Civil War.

Two

The Core Four

The American Civil War (1861–1865)

Understanding that the Republican Party opposed slavery, the Southern states did not want Abraham Lincoln to win the election of 1860. Only last year he reminded them that they did not deserve freedom if they denied it to others. Slavery, as Lincoln saw it, was the major difference between the North and the South. His position was strong enough, he believed, to win the election, and he was right. Within a few months, seven Southern states had seceded to form the Confederate States of America; four more would follow after the Civil War began.

Paramount to President Lincoln was preservation of the Union. Slavery, at least for the time being, would remain in its shadow. He, like many, understood that abolition could be a byproduct of a successful campaign. But just to be certain, he issued a preliminary emancipation proclamation in 1862, before making it official on January 1, 1863. It declared "that all persons held as slaves" within the rebellious states "are, and henceforward shall be free."

Although the Emancipation Proclamation did not end slavery in the nation, it cap-

A large contingent of African Americans, estimated at over 175,000 men in the Union Army alone, served in the American Civil War. A group of military men, likely from South Carolina, pose for a rare photograph (Library of Congress, LC-B818—0061).

19

A Black soldier guards a cannon at City Point, Virginia (Library of Congress, LC-B811—2583).

tured the hearts and imagination of millions of Americans and fundamentally transformed the character of the war. If it succeeded, life as they knew it, or so many believed, would change for the better. The document also announced the acceptance of Black men into the Union Army and Navy. By the end of the war, over 175,000 Black soldiers and sailors had fought for the Union and freedom, and more than 35,000 lost their lives in doing so.

On April 14, 1865, five days after the surrender of Confederate general Robert E. Lee, President Abraham Lincoln was shot by Confederate sympathizer John Wilkes Booth, and he died the next day. The war had ended but not the issue of slavery.

Reconstruction (1865 to 1877)

In an attempt to repair the Union, Reconstruction took place from 1865 until 1877. The injustice of slavery, and its legacy (economic, political, and social), needed to be solved. Only this would guarantee the successful readmission of the 11 states that had seceded to form the Confederacy. As simple as it sounded in theory, reality proved far more complex. President Andrew Johnson would preside over the beginning of a process that gradually seemed condemned to failure. As a former senator from Tennessee, Johnson was a Union loyalist. Yet he was also a states' rights advocate. Johnson would uphold the 13th Amendment, while being certain that the Southern states pledged their loyalty to the union and paid off their war debt. However, that was about as far as he was willing to push his cause. The southern states and their ruling class—primarily wealthy White plantation owners— were basically free to construct their government of choice.

Landowners ruled and built a system of government conducive to their needs. Since the labor force would fall under their control, Black Codes were passed, or laws with the intent and the effect of restricting African Americans' freedom and compelling them to serve in a labor economy based on low wages or debt. There was a cruelty to it: under Johnson's Reconstruction policies, nearly every Southern state would silence the voice of Black America. An all-White police or state militia, much of it made up of Confederate veterans of the Civil War, would see to that. White supremacist organizations, such as the Ku Klux Klan, did their best to undermine any Northern influence.

When the last federal soldier departed the South in 1877, he left behind many former slaves who were wondering just what was accomplished during the war. As a nation given to our myths, did we just add to it?

Three Amendments–A Trio of Disregarded Legislation

A proclamation was not enough to end slavery or curtail White supremacy. It needed a succinct amendment to the Constitution and the 13th Amendment was adopted on December 15, 1865. It *officially* abolished slavery. But it too was not enough. Former slaves received the rights of citizenship and the "equal protection" of the Constitution in the 14th Amendment and the right to vote by the 15th Amendment. But for the most part, this trio of amendments was ignored and routinely violated with little ramification.

Reconstruction failed for a number of reasons: it did not admonish those responsible for the conflict for fear of irreparable damage to the Union; it did not develop, sell, or implement a concise plan to the next generation—a period often considered to be 20 years; it did not quell the fear of both sides, nor establish common ground; and it did not chart an ongoing course for race relations after the abolition of slavery and the rise of Jim Crow. It forced freed slaves to use alternative solutions in order to exercise their right of suffrage as well as gain access to education, land, and employment.

Some believed these failures did not obscure a number of accomplishments with long-term consequences, including advances in African American representation in a variety of fields—though that may be considered debatable. Yes, it laid the groundwork for renewed struggles for racial equality during the civil rights movement. But had Reconstruction succeeded, some of those struggles could have been averted.

Defining the Color Line

To some, "the color line" was a barrier or non-physical wall usually created by custom or economic differences, to separate nonwhite persons from White persons. In the 1890s, this obstruction became commonplace in the Southern states of America. It was a legal line of separation with laws stating clearly where Blacks could and could not go in public. In time, the obstacle would evolve. By the turn of the century, Blacks were confronted with "Colored" signs on doors, water fountains, bathrooms, and waiting rooms in bus and train stations designating their places for standing, sitting, eating, and using public facilities. The

"Colored" sign was the most visible mark of racism imposed upon Blacks or African Americans by the abject Jim Crow laws, or the hateful practice of segregating Black people in the United States. The color line also existed in the mid-western and eastern states of the nation, but it was not so defined and was seldom enforced by law.

The phrase "the Color Line" was originally used as a reference to the racial segregation that existed in America after the abolition of slavery. By the 1870s, the locution was garnishing articles in newspapers such as the *New York Herald*:

> The phrase is often heard in the mouths of politicians, and it appears as a "catchword" in the newspapers. Its significance is not to be overlooked, especially at a time like this, when there is talk of a war of races in the South. Like the famous cross-bones and skull, it is a warning to those whom it most concerns and it is likely to prove most damaging to those by whom it was invented. But its full meaning is not conveyed to the mind by the words themselves. Anybody can see that it implies the organization of political parties on the basis of color, but it means more than this; its full significance is that the Whites are to be forced on the one side and that even the Negroes are to vote the other way at their peril.[1]

The phrase, borrowed from Frederick Douglass, gained fame after American sociologist, author, historian, civil rights activist, and editor William Edward Burghardt "W.E.B." Du Bois chose to repeat it multiple times in his book *The Souls of Black Folk* (1903).[2]

Giants Among Men

The great English novelist Edward M. Forster wrote in his novel *A Room with a View* (1908), "It makes a difference, doesn't it, whether we fence ourselves in, or whether we are fenced out by the barriers of others?" Two giants among men who saw no barriers were Booker Taliaferro Washington, an American educator, author, orator, and advisor to presidents of the United States, and Du Bois.

Washington was the dominant leader of the African American community between 1890 and 1915. Born in Hale's Ford, Virginia, around 1856, he was from the last generation of Black American leaders born into slavery and became the leading voice of the former slaves and their descendants. Deprived and oppressed in the post–Reconstruction Southern states, the group needed a voice and thankfully found one.

As a proponent of African American business, Washington was not intimidated by anybody or anything. He founded the National Negro Business League in 1900 "to promote the commercial and financial development of the Negro." His safe haven was the Tuskegee Institute, a college for Black students in Alabama that he, along with his friend Lewis Adams, helped establish.

In 1895, as the heinous lynching of Blacks in the South reached a peak, Washington gave a speech known as the "Atlanta compromise." It brought him national fame. The agreement was that Southern Blacks would work and submit to White political rule, while Southern Whites guaranteed that Blacks would receive basic education and due process of law. As anticipated, the accord was subject to tremendous scrutiny. Washington's objective was Black progress through education and entrepreneurship, or an alternative to attempting to challenge directly the Jim Crow segregation and the disenfranchisement of Black voters in the South. His rally call was welcomed by some but deplored by others.

Washington's long-term goal was to end the deprivation of the vast majority of African Americans, who then still lived in the South.

W.E.B. Du Bois was born in Great Barrington, Massachusetts, on February 23, 1868. Raised in a relatively tolerant and integrated community, he was not exposed to all the intolerance experienced by his peers. After completing graduate work at the University of Berlin and Harvard, where he was the first African American to earn a doctorate, he became a professor of history, sociology, and economics at Atlanta University.

As one of the founders of the National Association for the Advancement of Colored People (NAACP) in 1909, an American civil rights organization, Du Bois sought to advance justice through organized participation. Their purpose was to ensure the political, educational, social, and economic equality of rights of all persons and to eliminate racial hatred and racial discrimination.

Only four years before, Du Bois was the leader of the Niagara Movement, a group of African American activists who wanted equal rights for Blacks. Du Bois and his supporters opposed Washington's Atlanta compromise. He believed in full civil rights and increased political representation, which he hoped would be brought about by the African American intellectual elite. Not unlike Washington, Du Bois believed racism and its byproducts, such as discrimination, the Jim Crow laws, and violence, was evil.

As a prolific author, Du Bois reduced oppression with his words. Two of his works stand out to this day: *The Souls of Black Folk* (1908), a pioneering work in African American literature, and perhaps his greatest work, *Black Reconstruction in America* (1935).

Washington, the marketing genius, and Du Bois, the persuasive wordsmith, were eminent Americans enormously successful at eroding much of the hardship felt by the vast majority of African Americans, many of whom still lived in the South.

The Core Four

Although racism prevented many Blacks from climbing the social ladder, or even entering a boxing ring, a few remained undeterred. Charles A.C. Smith (1876, established, then claimed the title), Morris Grant (1878, claimed the title), Charles Hadley (1881–1883), and George Godfrey (1883–1888) built the foundation, as delicate and unrefined as it may have been, for the World Colored Heavyweight Championship. Four valorous souls hoped to exhibit their talent, or fighting prowess if you will, not only to their own race, but to all races.

So, what's in a title? A prefix or suffix, added to someone's name, often garnered veneration. It could note an official position, professional or academic qualification, or even be hereditary. Titles, under legitimate organizations, gathered more attention because they were presumed to exist as a result of a process. In other words, they were earned rather than applied. While these pioneers lacked organization, they didn't lack talent. They understood that meeting every challenge and conquering it legitimized aptitude.

Reconstruction was winding down in 1876, but the tension between the North and the South remained impassioned. Race relations were fragile. Nobody was anxious to alter any process that would racially bifurcate an existing entity.

The World Heavyweight Bare-Knuckle Championship had essentially been in place since 1719 and was dominated by White Englishmen. Americans began challenging the title in part thanks to the Hyer family. Jacob Hyer, the White patriarch of the genetically gifted family, was an accomplished bare-knuckle pugilist and generally credited as the first professional boxer on American soil. His 1816 match with Tom Beasley earned him the designation "The Father of the American Ring."[3]

Tom Hyer, Jacob's son, was born in 1819 and followed in his father's footsteps. He stood six feet, two inches and tipped the scales at about 185 pounds. Hyer had many successful minor contests, but his first real test took place on September 9, 1841, when he met George McChester, otherwise known as "Country McCloskey." Victorious after a grueling 101 rounds, or two hours and 55 minutes, Hyer claimed the Heavyweight Championship of America.[4] Later, on February 7, 1849, he defeated "Yankee Sullivan" (James Ambrose), and nobody questioned his assertion. Two years after that, Tom Hyer, the first American Heavyweight Champion, retired. As a consequence, Yankee Sullivan immediately claimed his title (1851).

John Morrissey and Joe Coburn, born in Ireland, and Mike McCoole and Tom Allen, born in England, followed in the shoes left behind by Hyer. Glancing at their significant battles indicates that Hyer, Morrissey, and Mike McCoole did not cross the color line; the closest Coburn came was an exhibition against Herbert Slade, whose mother was native Maori, and Tom Allen fought a losing battle against Bob Smith, "The Liverpool Darkey," very early in his career.

Take a look at the demographics. The Census of 1870 acknowledged the U.S. population at 38,558,371, a 22.62 percent increase since 1860. The Black population was at 4,880,009 (12.65 percent). As the Civil War concluded, some political change was noted: The 44th Congress included eight Black members. In sports, perhaps the most noteworthy athlete was Black jockey Oliver Lewis, who won the first Kentucky Derby race in 1875. Over the next 27 years, 14 Black jockeys would ride the wining horse at the Derby—a contribution that slipped from the pages of history as fast as Civil War promises.

Charles A.C. "The Black Thunderbolt" Smith

Chiseled like a Bernini sculpture, Charles A.C. Smith grew to the height of six feet and weighed about 185 pounds. Born in Macon, Georgia (c. 1852), and into slavery, he, like many Blacks, moved north at the end of the Civil War. During the conflict, Macon served as the official arsenal of the Confederacy and was known for Camp Oglethorpe, which was used as a prison for captured Union officers and enlisted men. It was not a comfortable environment for Blacks. So Michigan became an alternative.[5]

Like all youths, Smith was influenced by a number of factors: family (economic conditions, parenting); peers (friendships, interactions); school, if any (type, racial and ethnic composition); community (neighborhoods and structure); and media (when he learned to read newspapers). The experience of adolescence, for the literate or illiterate, was complex—for the disenfranchised even more so. Naturally, these factors had both positive and negative effects.[6]

Fighting primarily out of East Saginaw, Michigan, he gradually headed east to hone his skills.[7] In 1880, he penned a note to the *National Police Gazette* announcing himself and his wagers. Without takers, Smith made a bold claim to a designation called the World Colored Heavyweight Championship. In an era where land claims were common, why not boxing titles? Nobody, including the *Gazette*, took him seriously, so he headed to New York City in 1883 in search of competition and financial backing. Smith first tried to call out the widely known George Godfrey, but failed. Godfrey's avoidance of Smith actually worked in his favor, as he was pushed into the forefront of Black pugilists. A color-blind White backer, who went by the name of Hugh Reilly, initially took a liking to Smith; consequently, the association opened some doors for the fighter.[8] On August 16, 1883, Smith entered the ring, at the infamous Harry Hill's dance hall in the city's red light district, to face Canadian Jack Stewart, formerly of Galway. It was scheduled for six rounds, under Queensberry rules, using soft gloves. After five minutes and 25 seconds, or during the second round, Stewart knocked out Smith. Here is how the *Morning Journal and Courier* saw the final round:

> Stewart opened the ball by a hard hit to the pit of the stomach, Smith still foolishly fighting at the head and face. He fought gamely, but once or twice turned his back as the to avoid the shower of blows that fell on him. This was fatal as Stewart rushed at him, planting both hands in the face and ribs without a return. Smith tried all he knew to turn the tables in his favor, but he could do little more than push and paw. Seeing how matters stood Stewart changed his tactics by fighting at the head and face. This seemed to bewilder the darkey, who gradually retreated to his own corner, into which he was driven all in a heap and refusing to carry on the unequal strife his seconds threw up the sponge, Stewart being hailed the winner in orthodox style.[9]

The event, which attracted considerable attention, was claimed to be the first mixed race heavyweight encounter since 1811 (Cribb versus Molineaux). It put Smith on the front page of the newspaper.

Returning to East Saginaw, Smith's first major battle of 1884 came on March 10.[10] The handsome fighter was matched against Mervine Thompson at the Central Armory in Cleveland. The event, which attracted 2,500 spectators, saw Thompson knock out Smith in the eighth round. Under the subtitle "Smith, the Negro has grit, but was no match for the White bruiser," the *St. Paul Globe* reported the final round: "Smith went down, then knocked heavily through the ropes, and lay exhausted and unable to climb back. He was helped up, but failed to respond in time, and the match was given to Thompson, who was somewhat winded, but showed no sign of punishment."[11]

Tension between Reilly and Smith led to a split between the pair. For the latter, doors closed as fast as they were previously opened, and his name was disparaged. Over the next couple of years, Smith's behavior became erratic and his skills faded. Unfortunately for many boxers, this was an era when few fights were recorded, and the legality of boxing was in question. Finding solace and a bit of profit in his barbershop, Smith's name would surface again before the turn of the century.

Scrapping Across the Pond

Joe Goss, an English-born scrapper, was the World Heavyweight Bare-Knuckle Champion from 1876 until 1880. Standing five feet, eight-and-a-half inches, he weighed around the 150 mark. Cunning, quick, and adroit, the fighter had made his mark in his homeland by a trio of battles with the great Jem Mace. When Goss arrived in New York in July 1876, Smith, three years removed from turning professional, noted his entry. Goss was in the States to assess his pugilistic opportunities—his fistic accomplishments had made it into the American press by this point, so he was not a stranger.

Goss had drawn champion Tom Allen back in England on March 5, 1867. To provide a glimpse of the battle, along with the informality and legality of the sport in England, the *Chicago Tribune* reported: "At this point [third round] the police, who had up to this time remained at the bridge, crossed over into Glamorganshire. The men who had been fighting 17 minutes were at once ordered out of the ring by the referee, and the ropes and stakes removed. After going about a quarter mile, the constables staying behind, another spot, at the top of a hill, but sheltered from observation, was selected, and the antagonists, nearly an hour having elapsed, again faced each other."[12]

The police waited four minutes before once again reprimanding the lot. It was then off to Marshfield to conclude the match. Both men fought fast and furious up to the 32nd round, when exhaustion got the best of them. By this point, the referee, upset over the lack of action, had little choice but to call it a draw. The duration of the battle was one hour and 53 minutes, or 34 rounds. Two years after the Civil War, bare-knuckle brawling—at least in this case—wasn't always front-page news, but landing on page two wasn't bad. Goss would do battle with Allen at least two more times, even picking up the title from Allen via a foul on September 7, 1876.[13]

A Case of Mistaken Identity

The Fistic Editor of the *Buffalo Courier* received a letter from C.A.C. Smith, the "Michigan Thunderbolt" or "Black Thunderbolt," on February 15, 1898. It seems the former Colored pugilist, who was working as a barber and living in Chicago, Illinois, wanted to relay a concern. In his note, Smith claimed that Hugh Reilly, his former manager, also had a Black fighter named Amos Lavender, who fought under the name C.C. Smith and the moniker "Thunderbolt." Lavender, a heavyweight, had fought Smith back in 1883. Hailing from Albany, New York, C.C. Smith was touring New England, and the confusion was ruining the retired fighter's reputation.[14] Fight fans just could not separate the two. The former Colored champion further stated that his last official fight was against R.N. Harrison back on February 7 (or 11), 1887, at Walton Hall in Bay City, Michigan. Unfortunately, there was little anyone could do about the situation; subsequently, Reilly and Smith continued their practice.

Charles A.C. Smith died in Chicago in 1904. Although his ring record was incomplete, Smith's establishment and bold claim to the World Colored Heavyweight Championship, a subjective designation, set the stage for those who followed.

Got Smith?

Adding to the confusion, as if more was needed, it was while scraping in upstate New York, against some feisty White competitors, that a fighter by the name of Smith caught the eye of a celebrity trainer.[15] William A. Muldoon, the famed promoter, trainer, and physical culturist, who had his own traveling company of gladiators, was looking for two Black boxers. And he found them both. They were billed as Muldoon's "Thunderbolt" and Muldoon's "Pickaninny." Smith took the moniker of the former, and the son of Muldoon's cook the latter. Both talented glove men typically fared well against "all comers," as the company traveled from venue to venue. Both became rather popular.

In 1893, this Smith fought in a number of battles, often as a part of Dominick McCaffrey's numerous boxing productions. He took on Peter Maher at Madison Square Garden on April 29, 1893; on July 4, 1893, in an afternoon show at the Polo Grounds, he faced Con Riordan; and on September 4, 1893, Muldoon's "Thunderbolt" met Ed Watkins, the "Dangerous Blacksmith." Then this Smith seemed to slip away from the sport.

Three years later, a C.C. Smith emerged and was billed as Muldoon's "Colored Thunderbolt." This Smith was landing in places like Buffalo and Niagara Falls where he participated in bouts against far less experienced fighters. However, there was an exception.

On February 15, 1897, a fighter named C.C. Smith, "Muldoon's Black Thunderbolt," entered a Buffalo ring against Peter Maher, perhaps the most dangerous fighter of the 19th century. A lively crowd at the Empire Athletic Club watched as the Irish champion simply dominated his opponent for two rounds. Then both fighters appeared to tire. *San Francisco Call* reported the sixth and final round:

> The men were slow to get together and there were loud hisses from the audience. Peter jabbed Smith lightly on the face with the left, and the latter knocked Peter's head back with a left jolt to the chin. Peter swung his left on the ear, and Smith ducked a savage right swing. Peter jabbed his left on the mouth, and left and right on the head. The men were sparring for wind as the bell rang. Referee Doscher then declared Maher the winner.[16]

After the Maher engagement, "Muldoon's Black Thunderbolt" once again turned to fighting novice pugilists at places like the Maple Avenue Athletic Club in Elmira or the Olympic Athletic Club in Buffalo. An article in the *Elmira Morning Telegram* on May 23, 1897, elaborated on the career of C.C. Smith, the boxer who recently fought Maher. It stated he was alive and well and making his home in Buffalo, New York.[17]

Morris Grant

Although the legal importation of African slaves ended in 1808, few abided by the restriction. More than one million slaves were transported from the Upper South to the Deep South during the antebellum years to support cotton plantations. If an enslaved fugue pugilist had to exist in a challenging environment, this was it. Born on May 11, 1845, likely along the beautiful coast of South Carolina, Morris Grant would grow to a height of over six feet and weigh over 180 pounds. As the port of Charleston was a hub for slavery, he would learn early the challenges he faced as a result of his complexion.[18]

By the late 1870s, Grant had found his way to New York, attested to by his winning the *Police Gazette* Boxing Tournament of 1878. Like Smith, he saw himself unconquerable and thus claimed the World Colored Heavyweight Championship. Although he would never meet C.A.C. Smith in a boxing ring, Grant was conscious of his predecessor's talent and claim. Both fighters shared an acquaintance with pugilist Charles Hadley.

All contenders, Black and White, kept an eye on *the* title. Australian Laurence "Larry" Foley and a burly White lad named Paddy Ryan were challenging for the World Bare-knuckle Championship. It would be the latter, however, who would meet Joe Goss, the current champion.

On the morning of May 30, 1880, Paddy Ryan defeated Joe Goss over 87 grueling rounds in a skirmish held at Collier's Station, West Virginia (a mere six miles from Pittsburgh). Fast and furious—the battle timed in at an hour and 27 minutes—the engagement was witnessed by 1,000 spectators who arrived before daylight. With the victory, Ryan claimed the championship.

Ryan was more of a street—or should I say canal, as in Erie—scrapper than bare-knuckle boxer. Having emigrated from Ireland to Troy, New York—the area a haven for brawlers like John Morrissey—the pugilist enjoyed the atmosphere. Through much of the 19th and into the early 20th century, the city, located along the Hudson River, was not just one of the most thriving cities in New York State, but one of the most prosperous cities in the entire country.

It became an epicenter for trade. Commerce was vastly increased after the construction of the Erie Canal in 1825—its eastern terminus directly across the Hudson from Troy at Cohoes. Honing his defensive skills first along the canal, and later as a saloon owner, Ryan never fancied himself a prizefighter. It was a local athletic director, Jim Kiloran, who persuaded him to consider the transition. After the Goss victory, Ryan was more interested in lining his pockets with exhibition money than defending his title against White challengers. Unlike his successor, he would not make the transition to gloved conflict.

Meanwhile, Morris Grant toiled along the docks and picked up odd jobs while treating boxing as an avocation until about 1881. Not intimidated by wandering into the Five Points Area—a sanctuary for gambling dens and brothels—Grant was nevertheless cautious. "The Five Points" area of Manhattan was where four streets converged: Anthony (now Worth), Cross (now Mosco), Orange (now Baxter), and Little Water (now nonexistent). By the 1870s, a new wave of Italian and Eastern European (primarily Jewish) immigrants were settling into the area. Criminal gangs competed for control of the revenue to be taken from illicit activities, and if that meant a street fight, then so it was. Where there were fisticuffs, there was typically a wager. It is safe to assume that Grant lined his pockets on occasion.

Charles Hadley v. Morris Grant—World Colored Heavyweight Championship

Word traveled faster than one might think in those days, and nobody was particularly excited to meet Grant, on the street or in the ring—the disincentive being his size and color. As a result, the fighter found himself befriending a fellow Black pugilist called "Professor" Charles Hadley. Although Hadley had been born in Nashville, Tennessee, the stocky fighter had battled out of St. Paul, Minnesota, and Bridgeport, Connecticut, before establishing himself in New York. Since necessity was the mother of invention, both fighters stayed in shape by battling each other—by some counts, over a dozen times between 1881 and 1883.

During their first recorded match, on January 14, 1881, Grant lost on points in a three-rounder. So Hadley claimed Grant's title. As the pair's fight frequency and friendship—not to mention the lack of terms and conditions to hold such a designation—lent itself to speculation, neither fighter expressed concern. Prizefighting was in demand and for a Black fighter that meant a healthy paycheck.

The *Evening* Star reported on April 7, 1882, "The glove fight for the heavy-weight (colored) boxing Championship of America, in New York, yesterday, between Charles Hadley and Morris Grant, was won by Hadley.[19] By this time, a championship (*Police Gazette*) medal existed and was presented to Hadley."[20]

To illustrate how business was conducted, on December 7, 1882, the pair, both labeled Colored "light-weight" champions, met at Harry Hill's theater for a Thursday afternoon affair.[21] The friendly match was set for four rounds under Queensberry rules. As was often the case, Harry Hill acted as referee and called time at 5:15 p.m. Both fighters, wearing hard gloves, had earned solid reputations and developed followings of their own. Hadley, who was in complete control, dominated the affair. As the *Lancaster Daily Intelligencer* noted: "Some ugly blows were given and received, the men finally clinching and pummeling each other soundly, and finally retiring to their separate corners thoroughly 'blown.' When time was again called Hadley assumed the offensive and drove his antagonist all about the stage, chased him twice into the dressing room and wound up by stretching him upon his back on the floor."[22]

Clearly beaten, Grant's backers tossed in the sponge, while Hill turned to Hadley and declared him the winner. The *Police Gazette* medal was presented to Charles Hadley for the third time. The fighter was quick to note that he would defend it against all comers. Then all hell broke loose. As the *Lancaster Daily Intelligencer* continued:

> At this juncture George Cooley, a Colored man, who had acted throughout as Grant's second rushed to the front, in a heated condition and asserted that he could "lick any 120 pound nigger in the country." "You can have it now, if you like," shouted Hadley, angrily, throwing down his gloves and striking Cooley fairly in the face. The two men then jumped into each other furiously, and in an instant the place was thrown into the greatest confusion. Men mounted chairs and tables and screamed themselves hoarse, and the crowd hurried down the aisle, and, seizing the combatants, dragged them struggling behind the scenes.[23]

No stranger to such antics, Hill calmly took control and essentially apologized for what had just occurred. Then, as only Harry Hill could do, he dismissed the audience.

Grant's size alone was intimidating, and he was often viewed as a bully or insensitive. In early 1883, Grant had a disagreement with a White gentleman, William Degnan. Brought before a magistrate, Grant, with his head cut and his right eye closed, pleaded his case. Standing alongside the boxer, Degnan listened before denying that he took any money.

The *Sun* provided the details:

> Turning to justice Duffy, and mastering his emotion in a measure, Grant said that he had taken Degnan and another friend to a saloon on Seventh Avenue and treated them to drinks. He put a $5 note on the bar to pay. Degnan grabbed it. Grant expostulated, whereupon his friends struck him, one with a billiard cue and the other with a bottle. Grant called for a policeman, and he and Degnan were arrested. To a suggestion by Justice Duffy that he was a boxer and ought to be able to defend himself against two men, Grant replied that it was the bottle and the billiard cue that bothered him. Justice Duffy discharged Grant and fined Degnan $5. The latter had only $2, and asked Grant to lend him the balance necessary to his release. The colored boxer had no money, but hurried from the court to borrow it for the service of his friend.[24]

By 1885, Grant had left the ring. Census data suggest that Grant stayed in New York City for the remainder of his life. From waiting tables to bouncing bars in the Tenderloin section of Manhattan (the area originally ran from 24th Street to 42nd Street and from Fifth Avenue to Seventh Avenue), the pugilist became accomplished at using his fists outside the ring as well. Supporting a family that included a wife and three daughters required perseverance. The ring took its toll, however, as Grant was in need of support to walk later in life. Morris Grant died in the Bronx in 1915.

In addition to his title, Grant's achievements included: battling with his successor for the title, Charles Hadley (1881); establishing a relationship, or rivalry, with a fellow Black boxer as an alternative to facing a White fighter, and being recognized as a Colored "heavy-weight" boxer by a major newspaper before the turn of the century (1883).

"Professor" Charles Hadley

Born a slave on September 30, 1846, in Nashville, Tennessee, Charles Hadley stood five feet, nine and a half inches tall.[25] As a youngster, he escaped servitude and wisely headed to the northeast. The compact fighter, with his tremendous reach and superior arm development, preferred to fight at 160 pounds.

The *St. Paul Daily Globe* reported: "When a mere boy [sic] he landed in New York and was a bootblack on the streets of the metropolis. In 1862, he was employed as a jockey by Capt. T.G. Moon of Louisville, Kentucky, and continued with that gentleman until 1868. He went to Bridgeport, Connecticut, in the latter year, and received his first fistic instructions from Ed McGlinchy (also spelled McGlinchey), whom the writer knows to have been one of the most experts of the time."[26]

In 1882, *Morning Journal* noted Hadley's ring highlights: "On May 18, 1879, in a match for $150 with the bare knuckles at Waterbury, Connecticut, he beat J.H. Brown in 63 rounds, occupying 1 hour and 28 minutes. On May 17, 1881, he beat Prof. Anderson in 18 rounds, in 44 minutes, for a purse of $50, at Bridgeport, Connecticut. On June 5, 1881, he beat J.H. Brown, with gloves, for a silver cup, at Bridgeport, in three rounds, Brown being knocked out of time. Prof. Hadley is willing to fight any Colored man for $500 a side."[27]

Charles Hadley v. Morris Grant—World Colored Heavyweight Championship

In what was considered by some historians as the first major rivalry between two professional Black fighters, Charles Hadley squared off against Morris Grant. Among many fights, a trio of New York battles stands out: "First the aforementioned battle on January 14, 1881, followed by April 6, 1882, and December 7, 1882. The latter contest, at Harry Hills, had all the trappings of a championship event. A source stated, "Hadley had won the *Police Gazette* medal, twice, and it was his to keep if he won it again."[28]

By 1882, Hadley found a home at Harry Hill's in the city and wasn't bashful about taking on all comers—if that meant sending a letter to the *New York Herald* noting his whereabouts, then that was just fine. Grant, for all intents and purposes, was out of the Colored championship mix by fall 1882.

George Godfrey v. Charles Hadley—World Colored Heavyweight Championship

With regard to George Godfrey, who succeeded Hadley as champion, the *St. Paul Globe* reported: "On January 18, in the same year (1883), Hadley fought a draw with George Godfrey in New York. On February 23, the two men met again, this time at Boston, Massachusetts, and for a purse of $300 and fought six rounds in 27 minutes at the conclusion of which Godfrey was declared the winner, and now claims the championship of the United States for colored heavy-weights."[29] Another source reported, "Both men were badly punished. In the fifth round, Godfrey fought Hadley to a stand-still, winning the battle and $100."[30] Such was the nature of era ring reporting.

Late in 1883, Hadley headed west and found a home in St. Paul, Minnesota, one of the top prizefight markets in the country and a city enhanced by Black migration. There he tutored the art of self-defense, gave exhibitions and even refereed—the addiction of conflict never fades from the heart of any fighter, regardless of color. But by the end of August 1885, Hadley made it clear he was retiring from the ring. The local newspapers, which respected the fighter's talent, were quick to point out his decision. At the time, he claimed his record was 10–1–1 over a 17-year career.[31]

Less than a year after his decision, Hadley was back in the confine—retirement from prizefighting was always subject to a final offer. Of course, what he saw as a challenge or taking on all-comers, he likely did not view as an official battle. Record-keeping was just not that important. By 1886, Hadley had earned the moniker "The Professor" for his scientific approach to his trade and teaching ability. On December 31, 1886, Hadley, entered the ring at the Theater Comique to battle a stubborn Frank Taylor, aka "Black Frank." Lacing up pairs of four-ounce gloves, both Black fighters engaged for 15 rounds to a draw.

The *St. Paul Daily Globe* reported: "Hadley, in spite of his [almost] 40 years and superfluous flesh, took punishment like an ox, and received Taylor's sledge-hammer blows without going to the floor even once. He seemed to lack strength, and his delivery, especially with his right was ineffective. Taylor was in splendid condition. He threw his right with great force, and in the tenth and 12th rounds almost ended the fight."[32]

To Hadley's credit, he matched Taylor for the first five rounds. In the sixth round, however, Taylor began to penetrate his antagonist's defense. By the tenth, Hadley was clinching as a form of damage control.

The *St. Paul Daily Globe* continued:

> When the 15th round was called a cheer went up from the house at the pluck of the contestants. Both appeared to be winded and a clinch followed the delivery of every blow. Taylor did all the fighting, but could not swing Hadley off his feet. Time was held nearly a minute, but Hadley still held the fort and walked to his corner at the finish. Patsey Mellen, the referee, stepped to the front and asked if there was anyone in the house who felt he had not had his money's worth. There was no response, and then Mellen added, "I declare the contest a draw."[33]

For Hadley to enter the ring with Frank Taylor took a tremendous amount of courage. In 1887, Hadley also engaged multiple times with Harris Martin, aka "Black Pearl." Taylor and Martin were the two finest local Black pugilists.

In addition to his title, Hadley's achievements included battling with two former titleholders, rival Morris Grant and title pioneer C.A.C. Smith, along with his successor to the title, George Godfrey, and being recognized as a Black boxer by a major newspaper before the turn of the century (1885).[34]

George "Old Chocolate" Godfrey

George Godfrey was born in March 20, 1853, in Charlottetown, Queens County, Prince Edward Island, Canada—then a colony of the United Kingdom.[35] Sarah Byers and William Godfrey were his parents. As a boy, not finding the island, with a population of about 65,000 and primarily White, conducive to his needs, he traveled to Boston and found employment as a porter at Little and Hayes, a silk importing office.[36]

Records note a first marriage on February 6, 1872, in Boston, Massachusetts, to Hannah Allen (Brewster) of Saint John, New Brunswick, Canada, followed by a second union to Clara Jane Forbes, also in the Hub, in 1874. Godfrey, who became an American citizen, was a rare boxer who always seemed to strike a balance between his family and his occupation. Standing at 5 feet, 10½ inches, and tipping at about 165 pounds, he was coordinated and athletic. When Godfrey took an interest in pugilism it surprised few, as he seemed to love all sports. However, when he was introduced to Professor John B. Bailey, who operated the Hub City Gym in Boston, boxing became his primary interest.

Most historians note his professional entry into pugilism in 1879. That's when Godfrey knocked out Ham Williams, Joe Dougherty, and Mose Laborn during a heavyweight competition in Boston. The following year, fighting under the moniker "Old Chocolate," he fought numerous unrecorded battles—the fighter's record doesn't really catch up to him until 1883.

George Godfrey v. Charles Hadley—World Colored Heavyweight Championship

George Godfrey defeated Charles Hadley at Cribb Hall in Boston on February 23, 1883, to capture the World Colored Heavyweight Championship. It was the first significant step of his brilliant career. The *Morning Appeal* reported, in a brief article under the title "Boston Scandal," on February 24: "There was a hard glove fight last night [February 23] between George Godfrey of this city, and Frank [Charles] Hadley of New York, both colored. John L. Sullivan was referee. The fight was a slugging match and both men were badly punished. In the fifth round Godfrey fought Hadley to a stand-still [sic], winning the battle [and $100]."[37]

Following his achievement, Godfrey, who had young children, preferred to fight primarily out of the Hub. There he did battle with Black pugilists McHenry "Minneapolis Star" Johnson, George Taylor, and even Charles A.C. Smith.[38] Perhaps in an attempt to lure the bare-knuckle champion into considering him as an opponent, Godfrey sparred with John L. Sullivan's sparring mates, Joe Lannon and Steve Taylor, both White Boston fighters. But Sullivan, a die-hard racist who always drew the color line, vehemently refused.

Peter Jackson v. George Godfrey—World Colored Heavyweight Championship

Just when it appeared that every door of opportunity was closed to the Boston pugilist, one opened on August 24, 1888. Enticed by a fight purse of $1,500 and $400 to defray his travel expenses, George Godfrey was welcomed by the California Athletic Club to San Francisco, California. There, in the club's gymnasium, he would meet Peter "Black Prince" Jackson, Australia's premier Black heavyweight. Jackson was a marvel in the ring, and many considered him the greatest fighter of the era. It was the opportunity of a lifetime for Godfrey, and he knew it.

As the *Omaha Daily Bee* reported:

Exactly at 9:25 p.m., Hiram Cook ordered the men to shake hands, and, discarding their extraneous toggery, they stood up and walked to the scratch. The difference in size was discouraging to the Bostonian's friends and Arthur Chambers, who had been eyeing the tall Australian keenly from the moment of his entrance. Jackson towered three or four inches above his brown-skinned opponent. The Australian's ebony skin shone like satin, and the muscles of his back, his chest and his sinewy neck showed that he had not neglected his training.[39]

Far from intimidated, Godfrey also looked impressive and tipped at 160, or at a 15-pound deficit to his opponent. Jackson seemed to fight in alternate rounds to preserve energy. The fight began to heat up in the fourth round, and by the fifth round, Godfrey was spitting blood at the scratch.

As the *Omaha Daily Bee* continued: "Smash after smash from the huge Australian's fists sounded on his [Godfrey] face till he changed to the color of an Indian, and Jackson's gloves grew carmine. It looked as if the Bostonian could never last out the round. Though fairly slaughtered, he fought like a tiger. Jackson's white drawers were sprinkled with blood by every blow."[40]

Throughout the beating, Godfrey grinned as the blood ran down his face and chest. He just would not relent. Exhausted, the Bostonian had to be assisted to his feet to begin the 15th round. Jackson, aware of his dominance, was having his way with his opponent round after round.

The *Omaha Daily Bee* concluded: "He [Godfrey] astonished every one by remaining on his feet till the 19th round, when Jackson, after the usual tactics of drawing him back to the ropes, delivered him a right-hander over the region of the heart which ended the contest. The plucky Bostonian threw up his hands and gave up the fight."[41]

Despite losing the World Colored Heavyweight Championship, George Godfrey's reputation was bolstered. Those who viewed the fight were struck by the American's endurance and ability. Yet a somewhat dejected Godfrey was not particularly satisfied with his own performance. He took a few exhibitions to pick up some pocket change before heading back home. At one point, Godfrey pondered a European presence in hopes of drawing out a White champion, but he couldn't land the financial backing.

On February 4, 1889, he drew against White pugilist Joe Lannon over 15 rounds, and later knocked out White pugilist Jack Ashton in the 14th round of a November 7, 1889, encounter.[42] Both were Sullivan sparring partners—John L. Sullivan even refereed the Lannon bout. Fascinating was Sullivan's preoccupation with authority, he could comfortably count over a Black man, he just didn't want to be underneath one.

Taking two bouts in 1890, Godfrey knocked out Canadian Patsy Cardiff in the 16th

On July 8, 1889, John L. Sullivan faced Jake Kilrain (right) for the world heavyweight title in the last heavyweight championship held under London Prize Ring Rules, bare knuckles. Note the makeshift ring that was placed on a farm in Richburg, Mississippi (Library of Congress, LC-USZ6—8647).

round on May 8 and got the best of "Denver" Ed Smith (Edward Corcoran) over 23 rounds on November 25.[43] When the California Athletic Club offered him a shot at former heavy-weight champion (as recognized by the *Police Gazette*) Jake Kilrain, of Baltimore, it was tough to ignore.[44]

Godfrey was familiar with Joseph Killion, aka Jake Kilrain, as the pair, who both fought out of New England, had met earlier. But, this was not the same White heavyweight he tackled almost a decade ago, but a man who fought gallantly in a 75-round loss to John L. Sullivan at Richburg, Mississippi, for the world title—the last world heavyweight championship prizefight decided with bare knuckles under London Prize Ring rules. Branded by his strength and durability, Kilrain lost at the start of the 76th round. After over two hours of battling, in over 100-degree conditions, Mike Donovan, his second, threw in the sponge. To this day, the Kilrain v. Sullivan fight can rightly be listed among the greatest fights of the pre-modern era.

It was this Jake Kilrain who would meet George "Old Chocolate" Godfrey, for $5,000— the winner's take was $4,500—on March 13, 1891, in San Francisco at the California Athletic Club. A large and excited group of select spectators awaited the boxers, who donned five-and-a-half-ounce mitts.

As the *Rock Island Daily Argus* reported: "Both men showed up in fine form. Kilrain weighed 192 and Godfrey 173. Kilrain's seconds were Jim Hall and Muldoon. Peter Jackson and Frank Steele, of Boston, seconded Godfrey. The mill began sharp at 9 p.m. For the first five rounds Kilrain did all the fighting, getting in right and left on the Negro, the latter frequently clinching to save himself."[45]

For every blow Godfrey managed, his durable opponent answered with a pair. By the eighth and ninth rounds, the cumulative damage to both fighters was showing. Kilrain was going to the body, while Godfrey continued headhunting. From the 11th to the 16th, Godfrey took the bulk of the punishment. In the 17th, Kilrain went headhunting as well and was quite successful. Godfrey, who appeared numb to the pain, continued to endure while exhibiting that nervous laugh of his—a mannerism he perfected to convince his opponent that no damage was being done. By the 41st round, Godfrey had become familiar with the floor but not long enough to end the battle.

As the *Rock Island Daily Argus* concluded (under the subtitle: "Kilrain Knocks Him Out at Last"): "At the end of the 42nd round, Jake's efforts began to tell on him. In the 43rd round he did little work at first and appeared to be saving himself, but at the end he forced the fighting, following Godfrey all around the ring, smashing him wickedly and repeatedly and finally knocked him out. Jake's reach was much longer than Godfrey's and that advantage was noticed all through the fight."[46]

Following the seemingly endless Kilrain bout, Godfrey returned home. Entering the ring on May 16, 1892, in Coney Island, Godfrey knocked out Joe Lannon in the fourth round of a well-publicized event. The *Seattle Post-Intelligencer* reported: "At the call of time for the fifth round Godfrey responded and Lannon refused to get up, whereupon the referee awarded the victory to Godfrey. Lannon was very much exhausted, and could hardly have lasted another round."[47]

Having developed a following at the Coney Island Athletic Club, Godfrey was offered a match with Joe Choynski on October 31, 1892. Agile, clever, and fast afoot, Choynski was a popular pugilist. Having delivered four of his last five competitors by way of knockout in two rounds or less had grabbed a headline or two.

The front page of the *Helena Independent* read, "A Vicious Prize Fight, Joe Choynski whips George Godfrey in Fifteen Very Hard Fought Rounds." It was a very apt description of an excellent battle. "Chrysanthemum Joe" tipped at 168, while Godfrey weighed seven pounds to his advantage. A strong preliminary saw Kid Hogan barely defeat Dolly Lyons. The responsive crowd was provided with another thrill when Peter Jackson entered the venue and sat in a private box.

When the headliners began sparring at 10:10 p.m., it had all the makings of a scientific display. Then to everyone's surprise, Godfrey threw strategy to the wind. He rushed Choynski in the third round but was nearly decapitated. He returned to his senses during the following rounds. By the sixth round, Choynski was bleeding profusely from a wound to his eye. Frustrated by his antagonist's assault on his optic, Choynski went to Godfrey's stomach in the eighth. It wasn't a great idea as Godfrey sent his opponent to his knees with a powerful right. Choynski was dropped again at the very end of the 12th round. Back on his feet in the 13th, albeit briefly, Choynski had his lower lip split by a Godfrey straight left—he had been down again just prior to the blow. Godfrey began to slow in the 14th, leaving his adversary an opportunity to target his eye, while forcing him into the ropes.

The *Helena Independent* closed the account as follows: "Godfrey was totally blind in the left eye as he came up for the 15th. He rushed at Choynski like a blind bull, getting a straight jab on the closed eye, which staggered him. After several ineffectual attempts to land on Choynski's face and stomach the latter swung his right on the damaged eye and knocked the colored man completely out."[48]

In the last of his noteworthy challenges, George Godfrey fought Peter Maher on May 28, 1894. Maher, with over 50 bouts under his belt, was a formidable pugilist who could paralyze an opponent with a single blow. However, he was as graceful as a bull in a china closet and had a glass jaw. After destroying a few worthy opponents in Ireland and picking up a few titles, Maher headed across the pond in 1891. He held his own until crossing paths with Bob Fitzsimmons on March 28, 1892. Managing to last 12 rounds with "Ruby Robert," which was better than most, Maher finally surrendered. Since then, he had become a knockout artist, disposing of four by the form in his last six bouts.

Four thousand fans turned out to watch Peter Maher destroy George Godfrey in a gloved contest at the Casino in Boston. The *United Opinion* reported: "Maher clearly and completely bested Old Chocolate. In science, hitting powers, in generalship and in avoidance, Godfrey was outpointed. From start to finish it was Maher's fight. He punched Godfrey as often as he cared to. George was slow, and awkward and stiff."[49]

Later, Godfrey ran a boxing school in

John Lawrence Sullivan, generally recognized as the last heavyweight champion of bare-knuckle boxing under the London Prize Ring Rules (Library of Congress, LC-USZ6—19896).

Boston. Records state that he had six children. To Godfrey, being a father was always more important than being a pugilist. While he invested his earnings in real estate, equally important was his children's education. "Boston's George Godfrey" died at home in Revere, Massachusetts, of tuberculosis on October 17, 1901.[50]

All of George Godfrey's ring achievements can be summed up by his induction into the PEI (Prince Edward Island) Sports Hall of Fame in 1990. While he has yet to make it to Canastota, and the International Boxing Hall of Fame, it is only a matter of time

John Lawrence Sullivan, also known as the "Boston Strong Boy," was the first heavyweight champion of gloved boxing (1885–1892) and was generally recognized as the last heavyweight champion of bare-knuckle boxing under the London Prize Ring Rules. The Irish-American boxer was hell-bent never to fight a Black man in the prize ring and firmly drew the color line. George Godfrey did not live long enough to witness a Black man fight for the Heavyweight Championship of the World.

The Color Line, 1876–1888

These four men, Charles A.C. Smith, Morris Grant, Charles Hadley, and George Godfrey, were not only claimants to a designation, but pioneers of pugilism. Despite adversity and criticism, they persevered in the manly art of self-preservation. In doing so, they expanded the horizon of boxing—just acknowledging the obscure designation was an accomplishment, even if the sport remained segregated.[51] Smith created the title, Grant seconded the motion, and Hadley took it fair and square, as did Godfrey. Legitimacy was confirmed when the title, and its transfer, was recognized inside a major newspaper.

To witness one of the most popular periodicals of its time, the *National Police Gazette*, award a medal for the (World Colored Heavyweight) Championship of America—a Black sporting prize—was proof that the designation, or tool if you will, was accomplishing its task.

So what about the color line? By examining its evolution during the reign of these Colored Heavyweight Champions, along with those that will follow, the term can be placed in its proper perspective. And what better tool to use than period citations? From all across this great land, you will hear first-hand interpretations of the color line both in, and occasionally outside, the ring.[52]

For an initial perspective, we'll turn to the *Wheeling Register* on January 6, 1883:

> That the abolition of slavery has not abolished the color line in this country is a fact that is every day becoming more patent. Men, who maintain that it has, hold to a theory rather than a practical fact. We have simply decreed by law that the white line and the color line may run parallel; they never touch; and the tendency is to a wider space between. This, we say, is the practical fact, without reference to the differing views as to what should be or what was or is intended to be. Neither political, denominational, educational, social or business influences have served to change that relationship, or draw the lines more closely together.[53]

Jumping ahead two years and moving westward, the *Salt Lake Herald*, on January 4, 1885, noted: "The color line in society is as well defined now as ever, and it will never be less distinct than it is today. Nature herself has drawn it, and she makes no mistakes which legislation or society or sentiment can overcome. Men and women of the white and black races may associate with each other on occasions, and the colored people may be treated with as much respect and consideration as the whites, but the color line will exist; it can not be rubbed out until the natures of both races have been recast, and the prejudices which have existed and been cultivated for centuries are overcome."[54]

Skipping three years ahead, the *St. Paul Daily Globe* reported, under the title, "Sullivan Won't Notice a Coon," on December 30, 1888: "Sullivan's pugilistic backer here, apropos of the McAuliffe-Jackson fight today said that Jackson might challenge Sullivan, but that the Boston man would pay no attention to it as he had long ago declined to meet any colored men in the ring or any man who stands up with a colored fighter."[55]

THREE

The Black Prince

Making the journey all the way from Australia to San Francisco, Peter Jackson had only one thing in mind: winning the World Heavyweight Championship. But before the Aussie turned his attention to John L. Sullivan, he looked to George Godfrey and the World Colored Heavyweight Title. At the same time, as many others turned their observation to him. Jackson was just so handsome and charming that most women couldn't take their eyes off of him regardless of the setting. Although he stood a towering six feet, two inches, his long legs gave him the appearance of being taller.

The *San Francisco Call* noted his arrival: "He arrived in this city in 1888, and was then the picture of an ideal athlete. Tall, lithe, well proportioned, he attracted the attention of passersby on the street. Although not well educated he had mingled so much with men of the world that he acquired a polished manner. He was possessed of a quick wit and was a clever, well-informed conversationalist. He could talk on a variety of subjects, but could not be drawn into a discussion of his own prowess nor was he ever heard to speak slightingly of an opponent."[1]

Peter James Jackson, aka "The Black Prince," was born on September 23, 1860, in Christiansted, on the island of St. Croix in the Danish West Indies (U.S. Virgin Islands).[2] The son of Joseph, a warehouseman, and his wife, Julia, he was educated at St. Paul's parish school before seeking his dreams in Australia—then part of the British Empire.[3] Arriving at Sydney, located on the East Coast, about 1879, the youngster eventually found employment at the Greengate Hotel.[4] It was at the inn, some claim, that he was introduced to bare-knuckle boxing. Fascinated by the sport, he began reading every written tidbit about the fight game and even joined a gymnasium. In the fall of 1880, the youngster's skills caught the eyes of Larry Foley, a boxing manager and instructor. Knowing a thing or two about the sweet science, Foley, also the bare-knuckle champion of Australia, saw promise in the youngster.

Honing his skills at the Academy of Music, Foley's Hall, and other Sydney establishments, it wasn't long before Peter Jackson envisioned bigger and better things. On September 25, 1886, he captured the Australian (gloved) Heavyweight Championship by defeating Australian Tom Lees.[5] As Jackson developed into a very skillful and strategic fighter, Foley's instruction was paying off nicely. Casting swift and strong combinations, Jackson feinted and sidestepped with precision, all while mastering the valuable art of energy conservation.

Peter Jackson v. George Godfrey—World Colored Heavyweight Championship

Realizing that Sydney lacked the talent necessary to improve his ability, Peter Jackson headed to San Francisco. Unannounced, he arrived there on May 12, 1888. Taking at least two exhibitions and perhaps a minor contest, Jackson gradually acclimated to his new American surroundings. His first real challenge didn't take place until August 24, 1888, at the California Athletic Club. There, Colored heavyweight title in hand, George Godfrey awaited the Australian.

Under Marquis of Queensberry rules, and using two-ounce gloves, both fighters immediately went after each other hammer and tongs. In the only knockdown of the battle, Jackson sent Godfrey down with an enormous uppercut in the second round. Patient, Jackson exhibited tremendous control and accuracy with his left jab—taking command in the tenth frame, he had Godfrey's face battered and bleeding by the 15th round. The relentless Canadian, who needed assistance from his seconds to leave his corner during the final rounds, capitulated in the 19th frame. Swollen and exhausted at the end, Jackson marveled at the indefatigability of his rival.

A Quick Glimpse at John L. Sullivan

Born and raised in Boston's South End, John L. Sullivan became a Gilded Age American sports hero. As a heavyweight champion boxer for more than a decade, the Irish-American idol would push everyone off the mountain of pugilism—this while shoving over a million dollars into his Boston bank account. Then, by simply placing a pair of mitts over his outlawed bare knuckles, he confirmed his epic status.

His oversized personality, Herculean battles, and imperious challenges captured the public's imagination while igniting the virility of every male from England to Australia. Fans flocked to him like termites to springwood. Everyone wanted to touch him or even "shake the hand that shook the hand of John L. Sullivan." The Boston Irish drank to him, mimicked his poses, and loved him like a brother.

John L. Sullivan's return to home (Boston) just happened to coincide with Peter Jackson's arrival in America. The "Boston Strong Boy" had recently defended his Bare-Knuckle Heavyweight crown by drawing Charlie Mitchell over 39 rounds, or three hours, 10 minutes, and 55 seconds. Fought under London Prize Ring Rules, the event was held in Chantilly, France. In over 40 battles, John L. had yet to taste defeat.

Having to answer to no one, Sullivan, larger-than-life, continued to line his pockets with exhibition money for the remainder of 1888. The following year, he put up the bare-knuckle title for the final time against Jake Kilrain. The fight was halted in the 75th round and Sullivan retained his title. A stubborn racist who adamantly drew the color line, he refused to fight a Black man under any circumstances.

The *Evening Star* reflected:

With the advent of Sullivan came the uplift of prize fighting. John L. Sullivan became a prominent figure in the news of the day. When he visited England he was received by Albert Edward, Prince of Wales, afterward Edward VII, and John L. Sullivan was gracious enough to treat the prince as an equal. It was Sullivan's time that the late Marquis of Queensberry modified the London prize-ring rules by propagating the Marquis of Queensberry rules. After that prizefighting was permitted in many of the states. It was no longer necessary to hold them in isolated woods, on barges or secret places where the sheriffs or the militia could not run them down.

But there still remained a certain element of romance and glamour to the ancient game. Sullivan was what the boys would call a "colorful figure." Boiling drunk or gravely sober, he remained a big figure.[6]

In sharp contrast to "The Black Prince," his immense ivory frame appeared tempered by time and resolve.

Jackson's Initial Exposure to America

Following his bout with Godfrey, Peter Jackson met White heavyweight Joe McAuliffe at the California Athletic Club on December 28, 1888.[7] Initially, the local fighter drew the color line; however, a financial incentive altered his point of view. The club, which was criticized over concerns of fair play, had its president confirm that it was indeed a gentlemen's club and that the question of color was not an issue.

McAuliffe, to his credit (he had one hand bandaged), managed to take his adversary 24 rounds before facing defeat—he even dropped Jackson in the tenth frame. "The Black Prince" recovered from the embarrassment and eventually delivered the finishing blow to his opponent.[8] Prizefighting, at least in San Francisco, was no walk in the park. With the victory, Jackson added the enigmatic title of Heavyweight Championship of the Pacific Coast to his resume, while filling his wallet with $3,000 ($79,488 in 2019 dollars). More importantly, at least to local residents,

A rather stern-looking image of Peter Jackson as it appeared on a promotional button sponsored by High Admiral Cigarettes (author's collection).

he ignited a celebration in the Black community—the patina of a boxing ring took on a different hue.

After defeating Patsy Cardiff during 10 hard-fought rounds on April 26, 1889, Jackson decided to head east.[9] Cardiff was the fighter who only a couple of years ago gained fame by not being knocked out by Sullivan and even breaking the champion's hand. Jackson's victory over the Canadian was a clear statement of his ring prowess. Picking up bouts or exhibitions along the way, not to mention a manager (Charles "Parson" Davies), kept him occupied. By late July, Jackson was in Buffalo, then a hotbed of pugilism. There he picked up wins over Billy Baker, Tom Lynch, and Paddy Brennan. But fighting in Buffalo was no cake-walk for Jackson as Lynch bit him, he was involved in a street brawl, and Brennan was none too happy about getting his nose split. A lackluster victory over Jack Fallon, "The Brooklyn Strong Boy," on August 19, 1889, marked the end to his first trip to America. It was now off to the United Kingdom, then Ireland.[10]

Jackson faced Jem Smith, the heavyweight champion of England, on November 11, 1889. What many believed would be a spectacular fight turned out to be a London bust. As the *Salt Lake Herald* reported: "The fight lasted less than two rounds and Smith was so badly punished in the first round that in the second he deliberately cross buttocked Jackson, the referee at once giving the fight to the Australian amid a scene of great excitement."[11]

Using his height and reach to his advantage, Jackson took immediate command of the battle. He drew Smith in with feints and then completely abused him. His straight left was so damaging that Smith could not mount a successful retreat. At the end of the first round, Smith was visibly drained while Jackson remained stoic. In the second, when Smith went to the body Jackson countered with headshots. Sensing Smith's weakness, Jackson chased his adversary around the ring. Smith finally hung on to the ropes like a rock climber without a safety line. When Smith opted for wrestling tactics in the middle of the ring, Referee George Vize had little choice but to award the contest to Jackson.

As the *Salt Lake Herald* concluded:

> Jackson was the hero of an ovation, his manly style and fair fighting having gained him the good will of the whole company. Smith tore his gloves off and made a rush at Jackson, who had treated him so fairly as to get words of scorn from some of the fighters in the crowd. Before Smith reached Jackson a police inspector present promptly interfered, and Smith was advised to bottle his wrath. If Smith had laid a hand on Jackson after the latter had put down his hands on being proclaimed victor, there would have been a pretty rumpus as Jackson had made friends of the crowd by his manly style of fighting, whereas the crowd, English though it was, had as much of Smith as it wanted, and felt that he never deserved the title of heavyweight champion of England.[12]

Meanwhile, others who witnessed Jackson's ring prowess recognized his potential. Everyone, or so it seemed, understood—no, salivated at the mere thought—that a battle between Jackson and John L. Sullivan would be the fight of the century. Noting that there had only been three superior Black pugilists prior to Jackson—Molineaux, Robert Smith and Charles Jones, all Americans staking claims in England—spoke, at least to most, that Jackson would ignite a fervor never seen before in America. That is, of course, if the pair could be matched.

The *Appeal* claimed in December 1889, while Jackson was in England:

> Arrangements are being made by the New Erie County Athletic club for a glove-fight in this city [Buffalo] between John L. Sullivan and the Colored pugilist Peter Jackson. A purse of $30,000 is being raised, and the officers of the organization say that they have received word from Sullivan that he will meet the Colored fighter for that much money, which shall go to the winner.[13]

The discrimination that Peter Jackson had experienced in Australia was mild compared to what he encountered in America—the backlash of Reconstruction was reaching a pinnacle. Since racial animosity was common in the boxing ring, perhaps creative solutions, or so Jackson believed, needed to be considered. To silence the critics, Jackson became a versifier. With the assistance of Hugh Keough of the *Chicago Sporting Journal,* this poem was printed in America before Christmas in 1889:

> Peter's skin may be against him—
> Blacker than a rainy night—
> But the blokes that stood forninst him
> Learned too well they'd had a fight.
> There's that dusky gent from Boston,
> He don't want no more of Pete;
> Then McAuliffe ran against him-
> Do Him? Yes, like thrashin' wheat!
>
> Then before him Cardiff stands up
> Just to get it on the neck.
> Smith can hardly put his hands up
> When he got a sudden check—
> Smith, who carried cockney money
> By the hundred thousand pounds,

Proved to Pete as sweet as honey—
　　Punched out in a brace of rounds!

Fair and square he made his record,
　　Always treated people right;
Be his skin black, blue or checkered
　　Scratch him and you'll find him white.
Dignified you'll find him standin'
　　In the head set of the dance,
No concessions he's demandin'—
　　Give the colored gent a chance.

"Coon is coons?" Well that's amusin';
　　Now admit that pugs is pugs;
Men who make their livin' bruisin'
　　Got no right to put on lugs.
When a black man isn't lackin'
　　In the strength of head and heart,
When he's got the proper backin'
　　He should get a level start.

Color doesn't cut no figger
　　When it comes to make a fight;
Then the game and clever "nigger"
　　Is the equal of the white
Men who've got no social ratin'
　　You will find eight times in nine
Are the first to do the pratin',
　　First to draw the color line.

All admit that Pete's a fighter—
　　Well, I claim, that settles it;
If his skin was ten times lighter
　　'Twouldn't change the case a bit.
Straight-haired pugs may keep on sneerin
　　Jackson's comin' just as hard;
He is bound to get a hearin'—
　　Dusky Pete can not be barred.[14]

Jackson's comportment continued to catch Americans by surprise—White Americans that is. He didn't fit their mold of a Black fighter, and his counters, both in and out of the ring, were masterfully delivered. But his unpredictability was a social risk for White America. Should Jackson be placed in a ring with Sullivan, it would be the ultimate racial showdown. A loss by Sullivan could be viewed as a sign of racial inferiority, and that was simply intolerable. Still, the thought of such a match sold newspapers, and that was good enough to keep the fairy tale alive.

In his final fight of the year, on December 24 at Leinster Hall in Dublin, Jackson defeated the heavy-handed Peter Maher by way of a second round kayo. Fighting from San Francisco to Dublin, Jackson did not lose a single battle in 1889.

It was time to return to America. Jackson opened up 1890 with half a dozen battles, including a decision victory over "Denver Ed" Smith in Chicago, but many of his desired matches didn't pan out.[15] Dejected by the lack of competition, Jackson returned home to Australia in August.[16]

That fall, the nearest he came to defeat was an eight-round draw in Melbourne, Victoria, against Joe Goddard. The October 20 bout, at the Crystal Palace, was for both the

Australian Heavyweight Title (Goddard, first defense) and the Commonwealth (British Empire) Heavyweight Title (Jackson, first defense). Jackson, taller with a longer reach than his opponent, appeared out of condition, and his performance indicated the same.

The opening round was marked by vicious infighting as Goddard tried to overcome Jackson's reach. The *Los Angeles Herald* reported: "Jackson was perspiring when time was called for the third round. Goddard started in with both hands. Jackson lowered his head as he tried a body hook, and Goddard struck lightly on his opponent's head, getting a bad cut and going to the ground. Rising, he forced Jackson to the ropes with smashes on the ribs. He was, however, sent down again with a blow in the face. The round closed with Goddard rallying wildly."[17]

Following a fierce fourth round, both men found themselves down in the fifth. The sixth round was even, and the seventh was marked by a questionable blow—it happened as the referee was separating the fighters after a clinch—to Jackson that some believed was a foul. The claim was not allowed.

The *Los Angeles Herald* continued: "In the eighth and last round, Jackson tried hard to wind his man, but Goddard stood up to him, and got home with both hands in the face, stopping Jackson's rush. There were smart exchanges, and Goddard essayed a rush, but Jackson stopped him with his left on the ribs. Goddard landed his right and left on Jackson's face. Time was called, and the contest stopped. The referee said one of the judges had decided in favor of Jackson, and one in favor of Goddard, so he declared the contest a draw."[18]

From Melbourne, it was off to Sydney for his final battle of the year. Following a draw with Mick Dooley, on November 19, 1890, Jackson began looking back to America.

In San Francisco, an undefeated White heavyweight was turning heads. Standing six feet one inch, James John Corbett was as handsome as he was adept. Born to an Irish family that emigrated in 1854, the muscular 24-year-old held victories over Joe Choynski, Australian Billy Smith, and Jake Kilrain. His demeanor and interests, at least outside the ring, were similar to those of Jackson, some even viewing him as a pale reflection of "The Black Prince." Sensing an enormous opportunity, the California Athletic Club went about arranging a match they hoped would be conducted at their auditorium.

Corbett, a student of boxing, respected the skill of Jackson; just the thought of being matched with the talented Colored fighter aroused his curiosity. For the record, Jackson, also intrigued by the match, was not offended by his opponent's complexion. Mutual admiration aside, both fighters were galvanized by the $10,000 purse—$8,500 going to the winner and $1,500 to the loser. Most of the ring pundits saw the match as even.

Of course the winner was destined for a match with Frank "Paddy" Slavin—Jackson's Australian rival. Through the gates of Slavin, the *National Police Gazette*'s Golden Boy and recognized world heavyweight champion, was the only way to garner consideration by the great John L. Sullivan—at least that was how the newspapers played it.[19]

The *Helena Independent* wasn't bashful: "Peter Jackson was never one-half the man that John L. Sullivan was, and is not now, even in the heel of the remarkable American's career. Nothing but a look backwards at the eight-round contest between Peter and Goddard is needed to nail this statement."[20]

Peter Jackson v. James J. Corbett, May 21, 1891

It was greatest heavyweight boxing match ever made. That's how the local broadsheets saw the James J. Corbett versus Peter Jackson battle held at the California Athletic

Club on May 21, 1891. Both of the principals received salutes as they entered the ring a few minutes after nine o'clock. The club appointed Hiram Cook referee. As for the combatants: Peter Jackson tipped at 197 pounds and was seconded (assisted) by Sam Fitzpatrick and Billy Smith; James J. Corbett scaled at 185 and was supported by his brother Harry, John Donaldson, and Billy Delaney.[21] The *Salem Daily News* assessed the battle in this fashion:

> In the first six rounds Jackson had the best of it. From the sixth to the 25th the men fought fairly well, honors being easy, with Jackson showing less distress than Corbett. The latter was game and fought strongly, but it was plain that he was not such a seasoned slugger as Jackson. In the 25th round, in a rushing rally, Corbett punished Jackson with heavy body blows, and thereafter the black showed no eagerness for close work. It was not known until after the mill, however, that Jackson's ribs were broken, and that Corbett was also badly injured. The fight from the 25th to the 61st round was simply a standoff, no hard work being done. At the close of the 61st round the fight was stopped by the referee. (Ruled a No Contest!) The men were unfit to fight longer, and both were willing to stop. All bets were off, and the club holds on to the purses. So if either gets the cash they will have to fight for it again.[22]

For Corbett, the result was nearly as good as a victory—Sullivan would accept his title challenge.[23] However, the "Boston Strong Boy," who had ignored Jackson's provocations for years, would not alter his racial stance. Making his way to the East Coast after the fight, Jackson grabbed a few warm-up bouts and exhibitions before heading back to the United Kingdom on February 24. He was scheduled to meet Frank Slavin, for 20 rounds, inside the National Sporting Club at Covent Garden, London, on May 30, 1892. Jackson's only hope, so he believed, was for Corbett to capture the title, then allow him a rematch.

Jackson v. Slavin, May 30, 1892

Frank "Paddy" Slavin, aka "Sydney Cornstalk," was roughly the same size as Peter Jackson. While he had the same fundamental skill—the White pugilist was also trained by Larry Foley—and punching power as Jackson, he lacked his finesse. Capturing the Heavyweight Championship of Australia in 1888, Slavin picked up the *Police Gazette* championship belt by defeating Joe McAuliffe two years later. He was quick to assert his position as Britain's top heavyweight. Peter Jackson thought differently and was more than happy to defend his Commonwealth (British Empire) Heavyweight Title (2nd defense) against his Australian antagonist.

Slavin, rough around the edges, was considered a racist, and his relationship with Jackson was complex. As he saw it, what stood between him and immortality was Jackson, a Black fighter—there was more, however, as according to some, the pair once shared the same love interest. Jackson tipped at about 193 pounds and was seconded by "Parson" (Charles E.) Davies (manager), Joe Choynski, and Jem Young, while Slavin scaled at about 185 and was seconded by his brother Jack, Tim Williams, and Tim Burrows. The referee was Bernard John Angle. Lord Lonsdale provided an introductory speech prior to the bout.

The *Caldwell Tribune* reported: "Jackson's blows looked playful but they hurt. He countered well and took all the sting out of Slavin's tremendous lunges. Jackson gradually wore his opponent down, and when it came to the finish he gave Slavin one of the handsomest settlers—a right hook to Slavin's throat that sent him to the ropes—ever witnessed to finish the match. Despite the fact that Jackson is a Negro, his victory is extremely well received. Jackson invariably nailed his opponent as the latter came on, thus securing a blow of double impact."[24]

A few months later, on September 7, 1892, Corbett defeated Sullivan at the Olympic Club in New Orleans, Louisiana. By knocking out his undefeated antagonist in the 21st round, "Gentleman Jim" earned the Heavyweight Championship of the World, and he sent the "Boston Strong Boy" into retirement. Just what type of champion the San Francisco fighter would be remained to be seen.

Corbett dodged Jackson's immediate challenges by engaging in theatrical productions. Finally, amidst public pressure, the champion relented, with a caveat of course: he accepted an offer ($10,000) from the Florida Athletic Club knowing full well that Jackson would not fight in the South: For safety's sake, Jackson chose to fight north of the Mason-Dixon line in America, or anywhere in England.[25]

The *Fort Worth Gazette* quoted Jackson as stating: "Corbett may accept the offer of the Florida Athletic club, but I shall not agree to fight in any place in the South, no matter what inducements are offered, and Corbett is well aware of this fact. If Corbett was in earnest for the contest to take place, why doesn't he fight for the $20,000 posted and the $15,000 purse the National Sporting club has offered? Thirty-five thousand dollars should be inducement enough for him to fight in England."[26]

Uncle Tom's Cabin

Connecticut author Harriet Beecher Stowe wrote 30 books but was best known for her novel *Uncle Tom's Cabin* (1852), which depicted the harsh conditions for enslaved African

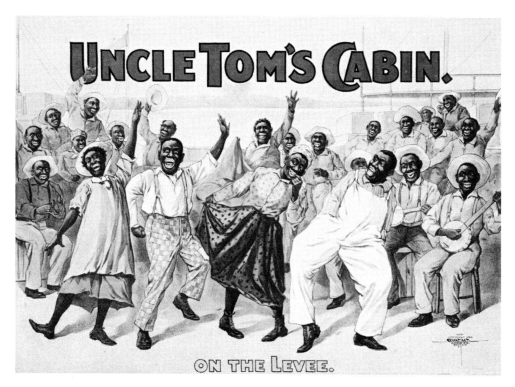

Theater poster for the play *Uncle Tom's Cabin*, based on an anti-slavery novel by Harriet Beecher Stowe. Starring in a production of the novel, Peter Jackson portrayed a character far different from his ring persona (Library of Congress, LC-USZ6—36250).

Americans. The book reached millions through print and theatrical performances. Influential in the United States, it energized anti-slavery forces in the American North, while provoking widespread anger in the South. As a White abolitionist from a famous religious family, Stowe was influential for both her writings and her public stances on social issues of the day. As it happened, she was so instrumental that many historians claim she laid the groundwork for the Civil War.

Uncle Tom's Cabin, the best-selling novel of the 19th century and the second-best-selling book of that century, following the Bible, featured the character of Uncle Tom, a long-suffering Black slave around whom the stories of other characters revolved. The sentimental novel depicted the reality of slavery while also asserting that Christian love can overcome something as destructive as enslavement of fellow human beings.

However, far more Americans saw the story as a stage play or musical than a book—this courtesy of hundreds of theater productions based on the work, or "Tom shows" that quickly became the rage.[27] How ironic that Peter Jackson, the era's premier boxer, would depict the era's premier fictional character. The man nobody could whip in the ring was "whipped to death" nightly before standing room only audiences.[28]

By 1893, Jackson focused more on exhibitions and his theater work than his ring genius. Later, it became clear that many of those attending the play hoped to see Jackson in action. So between acts, and even after the show, he would spar with boxer and stablemate Joe Choynski—both fighters were under the umbrella of Parson Davies.[29] Turning his back on pugilism, Jackson would part ways with his manager by 1895. As his theater work drew to a conclusion, the fighter pondered the idea of opening a boxing school in London and did so in 1897.[30]

In retrospect, had Jackson been an American and thoroughly comprehended the world of the stage character he was playing, he might have opted for a better choice; furthermore, the neophyte actor bore no physical resemblance to Uncle Tom. Jackson was being used merely as a pawn, or sales tool—he was billed as "the most famous Colored man in America."

When production ended, Jackson tended to some of his business enterprises before heading to St. Croix. From there it was on to England in 1894, where he sparred, drank, gambled, and enjoyed female companionship. Like every fighter who was pushed into the background, his mind was haunted by the past. When the heavyweight championship of the world passed to Bob Fitzsimmons, his former sparring partner, Jackson regained a sense of pugilistic optimism—this despite his age and waning ring skills. He left England and headed to San Francisco. Enter James J. Jeffries, an undefeated California heavyweight with championship dreams.

Sacrificial Lamb—Peter Jackson v. James J. Jeffries

Nobody truly believed—although many, such as those who saw him in his heyday, wanted to—that Peter Jackson was capable of giving anyone a competitive ring battle. After all, five years had passed since he last entered an ambitious conflict, his encounter with Frank Slavin. Scheduled to meet Jim Jeffries, a rising heavyweight star, at Woodward's Pavilion in San Francisco on March 22, 1898, Jackson believed otherwise.

Those who followed the fight game understood that the last person to recognize that the sport has passed him by was always the gladiator himself—a warrior never admits defeat. Was Jackson blind to his current ability? Nobody was certain, but the *Times* stated:

It is claimed that he has lost none of his wonderful skill or speed, and that his strength and staying powers seem to be as good as ever. All things considered, this information is surprising and gratifying to many ring followers. While Jackson has encountered all of the prejudices and drawbacks that his color has inspired, the words of Parson Davies uttered three or four years ago, that "the only thing black about Peter is his skin," is pretty generally conceded, and if he should win over the Los Angeles giant his victory will be hailed with pleasure by many who believe that he has not been shown the consideration that was due him.[31]

It was standing room only at the Pavilion as over 8,000 persons cheered both fighters as they advanced to the center of the ring and shook hands. Jeffries, who tipped 15 pounds to his advantage at 215, may have been the betting favorite (10 to 6), but Jackson received a larger ovation. The referee was Jim McDonald, the National League baseball umpire. Bill Delaney, DeWitt Vancourt, and "Spider" Kelly seconded Jeffries, while Patsy Corrigan, Vincent White, and Young Mitchell assisted Jackson.

According to the *Waterbury Evening Democrat*: "In one of the fastest and fiercest battles witnessed in this city in years, Jim Jeffries of California, young and brawny, last night knocked out Peter Jackson, Colored, of Australia. The knockout blow was delivered in the third round. That the end did not come earlier was surprising to the wildly excited and enthusiastic spectators of the battle. From the opening of the first round until the instant the decisive blow was delivered the men fought with energy of despair, each battling fast, as fiercely and as well as he knew how."[32]

This Was a Man

Most of the newspapers in the United States didn't report Peter Jackson's death until the first week of August. Few allocated enough print space to accurately portray his amazing life. He died on July 13, 1901, at the age of 40.

A special dispatch to the *Call* reported:

The death occurred at Roma, a sanitarium near Brisbane, Australia, early last month of Peter Jackson, once a candidate for the championship honors of the ring. Jackson, it will be remembered, suffered from an attack of pneumonia during a visit to this city a couple years ago, and he never fully recovered.

When it was discovered that he could not live very long he expressed a desire to go to his home in Australia, and friends in this city [Victoria, B.C.] and San Francisco made this possible. He set sail for the southern colony depressed in spirit and nearly a physical wreck.

The Brisbane papers say that his death had been expected for some time. Since his arrival in Australia he had received every attention from his former admirers and relatives. He had a comfortable home in the sanitarium. He was buried in Brisbane.[33]

This controversial memoir came from the *St. Louis Republic*:

Peter Jackson was the highest mental type of man that ever was a pugilist and the greatest pugilist that ever fought. He was a Black man, yet no pugilist, White or Black, bore so finely formed a head on his shoulders. Jackson was no common Negro, no dull African hewer of wood or drawer of water. In their native land his ancestors were Kings and Princes. A Black man, he was bred as well as the Black man can be bred. Naturally capable, he picked up a good education, was a keen observer, a delightful talker, interesting in what he said and the possessor of the perfect accent of an English gentleman. Dignified, well poised, courteous, diffident, but not cringing in the company of White men, he was a man who could make you forget he was Black.[34]

As for his fighting proficiency, the article continued, "Jackson was a straight puncher rather than a swinger, a wonder with the inside cross-counter and probably the best puncher for the head ever known in the ring. He could put them over or under the guard, inside or out, straight or swinging, with wonderful precision, speed and power. Never known as a body puncher, he could hurt there if he wanted to, and he had a nasty punch placed under the right or left breast that was enough to murder any man he could land it on regularly."[35]

Had Peter Jackson been born White, he would have ascended to the heavyweight throne. More than just a boxer, Jackson was an international figure—he was introduced to audiences by the Earl of Lonsdale, shook hands with Prince Albert Victor of Wales, and abolitionist Frederick Douglass even hung the fighter's portrait on a wall. Although he successfully crossed the color line in other aspects of his life, he could not conquer the title barrier of his own profession. Though his enormous worldwide popularity overshadowed his attainment of the World Colored Heavyweight Championship, Peter Jackson recognized what the designation represented. Indeed, this was a man.

The Color Line, 1888–1896

The Black community welcomed Peter Jackson. As they saw it, he came at a good time. He could carry some of their aggression into the ring and deliver it with proficiency. As a soft-spoken, well-mannered gentleman, his charm concealed his ambition—the heavyweight Championship of the World. "The Black Prince" couldn't dampen every element of frustration the community was experiencing, but he could quell some, and even some was better than none.

His first encroachment on the color line was a victory over Joe McAuliffe in December 1888, followed by another over Patsy Cardiff. Seeing the writing on the wall, White boxers were not forthcoming and Jackson needed to look elsewhere—this despite the efforts by Parson Davies to gain Jackson's acceptance from Whites.[36]

Outside the ring, things were even worse in his backyard. As the *Appeal* reported under the headline "The Color Line": "In the prizefight at New Orleans yesterday [January 23, 1891] the color line was drawn against admission of Peter Jackson, the Negro champion of Australia, and the Colored horse jockeys of the New Orleans racetrack. A Colored Mississippi politician of considerable prominence was also warned that he would be excluded if he sought admission. This is a new revelation of sporatastasis, or progress backwards. Hitherto the color line has been drawn among American men. Now it is drawn among American brutes. The 'gentleman' prizefighter forsooth has come to the front. The next evolution will be rebellion of white convicts against association with criminals of color."[37]

Despite the clear presence of a ring talent worthy of every opportunity the fight game had to offer, the color line could not be crossed. Looking at the barrier in other aspects of life, such as politics, the *Watauga Democrat* stated:

> But in government of the people it is the theory, and in the beginning it was the practice, that the fittest should rule. When Gov. [Fitzhugh] Lee said of the Southern States that the White men should govern he probably referred less to color than to character. He meant that intelligence the trained capacity and the ability to govern wisely, should control public affairs. These qualities happen to be possessed in incomparably the larger degree by the White race at the South. And, there is no Northern man settled in that section to live and conduct business who does not agree with Gov. Lee. He may think that governing White men should be republicans, but he stands on the color line with all the intelligent, just and patriotic natives of the South.[38]

Turning to labor, something everyone around the ring understood, the *Omaha Daily Bee* reported:

The assertion that the labor organizations of the country shut out the Colored people is absurd and only tends to create hostility toward the labor organizations and to give the Colored people the impression that the White race is striving to crush them under foot. And the idea advanced by another speaker that if the Negro race were in the majority the Whites would be trampled upon, is equally absurd. Look at Africa, where a few White men control, one might say, several millions of Blacks. Look at the South itself, for that matter. Aren't the Negroes in the majority there in many places, and have they subverted the Whites? The White man has always led and will continue to do so, simply because he is naturally the more capable. The salvation of the Colored man rests largely with himself. If he will go industriously to work, master a trade or some kind of a business or profession, race prejudice will soon be removed and the Negro will be respected as much as anybody.[39]

Sadly, like every World Colored Heavyweight Champion who sought to break the color line, Peter Jackson had to ride that delicate balance between being a racial hero or accepting the White standard for Blacks. Oppressed people, regardless of the ring they fight in, cannot remain subjugated forever.

FOUR

King of the Battle Royal

There was a city on the southeastern shore of Upper Klamath Lake, about 25 miles north of the California-Oregon border, that was originally called Linkville before changing its name to Klamath Falls. During the Twenties, the Oregon city, with its population of about 3,000, held an enormous July 4 weekend celebration. There was a water carnival, barbecue, ball games, and plenty of music and dancing. But boxing events were the highlight of the weekend, billed as "The Biggest Fistic Program Ever Held in Southern Oregon." People flocked to the 2,500-seat, open-air pavilion to witness an evening of pugilism that often included three main events, or about 20 rounds of fisticuffs. Part of the show was a special event called a "Battle Royal," where five local Colored fighters battled it out in a confine until only one man was standing—at times the participants were even blindfolded. The dynamic term, with its racist connotations, was used in the 19th century to describe forced combat between slaves in the United States. Although slavery had come and gone, this form of entertainment had not. Many a scrappy pugilist emerged from such events, including Joe Gans, Frankie Hunter, Kid Norfolk, and Bob Armstrong.

Born on September 4, 1873, in Rogersville, Tennessee, Bob Armstrong, son of an ex-slave, recalled little about the Hawkins County town except that it was old—indeed, it was settled in 1775 by Davy Crockett's grandparents. The reason was simple: He moved from the second-oldest town in Tennessee to Washington, Iowa, when he was about three years old. Armstrong attended school until he grew big enough to work, not unusual for the time period. Finding solace at the local racetrack like many men of Color, Armstrong, far too big to be a jockey, worked in the stables. Growing tired of real horses, he eventually jumped an iron version and headed to Des Moines, then on to Chicago.

Boxing to fill his pockets and his stomach, Armstrong found an avocation. Soon he stood a firm six feet, three inches and weighed about 200 pounds. Picking up a part-time handyman job at Professor Billy O'Connell's gymnasium and training quarters, suited Armstrong perfectly. O'Connell, a talented ring scholar, took a fancy to the youngster and believed in his potential. The cabbage patch, located in the heart of Chicago's business district, had more than its fair share of pugs drift through including Joe Choynski, Young Ketchel (1912), Joe Sherman (1913), and Johnny Dundee (1915), to name only a few. O'Connell was notorious for jamming about 300 spectators into his facility to watch an illegal prize fight—the admission tickets, which sold for 25 cents, were creatively masked as exercise coupons.

It was inside O'Connell's gym that "Parson" Davies' secretary, Harry Glickauff, spotted Armstrong. Davies, a boxing impresario, was in Chicago with his noted Jewish heavyweight, Joe Choynski, trying his best to land his fighter a title shot. Having long parted company with Peter Jackson, Davies wisely kept one eye open for new talent. When Glickauff informed his boss of his find, the manager immediately contacted Armstrong and placed him

Bob Armstrong (left), Edwin Van Dusart (alias Eddie McGoorty), and Ed McMahon are pictured here before a 1914 sparring session. As Armstrong's career drew to a close, he turned to various roles to assist other fighters (*Library of Congress, LC-DIG-ggbain-11841*).

in a ring to spar with Choynski. While Davies believed nobody could fill Jackson's shoes, he nevertheless saw plenty of similarities between his former fighter and Armstrong. With that, Armstrong, aka "King of the Battle Royal," acquired a fight manager and confirmed a career.

James J. Corbett

Fighting 61 rounds to a no-contest against Peter Jackson vaulted James Corbett into the fistic forefront. Nobody was more comfortable in a spotlight than "Gentleman Jim." John L. Sullivan, the Heavyweight Champion of the World, could draw the color line against Jackson, but he could not ignore Corbett. In retrospect, however, he probably wished he had. Corbett saw the champion's weakness as stamina, and believed that if he could wear him down, while avoiding his haphazard assaults, then victory was achievable. Corbett's observation proved correct as his scientific boxing overwhelmed the "Boston Strong Boy."

As comfortable on stage as in a ring, Corbett fed off adulation. In fact, even as champion he preferred the stage. Besides, there was limited risk and a lot more money associated with theatrical performances and boxing exhibitions, than defending a title.[1] Participating in an unregulated sport that many states saw as illegal, Corbett understood, had both advantages and disadvantages.

On January 25, 1894, the champion finally defended his title against Charlie Mitchell. It was a short and sweet success, a third round knockout. Later, he drew with Tom Sharkey on June 24, 1896. The former was Corbett's only successful title defense, and the latter was a result of police intervention after four rounds. It was inevitable that he would bow to public pressure and meet Bob "Ruby Robert" Fitzsimmons. The pair squared off in Carson City, Nevada, on March 17, 1897. Corbett took command, overwhelmed his antagonist, and sent him to the canvas in the sixth round. Although cut badly, Ruby Robert recovered and eventually wore Corbett down. Finishing him off with his trademark "solar plexus punch" in the 14th round brought a smile to Fitz's face.

"Sailor" Tom Sharkey, who stood only five feet eight inches tall, fought against Joe Choynski, Jim Corbett, Bob Fitzsimmons, and Jim Jeffries (*Library of Congress, LC-DIG-ggbain-04860*).

Corbett, who had done his best to dodge challenges as champion, was now issuing them daily to Fitzsimmons. Convinced his loss was a fluke, the former champion just couldn't accept defeat. For "The Freckled Wonder," who disliked Corbett and his unwillingness to defend the title, turnabout was fair play.[2]

On June 9, 1899, James J. Jeffries dropped Fitzsimmons in the second round, then unloaded on him in the 11th round to take the title. Corbett would fight for the title again, twice as a matter of fact. Both occasions were against Jeffries, his former training partner. Granting Corbett his first wish, on May 11, 1900, Jeffries put "Gentleman Jim" to sleep in the 23rd round (Jeffries' third title defense). Three years later (August 14, 1903), the champion sent Corbett into retirement via a 10th-round TKO (a technical knockout, or stoppage by a ring official).

"Big Bob"

Although Davies planned to work his fighter up in talent, if an exceptional opportunity materialized he considered it. By the fall of 1895, Armstrong was picking up press. This note ran in the *Philipsburg Mail*: "'Big Bob' Armstrong, the new Colored boxer, is a giant in stature. He stands 6 feet 3¾ inches in his bare feet and when he gets a little ring experience he ought to be able to give a good account of himself. So far he has only boxed Joe Choynski and Kid McCoy. Bob is a little bit diffident yet and hasn't cut loose real wicked, but the Parson says Tom O'Rourke has a big Black that he expects to pit against Armstrong and then we shall see whether Peter Jackson is to have a worthy successor."[3]

After losing to Peter Jackson in May of 1892, Frank "Paddy" Slavin, the celebrated Australian heavyweight, lost to Jim Hall, defeated Frank the "Harlem Coffee Cooler" Craig, and knocked out tomato cans Bob Marshall and Jack McCarthy. On November 5, 1895, Slavin tackled Bob Armstrong inside the Union Park Athletic Club in Hoboken, New Jersey. At the opening bell, Slavin, true to form, rushed Armstrong and began trading punches. Anticipating the strategy, Armstrong locked in with his left jab and delivered at will. By the tenth round, Slavin had slowed, and Armstrong capitalized by knocking him out. The loss couldn't have happened at a worse time for Slavin, as his team was negotiating a lucrative battle with Peter Maher, formerly the Irish Champion and claiming the championship of America. Wisely, Slavin persuaded the predominantly White press to focus their attention elsewhere until after a rematch. It worked, and Slavin signed articles for a 20-round bout against Maher to take place in England or South Africa. Certain fighters, and managers, had that kind of influence with the media, if of course you happened to be White.

An Armstrong-Slavin rematch was planned for November 23, 1896, at the Union Park Athletic Club in New York. To stay sharp, Armstrong took two battles, both in Madison Square Garden. He drew Black middleweight Fred Morris and disposed of Tommy Forrest, who was making his professional debut. As for Slavin, he fought seven times, including bouts with Peter Maher and Jake Kilrain.

The rematch with Slavin got off to a horrible start: Both fighters had signed articles to fight for a percentage, but Slavin was not satisfied with his cut and refused to go on, a common financial strategy utilized by fighters. Finally, he capitulated and entered the ring at 11:15 p.m. Armstrong weighed 185 pounds, while Slavin tipped at 178 pounds.

This is how the *Record-Union* recorded the affair:

> Frank Slavin of Australia wound up his career of defeat in this country by quitting in the fourth round of his battle with Bob Armstrong of Chicago before the Union Park Athletic Club tonight. Armstrong was by no means a star, and if Slavin had been a good second-rater he could have disposed of the Colored man. The Australian has seen his best days, and by no means entitled to make the demand he did before he went on. Having signed for a percentage he was dissatisfied with the house, and endeavored to back out.[4]

Armstrong dropped Slavin briefly in the first round and countered brilliantly throughout the bout. This is how the *Record-Union* saw the final round: "Round 4–Armstrong opened with a left to the nose, bringing blood. Slavin got in a hard body blow, but a left on the neck sent him to the floor. He got up and shoved his left three times on the Negro's wind. Armstrong then landed some terrific punches, and Slavin threw up his hands and quit, after two minutes and 56 seconds."[5]

Bob Armstrong v. Charlie Strong—World Colored Heavyweight Championship

Armstrong followed the Slavin bout with two knockout victories at the Broadway Athletic Club, the first against Charlie Strong (December 21, 1896), followed by Joe Butler (March 6, 1897). Of the two Black boxers, Butler, an athlete on the downside of his career, was a better opponent. As evidenced by his lack of challengers, word was traveling fast regarding Armstrong's skills.

After Peter Jackson essentially relinquished the World Colored Heavyweight Championship, confusion followed—the characteristic of an unsanctioned title.[6] Armstrong, noting the vacancy, stated his claim. Noting the proclamation was the *Evening Bulletin*: "Following his 19th round knockout of Charley Strong, 'the plucky colored boxer of Newark, New Jersey,' at the Broadway Athletic Club, Armstrong claimed the vacant title."[7]

However, not everyone was impressed by Armstrong's performance. The *Salt-Lake Herald* noted: "Bob Armstrong, of Chicago, the Colored heavyweight, who was heralded as a 'second Peter Jackson,' proved to be a vast disappointment to his friends, by his showing with Charley Strong, the New York Colored heavyweight at the Broadway Athletic Club

"Fireman" Jim Flynn (left) grappling against instructor and ring legend Tommy Ryan (right). Flynn, who wasn't afraid to cross the color line, fought Jack Johnson, Sam Langford, and Theodore "Tiger" Flowers (*Library of Congress, LC-DIG-ggbain-12202*).

tonight. With an advantage of seven inches in height, and 25 pounds in weight, it took the Chicago man 19 rounds to dispose of Strong, who is only a game second rater."[8]

In March 1897, James Barry (bantam champion), Charles E. "Parson" Davies, and Armstrong departed Chicago for Carson, Nevada, for the Corbett (KO in 11) v. Fitzsimmons fight. Both Barry and Armstrong planned to meet all comers along the journey.[9] Such a random opponent fight strategy, although profitable at times, lent itself to poor record-keeping.[10] By June, it was no secret that Davies hoped to see Armstrong do battle against Jim Jeffries. But "Jeff" and his fight manager, William A. "Bill" Brady, were not in a hurry—the fighter had been drawing some solid exhibition revenue sparring with the champion, Jim Corbett.[11] Davies did, however, pick up a couple of sound exhibitions for his fighters as he headed back east. The creative fight manager also saw opportunities outside the ring. Armstrong sparred with Black pugilist Frank Childs as part of a touring production of "A Bowery Girl." By October, Armstrong was assisting Tommy Ryan for his upcoming battle with Kid McCoy (September 8). Meanwhile, Davies was trying to match him with Peter Maher. In November, everyone's attention turned to an athletic carnival Davies had constructed. As the production entered a city, a local fighter would be chosen to spar a few rounds. For example, on November 18, while in St. Louis, Armstrong tackled local pugilist John Holtman for three rounds. In retrospect, without actually being there and having a sound understanding of both fighters, gauging the validity of these encounters is difficult. Armstrong was in the ring with Joe Walcott in December, not as an adversary but as a second—it was during his fight against Tom Tracy. Such was the year for the World Colored Heavyweight Champion.

Frank Childs, Armstrong's touring production partner, was a stocky, yet crafty Texan who was battling out of Chicago. Standing five feet, nine and a half inches, and tipping at about 180, Childs was six years older than Armstrong. After learning his craft on the West Coast, he headed to Chicago in 1894 and it was there that he caught the eye of manager Herman C. Roussellot.

Frank Childs v. Bob Armstrong—World Colored Heavyweight Championship

Having sparred with Bob Armstrong, Frank Childs was no stranger to his ability. But sparring wasn't fighting, or at least it wasn't intended that way. Childs was scheduled to meet Armstrong, for six rounds, in Chicago on January 29, 1898. Both men, over the then-heavyweight limit, would do battle inside the gymnasium at the Chicago Athletic Club. If a title was on the line, as some historians believe, Davies certainly did not confirm it. Here is how the *San Francisco Call* reported the encounter:

> After the second round had lasted one and a half minutes Childs landed his right squarely on the jaw, and Armstrong went down in a heap. He was down nine seconds, and, when he arose, Childs tapped him lightly and Armstrong went down flat on his face. He staggered up again, wobbled across the ring, and sat down helplessly in a corner. He was utterly unable to fight, and Referee George Siler awarded the fight to Childs. After the decision was given, Armstrong went tottering around the ring, and wound up in Childs' corner. Childs took him in his arms and let him gently down to the floor, where he remained. He was unable to leave the ring for several minutes.[12]

"Parson" Davies was also floored by the results—he had advised both fighters against such a reckless display.[13] Having recently been fired as Choynski's manager, Davies stated,

"I am going to wash my hands of the fighters as soon as I can."[14] He was livid at the treason exhibited by Childs.

Armstrong, clearly embarrassed, picked himself up by calling out many of the fighters he knew, like Choynski. He knocked out Yank Kenny in the fifth round on February 21 at the American Athletic Club in Chicago, took a slim newspaper verdict over Charley Strong on March 25 in the same venue, then headed to Syracuse to battle local fighter Ed Dunkhorst to a draw, held at the Central City Athletic Club on April 25.[15]

On May 27, after seven minutes and two seconds at the Arena in Philadelphia, Armstrong knocked out Joe Butler—two hard lefts to the jaw accounted for the damage. Fighting "Stockings" Conroy of Troy, in the same venue, to a six-round no-decision followed on June 10. Armstrong then headed west, to Cripple Creek, Colorado, and lost to "Mexican Pete" Everett on July 4. He had hoped to defeat Everett to gain access to Jim Jeffries. However, it was Everett, backed by the local mining contingent, who would next battle Jeff. As summer was drawing to a close, a patient Armstrong finally got his wish: He would do battle with "The Boilermaker."

A confident and aggressive James J. Jeffries planned to meet two fighters on August 5 inside the Lenox Athletic Club—both scheduled for 10 rounds. The first was Armstrong, while the second was Steve O'Donnell. But Jeffries shattered his left arm while defeating Armstrong and could not move on to O'Donnell.

Armstrong began the battle cautiously, trying to get a sense of his adversary. But by the ninth round, Armstrong had slowed. Sensing the weakness, Jeffries went first to the body, then to the face. "The Boilermaker" had an uppercut that was spot on, and he worked the left jab with precision.

The *Record-Union* saw the final round in this manner:

> Round Ten—They shook hands at the referee's bidding, and Jeffries hooked his right on the ribs. They exchanged lefts on the face, and after a great deal of footwork Jeffries put Bob on his back with a left swing on the head. Bob took eight-seconds to rest, and when he came up Jeffries hooked right and left on the jaw. These blows dazed Bob, and Jeffries kept pounding him, and Armstrong ran to the ropes without making an attempt to strike back. It was all one-sided now, and although Bob stayed the limit, he did so by running away from the big fellow. The referee declared Jeffries the winner, while Armstrong's friends were telling the Colored man that he had done well. Armstrong certainly stood the "gaff" fairly well, but he was far outclassed.[16]

Just over a year later, on June 9, 1899, Jim Jeffries captured the World Heavyweight Championship by defeating Bob Fitzsimmons, via an 11th-round kayo, at the Coney Island Athletic Club.

Armstrong would finish the year by battling Joe Goddard (August 29, 1898) over six rounds to a no-decision in Philadelphia and drawing Ed Dunkhorst (December 4, 1898) over 10 rounds in Syracuse, before disposing of "Mexican Pete" Everett (December 9, 1898) in Denver.[17]

Frank Childs v. Bob Armstrong—World Colored Heavyweight Championship

An honor, once held by Peter Jackson, took center stage on March 4, 1899, at the Stag Athletic Club in Cincinnati, Ohio. Bob Armstrong of New York met Frank Childs of Chicago for the World Colored Heavyweight Championship.[18] Both fighters set aside all criticisms of their previous encounters in favor of this 10-round competition. Unlike their previous contests, the environment had all the attributes of a championship, including delegations from all across the Midwest. Heavyweight contender Tom Sharkey, Armstrong's soon-to-be employer, and his manager, Tom O'Rourke, were also in attendance. In addition to the title, both participants fought for a division of the receipts.

Armstrong was seconded by both Sharkey and O'Rourke, while Childs was assisted by Harry Roussela, Sam Summerfield, and others.[19] Referee Johnnie Murphy, of Cincinnati, called the fighters to scratch at 10 p.m.

Armstrong, who towered over his opponent, started out strong with his left hand leads but was successfully countered in the first two rounds. Knowing he had the advantage at close quarters, Armstrong tried to draw Childs in. But the strategy failed. Childs assumed control in the third round. Following a heavy exchange, the Chicago fighter sent Armstrong to a nine-count with a solid right. Arising, Armstrong scrambled to stay out of range. Fighting back in the fourth, Armstrong swayed Childs with a right to the head. All the same, Childs resumed control in the fifth round and drove Armstrong around the ring with swift and accurate combinations.

The *Saint Paul Globe* saw the final round as follows: "In the sixth Childs rushed at Armstrong and landed a hard right swing on the jaw, which sent Armstrong flying across the ring. But for the ropes he would have tripped headlong into the audience. As he rebounded from the ropes, Childs landed his right again on the jaw, which sent Armstrong reeling about the ring with his hands hanging to his side. Childs was about to give the finishing punch when O'Rourke, seeing that his man was helpless, threw up the sponge and the title of the championship of the Colored heavy-weights was awarded to Childs."[20]

Armstrong's career descent had begun.

Billed as "Colored Giants Fight," Bob Armstrong defeated novice Ed Martin of Denver by way of a second-round knockout at the Lenox Athletic Club on June 6, 1899. Moving on to the Broadway Athletic Club in New York on July 21, "Big Bob" was given a 20-round decision over "Stockings" Conroy of Troy. But those who attended were critical of the decision; in their view, the victor endured the majority of the punishment. In the fall, Armstrong devoted a bulk of his attention to exhibitions and to Tom Sharkey and his efforts to grab the heavyweight championship from the hands of Jim Jeffries.

Finishing 1899 in New York, the "King of the Battle Royal" was slated to meet Jim Jeffords for 25 rounds before the Hercules Athletic Club on November 27. But the fight ended abruptly in the third term. The *Seattle Post-Intelligencer* noted the sensational ending:

> Both men went head foremost from a clinch over the ropes into a box at the ringside in the second round, and in the third Jeffords took another header from the effects of a right swing to the jaw. This took all the steam out of the big fellow, and when he regained his feet he was sent sprawling from a right swinging uppercut in the vicinity of the belt. Jeffords rolled over in agony, and his seconds claimed a foul, on the ground that he was hit below the belt. The referee decided that the blow landed fairly, and gave his verdict in favor of Armstrong, after Jeffords had been counted out and carried to his corner by his seconds.[21]

By the turn of the century, Bob Armstrong's ring days were drawing to a close. But his time around the fight game was not. The fighter was making good money participating in exhibitions and working with his fellow pugilists (Tom Sharkey in 1899, Bob Fitzsimmons in 1900, Jim Jeffries in 1901). Of note: Armstrong did battle "Denver Ed" Martin four more times—once in 1900, twice in 1902, and once in 1903—with the advantage nearly always in his adversary's favor.[22]

The Inside Track

Interesting was Bob Armstrong's viewpoint regarding "The Fight of the Century" between Jim Jeffries and Jack Johnson. Having assisted Jeff in preparation for his battles with Jim Corbett and Gus Ruhlin, Armstrong also trained Johnson to box Stanley Ketchel. The fight, which Johnson won, took place on July 4, 1910. Bear in mind that Armstrong was hired as an assistant trainer to Jeffries.

The *Evening Times* ran his thoughts:

> Clash of the races be hanged. I am a colored man and am always proud of a colored man's success, but helping to train pugilists is my business and I should be allowed to take my wares to the best market. I am with Jeff from inclination because I have trained with him many times before and he has always treated me as a man should be treated. I can't say as much for Johnson, but even that's not the point. Any man who earns his living the way I do aims to work on the winning side if he can manage it. Now, I have studied this thing out and I am as sure as the daylight that Jeff is going to defeat Johnson. That's why I jumped at the chance to go with Jeff when he asked me.[23]

Armstrong, after stating his feelings, believed he would be a joke among his race if Johnson won. Johnson, at least to Armstrong, had never met a fighting machine like Jeffries. When asked if it took Jeffries to emerge out of retirement in order to silence Johnson, he replied, "No, sir. I think Sam Langford will take Johnson's measure if he is ever given a chance."[24]

As the years passed, Armstrong surfaced periodically in the press, often for his views on training or a historical perspective. He spoke to the *Santa Fe New Mexican* during one such occasion: "Peter Jackson could have whipped Jack Johnson, the black heavyweight champion, the best day he ever saw. It was unfortunate for us colored folks that Jack Johnson won the heavyweight championship. Jackson was a gentleman. Johnson is not. Because of his actions, all colored boxers must suffer. If Jackson had won instead of Johnson there would have been no more prejudice than when Joe Gans or George Dixon won."[25]

Armstrong kept on training fighters and was chief second to King Levinsky in 1932. His death date has been given as January 5, 1933, in Chicago, following a long illness.[26] Although a talented and gifted trainer and a noted gladiator, Armstrong spent his last days in poverty. He was buried at Cook County Cemetery, which served as Cook County Potter's Field from 1911 until 1971—it was used for the burial of indigent and unidentified deceased people of Cook County. Bob Armstrong was one of over 90,000 burials in a pasture filled with unmarked graves.

The Color Line, 1896–1898

Following in the shoes of Peter Jackson was an impossible task. Although Bob Armstrong would enter the ring with the finest White fighters of his day, it wasn't during a championship fight, nor was it in any fight of substantial bearing. Yet he was talented enough to train the best White fighters and strong enough to enter a boxing ring and spar with them. Anyhow, Armstrong did enter the ring with numerous White pugilists, including Frank "Paddy" Slavin, Yank Kenny, Tom "Stockings" Conroy, Joe Goddard, and James J. Jeffries, to name only a few. When Frank Childs took the World Colored Heavyweight Championship from him, there was no bitterness. Perhaps Armstrong never felt the title was his to begin with.

So what of the color line during this period?

Looking over the ropes to the color line and, of all things, to the White House, the *Washington Bee* asks, "If Not Why Not?"

That is the question that seems to disturb a few jealous and political Afro American demagogues, why a colored man should not be selected for the cabinet. If not why not? Are we to continue to vote blindly for party supremacy and receive no consideration for it? We are told by some that it requires a colored man of superior ability to enter Major McKinley's cabinet. Great God have we no superior colored men? Especially when we consider how many ignorant, unpolished back woodmen, white men, who could hardly write their names have been placed in cabinets of presidents and become great by virtue of the position they held. Must the colored man be a law dictionary or encyclopedia, a map of the world, to become a cabinet officer, when we consider how many bums have been made cabinet ministers, assistant secretaries, auditors, etc…. Whenever a colored man aspires for a position of any responsibility the first thing some white man asserts is, that the colored line is being drawn. The color line is always drawn when we wish to better our condition politically.[27]

The *Times* couldn't resist running this piece:

Everybody laugh! Jim Corbett has drawn the color line. Drawing the color line is all right for some people, but in Mr. Pompadour Jim's case it is decidedly funny. The bank clerk, pugilist, actor, baseball player, never thought of drawing the color line or anything else for that matter, except his breath, in the old days out West when he was bidding desperately for fistic fame. He was only too glad to get a chance to meet Peter Jackson. In fact, he fell all over himself getting matched against the Negro, and although Peter was the toughest game he ever tackled he went up against him for another dose. But things are changed nowadays, and when Peter issues a wide sweeping challenge to the world and fixes his glittering eyes on "Gentleman Jim," the latter says nay, nay, and flees to the protecting wing of the "color line" excuse. Give us something easier, Jim.[28]

FIVE

Crafty Texan

By 1861, the state of Texas had seen and heard enough of Abraham Lincoln. It declared its secession from the United States of America on February 1, and joined the Confederate States on March 2. Citing the failure of the federal government to protect the lives and property of Texas citizens left, as they saw it, little choice. Texas, as everyone understood, was a state of mind and principle.

When the American Civil War ended in 1865, Federal troops arrived in Texas to restore order and establish ground rules. By that summer, Union soldiers had reached Galveston Island to take possession of the state and enforce the new freedom of former slaves. Sensing that this liberty would be harshly challenged in Texas, many slaves and their families chose to relocate. This was the environment that Frank Childs was born into on July 17, 1867.

Although the details are sketchy, it would be a mature and handsome Frank Childs who would journey westward in search of a better life. For this son of an ex-slave, innate fear of human subjugation had found a home in his soul. Standing a compact five feet, nine-and-a-half inches tall, Childs weighed about 180 pounds. Blessed with good genetics, he had solid, well-developed legs and fantastic arm structure, the latter enabling him to thrust short, powerful blasts with precision. Like many young adults, Childs was searching for answers. If that meant picking up a few dollars during a ring challenge, then such was the case. He set out for New Mexico, then on to California.

Climbing into a ring and defeating a seasoned fighter, George "Marine" LaBlanche, early in 1892 brought a level of acceptance for the youngster.[1] If Frank Childs wanted to learn his craft, trial by fire was certainly an option. At first, he was pinballing between the pugilistic epicenters of Los Angeles and San Francisco. Building a reputation, as he accepted, wasn't always convenient, but he needed to become familiar with the West Coast fight scene. At one point, he and noted Australian heavyweight Billy Smith were scheduled to meet, but the turnout was so poor they declined to do battle. It was too much, too soon. Yet California brought more opportunity than Texas, and that suited Frank Childs just fine.

Peter Jackson v. Frank Childs, An Exhibition

It took place at Turnverein Hall, over on 321 South Main Street in Los Angeles. Scheduled for one night only, on January 19, 1893, it was a must-see for every boxing fan: Peter Jackson, the champion of Australia, was conducting a scientific sparring exhibition with Frank Childs, a local rising star. Although it was a rare opportunity, spectator enthusiasm fell short of expectation. The *Herald* reported:

Jackson is not in condition, but showed up a wonderfully handsome figure, which is molded on such symmetrical lines as to hardly deceive one as to the extent of his muscular development. His arms are so long as to give them the appearance of being slender. Childs was fully a head, if not more, shorter than his opponent, but as regards breadth of shoulders, and probably circumference of biceps, he is not far behind the antipodean. The five rounds were characterized by friendly sparring, and served to show nothing as to the ability of either man, beyond their quickness and the fact that each was capable of hard work.[2]

Lackluster indeed, but for Childs it was still Peter Jackson, "The Black Prince," and that added instant credibility to his resume. As for the Australian, at this stage of his career he sought only a lucrative battle with Corbett. He stated, "I shall fight nobody again but Jim Corbett, and he doesn't seem anxious for it. It is rather late in the day for him to be drawing the color line after having fought me once for over three hours."[3]

Following the exhibition, Childs headed north again to San Francisco, where he once again planned to meet Australian heavy Billy Smith. The pair came to scratch at the California Athletic Club, on February 15, 1893. An impressive purse of $1,250 ($34,893 in 2019 dollars) had been arranged, and both fighters were eager to fill their pockets.

Childs went headhunting early and dropped Smith with a shot to the chin in the second round. But Smith recovered, and the two battled hard in the third. Both fighters went down in the fourth round with Smith worse for wear. The fifth round looked like a turning

A view of Chicago, at Monroe Street near State, during the period Frank Childs called it home. The "Crafty Texan" began fighting there in 1894 and stayed for the remainder of his career (*Library of Congress, LC-DIG-det-4a1970*).

point as the Australian endured tremendous impairment from Childs' targeted combinations. Witnessing the facial damage he administered in the sixth round, the "Crafty Texan" went for a knockout in the seventh. Although he failed to deliver Smith, the anguish endured by his antagonist was clearly visible. Bleeding profusely, with both eyes closing, the struggling Australian went down twice in the eighth round but somehow managed to endure. With both fighters exhausted by this point, the pace slowed.

The *Herald* noted the final rounds: "Smith went down in the 11th from a short-arm blow on the jaw. He arose weak and Childs soon sent him down twice more. He took nine-seconds on the floor each time and arose weak and bloody. Childs would have sent him down for a fourth time in this round, but the call of time saved him. The 12th round settled the fight. Smith was scarcely able to stand, and Childs soon landed a right on the jaw and sent him down and out. He had to be carried to his corner and it was several minutes before he could be taken from the ring."[4]

The elevated interest was in stark contrast to their first pairing. And the purse, well, that spoke for itself. With quality battles becoming scarce in 1893, Childs decided to head to Chicago. The move, he believed, would confirm his position as a contender. Engaging better fighters, regardless of their skin color, was the key.

As for the White heavyweight champion, James J. Corbett, he was feeling continued pressure to match with Peter Jackson. Confronted in nearly every city he visited, he needed to take a stand. In April, while in Cincinnati, Corbett confirmed that he would not fight outside of America and that the articles he signed with Jackson confirmed his position.

The *Comet* confirmed his stance:

Against the best wishes of my friends I agree to fight Jackson. I believe that a champion to be a champion must fight any and all comers for that name. I signed to fight Jackson. I have everything to lose and nothing to gain but as champion I must insist on the rights of a champion. I have a right to name the battleground and the time, and am not forced to go out of my country to fight. Americans believe in America, I first, last and all the time, am an American. When it is shown beyond the shadow of a doubt that I cannot fight in America then I will agree to go to some other country. Until that time America must stand as the battleground. In view of what has passed in pugilism, Peter Jackson, on account of his color, ought to feel highly flattered that I have recognized him as a fighting quantity.[5]

Looking into his bag of excuses, Corbett chose patriotism over race. However, his repugnant and indefensible final comment was that of a philistine when it comes to the manly art of self-defense and not that of a true champion.

Picking Up the Pace, 1897

Living and breathing in Chicago wasn't perfect for Frank Childs, but it was a fight town. Although he entered the ring often for exhibitions, regular work was scarce. Early in 1897, Childs signed on with "Parson" Davies and Company, as a sparring partner for Bob Armstrong. At times the fight was also outside the ring, as the *Pacific Commercial Advertiser* detailed Illinois life: "Today, there is an extreme prejudice against the Negro in the Northern States. He is excluded from many hotels, restaurants, theaters, schools and churches. At Alton, Illinois, only two weeks ago, Negro children were excluded from the public schools."[6]

Thicker-skinned than most, Childs was a fighter, and if that meant dealing with a bit of adversity, he believed he could handle it. Besides, even Peter Jackson was denied a hotel room. The *San Francisco Call* reported: "It is a law in all first-class hotels throughout the country, never to give accommodation to Negroes. Of course, the line is drawn in a delicate way, so as to not give offense or to render the manager liable to the law. The applicant is informed politely that there are no vacant rooms, and with this the answer must be satisfied, He is never turned away with a flat refusal to accommodate him, and hence no cause for complaint."[7]

The *Call* even added a valuable perspective, that of a Colored bootblack at one of the hotels: "It's a shame to refuse to give a room to such a gentleman as Peter Jackson. Didn't he walk arm in arm with the Marquis of Queensberry in Piccadilly? Didn't he shake the hand of the Prince of Wales? Ain't he the best fighter in the world? (Then in disgust he expectorated.) Some of these hotel men make me tired."[8]

During the summer of 1897, Childs was on the road as part of the successful play, "A Bowery Girl." As the *Copper Country Evening News* reported: "In the famous Bowery scene two interesting sparring exhibitions are given: The first by 'Jimmy' Barry, champion bantamweight of the world and Frank Fitzgerald, the second by Bob Armstrong, the giant colored champion, and Frank Childs. 'Parson' Davies will introduce the men."[9]

The Third Heavyweight Champion of the World, 1897–1899

Born in Helston, Cornwall, England, on May 26, 1863, Robert James Fitzsimmons, aka "Ruby Robert" and "Speckled Bob," seemed destined to attract attention with his stern scowl and distinguished widow's peak. A White man who decided to do battle in the White-dominated sport of boxing, he became perhaps the greatest boxer ever. On March 17, 1897, Fitzsimmons captured the Heavyweight Championship of the World thanks to a 14th-round knockout of James J. Corbett in Carson City, Nevada. At 167 pounds, he was a pure fighting machine, the lightest heavyweight champion ever.

During his incredible fistic journey, Fitzsimmons held three worlds championships—Middleweight, Heavyweight and Light Heavyweight—and was virtually undeniable in the prize ring. Although as champion he would hold the color line, he was not against entering a ring with a Black man and did so—by the end of his career—with "Starlight" (Edward Rollins), Peter Jackson (exhibition), Bob Armstrong (exhibition), Hank Griffin (exhibition), Jack Johnson, Joe Jeannette (exhibition), and Peter Felix (exhibition), to name a few. Like most White champions, he was also familiar with the pool of Black challengers.

After enduring tremendous punishment and even dropping his opponent in the second round, heavyweight James J. Jeffries knocked out Fitzsimmons in the 11th round to seize the title on June 9, 1899.

Gaining Recognition

On January 8, 1898, Frank Childs began the year strong by knocking out a novice fighter called "Klondike," aka John Haines (Haynes), in Chicago. Impressive in size and packing a powerful punch, Klondike, at this stage of his career, was fool's gold in the ring.[10] The pair went six rounds with Childs clearly getting the best of his antagonist. When "Klondike" demanded a rematch, Childs complied and disposed of his Black opponent even quicker.[11]

Frank Childs v. Bob Armstrong—World Colored Heavyweight Championship

Frank Childs and Bob Armstrong had sparred together so many times that people knew the "Crafty Texan" as the short one, and the "King of the Battle Royal" as the tall one. But on January 29, 1898, the pair, good friends, decided to mix it up a bit more. The Chicago Athletic Club opened their doors to both men who were over the heavyweight limit.

Following a few preliminaries, Childs knocked out Davies' meal ticket in the second round. The action was a shock not only to Armstrong but also to Davies, his employer. The victory brought Childs out of Armstrong's shadow and into the spotlight. But did it bring him a title? He was rumored to meet either Joe Butler or George Grant next.[12]

George Byers v. Frank Childs—World Colored Heavyweight Championship

On September 14, 1898, George Byers, of Boston, entered the ring at the Lenox Athletic Club in New York to do battle with Frank Childs, of Chicago. Both fighters tipped at 165 pounds and had similar physiques. For 20 grueling rounds, the pair toiled away. Childs was the aggressor during the first few rounds, as Byers seemed satisfied with his precision counters. Childs, who cut Byers' left eye in the second round, also appeared to be a more powerful puncher. However, a patient Byers finally started to time his straight left, and it began to do damage. Just prior to the bell to end the third round, Childs, anticipating a left, caught a right hand that nearly sent him to the floor. Byers continued to work the jab effectively as Childs' face mirrored the damage. In the sixth round, Childs managed to send Byers back with a hard right, but the fighter recovered quickly and countered with more jabs to the countenance of his antagonist. Childs could hardly see by the seventh round, and many felt the fight was drawing to a conclusion. Yet the Chicago fighter endured.

The *Sun* described the eighth and ninth rounds as follows: "'I can only see yer on one side,' gasped Childs, as he came up for the eighth and began piling in desperate swings. Byers quickly smashed the other eye and cut that open too. Childs was still very dangerous, however, and Byers watched for the swings with extreme caution. When the ninth began Childs rushed like a tiger, and with a right on the jaw he almost lifted Byers off his feet. The latter reeled, but got away and clinched to save himself and Childs came at him again. Byers recovered in a minute and drove Childs to a corner, where they fought like lions until the bell rang."[13]

By the tenth round, the pace had slowed. Childs, who was still having difficulty with his vision, controlled the 11th. Byers just could not slow his adversary's attack. Childs continued his assault into the 13th round, and his opponent continued to answer with his targeted jabs to the eyes. In the 14th, Byers went to the head and body, just trying to slow Childs. It was then that a pattern emerged: An aggressive Childs opened rounds with wild swings, hoping to land a single knockout blow, while Byers waited for the assault to conclude before firing a battery of accurate jabs and short punches.

The *Sun* described the final rounds: "Byers was satisfied with blocking nearly all of Childs's desperate drives in the 18th, and now and then rapping the eyes with knife-like jabs. Childs rallied in the 19th and kept up a fierce attack for over a minute. Then Byers put him on the defensive with some telling punches. Childs did as much fighting as Byers in the last round, but it was too late."[14]

Still undefeated, Byers received the verdict, but Childs received the sympathy of the crowd. The two Colored men had engaged in one of the finest fights at the club in years, and not a soul in the audience felt that they had witnessed anything short of an exceptional performance.

Childs seem to take the loss in stride. Ten days later, he stopped Henry Baker, in Chicago, in the third round of what was to be a six-round battle. He finished the year with a six-round decision over Tom "Stockings" Conroy, of Troy, New York.

George Byers

Any conversation about Frank Childs will eventually turn to George Byers, another very talented pugilist. The pair would cross paths just before the turn of the century and meet on a few occasions. Although Byers began as a middleweight and gradually worked up to the light heavyweight ranks, he wasn't afraid of mixing with the big boys. In contrast to Childs, he was smaller, lighter, with a more boyish, yet intelligent charm.

Born on Prince Edward Island, a British colony, on June 25, 1872, George Frederick Byers was just over a year old when his birthplace was federated into Canada as a province. Living in Charlottetown did not constitute an easy life for the large Byers family.[15] In fact, it was a challenge—crime ridden, poverty-stricken and violent—for most African Canadians living on the Island. Young George desired more, but just where to find it he wasn't certain. When the youngster discovered that his compact and muscular frame suited the sweet science, he decided to follow in the steps of George Godfrey. If Boston was good enough for "Old Chocolate" to achieve success, Byers believed, then why not for him?

As a young teen Byers set out to achieve his dream. Life in the hub wasn't simple either. After working his way through a variety of jobs, Byers found employment on the docks of the Boston waterfront. Handsome, he stood five feet, eight-and-a-half inches and was cut like a Michelangelo sculpture. Weighing between 130 and 155 pounds, Byers believed he could compensate for any physical disadvantage by fighting smarter, or more scientific as they used to say. To accomplish this task, Byers turned to George Godfrey. The former heavyweight champion loved what he saw in Byers and planned to model him after his own career—"Old Chocolate" even admitted that he saw a bit of not only himself in the youth, but Peter Jackson as well.

Byers trained hard and learned quickly. As early as 1897, he was gaining recognition, as the *Waterbury Evening Democrat* pointed out: "The sporting element about town are much delighted over the regular appearance of George Byers, the famous colored boxing expert of Boston, Massachusetts, who is to figure in a contest tomorrow evening in the Brass City [against Harry Peppers]. The young man goes through here at a rapid gait accompanied by two other gentlemen, probably trainers, and when not walking swiftly they run with the utmost of ease. The party getting in readiness for the coming exhibition and take these jaunts into the country for the refreshing air and exhilarating exercise."[16]

News traveled fast on December 9, 1897, when Harry Peppers, said to be the Colored middleweight champion of the Pacific Coast, knocked out George Byers in the eighth round of a contest held at the Waterbury Athletic Club. Or so the *Seattle Post-Intelligencer* reported. The date, players and venue were correct, but not the result of the contest.

It was far different, and there was more, much more. Both boxers appeared to be acting rather than fighting. If a fighter slipped to a knee, the other would help him arise. It was all a bit peculiar. Those in attendance were dumbfounded. Some blows were exchanged, but not many. When Byers pushed his adversary through the ropes in the fifth round, the pair shook hands. By the 12th round, the pace had dramatically slowed, and just two rounds later the referee was ordering both of them to fight. The *Waterbury Evening Democrat* elaborated: "In the 15th, they were again ordered to fight. Both men said they had broken hands. In the 16th Byers' left ear began to bleed from several right swings. In the next the referee wanted no live taps and said he would declare it a no contest. They mixed things up in this round and both were tired. In the 18th Byers had the best of it and in the 19th, after a few passes, he hit Peppers a light swing on the jaw and Peppers' head struck the floor with a thud. This stopped the contest and Byers was awarded the purse."[17]

Afterward, Byers' skills began to decline. Comfortably billed as a middleweight, he worked out of New England and New York, taking fights when and where he could. He battled more than once the likes of Johnny Gorman, Frank Childs, and George Gardner. Although Byers didn't win a single contest in 1901, he found himself in the ring with some impressive company: Jack Root, a White fighter who would capture the light heavyweight title; Frank Childs, in a battle some believe was for the World Colored Heavyweight Championship; and "Mysterious" Billy Smith, a White pugilist who won the welterweight crown back in 1892.[18]

Essentially retiring from the ring in 1904, Byers became a talented trainer—his prized student was Sam Langford.[19] He died at Boston City Hospital on April 10, 1937, from pneumonia.[20]

Child's Play

Frank Childs began 1899 as a participant in a two-day carnival of sport held inside the Tattersall building in Chicago. On January 21, he met and defeated Joe "King of the Middleweights" Butler, a Colored fighter from Philadelphia. Although it wasn't a great fight, disqualifications seldom are—the exposure was good. He was polishing a solid reputation in his own backyard.

Frank Childs v. Bob Armstrong—World Colored Heavyweight Championship

This was it! This 10-round contest for the World Colored Heavyweight Championship was between Bob Armstrong of New York and Frank Childs of Chicago. It had all the air of a meaningful event as delegations from all around the Midwest found their way to the Stagg Athletic Club in Cincinnati, Ohio, on March 4, 1899. Tickets ranged from $1 to $25, with the fighters battling for a division of the receipts. Johnny Murphy was selected as referee. Clearly, the event was meaningful. Coverage, at least by the bulk of the press, painted Armstrong as the titleholder.

The *San Francisco Call* reported the final rounds:

> The fourth round was furious one. Childs being staggered by a right on the head, while evidently holding back for a chance to land his right.

In the fifth Childs rushed and landed right and left repeatedly, driving Armstrong around the ring. Armstrong's replies were with right and left jabs. A hard right swing on the jaw staggered Armstrong, and Childs following it up, landed left and right, which made Armstrong very groggy.

In the sixth Childs rushed at Armstrong and landed a hard right swing on the jaw, which sent Armstrong flying clear across the ring. But for the ropes he would have tipped headlong among the spectators. As he rebounded from the ropes, Childs landed his right again on the jaw, which sent Armstrong reeling about the ring with his hands hanging on his side. Childs was about to give the finishing punch when [Tom] O'Rourke, realizing his man was helpless, threw up the sponge and the Colored Heavyweight Championship was awarded to Childs.[21]

So where does George Byers fit in to the World Colored Heavyweight Championship picture? Or does he? Did he ever, as some believe, hold the World Colored Heavyweight Championship? Or is this simply a good example of the subjectivity involved in interpreting the designation? [See appendix.]

Following the fight, Frank Childs took four fights—two wins and two draws before June. All eyes turned to Coney Island, New York, on June 9, 1899, as Heavyweight Champion Bob Fitzsimmons was scheduled to defend his title against Jim Jeffries. The hype, which had started months before, was unrelenting. Analyzed from every direction, it wasn't long before some familiar names crept into the study. The *St. Paul Globe* noted:

> The defeat of Bob Armstrong, the big Black, by Frank Childs, of Chicago, is significant in connection with the approaching battle between Fitzsimmons and Jeffries. It gives a fairly good line on the capabilities of the big boilermaker. It must be remembered that Jeffries failed to stop Armstrong in 10 rounds. Childs did the trick—and handily—in seven. Childs is a middleweight, and not such a big one at that. If Childs defeated Armstrong—almost without effort—in seven rounds—and Jeffries fails to conquer the big Black in 10—then Childs must be a wonder, or Jeffries is not as dangerous as the managers of the principals in the approaching match would have the public believe.[22]

James J. Jeffries defeated Bob Fitzsimmons by way of an 11th-round knockout to win the Heavyweight Championship of the World.

Meanwhile, a handful of matches finished the year for Frank Childs: The highlight was dual victories over "Klondike," aka John Haines (Haynes).[23]

A New Century

In 1900, Joe Walcott, later known as "Barbados Joe" Walcott, was challenging all heavyweights to fight for any amount under any conditions—nobody was quite certain whether it was the fighter's bold idea or that of Tom O'Rourke, his manager. Although it initially sounded a bit pretentious, a careful examination of this formidable fighter reveals a pugilist with exceptional power. Standing a mere five feet one and typically weighing less than 150 pounds, the "Black Demon" drew no boundaries. Childs' fight managers, Sam Summerfield and Charles T. Essig, answered the call but could not convince O'Rourke to take the offer—not even with a healthy forfeit and purse.[24]

Childs began the year by taking a decisive six-round decision over Jack Bonner on March 2. Bonner was floored in the first round by a right to the jaw during a breakaway. The talented middleweight was a tough White fighter who fought primarily out of Philadelphia. He had battled George Byers to a 20-round draw back on December 13, 1898. For Frank Childs, he was the perfect prelude to his next battle: a six-round contest against George Byers in Chicago on March 16.

Outweighing his opponent by 15 pounds, Childs fought Byers to a six-round draw at the Star Athletic Club. The crowd felt the Canadian got the best of his opponent, but Childs had no time to argue as he was scheduled to meet Jack Bonner again, over at the Chicago Athletic Club, the following evening. Unlike his first meeting with Byers, Childs appeared fatigued. Drawing Bonner on March 17 over six-rounds seemed to confirm the observation.

Childs was slated to meet Joe Choynski at the Fort Dearborn Athletic club but may have gotten into some unidentified trouble. The fight never took place. Instead, the Texan fought the burly Fred Russell, out of Denver, three consecutive times: On June 7, Childs took a very close six-round victory; on June 15, in a vicious six-round affair, he repeated the feat; and finally, on July 20, this time in Denver, the compact Texan defeated Colorado's golden boy over a 10-round distance.[25]

For Childs, who was having a challenging year, the term seemed destined to end in controversy. Sure enough, on December 15, the *Saint Paul Globe* described his next-to-last fight of the year in Chicago under the banner "Wasn't a Fake":

> Joe Butler, of Philadelphia, quit in the second round of his fight with Frank Childs, of Chicago, in the arena of the Chicago Athletic Club tonight. Childs had all the better of the fight in the first round, and in the early part of the second Butler went to the floor from a swing that barely touched him. He refused to rise, and Referee Siler counted him out. The club members raised a protest at the early ending of the fight, and as Butler expressed himself as willing to try again. Childs, who had taken off his gloves, began to fight again and knocked Butler out. This time there was no make believe about it. Butler was some minutes in recovering consciousness.[26]

On December 21, in Denver, Childs grabbed a 10-round decision over "Mexican Pete" Everett before the Colorado Athletic Association. The fight was rather uneventful. That is, until Childs broke his right hand. The injury forced him to cancel an upcoming engagement with "Klondike," the Colored heavyweight.

A broken wrist or hand is a common injury for a fighter. It can happen when he tries to catch himself during a fall or lands hard on an outstretched hand. Healing time varies and depends upon the care. The bones must heal in proper alignment or the fighter can incur complications. Childs hoped to return to the ring by the spring of 1901.

Frank Childs v. George Byers—World Colored Heavyweight Championship

What a way to start the year, when the fight set for 20 rounds only lasted 17. In that round, Frank Childs knocked out George Byers. It happened on March 16, 1901, in Hot Springs, Arkansas. Although Byers weighed less, he appeared lethargic and weak compared to his antagonist. As the *Saint Paul Globe* reported: "Childs, in the fourth round, stood perfectly still and let Byers hit him on the chin and mouth three times in succession, making no effort to defend himself or to avoid the blows. He knocked Byers down three times with left swings on the chin before the fight ended, and had it all his own way from the third round to the finish."[27]

Following the battle—which was his only recorded bout of the year—Childs was rumored to have reinjured his hand. If you believe Byers held the title prior to the match, it was certain he didn't leave with it.

As 1902 began, the rumors—often floated to draw an opponent out or test public opinion—about a match being struck between Childs and Joe Walcott filled newspapers—a Louisville club even put up a purse of $1,000. But Walcott didn't bite.

Childs was scheduled to do battle once again with Fred Russell for six rounds at the clubrooms of the Chicago Athletic Association on January 18. But Russell, the man who tackled Childs in three consecutive bouts in 1900, had other ideas and up and quit. So management secured the services of Walter Johnson of Chicago. The bout was about as interesting as watching grass grow. Which was probably good considering Childs' ring rust. As the *Indianapolis Journal* reported: "The first two rounds were Johnson's by a shade, but after that he tired rapidly. Childs did most of the leading, but was unable to land a knockout blow. At the end of the fourth round the spectators evinced much displeasure by catcalls, hissing and cries of 'Fake!' and many of them left the hall."[28]

In the end, it was Childs by a decision. After the fight, efforts were made to match Childs with "Denver" Ed Martin, the Colored boxer who was Gus Ruhlin's sparring partner and Billy Madden's candidate for a date with Jim Jeffries. It looked like the six-round battle was set for January 31, before McFarland's club in Philadelphia, but it was still being argued.[29]

As for Childs, his focus remained on boxing; accordingly, he had a six-round date with "Wild Bill" Hanrahan at the America Club in Chicago on February 3. One minute into the fourth round, "Wild Bill" was knocked cold—he had also hit the floor in Round One. When Childs went to the body in Round Two, Hanrahan was having difficulty recovering. Here is how the *Saint Paul Globe* reported the fourth and final round: "When they came together in the fourth round Childs continued to play for the stomach, easily avoiding Hanrahan's wild swings. After about a minute of fighting they got into a clinch, and on the breakaway Childs shoved a straight left into Hanrahan's stomach. The blow doubled Hanrahan up, and as his head dropped forward the colored man brought his right square on the jaw. Hanrahan fell flat on his back, and after being counted out his seconds carried him to his corner where they worked over him for fully 10 minutes before he was able to walk to his dressing room."[30]

"Denver" Ed Martin v. Frank Childs—World Colored Heavyweight Championship

Following months of negotiation, Billy Madden finally landed the fight he was looking for. It was just a six-round contest, before the America Club in Chicago on February 24, 1902, but it was long enough for "Denver" Ed Martin to capture a decision and perhaps a title.

Martin easily grabbed the first two rounds by wisely keeping Childs out of range. Using his jab effectively to induce damage, he retreated before the Texan could counter. Childs just could not penetrate Martin's superb defense or draw him to close quarters for an assault. Frustrated in the third round, Childs resorted to some wild and off-balance swings in hope of catching his adversary off-guard. However, the strategy failed. Martin seized the opportunity and fired a right that caught Childs squarely on the jaw before dropping him. Embarrassed by the plunge, Childs arose determined to destroy his antagonist. Yet the Denver man remained calm and worked that left jab of his to perfection.

The *Salt Lake Herald* reported the conclusion: "The fourth round was Martin's although little damage was done by either man. In the next Childs reached Martin's neck with a right swing that jarred the Denver man, but Martin pulled himself together in a hurry and retreated until he had collected his faculties. The last round was rather tame. Martin seeing he had such a big lead, made little effort to increase it. Childs worked hard to even up matters, but Martin either dancing out of reach or locked in Childs' arms. A good portion of the audience was hissing as the contest came to an end."[31]

The decision, by Referee George Siler, to award the fight to Martin was the right call.[32]

A Trio of Hall of Famers

For a professional athlete, there are many ways to end a career, but most would prefer a memorable conclusion. Facing three consecutive elite fighters (members of the International Boxing Hall of Fame), Frank Childs accomplished just that in 1902—his career essentially drew to a conclusion two years later.[33] In a period of just over 50 days, Frank Childs would enter a ring against Joe Walcott, Jack Johnson, and Joe Choynski. A fighter could spend a lifetime just bragging that he faced one of these great boxers.

Frank Childs v. Joe Walcott, October 9, 1902

It wasn't the perfect way to start off a boxing trifecta for Frank Childs, but it wasn't bad either. On October 9, in Chicago, Frank Childs fought Joe Walcott for two-and-a-half rounds to a "no contest." Walcott was unable to continue fighting due to a left arm injury—some sources stated he deliberately quit under punishment.[34] To the skillful fighter's credit, he donated his share of the purse to charity. Although staring across a ring at Joe Walcott could be intimidating, Childs showed no emotion.

The *Arizona Republican* reported:

"Barbados" Joe Walcott, a tough welterweight fighter, was willing to take on all comers from welterweight to heavyweight. He's pictured here on a cigarette card for Mayo's Cut Plug tobacco (*Library of Congress, LC-DIG-ppmsca-55332*).

Childs changed his tactics in the third and forced the fighting. He had little trouble in locating Walcott and landed three straight rights on the latter's stomach. The blows weakened Wolcott and Childs assumed the lead, when his opponent suddenly discovered that his arm was useless and asked the referee to stop the fight. The referee ordered Walcott to continue the fighting, but the pugilist declined and walked to his corner. The officials of the club believed that Walcott was faking and announced that his share of the purse would be given to any charitable institution that Referee George Siler should name.[35]

The *Evening World* went so far as to title their coverage of the battle, "Walcott Fakes Another Fight, Colored Welter-Weight Works the Injured Arm Trick in Bout with Childs, so His Share of Purse Goes to Charity." The newspaper also observed: "Walcott did the same in a fight with Tommy West at the Garden two years ago."[36] An x-ray and subsequent examination, however, by a Dr. Bennett concluded that the fighter's arm was indeed broken.[37]

Jack Johnson, pictured here, defeated fellow Texan Frank Childs twice in his career, once in 1902 and again in 1904. Both fighters rose to prominence at the height of the Jim Crow era (*Library of Congress, LC-DIG-gg-bain-08094*).

Frank Childs v. Jack Johnson, October 21, 1902

As fate had it, Joe Walcott was scheduled to meet Jack Johnson on October 21, at the Century Athletic Club in Los Angeles. Naturally, Walcott could not make it, so Manager "Uncle" Tom McCarey wired both George Gardner and Frank Childs, informing them of the dilemma and offering them a chance to substitute for the fighter. Childs was scheduled to meet Jack Gardner in Los Angeles before heading north to do battle with the winner of the Gardner v. Choynski bout in San Francisco. Thankfully, the opportunity caught up to him in Kansas City on October 15.

The "Galveston Giant," Jack Johnson, fought out of his hometown in Texas until the turn of the century. It was there that most first learned of the Black fighter, when he was arrested and jailed with Joe Choynski. Since then, Johnson had opted for the California boxing scene. His reputation was growing, and many of the White fighters were keeping their distance. To stay in shape, Johnson turned to others his own size and color, such as Hank Griffin, the Michigan heavyweight. Johnson hadn't lost a fight all year and looked forward to meeting Frank Childs.

A bulk of the fight coverage was limited to two sentences, such as what appeared in the *Topeka State Journal*: "The fight last night between Frank Childs of Chicago and Jack Johnson of Bakersfield ended in the 12th round when Childs' seconds threw up the sponge, claiming that their principal had dislocated his elbow. The injury was supposed to have been received in training, and Childs claimed that the arm went back on him during the fight."[38]

The fight, which was held at Hazard's Pavilion, would enter the record books as a 12th-round victory in favor of the "Galveston Giant." Soon, Jack Johnson's press coverage would improve dramatically.

Frank Childs v. Joe Choynski, December 1, 1902

Some viewed them as second-class heavyweights, but Frank Childs and Joe Choynski, when healthy, could match with anyone. Both agreed to meet at catchweight—Choynski 15 pounds the worse of it—inside the Glickman Theater and under the auspices of the Lyceum Athletic Club in Chicago.

Choynski swarmed Childs like a bee to honey and even floored him in the second round. At the end of the six rounds, it was Choynski by a decision. It was the veteran's cleverness that enabled him to dance out of danger whenever he felt threatened. Childs went all-out in the third round, but Choynski aggressively countered as the two went at it hammer and tongs. Many felt it was the best round of the evening.

The *St. Louis Republic* noted: "The fourth round was the slowest of the lot, the fast pace set in the preceding round having told on the fighters. Childs did not meet with the approval of the crowd and cries of 'Fake,' and 'Why don't you fight?' were heard throughout the house. The last two rounds were extremely fast for big men, and enough blows were delivered by each to suit the most fastidious 'fan.' Frank tried his best to put Joe away in the final round, but the blond boxer met his every rush with straight left handers [*sic*] and easily won the decision."[39]

Following the trifecta, Frank Childs had a lot to think about and plenty of time to do it—he chose to be inactive in 1903. Later, the aromatic bouquet of the ring, not to mention its remittance, beguiled the pugilist.

It was viewed by some, including the *Evening World*, as "the slowest fighting imaginable."[40] On June 2, 1904, Jack Johnson captured a six-round decision over Frank Childs inside the Empire Athletic Club in Chicago, Illinois. Those present, many of whom had high expectations, were disappointed by Johnson's performance—they wanted a line on the big Black man and his chances, should he ever meet Jeffries. Perhaps it was a favor to Childs, who hadn't been in the ring with real competition since December of 1902. Nobody was quite sure. According to the *Evening World*, "During the entire time four light blows were landed, and as Johnson landed them the referee was forced to give him the decision."[41]

A few days later, Childs knocked out "Klondike" in the eighth round of a battle held in Michigan. The tall Black boxer, who had been ringside at the Johnson v. Childs battle, had known Childs for years and always welcomed a go-around with the fighter.

Frank Childs died on June 20, 1936, in Waukegan, Illinois, almost a year to the day before Joe Louis captured the NBA, NYSAC and *The Ring* world heavyweight titles.

The Color Line, 1898–1902

Frank Childs fought some good White fighters: George LaBlanche, Jack Bonner, Tom "Stockings" Conroy, and Fred Russell. He also fought some good Black fighters: Hank Griffin, "Klondike," and Joe Butler. The "Crafty Texan" also entered the ring with some outstanding pugilists: Peter Jackson (Exhibition), Joe Choynski, Bob Armstrong, George Byers, "Denver" Ed Martin, Joe Walcott, and Jack Johnson. But Frank Childs would not enter a ring against the recognized White heavyweight champions, Bob Fitzsimmons (1897–1899) or Jim Jeffries (1899–1905). The color line was rock solid, and neither champion would cross it.

Fitzsimmons, the fight game's first three-division world champion, was a fighting machine. However, he told the *Topeka State Journal*: "I draw the color line and will not fight Bob Armstrong, but I will back 'Yank' Kenny, who is my sparring partner, against him to any amount in a finish fight."[42]

As for James J. Jeffries, who turned down a $20,000 offer to fight Sam McVey, he was never hesitant to state his position, and did so in the same newspaper: "I have made up my mind never to fight a Negro again as long as there are White men in the field. Then, again, [Sam] McVey is not to be regarded as a championship possibility. His last fight resulted in a defeat by Jack Johnson. The latter is a little fellow compared to McVey, so I don't see where he figures at all."[43]

What color line? Looking south, the *Ocala Evening Star* printed:

As to the "color line," there is no color line, only as drawn by nature. The South doesn't draw any either. The line they draw is on the Negro's conduct and condition. Being a White Negro doesn't make you a White man. You are a Negro and the line is drawn just the same. They have nothing against "Black" as a color. They wear black hats. They admire a black span harnessed to a black carriage, they wear black dresses, etc. Where is the color line in these things? If they acted as the Negro does, they would draw the color line on these things, too. Let us stop sitting down [and] whining about "discrimination" and "color line" and set about to improve our conduct by acting gentlemanly and lady-like, better our condition by buying homes and beautifying them, and sending our children to school. Work and make an honest living, keep away from the courthouses and out of the chain gangs and jails, and see if the imaginary "color line" will not disappear as the flying cloud before the rising sun.[44]

Six

Colorado Giant

The boom in gold prospecting and mining in the Pikes Peak region of western Kansas Territory and southwestern Nebraska Territory of the United States was labeled the Colorado Gold Rush. It began in July 1858 and lasted until roughly the creation of the Colorado Territory on February 28, 1861. Everybody, or so it appeared, headed west to strike it rich—an estimated 100,000 precious metal seekers took part in one of the greatest gold rushes in North American history. Ironically, many were not those initially lured during the California Gold Rush of 1849.[1]

The influx of fortune seekers created a few mining camps such as Denver City and Boulder City that would develop into metropolitan areas. These regions, often rough in nature, became known for conducting their fair share of boxing contests. As a busy day in the mine often led to a hectic evening in a saloon, an impromptu challenge was never more than a few whiskey shots away. Some camps even held exhibitions and invited the most prominent fighters of the day.

Born on September 10, 1881, Ed Martin, the son of a former slave, grew to well over six feet tall—some claim as high as six feet, six inches—and tipped over 200 pounds. Originating from Denver, it seemed only logical for the common-named pugilist to acquire it as a moniker, so the pugilist did just that. Having acquired some skills at a local gymnasium, the lanky youngster showed promise. Heading east just before the turn of the century, he intended to quarry his potential in the opposite direction.

On June 6, 1899, "Denver" Ed Martin found himself staring at Bob Armstrong, of Chicago, at the Lenox Athletic Club in New York City.[2] How many amateur or bootleg contests the fighter had prior to this match was unclear. The result of this battle was not: in the second round, the Colorado pugilist found himself flopped on the side of the club's ring and counted out.[3] Welcome to New York, Mr. Martin.

His follow-up performance came at a "'Culled' Event at Coney" on July 24. Martin was part of a show where all six fighters, at the Coney Island Sporting Club, were Negroes. The feature event was intended to be Frank Childs versus George Byers; however, the former was missing in action and had to be replaced. Martin met Charles Stevenson, of Philadelphia, in a battle scheduled for 15 rounds. The *Kansas City Journal* reported: "The men were very slow. Martin was the cleverer, but he made a very poor showing, as he missed several opportunities of settling the mill in short order. In the 13th round he floored Stevenson with a smash on the jaw, but the bell saved the Philadelphian. Martin went to his man in the next round and had Stevenson all but out when the referee stopped the fight, which he awarded to Martin."[4]

Martin next defeated Walter Johnson, a Colored fighter from Philadelphia, in a seven-round bout held at the Broadway Athletic Club. Conducted on August 25, the bout

74

072145 WASHINGTON ST. FROM FULTON, BROOKLYN, N. Y.

Not unlike Denver, Brooklyn also had its share of rail cars with easy access to local athletic clubs (Library of Congress, LC-DIG-det-4a23886).

was a preliminary to the feature that saw Dan Creedon, of Australia, defeat Black fighter Fred "Cyclone" Morris in six rounds. Martin performed well, and as a result found himself on some talented future fight cards—his size, no doubt, added to the appeal. The caveat to such a performance: As a Black fighter's reputation grew, it became harder to match him— many White fighters, who exceeded the number of Blacks, drew the color line.

As the century turned, the "Colorado Giant" took his first two fights in Philadelphia. There he snatched two six-round no-decisions: The first against "Klondike" on January 27, followed by a lackluster rematch with Bob Armstrong on March 23.[5] Returning to Brooklyn, Martin lined his pockets with a couple of insipid battles before ending the year against Gus Ruhlin's punching bag, Yank Kenny. A White fighter who was at the tail end of a good reputation, Kenny was also well-known for being a sparring partner of Bob Fitzsimmons during the late 1890s. The Michigan scrapper wouldn't win a single battle in 1900; moreover, he would box four more years without a victory. With the fight planned for August 31 inside the Hercules Athletic Club, Kenny wasn't thrilled by the pairing but took the fight anyway. As the *Waterbury Evening Democrat* reported: "They were to have fought 25 rounds. Martin sailed in like a demon. Both exchanged lefts and Kenny clinched. Then Martin roughed it and hammered Kenny's side until it was nearly raw. Both let go swings. Martin got there first and with a heavy blow knocked Kenny out. The round only lasted one minute and 30 seconds."[6]

In contrast to Kenny, the "Colorado Giant" hadn't lost a ring battle since his encounter with Armstrong last year. Not only was Martin improving with every skirmish and getting

Denver and Brooklyn were two cities Ed Martin became familiar with. The street railroads of Denver promoted athletic events and were a common form of transportation (Library of Congress, LC-USZ6—05405).

stronger, but his contacts, and thus opportunities, were improving. By December, he was being touted as a contender for the World Colored Heavyweights Championship—attempts were being made to match him with Frank Childs.[7]

An Advantageous Affiliation

Enter Gus Ruhlin, the "Akron Giant," a large, White, Irish American warrior who stood six feet, two inches and tipped at about 200 pounds. Ruhlin was destined for fame, or at least he thought so. However, the Ohio-born pugilist had to overcome some of the obstacles of his era to get there, as did Bob Fitzsimmons and James J. Jeffries.

The handsome, widow's-peaked giant had thighs like tree trunks and moved about the ring with precision. Ruhlin's downfall was his spasmodic performances—he was either consistently bad or good. Former champion James J. Corbett, who taught and trained Ruhlin, commented to the *Topeka State Journal*: "But what I hope for is to see Ruhlin in the same condition he was when he fought and beat Tom Sharkey, and to use the same judgment. If he is in shape and uses his head rightly neither Jeffries nor any other man on earth can knock him out in 20 rounds. Then after it's all over the very worst Gus can get is a draw."[8]

Ruhlin was scheduled to meet Jeffries on February 15 in Cincinnati, but Governor Nash of Ohio prevented the bout. The pair would convene on November 15 in San Francisco instead. Ruhlin's manager, Billy Madden, believed Ed Martin could assist his fighter in training. So the "Colorado Giant" became part of Ruhlin's team—Martin was an inch taller than Jeffries.[9] The fighter would also accompany Ruhlin on a western exhibition tour. To pick up some extra pocket cash, Martin "would take on any local man for two rounds and give him $50 if he stayed."[10] In addition to these skirmishes, the fighter would grab a ridiculous victory over a fouling, or should I say kneeing, Fred Russell on August 12, 1901, then head to Los Angeles to tackle Hank Griffin on October 2. The latter fight was billed as for the "Colored Heavyweight Championship," although no specifics regarding the views of Frank Childs were given.

According to the *Evening World*:

> The fight was one of the best ever seen here. It was action from the first round until the finish. Griffin was made to feel weary by the succession of left jabs sent by Martin. That is Gus Ruhlin's game, and the aspirant for Jeffries title was in "Denver Ed's" corner giving him tips.
> The blows cut Griffin badly and his face looked a horrible sight before the fourth round had finished. It will be remembered that Jeffries could do nothing with Griffin in that number of rounds in their meeting a week or so ago.[11]

Martin's affiliation with Ruhlin turned out to be exceptionally beneficial, not only for the corner tips, but also for the publicity he was able to earn. *Butte Inter Mountain* noted during his exhibition with challenger Denis "Ike" Hayes: "Martin showed himself to be a clever fighter, not only in his go with Hayes, but in his three round exhibition with Ruhlin. The big Negro handles himself well, is quick and is shifty on his feet. His sparring with Ruhlin was a revelation and there are many who believe Madden's prediction that Martin is a coming heavyweight. In his go with Hayes, Martin showed that he can hit hard and often. He beat the former Montana State champion to a whisper and would have made a chopping block of him had not Hayes thrown up the sponge."[12]

Not to lose sight of the mission: On November 15, in San Francisco, James J. Jeffries, held to a 20-round draw by Gus Ruhlin back in 1897, simply dominated his foe in their rematch. Ruhlin tried desperately to avoid a knockout—he even managed to stay on his feet until the fifth round. However, when he returned to his corner, Billy Madden tossed a sponge into the ring.

It was time for Martin to shift his attention back to his own career.

"Denver" Ed Martin v. Frank Childs—World Colored Heavyweight Championship

The Colored Heavyweight Championship of the World was transferred via a six-round decision to "Denver" Ed Martin on February 24, 1902. As formal as the transaction may sound, few recognized it as such. Frank Childs, the local favorite, fought gamely but failed to defend his title. His artillery fell short, and when Martin was within range Childs got entangled in his tentacles. *Omaha Daily Bee* noted: "Martin's performance during the first four rounds was so far superior to that of Childs that he made the latter look rather cheap. During the last two rounds Martin took few chances and contented himself with keeping Childs at a distance, where the Chicago man could do no damage."[13]

Martin worked with precision and was destined to acquire the designation. Speaking of which, what better place to polish any crown than the United Kingdom. In 1901, Queen Victoria died, having served as queen for 63 years. Her son, Albert Edward (1841–1910), became king in 1901, but was not crowned king until August 9, 1902. As part of the coronation festivities (The Coronation Sporting Tournament), a group of American pugilists, including Gus Ruhlin and "Denver" Ed Martin, both members of Billy Madden's stable, were invited to perform, as were Bob Armstrong, Pat Daly, Frank Erne, Tom Sharkey, Joe Walcott, and Tommy West. While it was indeed an honor to be asked to the event, some members of the press felt differently. According to the *Albuquerque Daily Citizen*: "It would be difficult to get together a more representative lot of 'has-beens' than the American fighters named, while the few Britishers to appear are of no larger caliber, having taken their turn a long time ago at being walloped by second-raters from this side of the water."[14]

As part of the festivities Martin defeated Sandy Ferguson, of Boston, in five very spirited rounds. Floored multiple times, an unconditioned Ferguson was so weak that it justified the referee's decision to stop the battle.

On July 25, Ed Martin, the World Colored Heavyweight Champion, defeated Bob Armstrong in a 15-round title defense at the Crystal Palace in London. Picture 22,000 animated fans surrounding a 24-foot ring; hence, a championship vista. Following the victory by decision, Martin challenged the winner of the Jeffries v. Fitzsimmons contest.[15] Why not?

As for how Billy Madden saw his fighter's accomplishments, the enterprising manager was quoted in the *Saint Paul Globe*: "The leading sporting papers here [Ireland], as well as in England, concede Martin the undisputed championship of England. I have secured two titles for Martin since he has been under my management—Black champion and English champion. So, consequently Jeffries is only champion of America until he meets and licks Martin."[16]

Martin finished his tour by defeating Frank Craig, aka the "Harlem Coffee Cooler," on August 30 in a bout held in Newcastle, England. Craig was a quick and talented Black boxer who fought mainly out of New York and Philadelphia early in his career, before heading to England. He gained a level of notoriety on February 19, 1894, when he defeated Joe Butler, "King of the Middleweights."

Billy Madden could not curtail his excitement, or his narcissism, over his European trip, the *Butte Inter Mountain* reported: "There are no flies on Martin, even if I say so myself. He is the cleverest Negro pugilist in the world, not even overlooking the late Peter Jackson. Since I took hold of Martin he has developed into a wonder. He knows how to punch, is game and is up to date."[17]

On December 10, 1902, Ed Martin closed out the year with an action-packed, six-round no-decision against Bob Armstrong at the Penn Art Club in Philadelphia. According to the *Minneapolis Journal*: "The bout was fast from start to finish, and both men narrowly escaped a knockout. The bell saved Armstrong in the third and fifth rounds, and Martin was floored six times in the fourth round. When the bell sounded the fighters were extremely groggy and showed evidence of exhaustion."[18]

In 1903, "Denver" Ed Martin, having become one of the most popular Black heavyweights, would face three of the greatest fighters of their era: Jack Johnson, Bob Armstrong, and Sam McVey. All three pugilists would put Martin's skills to the test while altering his career path.

Jack Johnson v. "Denver" Ed Martin—World Colored Heavyweight Championship

"The Galveston Giant," Jack Johnson, with fewer than a couple dozen recorded battles under his belt, was on his way to becoming one of the most intimidating pugilists ever to enter a ring. Although that wasn't clear in 1903, what was certain was that he was an enormous obstacle in the heavyweight division. Having tackled some tough Black boxers in "Utah" Bob Thompson, "Klondike," Hank Griffin, and Frank Childs, along with some challenging White pugilists in Joe Choynski, Joe Kennedy, Jack Jeffries, George Gardner, and Fred Russell, Johnson feared no man.

On February 5, 1903, Jack Johnson met "Denver" Ed Martin in a 20-round bout before the Century Athletic Club of Los Angeles, California. Most newspaper coverage of the fight was 10 lines or less. The *Evening Star* noted: "The contest went the limit and Johnson outpointed Martin at every stage. Owing to Johnson's recent victories over George Gardner, Frank Childs and Hank Griffin, he was made a 10 to 8 favorite. For the first 10 rounds Martin easily held his own and shoved his long left often into Johnson's face and mouth. But his punching powers were no avail, and Johnson soon had him tired. In the remaining rounds Johnson was the aggressor, and had no trouble in getting the verdict. Madden is disappointed with the result, and has challenged Johnson to tackle Martin again."[19]

Martin simply lacked the power necessary to have his way with Johnson. The "Galveston Giant," having picked up the Colored title, was in another league, as they say, and that's meant as no insult to the "Colorado Giant."

In late spring, Madden tried to land his fighter a match with Fred Russell, but that didn't fly. Later, he was successful at matching Martin against the familiar face of Bob Armstrong. The fight was scheduled for 12 rounds under the auspices of the Tammany Athletic Club of Boston, on June 10.

Martin entered the fight with Armstrong like a man on a mission. He was all over his nemesis in the first two rounds, firing artillery in the form of combinations into his face. Stoic, Armstrong appeared to welcome the assault. Granted, the Philly fighter sneaked in a few solid jabs to the body, but that was about it. Two minutes into the third round, Armstrong saw a shot at Martin's stomach and took it. Kaboom! The thud as a result of Armstrong's left could be heard in Springfield. The fighter went down and out. A weakness had been found in Martin's armor.[20]

Having plenty of time to recuperate, Martin had one last battle before the end of the year: The Century Athletic Club, of Los Angeles, California, was able to match him with Sam McVey for 20 rounds on September 15.

It ended nearly as quickly as it started. Three short-arm right hands delivered the damage to Martin's solar plexus, his recently revealed weak spot, and it was over. The event, held at Hazard's Pavilion, saw the big Black boxer from Oxnard, California, deliver Martin in the very first round. Having taken control right from the opening bell, McVey looked impressive—unusually sharp for someone with fewer than 10 recorded bouts. Martin managed only one clean blow, a straight left to his antagonist's face.

The *San Francisco Call* reported the final moments: "McVey met him, avoiding his straight left for the face and sending in two right hand body blows in quick succession. They were at such close quarters that as Martin fell forward he clasped his arms about McVey's shoulders. McVey shook him loose and Martin went down, rolled over on his face and lay perfectly still. He was counted out but did not get up. His seconds climbed through the ropes and administered the usual remedies in the case of a knockout. After about a minute Martin was lifted up and placed in his chair in his corner."[21]

After two minutes and 30 seconds, it was done. Cries of "Fake!" soon overtook the hush of genuine concern for Martin. Even so, there was no hoax, only a defeated man trying to reclaim a sense of dignity.

The following year (1904), Martin hoped to prove that his recent performances were nothing but a fluke. So he scheduled a pair of rematches. The first was a 10-round event slated for the arena of the Outing Athletic Club in Los Angeles on August 12. Across the ring from him was the local favorite, Sam McVey. Billy Madden, who hadn't lost faith in his fighter, did well by his side. His faith seemed to work as Martin took the decision. According to the *Call*, "Martin had all the cleverness and speed and made McVey look like a novice at times. McVey put up the worst fight of his career."[22] In a bit of a surprise, the press paid little attention to the fight.

Jack Johnson v. "Denver" Ed Martin—World Colored Heavyweight Championship

Martin's rematch against Jack Johnson, on October 18, 1904, drew far greater interest— Johnson had added 10 more victories to his record. Spectators packed Hazard's Pavilion in Los Angeles. Treated to a whirlwind affair that lasted only two rounds, most fans had barely enough time to drop a wager. Martin tried to take control early but was drawn to close quarters, where he took some savage body blows. Johnson was clearly aware of Martin's weakness and had every intention of exploiting it. The Galveston fighter's blows were so hard that they sent Martin to his knees twice in the first round. The *Salt Lake Herald* said: "In the second Martin started the fighting with a straight left to the face, but got a hard right over the heart which put him down for a count of seven. He got up and rushed again, and again went down from a left in the stomach. He arose at the count of six and immediately got a right to the body and a left to the jaw which put him out."[23]

Johnson simply dominated the fight because he had to, Martin was that good. He couldn't ride his opponent for a round or two as he had done in other battles. Also, if he was going to call out Jeffries, he needed to make a statement, and this was it. The Century Athletic Club, under manager Tom McCarey, offered a $15,000 guarantee should Jeffries take up Johnson's gauntlet.

Martin was hit so hard that some believed the fighter was dead—it took 10 minutes to revive him. When it was clear that Martin was still alive, those remaining in the building called for a few words from the victor. The *Washington Times* noted Johnson's position:

> I will not rest until popular public opinion forces James Jeffries, the world's champion, to recognize the validity of my claim for a fight with him. His drawing the color line is all bosh. His famous battle with Peter Jackson out here, his fight with Bob Armstrong in New York, and his tussle with Hank Griffin, all Negroes, makes his drawing of the color line ridiculous.
> Jeffries says that if any man comes along better than Bob Fitzsimmons he will fight again. Well, I am better than Bob Fitzsimmons. I knocked out George Gardner, a feat Fitzsimmons was unable to accomplish. I have never been defeated and am the one man in the world fit to make James J. Jeffries extend himself to his limit. The champion knows this and, accordingly, side-steps with that time worn, old, cowardly, four flushers' stand by, the color line.[24]

Martin's career was drawing to a close. He would not fight in 1905, battle only Sam McVey in 1906 (KO4) and 1907 (KO16), and face only one notable fighter in 1909 (ND4), Ed "Gunboat" Smith—the latter winning the White Heavyweight Championship by defeating Arthur Pelkey in 1914.

In 1911, Martin turned to wrestling under the management of Frank Riley. The enterprise allowed him to stay close to home, which was Washington State. He turned up in the sports section once again, but not in the manner he would have hoped: "'Denver Ed.' Martin' Forfeits His Bail." The fighter was arrested in Tacoma, on October 16, 1911, on a charge of shooting craps. Martin ended up forfeiting his $30 bail. Martin also continued to throw out challenges to Jack Johnson, which he did on December 9, 1911. If accepted, not only would it be for his title but also for a side bet of $2,500.

In his later years, Martin filled the hours by training young fighters at a club in Seattle. Of course, he was always an offer away from an exhibition and even contemplated a comeback numerous times. In 1921, the ring veteran actually gave it a serious try. But only a few fights into the resurgence, an aggressive Harry Wills knocked him out in the first round—Martin was down six times before being put to sleep. That fight took place on November 18 in Portland, Oregon, and "The Black Panther" was at the pinnacle of his career.

"Uncle Tom" McCarey (1872–1936)

When he strolled into a room in his three-piece suit, you immediately noticed his long White face beneath a carpet of dense, wavy hair. His protracted nose, garnished with a pair of bushy eyebrows, seemed to move in unison with his mustache. His eyes, lit like stars, filled with opportunity. That was Thomas Jefferson McCarey. The name McCarey comes from the ancient Dalriadan clans of Scotland's west coast and the Hebrides Islands. In Gaelic, it is a word for son of the young, manly one. As a surname, it appeared to fit the lanky businessman perfectly.

McCarey was born on September 22, 1872, in Edwardsville, Illinois. Traveling from the Midwest before the turn of the century, McCarey delighted in the climatic conditions of the West Coast. The drier weather also seemed to solve some respiratory issues he occasionally struggled with. Ambitious, he began his California career in the laundry business, which is appropriate for someone so dedicated that he would give a friend the shirt off his back. Noting the area's fascination with boxing, McCarey pooled his resources and turned to Hazard's Pavilion as a home for fistic entertainment.

McCarey told the *Los Angeles Herald*: "As the idea [fight promotion] grew I wanted to become familiar with the various angles of the sport, so I took the management of four colored boxers, and began to get a real insight in the game. I never made any money as a manager but I did familiarize myself with boxing and boxers, and was only waiting an opportunity to get into the sport as a promoter, as I wanted to carry out my own ideas as to how a club should be run."[25]

He became "known from one end of the country to the other as 'Uncle Tom,' friend of pork and bean fighters, and general relief committee to hundreds."[26] Not minding the moniker, McCarey opened his arms to Black fighters, recognized their talent, and gave them a stage to exhibit their virility. He accepted their willingness to challenge the falsehood of White superiority. Race sold, and McCarey understood this, as exemplified in his passion for all Black or mixed bouts. More importantly he was fair to everyone. Speaking to the *Los Angeles Herald*:

This fighting business is just the same fundamentally as any other. Nothing in the world succeeds unless you are honest. Now most fighters are boys who have grown up without education other than the world's hard knocks have given them and are naturally inclined to go wrong when the chance presents itself to make a lot of money for one crooked act. The tempter is ever present the shape of some rich gambler, and only by watching all the time can he be foiled of cheating the public through his poor tool. I watch the fighter and his associates, and the least suspicious action is enough for me to interfere and spoil what they call a "frame-up."[27]

Every boxing market depends on successful promoters. From 1901 until 1914, Thomas Jefferson McCarey brought his pugilistic genius to the Los Angeles area, staging confrontations at Hazard's Pavilion (1901–1904), Naud Junction Pavilion (1905–1910), and Vernon Arena (1910–1914). Only legislation could keep him from the sport he loved; in the November 1914 election, the California voters passed an anti-pro boxing amendment. Such began the "Four-Round Era" (1914–1925), as some historians call it, a name synonymous with the maximum allowable length of a battle.

During McCarey's time, he was one of fewer than a handful of good promoters in California, along with James Coffroth of San Francisco, Eddie Graney of San Francisco, and Chet McIntyre of Vancouver, British Columbia.

McCarey was the brains behind the Century Athletic Club. The impresario conducted many bouts featuring Black boxers such as "Dixie Kid" (Aaron Brown), Frank Childs, Jack Johnson, Sam McVey, "Denver" Ed Martin, Joe Walcott, and Billy Woods. Later, he would operate under the auspices of the Pacific Athletic Club at the Naud Junction area of Los Angeles. It was during this period that Southern California began to rival San Francisco as the epicenter of boxing.

To say that Tom McCarey created his fair share of White anxiety would be an understatement. The migration, not to mention success, of many of the Colored fighters drew attention to Southern California and created a comfort level for Blacks. By 1900, Los Angeles had the second-largest Black population in the state.

When people think of the history of Southern California boxing, various places are drawn to mind, including the old Vernon Arena. The Los Angeles–area landmark, which hosted hundreds of bouts and brought in thousands of dollars, burned to the ground in October 1915. During its seven-year run, many boxers reaped its benefits, including Johnny Kilbane, Luther McCarty, Joe Rivers, and Kid Williams. McCarey leased the facility from the Huntington family and conducted some of the finest boxing available anywhere—it had a capacity of 8,500.

An added benefit from Vernon was that it allowed 25-round bouts with decisions beginning in 1908—only months before, in 1907, the city of Los Angeles mandated no-decision bouts with the maximum number of rounds set at 10.

Charming, soft-spoken and educated, McCarey often found solace with his family. Living in a beautiful home in the Southwest part of Los Angeles suited him just fine. There, he and his wife, Leona Mistral (1876–1954), raised their children. McCarey always loved a wager, or risk if you will, as evidenced by his time spent at racetracks betting on horses. Perhaps he passed some of that feeling to his sons. When McCarey passed in 1936, his two sons, Leo and Raymond, would carry on the family legacy. However, it would not to be in a ring but in a cinema. Leo McCarey directed a number of well-known movies, including *Duck Soup*, *Going My Way*, and *Bells of St. Mary's*. He won two Academy Awards as Best Director and another for best story.

The Color Line, 1902–1903

"Denver" Ed Martin entered a boxing ring with some good White fighters, including Yank Kenny, Fred Russell, Gus Ruhlin (exhibitions), and Ed "Gunboat" Smith. But he also slipped between the ropes with some great Black boxers, including Bob Armstrong, Hank Griffin, Frank Childs, Sam McVey, and Jack Johnson. His popularity drew attention to the color line, even if he never crossed it to battle Jim Jeffries.

With regard to the White champion, manager Bill Delaney spoke to the *Spokane Press*: "There is not the remotest possibility of Jeffries meeting Jack Johnson or any other colored man. It's simply that we are never going to give a Negro a chance to be champion. Jeff has fought Negroes—we're willing to admit that—and he would fight a Negro again if the Negro was champion. But there'll be no Negro champion while we hold the belt."[28]

Tom McCarey took considerable criticism for his matches, yet through them the color line faded a bit. In his early years, the White promoter wasn't hesitant at enlisting the services of the best Black fighters, something that was unheard-of at the time. On June 20, 1902, he even conducted his first all-Black card that featured Jack Johnson versus Hank Griffin. Seven years later, Jack Johnson noted it as "one of the hardest battles and which I consider one of the best in my career in the prize ring."[29]

As for titles, the *Seattle Republican* noted: "It is strange indeed, says an exchange, to see that those Negroes who have attained distinction in Art and Science, Music, Oratory, etc., persist in denying originality to the Negro race by styling themselves the 'Black Patti,' the 'Black Jennie Lind,' the 'Black Beecher,' the 'Black Cicero,' or 'Black Moses.' Why should a great Negro orator be called a Black Phillips or a Negro statesman be called the Black Blaine, etc., etc.... These titles add no dignity to the Negro race and by claiming them we appear ridiculous."[30]

Some Black boxers, such as Frank Craig, were doing extremely well overseas—the fighter reported making $6,000 annually in England. So were things really any better over there? The *Sedalia Weekly Conservator* printed this:

> It has been the boast of England in the past that it never drew the color line, Whites and Blacks being treated alike in hotels, theaters, restaurants, saloons and other public places. Nevertheless, the color line is being drawn, and Negroes are beginning to be discriminated against in public places, as in the United States. The courts have just upheld such discrimination as legal. A saloonkeeper in the West End refused to serve two Negroes drinks at the bar. Negroes brought suit (they lost).[31]

Seven

Galveston Giant

It was likely true that he played into the White man's hands and was his own worst enemy, though his behavior, so much criticized then, seems by the modern Richter scale of athletic behavior mild enough.[1] But there comes a time when a man's conscience tells him what is right. That man, who happened to be Black, was Jack Johnson.

He never dreamed that he would become one of the most important figures of the 20th century, yet Arthur John Johnson, born on March 31, 1878, in Galveston, Texas, became precisely that. His parents, Henry and Tina (Tiny), were ex-slaves and understood the value of freedom. They were hardworking—Henry was employed by the school district, and Tina took in domestic work when time permitted. Keeping a home for a large family was no simple task. Young Jack, the third child and first son, was blessed with superb genetics; as a result, he grew to a height of just over six feet and maintained about 200 pounds. Handsome, muscular and athletic, he commanded attention just by being there.

Raised in the racially mixed Twelfth Ward in Galveston, Johnson had a more relaxed view on racial separation—it was a far cry from those he met from the polarized Deep South—and it would work to his benefit.[2] Like most youngsters, he found employment when and where he could. Johnson worked in the livery stable, where he emulated the star Black jockeys of the day and became mesmerized by speed. Watching the horses sprint majestically over a race course, Johnson marveled at both their acceleration and tempo. Oh, if I could only harness that type of power, he thought.

Later, a gymnasium would become his racetrack as he honed his boxing ability while working inside its walls. He learned how to use his muscular arms to confuse or tie up an opponent, and how to exploit his power. It was in this environment that he found a passion for prediction—he became so skilled that he could tell an opponent where and when he would hit them, and do just that.

Unlike the past, when Black pugilists had few to emulate, Johnson had names like George Dixon, Joe Gans, and Joe Walcott—talented and formidable athletes who commanded respect. The footsteps were there to follow, if he had the aspiration. He did. To his credit, Jack Johnson, with his unmitigated desire, never felt the mountain was too far away or too high to climb.

The Road to Respect

Johnson fought primarily out of his hometown until the fall of 1900. His most talented opponent to this point appeared to be "Klondike." The competitive pugilists met in three different cities, each fight ending in a different outcome. Johnson, like Haines (Haynes), was trying to establish himself in the fight game. So he took advantage of every opportunity—if that meant battling each other, that was fine.[3] Conquest, either in or out of a boxing ring, was a trait Jack Johnson found hard to ignore. His love of the ring was matched only by his passion for women, speed, power, and the spotlight.[4] Johnson's first big break, not to mention major press coverage, came on February 25, 1901, when he entered a local ring against White pugilist Joe Choynski.

The *Daily Morning Journal and Courier* was one of the newspapers that carried the three-line synopsis: "Before the Galveston Athletic Club Joe Choynski put Jack Johnson out in the first few seconds of the third round tonight. Both men were arrested by state officers at the close of the contest. The event was entirely bloodless and was a splendid exhibition up to the time Choynski made a feint with his left and put a right-hander to the pit of Johnson's stomach."[5]

More than 800 spectators watched the event that ended with both fighters traveling to police headquarters. Prizefighting, as everyone understood (wink, wink), was contrary to the laws of the state.[6] Seldom mentioned, the penalty for engaging in a prizefight was from two to five years imprisonment in the penitentiary at hard labor. Bond for both pugilists was finally fixed at $500. Since neither fighter could furnish that amount, both were placed in jail. (The photograph of both fighters staring out from behind bars and fronted by armed guards became a classic image.) When the grand jury failed to return an indictment, Choynski and Johnson were released on $1,000 bond each on March 22, 1901.[7]

Johnson left Galveston and headed northwest to the popular fight market of Denver. There he met White fighter Billy Stift at the Colorado Athletic Club on April 26. More of a middleweight than a heavy, Stift managed to battle his adversary to a lackluster, 10-round draw.[8] A pair of California battles against the large and skillful Black boxer Hank Griffin would close out the memorable year for Johnson. Losing the first battle over 20 rounds in Bakersfield on November 4, Johnson next drew Griffin over 15 sessions in Oakland on December 27.[9] Johnson, who would fight out of California in 1903, would not lose another boxing contest until March 28, 1905 (to Marvin Hart).

Outside of Galveston, Johnson was just another Black fighter. Granted the Choynski fiasco brought him some press, but it wasn't the kind he needed. Not right now, not at this stage of his career. He needed a boost, something to push him to the forefront. Johnson's brief-tenured manager, Frank Carillo, agreed. So in 1902, following a few knockouts, Carillo penned a note to Tom McCarey; consequently, it came at the right time, as the fight promoter had the perfect opponent.[10]

Jack Jeffries, brother of the heavyweight champion and his foremost sparring partner, accepted a challenge from Jack Johnson. The Jeffrieses' reasoning was as clear as their complexion: If Johnson won, it was against Jack, not Jim. If the "Galveston Giant" lost, something many believed could—and there's always a "could" in boxing, isn't there—happen, it would push any thought of his brother ever meeting Johnson off the sports pages. However, Johnson, who fully realized the opportunity and its consequence, had no intention of losing.

Showing up in a pair of pink trunks, Jack Johnson premiered his trademark defiance. The fight, held on May 16, 1902, at Hazard's Pavilion, was under the auspices of the Century Club and drew an enthusiastic crowd of 4,000 spectators. Salivating at just the thought of Johnson being dismembered by their White hometown fighter had many Southern California fans at the edge of their seats.

The champion, who accompanied his brother, announced before the fight that he and Bob Fitzsimmons would do battle for the crown. It was an intimidating reminder—don't you think for one second that Jeff didn't fully understand the psychological benefit of the display—of just what the Jeffries family legacy was all about. The cheers were deafening.

Four rounds of unimaginative boxing commenced with the opening gong. Exhibiting his defensive skill but little else, Jeffries, nothing more than a novice boxer, mimicked a sparring partner, his power clearly ineffective against his antagonist. Patient, yet calculated, Johnson worked his combinations with precision. He was as calm as a plumber who says he thinks he can fix a leak.

The *San Francisco Call* reported the final round as follows: "In the fifth round, while the men were sparring cautiously, Johnson forced Jeffries into a corner, and, feinting with his left, sent in a hard right to the neck below the ear. Jeffries fell like a log. After he had been counted out the champion carried his helpless brother from the ring. It was thought for a time Jeffries had sustained severe injuries, but he soon came around."[11]

The image—as discreetly symbolic as it would become—of the champion assisting his helpless brother was profound. With the victory, McCarey had found a new star. On May 24, it was reported that Bob Fitzsimmons selected Jack Johnson as his sparring partner—Fitz was training for his championship battle on July 25. Johnson couldn't have been happier and closed out the year strong against both White and Black boxers. He was becoming his own man, exhibiting courage and solid ring skills. Although there were times, especially in fights against White opponents, when the crowd was more hostile than his antagonist, Johnson never let the threats—and there were many—overtake his comportment.

Jack Johnson v. "Denver" Ed Martin—World Colored Heavyweight Championship

On February 5, 1903, Jack Johnson, now under the management of Zeke Abrams, was matched against "Denver" Ed Martin for the World Colored Heavyweight Championship.[12] The battle would take place at Hazard's Pavilion in Los Angeles. The referee was Harry Stuart. Martin was the favorite and looked the part at 20 pounds heavier (203 pounds) and four inches taller. At the end of 20 rounds, the decision and championship belonged to Jack Johnson. A highlight was the 11th round. According to the *San Francisco Call*:

> Early in the 11th round Johnson sent in a terrific right to the jaw. Martin fell forward and clasped Johnson around the neck. He hung on for dear life and when finally shaken fell to the floor. At the count of six he got up upon his knees, but fell to the floor again. Seven was counted before he stood upon his feet. He kept his head and clinched, but went again from a shower of blows, none of which landed squarely. Four times he got up, only to go to the floor, partly from weakness and partly from a rain of blows. At the call of time Martin was hanging to Johnson, trying to save himself.[13]

The record-breaking crowd was a feather in the cap of the Century Club who handled the championship. McCarey would next match Johnson against the formidable figure of Sam McVey, (also spelled McVea). The two Black pugilists, matched for the first time, would meet at Hazard's Pavilion on February 26—it would be Johnson's first Colored title defense.

Jack Johnson v. Sam McVey—World Colored Heavyweight Championship Trilogy

Without parameters—although some benchmarks were set by White designations—World Colored Heavyweight Championship defenses were subjective. Naturally, a fight promoter wanted to sell tickets, and saying a battle was for a title could accomplish the task, but the public wasn't going to buy a setup. Matches had to make sense; therefore, Jack Johnson versus Sam McVey was a sound choice.

McVey stood 5 feet, 10½ inches and tipped over 200 pounds. With fewer than a dozen professional fights to his name, it was difficult at first for some to believe he was in the ring against a fighter as imposing as Johnson. That was until you saw him. Muscular, compact, strong, and agile, McVey was a daunting figure. With punches that could split rocks, not to mention a glance that could melt steel, none of McVey's opponents had lasted longer than six rounds.

Johnson took command early and found considerable success in landing his arsenal. While McVey could take a punch, his lack of experience made him appear a bit awkward. At the end of 20 rounds, it was a decision for Johnson. He would rematch with McVey again on October 27, with an identical conclusion. The trilogy would conclude the following year with little fanfare but considerable skepticism.[14]

Jack Johnson fought seven times, or 99 rounds, in 1903, against four different opponents, and did not lose. Three of his opponents were Black, and only John "Sandy" Ferguson was White. As the World Colored Heavyweight Champion, his fights received some press coverage but it was often limited to a few lines. There were exceptions, like those surrounding the major boxing markets that ran more print, like the *San Francisco Call*. Clear, at least to most who followed boxing, was that Johnson was the top contender for Jeffries' crown. It was during this time that Johnson met two Colored girls who caught his fancy, Etta Reynolds and Clara Kerr—the former would slip away, while the latter would occupy a considerable amount of the fighter's time by living in his home at Bakersfield, California.

The following year (1904), Johnson participated in five recorded battles and posted a record of 3–0–0, with two no-decisions and two successful title defenses. His only White opponent was John "Sandy" Ferguson (ND6), and all the rest were Colored—"Black Bill" (February 16, ND6), Sam McVey (April 22, KO20, title defense), Frank Childs (June 2, W6) and "Denver" Ed Martin (October 18, KO2, title defense).[15]

With his victories, Jack Johnson had made a position statement. Champion James J. Jeffries, not to mention other White pugilists, found it hard to overlook. It became harder and harder to match Johnson with solid competition unless, of course, they were fellow Black participants, or what would become to be known as pool fighters. As history would prove, this group played an essential role in the World Colored Heavyweight Championship.

Jack Johnson v. "Denver" Ed Martin—World Colored Heavyweight Championship

Johnson's final fight of the year came on October 18, 1904. With a second-round knockout victory over "Denver" Ed Martin, Johnson confirmed his position as a perpetual threat to natural order. It was as clear as the White skin on Jeffries' cheeks. The *San Francisco Call* reported: "It was stated after the fight that Johnson fought as he did tonight in order to demonstrate that he was entitled to consideration by Jeffries. Johnson's manager stated he would issue a formal challenge on behalf of Johnson at once to fight the champion of the world. Manager McCarey of the Century Club announced that he would offer $15,000 guarantee for a match between Jeffries and Johnson, the battle to come off here some time this winter."[16]

Earlier in the year Johnson had stated, according to the *Los Angeles Herald*: "Unless Jeffries consents to withdraw his color line declaration and fight me, I shall claim the world's championship. It was not my fault that I was born Black, and Jeffries will have to meet me in three months or drop the championship title."[17]

Despite all the newspaper articles and offers, Jeffries held solid to his convictions. He routinely dismissed claims that he had agreed to fight Johnson. He reiterated his statement often, as was printed in the *Los Angeles Herald*: "I never will fight a Negro—back to the boiler works first. I am entirely in the hands of the press and the people. Any White man they choose I will fight on six weeks' notice. Unless this is done before a great while I will retire from the ring and be the only retired champion."[18]

In 1905, Marvin Hart, aka the "Fightin' Kentuckian," was the premier White contender for Jeffries' crown. A bit awkward at times, he nevertheless packed a powerful punch. At 5 feet, 11 inches, Hart was a stocky scrapper with tremendous endurance—when he took command of a fight, he never relented.

Hart had no intention of fighting a Black man and made that clear when Joe Walcott challenged him. But Johnson thought he could persuade the Southerner to change his mind; he showed up at his training facility one day and called him a coward to his face. It was an incredibly bold move, but it worked. His masculinity challenged, Hart capitulated. In summing up the March 28, 1905, contest held in San Francisco, the *Los Angeles Herald* reported:

> Marvin Hart was awarded the decision over Jack Johnson in a 20-round contest tonight that went the limit, but he was far from demonstrating that he is qualified to meet Jim Jeffries. Hart was as badly punished a man as has been seen in the ring for a long time, but he was game to the core and kept boring into the big colored man all through the fight. Johnson's much vaunted cleverness did not manifest itself. Hart's face was battered to a pulp, but Johnson's blows did not seem to have much sting to them. Johnson did a great deal of upper cutting, but Hart covered up and the blows did not seem to hurt him.[19]
>
> Referee and promoter Alex "Alec" Greggains, viewing Hart, bloodied face and all, as the aggressor throughout, declared Hart the winner. Johnson was simply crushed by the verdict, and to little surprise some disagreed with Greggains' appraisal. But Greggains was a noted figure in San Francisco boxing and his opinion, as swayed as it might be, was valued. Champion James J. Jeffries was quick to state for the *San Francisco Call*: "I am glad Hart won, not that it necessarily means we will get into the ring in a fight for the championship, but because it puts the Negro out of the running. If Johnson had won he would never have fought me, as my decision never to fight a Negro would have been faithfully kept. If Hart is considered out of my class I will retire from the ring this year forever."[20]

On May 2, 1905, James J. Jeffries announced his retirement and relinquished the Heavyweight Championship—he had run out of White contenders. The door to the Heavyweight Championship of the World appeared to be open a crack, or so Johnson believed. From the time of Jeffries' retirement until his re-emergence in 1910, four great Black fighters would surface: Jack Johnson, Sam Langford, Sam McVey, and Joe Jeannette. Convinced he was not being treated fairly on the West Coast, Johnson moved to his third major fight market, Philadelphia. In his remaining 1905 fights, only two of which were outside the solace of the patriotic city, Johnson would lose only one contest—to Joe Jeannette on a second-round, controversial foul.[21] His only focus was on *the* prize, the Heavyweight Championship of the World. However, Jack Johnson was growing concerned: The big-money fights were fading, as was his relationship with Miss Clara Kerr. Under an umbrella of self-pity, Johnson's behavior became erratic, and he began to drink heavily.[22]

On February 23, 1906, Marvin Hart, having knocked out Jack Root and claimed the Heavyweight Championship, lost a 20-round fight and the title to Canadian Noah Brusso, aka Tommy Burns. At five feet, seven inches, Burns became the shortest heavyweight champion ever. With the transition—Burns initially claimed he would defend against all comers—Johnson's attitude improved. Nevertheless, the Galveston contender had to remain patient, as Burns inked a 25-week vaudeville contract as a result of his victory.

In 1906, Johnson took at least a dozen fights—four against Joe Jeannette—and did not lose a single contest.[23] He did not defend, nor press, the World Colored Heavyweight Championship; the goal was to sustain the media pressure that had been placed on Burns to accept his challenge.[24] Of the fighters he faced, one stuck out, Sam Langford. On April 26, at the Pythian Skating Rink in Chelsea, Massachusetts, Langford, outweighed by nearly 40 pounds, got off the canvas twice in the sixth round to administer quite a beating to Johnson.[25] While the "Galveston Giant" pulled away with the win, he would wisely never again fight the "Boston Tar Baby."[26]

Feeling his career had stalled, Johnson looked overseas.[27] He was getting tired of the same old faces, stories, venues, and small purses. Australia, officially the Commonwealth of Australia, was the world's sixth-largest country by area and, to many, worlds away. Dominion of the British Empire and under the reign of Queen Victoria, the city of Sydney was its epicenter. Johnson, under the eye of manager Sam Fitzpatrick (Alec McLean also claimed management of Johnson), targeted this destination first. Black fighters, especially good ones, were still a novelty overseas, so perhaps the slow journey to Australia's east coast would pay dividends. Also, if he could grab an arbitrary title or two, he could use it as leverage—or so Johnson hoped—to match against Tommy Burns.

Jack Johnson v. Peter Felix—World Colored Heavyweight Championship

Australians loved boxing, so an entertainment program that consisted of fight films mixed with exhibitions was arranged for Johnson. This, along with the fighter's public training sessions, stirred the pot of enthusiasm. (As the Immigration Act of 1901 had effectively barred Nonwhites, Johnson's magnificent Black physique may have added a touch of intrigue as well.)

On February 19, 1907, Jack Johnson met "Australia's Coloured Champion" Peter Felix (a first cousin of Peter Jackson), in Sydney. In defense of his title, Johnson was magnificent. However, the fight coverage, at least in America, was not. The *San Francisco Call* noted, "Jack Johnson, the American pugilist, today [February 19] defeated Peter Felix, the Colored Heavyweight Champion of Australia, in two minutes of fighting."[28] That was it. Just a single line—note the word knockout was omitted—ran in a majority of newspapers across the United States. Following their visit in Sydney, the team headed to Melbourne. After a short stay there, which included a ninth-round knockout of Bill Lang, a popular footballer, Team Johnson headed back to America.

Upon his return, Johnson met Bob Fitzsimmons, the ex-champion who was now 45 years old, in a bout before the Washington Sporting Club in Philadelphia on July 17. According to the *Nashville Globe*: "Fitzsimmons did not show the trace of his former prowess, and it is probable that Johnson could have stopped him in the opening round if he had cared to do so. The blow that put Fitzsimmons out was a right to the jaw. The old man fell to the floor, and as he made no attempt to rise the referee stopped the bout."[29]

Fitzsimmons suffered from a badly sprained arm and was essentially defenseless. Yet, for Johnson to add the name of Fitzsimmons to his list of victims wasn't such a bad thing.

Taking a first-round knockout over tomato can Charlie "Kid Cutler" and a no-decision against Frank Loughnane, aka "Sailor Burke," Johnson headed west to meet Andrew Chiariglione, aka "Fireman" Jim Flynn, at Coffroth's Arena at Colma, California, on November 2. The *Salt Lake Herald* reported the result:

A ringside ticket to the World's Championship fight, Jim Flynn versus Jack Johnson, in Las Vegas, New Mexico Territory, on July 4, 1912 (author's collection).

On July 4, 1912, in Las Vegas, Jack Johnson defeated "Fireman" Jim Flynn by way of a ninth-round disqualification. The bout was scheduled for 45 rounds (Library of Congress, LC-USZ6—8931).

"You're a clever nigger," were the last words uttered by Jim Flynn, the Colorado fireman, in his scheduled 45 round contest with Jack Johnson, the Colored heavyweight at Colma this afternoon. A straight right flush to the jaw cut off further speech, and Flynn toppled to the floor completely knocked out. The finishing blow was delivered in the 11th round, and it took four minutes to resuscitate the defeated pugilist.

Throughout the contest Johnson toyed with his antagonist as a terrier would with a rat. In the initial round, he practically closed the Colorado man's left eye, and thereafter made it a target for his unerring left jabs. Johnson landed at will on his man, and seemed to have the contest well in hand at all stages. He left the ring without a mark, and only once did he receive a telling blow from his opponent.[30]

Afterwards, Johnson's attention returned to Noah Brusso, aka Tommy Burns. While Johnson kept one eye on the champion, he kept another fixed on Anna Peterson, aka Hattie McClay, a White love interest and prostitute working in Manhattan. To little surprise, the new distraction didn't bode well for Lola Toy, Johnson's current companion.[31]

Heavyweight Championship of the World

In 1908, the Heavyweight Championship of the World took center stage. Following a three-round draw with Joe Jeannette on January 3, Johnson packed his bags for Europe. The goal was to keep the pressure on Burns, while attempting to maintain the same time zone—the champion split his time between Europe and Australia.[32] Johnson went first to England, then to France, then back to England until the end of July. The newspapers hounded the champion, as article after article questioned his courage and honor. It was precisely what Jack Johnson had hoped for: Without the relentless social pressure, although there was some, to maintain the White supremacy of the title—Burns was not an American—challenging the champion's manhood was destined to yield opportunity.

Finally, at the end of September, Burns confirmed that only a figure of $30,000—a ridiculous sum that no fighter had ever received for a single contest—might alter his mindset. The champion was absolutely certain that level of backing could not be obtained. He was wrong. Funding, thanks to Hugh D. McIntosh, was found and a deal—it was $30,000 (win, lose or draw) for Burns, and $5,000 to Johnson—was struck.[33] Thus, Tommy Burns became the first gloved era heavyweight champion of the world to allow a Colored man to fight for the title.[34]

All of Burns' predecessors drew the color line as champions and were confounded by his behavior. The Canadian-born pugilist, who wasn't hesitant about defending his title across the globe, had overstepped a sacred boundary. The championship, at least in their minds, wasn't about income or inclusion. It was about power. The title was a reflection of racial superiority and needed to stay in the mitts of those who could control it. And those hands were White.

Retired champion James J. Jeffries wasn't bashful about Burns' violation of the color line protocol. The *Detroit Times* documented his remarks: "All fighters are the same color after they have climbed through the ropes at the ringside. The time to draw the color line is when the Black man first asks for a match. Burns, in his wild greed for gold, has trampled upon all traditions of the ring. He must expect no favors after the gong rings. He has his man in front of him, he is facing a match that he himself has made possible, and Burns must fight the giant Negro without expecting any sympathy from the public in case of a defeat."[35]

While opinions differed around the world, Americans had a hard time believing the scrap was on the level. The skepticism centered, as one might anticipate, on the economics of the event. The *Waterbury Evening Democrat* examined the issue: "Burns could easily hand over his share of the money to Johnson to induce the Negro to quit and afterward Burns could refuse to fight Johnson again and could tour the world picking up a fortune in gold. Burns is worth probably $200,000 today, while Johnson hasn't got a nickel."[36]

This cablegram was received by Robert Edgren, and printed in the *Evening World*: "Am feeling great. Johnson insisted on McIntosh as referee. Advance sale is over ten thousand pounds. Tell the American public I will uphold the White supremacy. Am 2 to 1 favorite. TOMMY BURNS."[37]

Up to the very moment of the fight, many believed Tommy Burns would win. He was, above all, a favorite with the Australian public. But opinions differed, especially the American newspapers where a sense of nationalism surfaced. The *Salt Lake Herald* noted: "It is the first time in the history of the fighting game where a great part of the sporting public is plugging for a Negro to whip a White man. Usually the Black man has to fight with the handicap of public opinion against him, but men who ordinarily are against a Negro first, last and all times are pulling for Jack Johnson to beat Burns tomorrow."[38]

Crossing Over

It was 20 rounds, under the Marquis of Queensberry rules, on Saturday, December 26, 1908, at 11 a.m., at an arena built at Rushcutters Bay in Sydney, Australia. Both participants wore four-ounce gloves and fought inside a 24-foot ring. Johnson, at age 30, was three years older than Burns. The estimated attendance was between 18,000 and 20,000 persons.

In the "Tale of the Tape," or analysis of key physical measurements, Johnson equaled or exceeded Burns in every category except hips, thighs, and calves. Simply put: Burns drew his power from below the waist. He also had a slight reach advantage.

The champion held victories over Jim Flynn, Jack O'Brien, Gunner Moir, and Marvin Hart, while Johnson held victories over Sam McVey, Denver Ed Martin, Bob Fitzsimmons, and Jim Flynn.

The *Salt Lake Herald* proclaimed the result with this headline: JACK JOHNSON DEFEATS BURNS, World Has a Colored Heavyweight Champion—Wins Decision in Fourteenth.[39]

From the outset, it was made clear that if during the contest the police should interfere and stop it, Referee McIntosh would give a decision based on points.

Burns was floored during the first moments of the first round by a sharp uppercut; nearly dropped by a right to the chin in the second; struck by powerful kidney punches in the third; hammered by a heavy right to the ribs in the fourth; floored briefly in the seventh; bleeding in the eighth; limping to his corner in the 11th; and groggy in the 13th.

In the 14th round, Burns was dropped with a right to the head. He arose groggy after a count of eight. Johnson then attacked his prey unmercifully until the police had little choice but to stop the fight.

Following the contest, Johnson's accomplishment took a backseat to his race. Former champion James J. Jeffries spoke to the *Seattle Star*:

> The Canadian never will be forgiven by the public for allowing the title of the best physical man in the world to be wrested from his keeping by a member of the African race. The same people who have been condemning Burns for heretofore refusing to meet Johnson will be the first to condemn him for having allowed an Ethiopian champion to wrest the ring supremacy from the Caucasian race.

Tommy Burns [sic] mistake—the one great mistake of his career—was in allowing Johnson the opportunity to fight for the title. I refused time and time again to meet Johnson while I was holding the title, even though I knew I could beat him. I would never allow a Negro a chance, even it be a desperate one, to fight for a world's championship, and I advise all other champions to follow the same course.[40]

While these statements were disturbing, he crossed the line with this befuddling comment: "The fact that Johnson is a Negro cannot be held against him by the followers of the fight game."[41] It was one of the most hypocritical and ignorant quotes from the world of 20th century boxing.

Even the great John L. Sullivan was quick to drop a disclaimer to the *Seattle Star*: "Even with the victory over the so-called champion of the world, though in my opinion Burns never was champion of the world, the Negro can't assume that title."[42]

As for the new Heavyweight Champion of the World, he would take a five-week engagement at the Sydney Music Hall. At $1,750 per week ($48,406 in 2019 dollars), Jack Johnson wasn't going to turn down such an offer.[43] He would then travel to various parts of Europe and on to Vancouver, British Columbia, Canada before heading back to Galveston. His arrival in Vancouver was notable for the absence of Sam Fitzpatrick, his now ex-manager, and the company of a White woman whom Johnson identified as his wife, or the former Nellie O'Brien. As interracial marriage was officially outlawed in 30 of the 46 states and frowned upon by society, the association was instant news.

On April 19, 1909, in New York City, James J. Jeffries announced that he might be in a position to tackle Johnson for the title in about eight to 10 months. But, would he? Johnson saw it as nothing more than a publicity stunt for the retired champion's vaudeville tour. With the fine line between exhibitions, no-decisions and actual battles difficult to identify, the Champion met "Philadelphia" Jack O' Brien (ND6), Tony Ross (ND6), Al Kaufman (ND10), and a few others before facing Stanley Ketchel in Colma, California, on October 16, 1909.

There was also the issue of film revenue, which was huge at the time.[44] Legend has it, and from some good sources, that the two fighters agreed to extend the fight for the full 20 rounds for the sake of the motion picture exhibitors. However, Willus Britt, Ketchel's shrewd manager and no stranger to the California boxing scene, had other ideas. Even if the film revenue was enormous, the value of the heavyweight title was worth even more. Britt counseled Ketchel, one of the best ever, that if he saw an opening to take it, but make it count. Fully realizing that the situation mandated a knockout, Ketchel waited until the 12th round. Seeing an opportunity, he took it. Unfortunately, his imperfect right hand was good enough to floor his target but not powerful enough to keep him there.[45]

Floored, or you might also say double-crossed, by middleweight champion Stanley Ketchel early in the 12th round of their scheduled 20-round bout, Jack Johnson was confounded. Arising in a fit of anger from the Mission Street Arena ring, Johnson felt betrayed. So he sent a lethal right uppercut into Ketchel's face that dropped the "Michigan Assassin" like an anvil from a rooftop. As Ketchel was counted out, Johnson brushed off a pair of Ketchel's teeth that had embedded in his glove.[46]

As the year drew to a close, Johnson's first as champion, he had a new manager in George Little, a new main squeeze in Belle Schreiber (Becker), and a few new wheels in his garage. (One might also add White Brooklyn socialite Etta Duryea into the equation.) Overindulgence in the fruit of life, Johnson believed, was simply part of being a champion. The sporting lifestyle, from his perspective, suited him just fine.[47]

The Battle of the Century

Johnson had a theatrical contract to fulfill early in 1910, but once he completed it in March, he planned to begin training for his battle with Jeffries. That duel was scheduled for July 4. As boxing was legal only in Nevada, the fight had difficulty finding a home. Eventually Reno was selected, but only weeks before the contest. From January until the day of the fight, newspaper articles dissected every aspect of the event.

As the engagement approached, some of the anxiety Johnson faced came to light. The *Seattle Star* noted: "Much of the mail that reached the Seal Rock house for Johnson contains threats. Some letters advise the champion that daylight will sift through his carcass, pulverized via .45-caliber bullet hole routes, should he knock out Jeffries. Others threaten his annihilation for other offenses."[48]

The champion hired people to guard him and even test his food—additives that concerned the fighter included rat poison, carbolic acid, pulverized glass, cyanide of potassium, mercury bichloride, and a few others. The *Star* even noted: "That there may be no chance for sleight of hand his manager installed a 'taster-in-chief' of Johnson's food. Every bit of chuck that reaches Johnson is tried 'on the dog,' and if he lives long enough for the medical expert to decide he isn't going to kick off, the food wends its way to the Johnson table."[49]

Also for safety's sake, Johnson packed a very large Colt equalizer.

Reno was selected as the host city despite the fact it was inclined to draw the color line. Johnson learned of this rather quickly when he was declined accommodation at Lawton Hot Springs. Livid, the fighter just bit his tongue. As the *Tacoma Times* noted, "The color line always has been drawn tight in Reno. Old-Timers relate that a Black face was never seen here in the early days, and up to four years ago a Colored hotel porter was the only Negro in the city."[50]

The June 19, 1910, the headline of the *Salt Lake Tribune's* sports section said it all:

ENTIRE NATION APPEARS TO BE FIGHT MAD

The Battle of the Century was on the tip of the tongue of everyone across the country. Everyone had an opinion, including experts like James J. Corbett. In an article reprinted in the *Evening Star,* the former champion stated: "Now, I certainly must know something about Jeffries, and I assure you all who read my weekly letter to this paper that, although I do want Jeffries to win badly, and I dislike Johnson not so much because he is a Negro, but simply because I think he is one of those fresh Negroes that not alone thinks he is as good as a White man, but is better; that, admitting all of these things, I am not letting my prejudice interfere with my judgment."[51]

Other popular pugilists chimed in as well. Bob Fitzsimmons stated, "Jeffries will tear a hole in Johnson—why, the nigger will turn white in the ring when he goes up against Jeff."[52] Joe Gans, suffering from tuberculosis, stated, "If Jeffries were in his prime he would be a 10 to 1 favorite over Johnson. But six or seven years without a battle makes more difference than the average man can conceive."[53]

Joe Jeannette noted, "Jeffries has the head and the heart to whip Johnson. I think Jack is a wonderful boxer and that he will make Jeffries look awkward for a couple of rounds. Then Jeffries will sail in and beat him to a frazzle. Johnson can't stand the gaff. Give him a couple blows in the stomach and he will wilt."[54]

Reno, as a final destination, wasn't particularly hard to get to; however, transportation wasn't economical for every fight enthusiast. There were plenty of Black fight fans interested in the journey.

On June 24, a rail alternative became available, according to the *Spokane Press*: "Every Colored man in Los Angeles, who can scrape together the coin necessary to pay his passage to Reno and buy a ticket for the big fight, will travel in state to the capital of the fight world in a special car. The 'Jim Crow' special will leave the Arcade station on the evening of July 1, and will begin the return trip the day following the fight."[55]

While Johnson faced more than his fair share of racism in the newspapers, opinions such as this, printed in the *Morning Examiner*, were certainly food for thought:

> The big affair is a contest between men, not races of men. Those fighters who have drawn the color line in the past have, almost without exception, done so because there happened to be a Negro of their weight whom they feared. Take Billy Papke tabooing the Colored fighters, for instance. Without closing your eyes in thought for an instant you can conjure a picture of Sam Langford. Sam is Papke's color line reason. It is not any little nicety of sentiment. Jimmy Britt advertised his mother's aversion to the Negro widely as the real cause of his dodging Joe Gans. Yet, when he was able to "frame" his fight with the Baltimorean, so that his record might be untarnished, he took the bait with one gulp.[56]

A Chicago writer, H.E. Keough, assessed the situation this way in the *Evening Times*, while visiting the area: "On the surface, it is all Jeffries out this way. To give voice to a contrary opinion is to be accused of personal animosity to the hope of the White race, but a lot of them who will cheer as loudly for Jeffries if he wins as those who are cheering for him now are stringing along quietly for the black fellow and waiting for the price to go up to unbelt on him. They, too, have seen Jeffries in training and will grant you he is 'back,' but they also will have seen Johnson and believe that there is more to him to lick than ever was pitted against Jeffries before his retirement."[57]

The Fight

James J. Jeffries, past his prime and lured out of retirement for all the wrong reasons, found Jack Johnson's defense too powerful to overcome. Try as he may, and indeed his courage was clearly on display, he was ineffective. Johnson countered magnificently and tied Jeffries up like a runner tying a shoe lace—tight, snug and secure. Taunted relentlessly from Jeff's corner, Johnson, unfazed, fired back at will. One-sided from the start, a beaten and bloodied Jeffries was mercilessly butchered during the final five rounds. Floored for the third time in the 15th round, Jeffries hung on the ropes in desperation as his corner threw the towel into the ring. His seconds then rushed the ring to prevent the former champion from taking a full count.

The Repercussions

Almost immediately, the authorities scrambled to stop the exhibition of the Reno prizefight pictures. Anti-black and anti-boxing crusaders also did what they could to block local screenings of the film. Later (1912), citing the same motion picture, Congress passed the Sims Act, which banned the transport of fight films over state lines. The last thing, some believed, the country needed was for everyone to have a chance to witness the Colored man's victory over the so-called "Great White Hope"—the event was far more, as everyone understood, than just a successful title defense for Jack Johnson. The *Salt Lake Tribune* reported: "As word spread, celebrations turned into demonstrations, as Blacks and Whites fiercely engaged in bloody contests across the land. The struggles even gave rise to fatal injuries. Across the country, people were seriously injured: Fierce fighting in Bessemer, Colorado, saw two White men stabbed; Savage rioting, in seven separate places in New York City, saw one Negro badly beaten and a Negro tenement burned by Whites; One man was killed, another mortally wounded in Mounds, Illinois, as four Negroes shot up the town and much, much more."[58]

Ironically, the first prominent mention of potential fallout from the battle came from a fictional and racist story printed by the *Los Angeles Herald* on June 27, 1910:

> When the bulletins of the eastern papers pictured the weakening of the White champion during the latter rounds of the battle the Negroes that peppered those seas of humanity [a riot was predicted and took place] gave vent to their feelings in the ultra emotional so characteristic of that race—with resounding slaps on the back and embraces where space permitted they triumphantly shouted:
> "One mo' of dem uppe' cuts and de po'k chops and bacon do come home to de colo'd man."[59]

The newspapers, having continually placed the White challenger in the winner's circle, never dealt with the possibility of a loss. Consequently, there was no contingency plan. From the press to the police, everyone appeared stunned. New York boxing fans had their reaction recorded by the *Ogden Standard*: "For the first time in the prize ring a Negro is the undisputed heavyweight champion of the world. [So much for Johnson's victory over Tommy Burns.] And what White man is there in sight today who can wrest that title from John Arthur Johnson? That is the question the fight followers of New York, as well as of the whole country, are asking today. The only answer is an echo—'Who?' The only hope any of the fans can see today lies in Al Kaufman, but it is admitted generally that his hope has not a valid foundation."[60]

The *Spokane Press* ran the subheadline, "24 Deaths Because of Jack's Victory," on the front page of their home edition on July 5. Society had been shaken to its roots, stirred, and brought to a boiling point. Credibility for the Black man brought anxiety for the White man—the shoe was on the other foot.

If you don't know where you are going, any road will take you there. Everyone seemed to be traveling down a road, with Johnson, as usual, traveling faster than anyone else. All Caucasian challenges to the heavyweight championship, including Al Kaufman's, were accepted by Johnson but ignored by fight promoters—nobody wanted to take the risk of feeding the champion an endless stream of "White Hopes."

Following his victory, Johnson continued his life of excess. He raced automobiles at Coney Island with pioneer auto racer Barney Oldfield, the first man to drive a car at 60 miles per hour. Oldfield, a white hope of a different sort, won his race against Johnson. As always, Johnson fed off the adrenaline rush.[61]

Meanwhile, beautiful and charming Etta Duryea, who was always elegantly dressed, did her best to remain in Johnson's life—an existence that still included Belle Schreiber, Hattie McClay, and a plethora of female distractions. Following a near-tragic confrontation on Christmas Day 1910 in which Johnson beat Etta so badly that she was hospitalized, the couple somehow managed to reconcile.

Johnson did not log an official fight, nor defend his title in 1911. In January, he married Etta Duryea in Pittsburgh. While the nuptials may have brought a level of stability to their relationship, the mixed marriage was subjected to enormous criticism from both races. While the champion enjoyed the grandeur brought by the crown, the public hostility and Johnson's abuse and infidelity took a toll on his wife.

In stark contrast to the previous year, the next 12 months proved far more eventful for Johnson. The *Tacoma Times* noted the champion's status on January 1, 1912: "With theatrical contracts for 90 weeks at $2,000 a week in sight, Jack Johnson, pugilist [his status as champion not acknowledged], today turned up his nose at an offer by Jack Curley of a paltry $20,000 for a 20-round bout with Jim Flynn. Following the turndown by the big smoke [Johnson], Flynn wired his Salt Lake backers that Johnson positively would not accept less than $30,000 for his end of a fight."[62]

Sam Langford, the last man the champion wanted to crawl between the ropes with, remained the premier challenger to Johnson's prized possession. But the Heavyweight Champion of the World drew the color line. Ironically, Jack Johnson refused to do battle with a fellow Black gladiator. "No, siree. I'm going to be the only Black heavyweight champion in history. Langford or Jeannette couldn't beat me, but they jest ain't a-goin' to have a chance," Johnson told the *Evening World*.[63]

Flynn's manager, Jack Curley, continued to dangle offers in front of Johnson until he eventually took the bait. His battle with "Fireman" Jim Flynn, and his only ring battle of the year, took place on July 4, 1912, in Las Vegas, New Mexico Territory.

On June 21, the *Evening Standard* reported news out of Chicago: "Jack Johnson, champion heavyweight pugilist, and his wife, Etta Johnson, were indicted by the federal grand jury today for alleged smuggling. Johnson while abroad bought a diamond necklace for his wife and brought it home without paying duty…. The authorities said the indictment would not interfere with the Johnson-Flynn fight July 4."[64]

It was a distraction, but not a showstopper. The *Topeka State Journal* summed up the Flynn battle in two sentences: "Jim Flynn's whole hope expired today in the ninth round of his scheduled 45 round bout with champion Jack Johnson. Flynn's face was chopped and cut frightfully by the champion's deliberate blows and in the ninth round Captain Cowles of the New Mexican State police pushed his way to the ring and declared the contest ended as a brutal exhibition."[65]

Flynn's new approach to fighting Johnson was leaping off the ground in hopes of having his head meet Johnson's chin. When warned of his latest butting technique, Flynn claimed he was being fouled. The fiasco, according to some, was just another sign of the White man's desperation.

The Cafe de Champion, catering, according to proprietor Jack Johnson, "to de African aristocracy and de flowah and chivalry of de vanquished but aspiring White race," opened on July 11, at 41 West 31st Street, in Chicago.[66] (Although the racist White press printed Johnson's remarks in this manner, it was not the way the articulate champion spoke.) Restaurant ownership quickly occupied a bulk of his time and took him away from his wife. It also increased Johnson's exposure to the public, and they to him. Temptation, or so it appeared, was always just a table away. Meanwhile, Etta was beginning to feel more and more isolated. Following the death of her father and fallout from her marriage, Etta Duryea slipped into a state of depression and committed suicide on September 11, 1912. The *Detroit Times* provided the details: "Dismissing her maids last night with the injunction that they 'Pray for her,' Mrs. Johnson went to her rooms above her husband's new cafe—the Cafe de Champion. At 3:30 this morning late revelers were alarmed by the sound of a shot. Rushing upstairs they discovered the pugilist's wife unconscious on the floor, a bullet in her brain. She was rushed to the hospital and died without regaining consciousness."[67]

The champion's expressions of genuine remorse over the death of his wife were accepted initially. But later they were questioned. During the summer, he had become infatuated with an 18-year-old Milwaukee prostitute, Lucille Cameron. She strolled into his Cafe one day, captured his attention, and was hired as the champion's stenographer. When she was seen on the champion's arm, a month after the death of his wife, it created quite a stir. Cameron's mother, Mrs. F. Cameron Fallconet, was the most upset. She took action by going to the police and claiming her daughter had been kidnapped. Johnson was arrested for violating the Mann (White slave) Act and taken to City Hall. A bond of $800 was initially arranged, then raised to $1,500. The case fell apart when Cameron refused to cooperate. Johnson was arrested again less than a month later. Again the charge was violating the Mann Act. This time, however, it was in transporting Miss Belle Schreiber—formerly employed by the Everleigh Sisters Club.[68]

On December 4, 1912, Jack Johnson, 34 years of age, married 19-year-old Lucille Cameron. The action would not affect the case in federal court, though it would create a public outrage.

The *Broad Ax*, a noted Black publication, summed up the whole incident in this manner: "In conclusion, after all that has been said and done, in this whole affair, and that as Jack Johnson, seems to have been, the chief stumbling block, in the pathway of Miss Cameron, causing her to become an outcast forever, among her own people and race, he must be given the credit however distasteful it may seem to many; for having the courage and manhood, to stand by her and to lawfully marry her; after he had gotten her into so much serious trouble."[69]

Jack Johnson skipped bail following his Mann Act conviction in June 1913. Turning up in Montreal, where his bride was waiting for him, he would spend the next seven years in exile.

Mississippi's *Jones County News* concluded: "Jack Johnson is by nature a brute, and it was only a question of time when he would run to the end of his tether and have justice meted out to him. We are glad that the South is free of such characters as this Negro and his White concubines. We doubt if there is a White woman so low in this broad Southland of ours who would thus prostitute and sell herself for ease and money. The North has been given a dose of Black draught in Jack Johnson, and we hope it will act as a purifier. When you lay down with dogs you must expect to get up with fleas."[70]

The incident created an international stir. The French Federation of Boxing Clubs stripped Johnson, who was in France at the end of 1913, of the Heavyweight Championship. Yet the IBU declined to do so.[71] In Paris, on December 19, Jack Johnson met "Battling" Jim Johnson, a Boston-imported sparring partner, who was also Black. Although scheduled for 20 rounds, the encounter lasted only 10 due to an injury suffered by the champion. The fight entered the record books as a 10-round draw—Johnson retained his championship.[72]

As his money supply dwindled, a distressed Johnson looked at alternative sources of income. He even briefly tried wrestling in Sweden. The reality was that the controversy that surrounded the fighter scared boxing promoters.

Finally he was matched with Frank Moran on June 27, 1914. A White dentist from Pittsburgh and gifted college athlete, Moran was far from a tomato can, but also far from a champion. After 20 rounds at the Velodrome d'Hiver in Paris, Johnson took the battle on points. There were no knockdowns during the fight, the champion's only bout of the year. Moran showed up in the first 10 rounds, but slowed during the final half of the fight.

In 1915, the Johnsons moved on to Buenos Aires, Argentina, before heading to Cuba in April. Still economically challenged, the champion had agreed to meet Jess Willard, for a guaranteed $30,000, plus one-third of picture privileges on April 5, at Oriental Park in

Havana. Jack Curley was behind the promotion. The *Daily Telegram* printed the ringside report:

Jess Willard, the Kansas cowboy, is the new heavyweight champion pugilist of the world. He knocked out Jack Johnson, the Black champion in the 26th round of their championship bout here Monday. It was Johnson's fight all the way until the 22nd round when his vitality left him because of the hard pace which he carried throughout the early rounds. Then, the giant plainsman opened his heaviest attack and in the next few rounds carried the fight away from the Black man and toppled him over with rights and lefts to the body and blows to the face. Seventeen thousand persons saw the combat and when Johnson crumpled up on the floor from a terrific right swing to the jaw the crowd burst into the ring. Soldiers cleared the ring.[73]

Willard, "The Pottawatomie Giant," stood six feet, six inches and tipped at just over 238, or 13½ pounds heavier than Johnson. The end came at the 1:26 mark of the 26th round—the battle having been scheduled for 45 sessions. When the final blow struck Johnson's head, it snapped violently to the side while his hands reached out in desperation to cling to Willard. The effort to bring his adversary down with him failed, and his unconscious frame slid down Willard's torso and legs before landing on his back. As Johnson's arms instinctively shaded his eyes from the blinding sun, referee Jack Welsh tolled the count. Once the arbiter reached "10," he immediately raised Willard's right arm. And just like that, the Black man's reign was over.

The victory wasn't front-page news—Johnson's exile had seen to that—but word traveled fast. One reaction, or recommendation, came from the *Ocala Evening Star*:

If Willard and all other White fistic champions will draw the color line they may be forgiven for some of the depravity they have shown in the past, but such men as Jeffries who deliberately create situations that cause and add to friction between races, are enemies of both. From the day of his triumph

On April 5, 1915, Jess Willard knocked out Jack Johnson, Heavyweight Champion of the World, at the 1:26 mark of the 26th round. Johnson had underestimated Willard's strength and conditioning (Library of Congress, LC-USZ6—3753).

in Reno, it was only a matter of time before Johnson should meet his Waterloo, as the chief concern of fistic circles ever since has been the training of White hopes to knock him out. Increasing age and dissipation told on him, and he was not near as strong and active as when he faced Jeffries, nevertheless, he gave Willard about all he could.[74]

As Willard sailed to Key West, then north on to Jacksonville for a vaudeville run, Johnson, still in exile, contemplated his future. But the book was closed on the first Black Heavyweight Champion of the World.

As World War I, which began in 1914, continued to rage, Johnson headed to Spain. While there, he even tried his luck as a bullfighter. Then it was on to Mexico in the spring

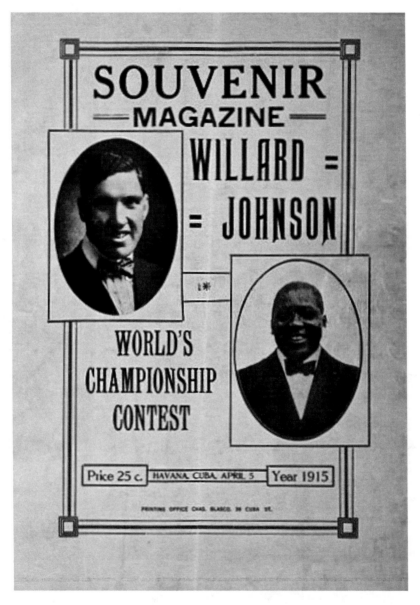

Souvenir magazine for the Willard versus Johnson World's Championship Contest held in Havana, Cuba, on April 5, 1915 (author's collection).

of 1919. As you get older, the sins of the past have an ugly way of surfacing, then lingering. Living in Tijuana, Mexico, the proximity reminded him daily of the freedom he left behind. Jack Johnson surrendered to the authorities on July 20, 1920. The *Rock Island Argus* noted his action on the front page: "Jack Johnson, fugitive pugilist reported arrested today in California, will be turned over to the United States marshal on his arrival in Chicago to be taken immediately to Fort Leavenworth prison, it was declared at the office of District Attorney Charles F. Clyne today."[75]

Johnson's life at Leavenworth, where he knew the warden, proved rather cozy. He arose around 8:30 a.m., cleaned up, and ordered breakfast from a restaurant. Reading and writing occupied most of his mornings. In the afternoon, following lunch at a nearby cafe, Johnson trained. After sunset, it was walking about town or an automobile ride. Jack Johnson was released on July 9, 1921, and headed back to Chicago.[76] Lucille was patiently waiting. However, her tolerance only lasted four more years. She filed for divorce—on the uncontested charge of infidelity. Unfazed, Johnson greeted Helen Matthews, then Irene Pineau, and married the latter in 1925.

Exhibitions or stray battles occupied a bulk of his time until his death, as a result of an automobile accident, on June 10, 1946. Johnson was en route to New York from Texas, where he concluded a personal appearance tour. He lost control of his vehicle and crashed into a light pole—the vehicle overturned.

Forever recognized as the first pugilist to cross the color line of the World Heavyweight Championship, Jack Johnson was flamboyant, crafty, and enormously talented. As one of the greatest pugilists of all time, he has been inducted into every elite boxing institution.

The Color Line, 1903–1908[77]

Courage was what Jack Johnson was all about. Never had anyone faced such cruelty, such unabated racism, or such hate. His greatest fight was not in the ring, but outside it—against the endless bigotry. As the first Heavyweight Champion of the World who was Black, Jack Johnson was the most powerful physical specimen on the planet, and he was also a role model. His actions, like it or not, would set the standard by which all others will be compared. However, Jack Johnson wasn't interested in the White man's standards, nor that of the Black man, only his own.

The reaction to his boxing match against Jim Jeffries was the most widespread racial uprising that the U.S. had ever seen—or ever would see, until the 1968 assassination of civil rights leader Dr. Martin Luther King, Jr. If you thought the sexual anxiety of the White man tipped when folks saw Johnson accompanied by a White women (when he returned from Australia), it overflowed at the destruction of Jeffries. Johnson became the poster child for state statutes forbidding miscegenation and even managed to upset Negro educator Booker T. Washington for his misrepresentation of his race.

Johnson didn't just beat his opponents, he humiliated them. The larger the fight film revenue projections, the longer his adversary had to live. Wearing them down was far more satisfying than their immediate destruction. As a master defenseman, he predicted the rounds in which his antagonist would fall, then dropped them right on time. He could trash-talk with the best of them—his corner conversations with Corbett, during the Jeffries battle, were not for the faint of heart. As the essence of male narcissism, Johnson knew all the buttons to push when it came to the White man, and he could do so at will.

Boxing gives you the ring but it's up to each fighter to chart their own course—to rise and fall at their own pace. Those who witnessed Jack Johnson's behavior were certain that he was doomed for the toxic fallout of public notoriety—enemies multiply, friends do not. The Mann Act became the iceberg in Johnson's ocean.[78]

When he was reduced from heavyweight champion to a sideshow off Times Square, his penance wasn't fun to watch. It also wasn't fair.

During his tenure as champion, Jack Johnson challenged many views on the color line. In 1905, Bob Fitzsimmons shared his wisdom with the *Los Angeles Herald*: "To begin with, we've got to admit there is a color line and as long as there is pugilism in this country there will be one. Why? Simply because there will always be Negro fighters, for the Negro is peculiarly fitted to be a pugilist in some ways and just as unfit in other ways, but there will always be a few of them with both qualities combined."[79]

In 1906, John L. Sullivan, never bashful, shared his views with the *Salt Lake Tribune*: "With Gans put where he belongs, there isn't a chocolate fighter in sight to take the place of Jackson, Dixon, Craig, Godfrey, Armstrong, Johnson, Walcott, Martin and other Negro fighters. Peter Jackson was the best of all the smoked pugs, and I say this in spite of what has been said about me being afraid to meet him. I was never for one minute afraid of Jackson, or any other fighter, but I never would go into the ring with a Negro, and my record is clean in that respect."[80]

In 1907, outside the ring, the color line varied city-to-city, like this view of Atlanta that appeared in the *Broad Ax*:

The color line is drawn, but neither race knows just where it is. Indeed, it can hardly be definitely drawn in many relationships, because it is constantly changing. This uncertainty is a fertile source of friction and bitterness. The very first time I was on a car in Atlanta, I saw the conductor—all conductors are white—ask a Negro woman to get up and take a seat further back in order to make a place for a White man. I traveled a good deal, but I never saw a White person asked to vacate a back seat to make place for a Negro. I saw cars filled with White people, both front seats and back, and many Negroes standing.[81]

In 1908, even Highland Park College in Des Moines, Iowa, drew the color line, according to the *Topeka State Journal*: "President Longwell, in announcing the drawing of the color line, declared he had nothing personally against the Blacks; that they had conducted themselves well, but that the White students compelled the action by refusing to attend chapel or to walk into classes with the Negroes."[82]

In 1910, and back into the ring, the *Evening Times* viewed the color line this way:

Every few years a terrific howl about the color line goes up from one weight division or another, but you never heard a bunch of fighters set up that color line oratorio unless there was concealed in their particular woodpile a Colored man who could flay them alive. You never knew a fighter to howl about the color line unless he was being systematically prodded into a match with a Colored man whom he had a might good reason to fear.... It is the White goose who lays the golden egg for the Colored fighter. Two colored men, no matter how good they may be, will never prove a strong drawing card. A Colored man, in order to get money out of the game, must fight White men, and if he handles the first crop too roughly he may find the rest of it blighted.[83]

EIGHT

The Idol of Paris

As imagined by its early claimants and titleholders, the World Colored Heavyweight Championship accomplished its goal when one of them became the Heavyweight Champion of the World. The initial phase of its existence spanned from 1876 until 1908. During Jack Johnson's reign as the Heavyweight Champion of the World, the Colored designation faded into obscurity for a number of reasons. However, it did not die. Three fighters, any of whom could defeat the other on a given day, shared the inconspicuous designation. They were Sam McVey, Joe Jeannette, and Sam Langford. Any or all of these gifted pugilists could have been Heavyweight Champion of the World if given an opportunity.

Fallout

By capturing the World Heavyweight Championship, Jack Johnson rocked the social balance of power. Not since Abraham Lincoln had a single man ignited so much fear, yet so much expectation. In response to the apprehension, a search began for a "White Hope" to take back the title. The talented author and *New York Herald* reporter Jack London, covering the Jack Johnson versus Tommy Burns World Heavyweight Championship fight, penned his now-famous words in a special cable to the *San Francisco Call*: "One criticism, and only one, can be passed upon Johnson. In the 13th round he made the mistake of his life. He should have put Burns out. He could have put him out. It would have been child's play. Instead of which he smiled and deliberately let Burns live until the gong sounded, and in the 14th round the police stopped the fight and Johnson lost the credit of a knockout. But one thing remains; Jeffries must emerge from his alfalfa farm and remove that smile from Johnson's face. Jeff, it's up to you."[1]

London never hid the fact that he favored Burns, even when his snowy White skin turned a shade of crimson.

An article in the *Detroit Times*, titled "None but Negroes to Fight Dusky Winner of the Title," said it all and more:

The two men who loom up as candidates for Johnson's title are of his own color. There is Sam Langford, now on the Pacific coast, who has already admitted that Johnson is his master. Then there is Sam McVey, who has been beating everyone in France. McVey has made so much money that he is likely to take a chance for the loser's end. Langford may also take a similar chance. Johnson's willingness to meet anyone seems to indicate that he may be matched with some other heavyweight shortly.

Just at present the whole talk in Sydney is of the fact that the colored men now practically dominate the ring. It is generally conceded that the only reason Ketchel, Papke and Kelly sidestep Sam Langford is because they are afraid of him. The same applies to the lightweights and welterweights who will not oppose Jack Blackburn. Sam McVey has all the heavyweights and middleweights "buffaloed" on the

English and French side of the water. The lighter classes alone in America keep up the supremacy of the white men.[2]

By 1915, many witnessed firsthand the impact of Jack Johnson's reign. However, his brash lifestyle was wearing thin on society's moral compass. Having accomplished the difficult task of crossing the color line, it was his goal to stay World Heavyweight Champion. If that meant turning his back to his own race, or the only serious contenders to his crown, such it would be. It was his reign and his parade. And he knew it.

Samuel E. McVey (McVea)

Saving him from Potter's Field, disconsolate Jack Johnson traveled all the way from Cincinnati to New York to provide a decent burial for an old foe and ring associate, Sam McVey.[3] The very man who crossed the color line of the Heavyweight Championship of the World wanted to be certain that McVey's funeral expenses were paid. Johnson's thoughts at the tearful hour were published in the *Bridgeport Times and Evening Farmer*: "Sam meant much to me. The old Black guard is waning. Athletic decay has set in the race that was once physically great. He was the toughest man I ever fought. He hit me harder than I was ever hit before or since. I returned the compliment. Sam had the worst left hand I ever encountered. It was a short chop, loaded with TNT. Sam Langford had just such a hook in either hand, but Langford, great as he was for his weight and inches, had neither the weight nor leverage to drive his sock home."[4]

They officially fought three times (1903–1904), but also performed exhibitions and sparred together. The encounters were so impactful that Johnson could recall the distant contests like they were yesterday. The *Bridgeport Times and Evening Farmer* continued: "Twice I gained the decision over limited distances [20 rounds]. Once I knocked him out in the 20th round at Mechanics' Pavilion in San Francisco. And I wish to tell you in that fight I was hit the hardest blow I ever took in my life. It was one of those short, left chops to the mouth that stove in my teeth and left my head dizzy and body numb for 10 rounds or more. Finally, when I nailed McVey I hit Sam on the jaw harder than I ever hit any man, and at that the count scarcely beat him. A good, game man McVey. That's why I'm here."[5]

A member of the famed "Black Teen Foursome," a moniker hung on perhaps the greatest quartet of heavyweights ever, Sam McVey, along with Jack Johnson, Sam Langford, and Joe Jeannette, devoured antagonists like a wolf awakening from hibernation. If his five feet, 10½-inch frame, mounted on over 200 pounds didn't intimidate you, his piercing glance, that could melt steel, resembled that of the Grim Reaper.[6] If you entered a ring against Sam McVey, you were destined for dreamland.

Born on May 17, 1884, in Waelder, Texas, Sam McVey (also spelled McVea) was reared briefly in the small town.[7] Small it indeed was, home to just under 300 residents. As the son of a former slave, his first job was as a farm laborer. By 1902, living in Oxnard, California, the teen, growing like a weed, was convinced he could use his size to his advantage. Settled by American farmers, Oxnard was known for its barley, lima beans, and beet production. McVey, like others, capitalized on the opportunity to work the fields. When the youngster had enough of picking, packing, and transporting crops, he looked to alternatives.

McVey would become a professional boxer more than a year before Oxnard became a California city.[8] Following a series of knockout demonstrations against no-name pugs, he went up against Fred Russell on November 1, 1902, in Oxnard. The handsome Colorado puncher wasn't bashful about crossing the color line; Russell had already confronted Frank Childs, Klondike, Hank Griffin, and the great Joe Walcott. At this stage of his career, while Russell looked impressive, he couldn't box his way out of a wet paper bag, and he proved more of a White sacrificial lamb than anything else. McVey knocked him out in the fifth round. It was his first battle to attract media attention—the *San Francisco Call* ran this blurb on November 3: "Fred Russell was defeated in the fifth round last night by Sam McVey, the Colored heavyweight. McVey's record is one of unbroken victories, having never been defeated. His victory places him among the promising pugilists of the Pacific Coast. Harry Stuart of Los Angeles refereed the match."[9]

About a month later, the *Minneapolis Journal* noted, "Down in Los Angeles they have a couple of promising Colored heavies. These are Jack Johnson and Sam McVey."[10] Naturally, it didn't take Tom McCarey long to notice McVey. He immediately went about trying to match the fighter on behalf of the Century Athletic Club.

Jack Johnson v. Sam McVey—World Colored Heavyweight Championship

In 1903, McVey, who was working with boxer and instructor Hank Griffin, knocked out highly touted "Toothpick" Kelly, who stood six feet, six inches and scaled at 240, and tomato can Jack Lavelle.[11] This positioned him for a battle against Jack Johnson on February 26—it would be the first of three believed title fights against the World Colored Heavyweight Champion. Although the relatively inexperienced fighter outweighed the "Galveston Giant," he could not effectively harness his power. The champion, with his superlative defensive skills, took the 20-round decision. However, having gone the distance with Johnson was certainly noteworthy.

On May 5, an 11th-round knockout of "White Hope" Kid Carter elevated McVey's status. Touted as a possible Jeffries adversary, his rise was that quick and that impressive.[12]

The *Washington Times* noted: "McVey is more on the giant order, impervious to punishment and able to land hard at short range. No clever man can beat the present champion [Jeffries] without the aid of an effective blow but a chap almost as large as himself, and one with strength rather than science appears to be one to be feared. Should McVey win both of his coming battles ["Denver" Ed Martin and Jack Johnson] pressure will be brought to bear on Jeff and the color line will probably go a glimmering."[13]

On September 15 in Los Angeles, it would take only three short right-hand blows, at close quarters, to send Denver Ed Martin down for the count in the first round. Martin's weakness, as discovered, was the solar plexus (the pit of the stomach), and McVey, cognizant of that fact, hit his target with a vengeance.

Jack Johnson, on the other hand, would not be so easy. The pair met again on October 27, also in Los Angeles. McVey was struck like a heavy bag and dropped three times. Following 20 grueling rounds—which at least proved McVey had a concrete chin—Johnson, a more scientific fighter, was granted the decision.

Only two ring battles occupied McVey's time in 1904, and both foes were familiar. The first was on April 22, in San Francisco at Mechanics' Pavilion, against Jack Johnson. Not only was the battle another defense of Johnson's Colored title, but the last formal time the pair would meet inside a boxing ring—later, they would meet only in exhibitions. The fight, which was said to be one of the worst fights seen in San Francisco in years, saw Johnson knock out McVey. The result wasn't the issue, but the timing was: He did so with a mere 20 seconds left in the final round. As usual, Johnson led with his left hand and tied up his rival. McVey, who exhibited little power, simply endured 20 rounds of punishment. Halfway through, the dance, or display, by the fighters was so pathetic that half the spectators left. If Johnson was defending his title, which some believe he was, it certainly didn't appear that way.

Despite his poor performance against Johnson, McVey was matched with Denver Ed Martin for 10 rounds at Hazard's Pavilion on August 12. Recalling his first-round knockout of the fighter, McVey didn't take the fight seriously. However, unlike their previous meeting, Martin trained hard for the battle; consequently, it paid off as the Denver pugilist took the 10-round decision. McVey's languid performance, perhaps his worst to date, sent the fighter into a tailspin—he had lost four of his last seven conflicts. Losing confidence and questioning his career choice, McVey turned his back on the fight game in 1905.

A New Perspective, 1906–1907

So the story goes: Frank Carrillo, the Bakersfield sportsman, caught wind of McVey's decision and talked him back into the ring. He told the *Los Angeles Herald*: "You know that McVey was a green fighter. Nobody ever taught him anything, and he depended on his great strength and endurance to win fights. When he came up to Bakersfield I put him to boxing, and taught him something."[14]

Coming back to the ring in 1906, McVey looked sharper than ever. On January 25 in San Diego, he met Denver Ed Martin once again. Scheduled for 20 rounds, McVey would need only four. That's when he delivered a crushing left to his opponent's jaw that sent him crashing to the canvas for the full 10 seconds. The *Los Angeles Herald* saw it like this:

> Martin was twice to the carpet in the first round and took the count each time. In the third round the two men came together with such viciousness and force that McVey was knocked out of the ring and Martin was knocked flat, where he remained while his opponent was climbing back into the ring. Martin got the best of the game in the last portion of the round, but the gong sounded before he could deliver the knockout blow. There was vicious fighting in the fourth before the final blow toward the close of the three-minute session.[15]

Still a bit apprehensive, McVey concluded his year with a first-round knockout of tomato can "Tornado" Smith in Bakersfield, California, on February 24, and later, a second-round kayo of "Sailor" Matt Turner on November 29.[16] Of the latter, Turner was an undefeated Black Navy fighter who drew solid local support—many believed he would bury his adversary in less than 15 rounds. They were wrong. McVey, growing in confidence, looked sound and was in good physical condition.

Residing in Bakersfield, California, McVey would take only two fights in the States in 1907 before heading to Europe.[17] On February 28, he met Denver Ed Martin in Sacramento and knocked him out in the 16th round. It was the pair's fourth meeting. On April 15, it was off to New York to dance to a 10-round no-decision with Joe Jeannette, a noted local Black pugilist. While in the city, he also switched managers, from Frank Carillo to Frank Bernard. McVey was in search of better opportunities and knew that Bernard had a solid relationship with Jeannette's manager, George Armstrong—the pair agreed to match their fighters when necessary. Read into that what you may. Bernard was with McVey over in London when he learned that many of the United Kingdom's clubs were also drawing the color line. Manager

Bettison of the National Club said, "The London sports won't have their champion beaten by a Negro."[18]

Proceeding to Paris, McVey defeated Marc Gaucher, a former French champ and Jeannette's sparring partner on October 24, by way of a fourth-round knockout to become, in his words, the Heavyweight Champion of France. On December 28, he defended his new title with a second-round knockout of Englishman Jack Scales. The French just loved McVey, so he promised to stay there and defend his crown. In truth, he remained until the spring of 1911 before heading off to England and on to Australia (September 1911). McVey would not return to the United States until December 1914.

The Idol of Paris

A bulletin from across the pond in January 1908 was printed in the *Detroit Times*: "From Paris comes the news Tommy Burns has put up the bars that separate the Black pasture from the White, and is now willing to take on no Colored man excepting 'Lil' Arthur Johnson. And if Sam McVey, the husky Bakersfield Negro now bidding for the championship honors across the pond can be believed, he is the one responsible for Tommy's sudden change of mind."[19]

Not just a Parisian novelty or a fierce Black fighter who ate Frenchmen for dinner, McVey was a talented pugilist who was pulling down big money for his appearances. The French viewed ring contests similarly to the way New Yorkers saw horse shows—a social environment catering to city gentry. For Parisians, McVey was a freshness they hadn't seen since Benjamin Franklin. And he lived up to expectation—he knocked out every opponent he faced. The *Times* continued: "McVey appears to be the whole show in affairs pugilistic in Paris, and since his sojourn there has gathered much influential support. He has felled all available heavyweight timber and is now reaching out into the isles of England and Ireland."[20]

The jealous American boxing press, none too happy about the talented European migration, went so far as to accuse McVey of padding his resume. The *Los Angeles Herald* stated, "For instance, it is understood [no source given] that Sam McVey is posing as having beaten Jeffries, and the admiring Parisians look on him as the greatest fighter in the world."[21]

In 1908, McVey continued to challenge Tommy Burns while destroying about a half-dozen opponents along the way, including Joseph "Jewey" Smith, claimant to the Heavyweight Champion of Great Britain. A deprecatory letter, penned by Willie Lewis, a White American boxer and Jeannette's second, who also went to France in search of the Golden Goose, appeared in the *Detroit Times*:

> Everybody here is crazy over McVey. They never saw anything so big and ugly. You ought to see him. He's got clothes that would make a Sixth Avenue dark dude look like a rag picker. Last time I saw him he wore a cream-colored suit that looked like a silk—sort of a pajama rig. He goes to fights in a carriage with a dress suit on and a big bouquet in his hand. They say society has taken him up and he is taken to dinners in the best houses and allowed to sit at the table without wearing a muzzle and chain. It must be a treat to see McVey dining with a Duke.[22]

Riding on his newfound stardom, McVey, who could care less what Willie Lewis thought, also became a trainer. When a young Frenchman named Georges Carpentier decided he wanted to tackle the bantamweights, he looked no further than McVey. In 1921, he would assist Carpentier for his bout against Jack Dempsey.

The Palace of Versailles, the principal royal residence of France from 1682 until the start of the French Revolution in 1789, was the perfect backdrop for Sam McVey, "The Idol of Paris" (author's collection).

A Title in Transition

Jack Johnson's only ambition in 1909, or so he claimed, was to return to America as champion—the "recognized" Heavyweight Champion of the World, that is. In the eyes of some, Johnson relinquished the World Colored Heavyweight Championship after he defeated Tommy Burns. He had a new title, one he would safeguard against any White challenger.

Rather than defending his crown against the leading Black boxers of the day, Johnson drew the color line. The same slap that so often reached his face, he chose to return. He claimed the fights wouldn't draw crowds and therefore wouldn't be profitable. The contradictory behavior was an enigma to most and reason enough, some believed, to continue the World Colored Heavyweight Championship. But that strategy needed to be evaluated.

Proven successful for leveraging the championship, some were afraid it could also segregate the designation. What if Johnson turned to McVey and said, "You have your title and I have mine." While the forum it represented was important, caution surrounded its presentation—none of the Black contenders could afford to give up a championship opportunity.

A couple of handfuls of battles occupied Sam McVey's time in 1909, including a trio against Joe Jeannette.

Sam McVey v. Joe Jeannette—World Colored Heavyweight Championship

Sam McVey met Joe Jeannette for 20 rounds at the Cirque de Paris, on February 20, 1909. It was a catchweight confrontation billed as for the "World's Championship"—no specifics were given as to what crown the winner would be wearing. The 20-round decision went to McVey, but the event lacked the intensity of a championship fight. In fact, the *Times Dispatch* reported: "clinches were the main feature of the last two rounds."[23] Later, to complicate matters, a cablegram stated that the fight was initially awarded to Jeannette, then reversed. Which begs the question: who got what cut? The winner supposedly put $3,000 ($82,824 in 2019 dollars) in his pocket, while the loser grabbed $2,000 ($55,216 in 2019 dollars).[24] What exactly was placed on the line?

With the victory, McVey claimed the World Colored Heavyweight Championship and a very healthy paycheck.

Joe Jeannette v. Sam McVey—World Colored Heavyweight Championship

Joe Jeannette defeated Sam McVey in the 50th round of a three-and-a-half-hour battle. Initial reports called it "the greatest fight witnessed in France since John L. Sullivan and Charley Mitchell fought in Chantilly in 1888."[25] What of the details?

It was a fight to the finish, the first of its kind since Fitzsimmons met Corbett in Carson City many moons ago, when Sam McVey met Joe Jeannette on April 17, 1909, at the Cirque de Paris in Paris. The atmosphere was intoxicating despite attendance falling short of expectations (estimated at 2,500 or about half capacity). Rumors that the pair's first encounter wasn't on the square—not surprising considering the friendship between fight managers—likely contributed to the reduced gate. As there was no chance of interference by authorities, it vowed to be the ultimate confrontation and was just that.

The account picked up by most newspapers, including the *San Francisco Call*, stated: "McVey had the better of the fight up to the fortieth round, and in both the 21st and 22nd rounds he had the New Yorker so groggy that he barely could keep his feet. Jeannette bore the punishment bravely and recuperated in a wonderful manner. McVey had almost worn himself out after 40 rounds, and by this time the New York fighter was coming back. By effective fighting he gradually beat the Californian and practically had him knocked out when the fight ended, McVey's seconds throwing up the sponge."[26]

The description sounded like a rewritten version of a very long piece—perhaps it was condensed to meet a word count or a deadline. Some sources described it as a war that included 38 knockdowns over the course of 48 three-minute rounds.[27] Common among every credible account was that it was a fight for the ages, a magnificent exhibition and a testament to the endurance of two of the most talented pugilists in the fight game. The victory and the title were now in the hands of Joe Jeannette. More observations would follow from those who actually witnessed the event.[28]

Less than a week later, McVey's manager was talking a return match. According to the *Washington Herald*: "It can be for 20 rounds only, and there shall be no 'doping,' as he attributed McVey's defeat to the oxygen, caffeine and ether that were administered to Jennette and to the cold water that was thrown on him by his seconds when he had been virtually knocked out in the 19th round."[29]

To clear the air, a return match was indeed scheduled.

Joe Jeannette v. Sam McVey—World Colored Heavyweight Championship

The *Daily Missoulian*, like so many other newspapers, described this event as follows: "In the fight here [Paris, France] tonight [December 11, 1909] between Sam McVey and Joe Jeannette, the American Colored heavyweights, the referee declared the bout a draw after 30 rounds. The decision created an uproar."[30]

When Jeannette returned to New York for the holidays, he spoke to the *Evening Star*: "They handed me a draw, when all my friends, as well as myself, were satisfied that I beat McVey to a frazzle. In that fight I had McVey hanging around my neck like a creditor in the last six rounds, and he didn't put a glove on me during that period."[31]

American reporters were particularly hard on McVey. They were resentful of all the attention he was receiving in France, not to mention his bankable purses. Also, the rivalry was wearing a bit thin, many believing both managers were choreographing each event.

About a dozen French victories and a draw were added to McVey's record in 1910. His most interesting battles were a 15-round draw (August 7), followed by a 21-round knockout victory (November 19) against big "Battling" Jim Johnson. The New Jersey boxer had spotted a weakness in McVey's armor: His opponents had not learned how to block his left hook effectively. Johnson properly positioned his left arm to counter its effectiveness.[32] Six foot, three-inch Johnson, more of a sparring partner than a boxer, matched well against McVey from an entertainment perspective—the Parisians, some of whom mistook "Battling" Jim for Jack—loved watching the two enormous Black men browbeating each other about the ring.

Sam Langford v. Sam McVey—World Colored Heavyweight Championship, 1911–1913

Even though Sam McVey's main focus was always positioning himself for a title shot against Jack Johnson, he still had bills to pay. Often fighters have a rival, or rivalries, that they are associated with, and McVey was no different. Beginning in 1911 and ending in 1913, McVey fought a series of seven recorded contests against the fearless Sam Langford. Their battles ranged from short, no-decision bouts to 20-round stamina drainers. Adding to the enmity of the contests was the international flavor—one took place in France and six in Australia. Although Langford was commonly the victor, there were no spoils for McVey. How could there be? He battled the best his weight class had to offer, and the purses often reflected that fact.

Against Langford, McVey posted records of 1–0–1 in 1911, 0–4–0 in 1912, and 0–0–1 in 1913. Two of the battles surfaced as possible, although not billed as such, World Colored Heavyweight titles exchanges: McVey's trouncing of Langford during a 20-round decision on December 25, 1911 (billed as an elimination contest for the right to challenge Champion Jack Johnson) and Langford taking a convincing 20-round decision over McVey on April 8, 1912.[33] Following the latter, all eyes turned to Johnson to accept an offer to fight Langford. But the champion would not relent.

In 1911, Sam McVey also picked up the Australian Heavyweight title by defeating Bill Lang. He successfully defended it multiple times before relinquishing it to Sam Langford in 1912.[34]

On February 7, 1913, the New York State Boxing Commission placed a ban on ring contests between Whites and Negroes. These "mixed" contests had given rise to debate for some time, so the NYSAC (New York State Athletic Commission) finally felt compelled to act. The action confirmed McVey's intuition: Australia was the perfect location to conduct business.

By the end of 1913, matching McVey with Langford had a diminishing appeal, and the pair fought to a lackluster draw on March 24 in Brisbane. In America, the press viewed the match more as a vaudeville act than an actual rivalry. An article in the *Honolulu Star-Bulletin* viewed "Jack, Joe and the two Sams" in this manner: "It is difficult to pick the best man. Many believe that McVey would have been Johnson's master if they had fought about the time of the Jeffries-Johnson battle,

Sam McVey, pictured here in a passport photograph, left Paris in 1911 as a popular and wealthy man (author's collection).

yet others would have backed Langford and Jeannette against Johnson. McVey's fighting career was waning, and he has ceased to be useful even as a meal ticket for Sam Langford. Johnson is the oldest of the bunch, having been born in 1878, while Jeannette was born in 1881, McVey in 1885 and Langford in 1886."[35]

Despite the obvious—or the presence of Jack Johnson—the White newspapers continued their efforts to bury the Black pugilist. The *Bridgeport Evening Farmer* said: "The Negro fighter is gradually dying out. Less than 10 years ago the names Joe Gans, Joe Walcott, Jack Blackburn, Jack Johnson, Sam Langford, Sam McVey and Joe Jeannette were common to boxing fans. The last of these are Langford, Jeannette and the champion. Langford and Jeannette are slowly fading, and inside of another year the pair will probably be forgotten. Their exhibition two weeks ago gave evidence that they are about ready to join the down and out club. True, Langford did not train for that bout, but those who watched Sam in his fights since he returned to this country declare that he's done. Langford stalled along for many years, failing to give the fans the best he had, but now his star is gradually dying out."[36]

Posting records of 2–0–1 (draw versus Langford) in 1913 and 2–0 with a no-decision in 1914, McVey's most impressive victories were over former White Heavyweight Champion of the World Arthur Pelkey (KO4, 1914), and rising star Harry "The Black Panther" Wills (W20, 1914).[37] The Pelkey victory made it clear that the White designation had yet to find its savior, while the Wills victory, in his hometown, cast a shadow of weakness on the development and management of "The Black Panther."[38]

Title Resurrection

With World War I (1914–1918) still raging in Europe and McVey's opportunities in Australia not panning out the way he would like, he turned to Cuba, America, and Canada in 1915. He took a 20-round victory over "Battling" Jim Johnson, before a six-round exhibition against Jack Johnson—the latter event a mere 48 hours before the Heavyweight Champion of the World would climb into the ring with Jess Willard. Both events were held in Havana, Cuba.

Both McVey and his trainer David Mills claimed Johnson "laid down" to Willard. The *Washington Herald* noted McVey's remarks: "Jack never did train like a man who was getting ready for a fight. He didn't do any road work. He just took a walk every day.... I think something happened.... When Jack was walking back to his corner after the knock-out, he winked at me and Bob Armstrong says: 'There you see what money will do.'"[39]

The article penned by Damon Runyon also noted Johnson signing an agreement that gave him 50 percent of the pictures and the management of the European rights just before the fight, the champion's peculiar behavior between rounds, and his lack of any remorse after the fight. McVey also stated, "I tried to get a fight with Johnson and he promised me a match, but said it had to be for ten rounds and that it would have to be fixed."[40]

With no clear direction in mind, McVey returned to Boston in April. He drew Joe Jeannette over 12 rounds, fought a no-decision with Harry Wills in New York, and a no-decision against "Battling" Jim Johnson in Canada. Returning again to Boston at the beginning of summer, McVey took victories over Sam Langford (W12) and John "Sandy" Ferguson (W8).

Harry Wills v. Sam McVey—World Colored Heavyweight Championship

McVey felt good, and his newly found American audience enjoyed watching him. But a 12-round loss to Harry Wills, on September 7, soon changed that. With Johnson's loss to Willard, Harry Wills resurrected the World Colored Heavyweight Championship. It seemed logical, as he just beat Sam McVey, who some believed held the title, and if he could use the designation to garner the spotlight, why not? Of course, Jeannette, who still held his version, disputed the claim.

Finishing up his year by drawing Langford over 20 rounds in Denver, then defeating Black fighter Jeff Clark (W10) in Kansas City, McVey headed back in New York City. It had been a long year and it still wasn't over. He glided to a no-decision over 10 rounds with Langford on November 23.[41] The Langford v. McVey combination may have been wearing thin in Australia, but it still had drawing power in the states.

In an article by Brown Holmes titled, "Sable Sams Are Last Notable Survivors of Race Fighters," the *Tacoma Times* noted:

> Everybody laughs when, every few weeks, Sam McVey and Sam Langford are matched, but there is a good reason why these two Negro fighters keep pummeling one another. There is nobody else for them to fight. Langford and McVey are the last notable survivors of a race that produced some mighty clever performers—Joe Gans, Peter Jackson, George Dixon, Joe Jennette, Young Peter Jackson, Joe Walcott, Jack Blackburn, Bob Armstrong and others. Harry Wills, a New Orleans heavy is still in the game, but he came too late to gain prominence. Jack Johnson, Jeannette and all the others, except a few smaller fellows, are through. In some states bouts between white and black fighters are prohibited. There is no demand for the black scrapper and many White fighters draw the color line.
>
> Jack Johnson hurt the game for the men of his race. His actions put the Negro boxer in dispute. He tore down prestige built up by Gans, Dixon and others. McVey and Langford were real stars. McVey at one time held the championship of France. Few white heavies wanted any of his game. Langford ruined his chances for matches by trimming Gunboat Smith. The two sable Sams have met about 15 times. They have faced one another in about 150 rounds. At first one would win, then the other. Lately they have been boxing draws. Langford has been in the ring 13 years. McVey 12. They are slowly fading and when they are gone, the day of the Negro fighter of prominence will be over.[42]

The Final Rounds

The Langford versus McVey caravan, far from concluding its business, conducted its no-decision engagements in New York City, Syracuse, and Akron, before heading to South America in 1916.[43] "White Hope" and Kansas City heavyweight Bob Devere tagged along with the pair on their excursion to Santiago, Chile.

The following year, the group headed to Panama to exhibit their talents. On that occasion, pool fighters Kid Norfolk, Jeff Clark, and "Battling" Jim Johnson joined them. Before the Central American visit concluded, late in 1918, Harry Wills also joined forces with McVey.[44]

The final years of a boxing career are hard on every fighter, but they were particularly hard on many Black fighters during this era. There was never a definitive end, and few planned for retirement. Although McVey entered the ring with a few familiar names after 1918, doing so was merely a sign of existing and not living. On August 2, 1921, he fought Jeff Clark to a 10-round no-decision in Lancaster, Pennsylvania. Less than five months later, he was dead. Destitute and suffering from pneumonia, Sam McVey died on December 23, 1921.

Many of his fellow fighters, including Panama Joe Gans, Kid Norfolk, and Jack Johnson, planned a benefit for his family.

Jess Willard

On April 5, 1915, in front of a large and intimidating crowd at the new Oriental Park Racetrack in Havana, Cuba, Jess Myron Willard knocked out boxing champion Jack Johnson in the 26th round to win the World Heavyweight Championship.[45] Few could get past his enormous size in order to properly evaluate his skills—he stood six feet, six inches and weighed between 225 and 275 pounds.

Prior to Willard's battle with Johnson, William Muldoon, formerly the world's champion wrestler and authority on conditioning, stated this regarding Willard's physique to the *Washington Herald*: "He is entirely too long between the joints. His bones and tendons are soft: his vital organs are easily affected. His mind is simple; his power of concentration is easily disturbed. His knowledge of coordination, cooperation is sadly neglected. In fact, the art of the profession, which he is following, is not apparent in any way in his actions within the ring, and cannot be any part of his performance until it has been thoroughly drilled into him by hard knocks and experience."[46]

Perhaps Willard's 83 inches of reach, dynamite right hand, and effective left jab were underestimated. Jess Willard would not lose a fight until July 4, 1919, when he lost the title to Jack Dempsey.

"The Pottawatomie Giant" was born on December 29, 1881, in St. Clere, Kansas. Deceptively quick for a big man, he was not an aggressor but a solid counter-puncher. Honestly, he didn't like boxing. Willard didn't even begin his career as a pugilist until the age of 29. Forever known as the man who ended Johnson's nearly seven-year title reign, Jess Willard transformed his new-found popularity into an entertainment career. Touring the country with circuses and shows such as Buffalo Bill's Wild West Show was far less stressful.

According to the *Star-Independent*, following his battle with Jack Johnson, promoter Jack Curley stated: "Willard will take a brief rest and then will meet any White fighters. He will draw the color line. The fight was a big success. Willard deserves the thanks of the entire White race for his glorious victory, bringing back to the White race the heavyweight championship title."[47]

Willard found solace in the supermarket business during retirement, along with refereeing wrestling matches. He died on December 15, 1968, in Los Angeles, California.

The Color Line, 1909–1915[48]

Speaking to the *Washington Herald*, the aforementioned William Muldoon lent his perspective to Johnson's championship reign: "That particular boxer that Johnson is afraid of will never have an opportunity to try his skill, strength and endurance with Johnson as demonstrator. That boxer is also a Colored man [Sam Langford]. Then there are two more Colored men [Sam McVey and Joe Jeannette] in the boxing profession that have an even chance of defeating the champion in a fair contest, and these Colored men are the only ones in the boxing profession that have anything near a chance with Johnson."[49]

Fully understanding this, the champion drew the color line. For Johnson, pride always took a back seat to power and profit. Boxing was a business, and Johnson was a business-man first, pugilist second. The man in the mirror represented Jack Johnson, not his race. Because of this, Sam McVey would never fulfill his dream.

C.E. Van Loan penned this in the *Evening Statesman*:

> While the White Men have not been blameless in this respect [stalling], the Blacks have been the worst offenders. There are plenty of good healthy reasons for this state of affairs. If a Negro is "too good" and lets everybody find it out, he is going to find himself up against the grand old life-saver—the color line. There is always a fine tailor-made excuse for sidestepping a tough Black man. Very possibly Ham's grandson discovered the color line and the Black men have been starving behind it ever since. All the Colored fighters fear the drawing of the line; some of them are worldly wise enough to "pull" to an opponent now and then in order to keep the sucker crop coming.[50]

Nobody anticipated this when it appeared in the *Evening Standard*: "The die has been cast by one New York newspaper, one of the oldest and most trusted in the country, and it is our sincere hope that the policy will be taken up by every other publication throughout the length and breadth of the land. The paper in question has decided to draw the color line in pugilistic matter that appears on its sports page. Negro's [*sic*] names are barred absolutely. Never again will the besmirched 'Jack Johnson' be set up on its Linotype machines as part of a boxing story, and the only way it can creep into the general news pages of the paper is as an essential integer in tales of justice meted out for criminal acts."[51]

Less than a month before this nation celebrated the Jubilee year, or the 50th anniversary of the Emancipation Proclamation, and under the subheadline "Johnson a Disgrace," the same article continued:

> There is no doubt that Johnson has been the most prominent Negro before the public eye in recent years in this country. And his dastardly acts have been about as low as one can conceive.... It is not Negroes as a whole that Johnson has shamed most, but Negro boxers. Nobody can think of another Negro fighter without his thoughts flashing to Johnson and then having a distasteful opinion of Negro fighters as a whole. If the color line is drawn definitely and firmly for a few years—or a few months may be enough—the situation as to the heavyweight championship can be cleared up. White men will fight only among themselves, and Negroes and Whites should not box each other any more than they should marry each other. Moreover, White promoters should not try to offer Negro fights if the great majority of the spectators are to be White persons, and vice versa.[52]

Oscar Wilde once quipped, "Selfishness is not living as one wishes to live, it is asking others to live as one wishes to live." Perhaps Sam McVey would agree.

NINE

Joseph "Joe" Jeremiah Jeannette

When Joe Jeannette sat next to Walter Johnson, in the dark and dank dressing room of the Knickerbocker Athletic Club on May 9, 1905, both fighters found it difficult to control their emotions. The club, located at Grays Ferry Avenue and Carpenter Street in Philadelphia, was a premier pugilistic platform. The atmosphere was completely intoxicating, the sounds and smells simply electrifying. That was understandable, as Jack Johnson, the World Colored Heavyweight Champion, was to separately meet both Colored men for three rounds—the champion's adversaries viewed as nothing more than sacrificial lambs. In front of a large crowd, Jeannette was first on the card. Determined to be more than an appetizer, the local pugilist took a deep breath and a firm stance. Aggressive, yet cautious, Jeannette was given mixed newspaper accounts at the end of the encounter—the *Washington Times* stated that he deserved at least a draw. Next came the more experienced and self-assured Walter Johnson, who was knocked cold by a powerful right hand by the champion. For Jeannette, in his fourth recorded professional fight, it was his fourth straight loss—he lost a pair to Morris Harris, one to Black Bill and now Johnson. But it was also the fighter's first decent press coverage—thanks to his acclaimed antagonist.

Joseph "Joe" Jeremiah Jeannette, aka Joe Jennette, was born on August 26, 1879, in West Hoboken, New Jersey. His father, Benjamin Jennette, was a blacksmith. Joe loved his family and loved animals—he even dreamed of becoming a veterinarian. Like any youth, he roughhoused when provoked but had no inclination about making such action a career. When he became of age, Joe apprenticed with his father and even learned how to drive a coal truck. At the time, Hoboken was a bustling terminal port that employed many German immigrants. In many ways, the survivalist mentality of the harborside contributed to Jeannette's maturity—he would learn quickly to stand his ground.

Growing to a height of 5 feet, 10 inches and tipping at around 190, Joe Jeannette began boxing and turned professional in 1904. Handsome—a light-skinned, Black Adonis cut to perfection—and humble, his quiet lifestyle suited him just fine. Fighting out of Philadelphia, just over 90 miles from Hoboken, he wasn't quick to impress—he won only half of his first 10 recorded engagements. However, when you took a closer look at his opponents—Black Bill, Jack Johnson, George Cole, and Jim Jeffords—and their experience, it painted a picture of trial by fire. Black Bill, aka Claude Brooks, was an experienced pool fighter battling out of Merchantville, New Jersey; Johnson, just over 40 bouts into his career, was vanquishing his opponents; Cole was a seasoned middleweight fighting out of Trenton; and Jeffords was a tall White fighter from California who had traveled east in search of better ring talent. The *Washington Times* noted on July 7, 1905: "Jeannette has shown improvement in every one of the last few bouts he has been in, and last night he showed up to particular advantage. [George] Cole was floored in the fourth from a glancing blow on the head, and

116

again went down in the fifth from a half-slip and punch. These were the only knockdowns during the bout."[1]

On October 11, Jeannette's intimidating reputation formalized. In the seventh round of a battle against "Black Bill" (Claude Brooks) at the Wilmington Athletic Club, he pulled off an incredible middleweight performance topped off by catapulting his adversary through the ropes. Furious, not to mention embarrassed, "Black Bill" gathered his thoughts and returned to the ring. It was a bad idea. Jeannette reloaded the chamber and dropped him like a cement block from a third-story window.

With well over a dozen competitive contests in 1905, Jeannette established a reputation as a solid pool fighter with higher aspirations. In 1906, his popularity, not to mention ring ability, garnered more ink. The *Evening Star* noted:

> Joe Jeannette, through his manager George Armstrong, has issued a challenge to Jack O'Brien. Jeannette weighs about 165 pounds and agrees to make that weight. His easy victory over Sam Langford at Lawrence [December 25, 1905] opened the eyes of some of the fight followers. But they evidently forgot that he won from Jack Johnson, and had all the better of a go with the "Pink Pajama Man" until Jack remembered how Sandy Ferguson lost, and fouled Jeannette. Armstrong ridicules the claims that Jeannette had 20 pounds on Langford. He declares "Laughing Ho Ho Sam" is a middleweight, and that he would have hard work to weigh in under 155 pounds. Jeannette has a fine record, and has defeated Jim Jeffords and other heavy men. Armstrong realizes that O'Brien has drawn the color line, although why at this late day he cannot understand, for he has met George Cole, Young Peter Jackson and others in the ring.[2]

Facing only three different Black adversaries—Jack Johnson, Sam Langford, and Black Bill—in 1906, Joe Jeannette posted a record of 1–2–1, and two no-decisions.[3] This as he re-

Philadelphia Jack O'Brien, who typically weighed in at 165 pounds, possessed a strong left jab and solid right. Skilled at defense and countering attacks, he often fought light heavyweights and heavyweights (*Library of Congress, LC-DIG-ggbain-09701*).

alized the city of Philadelphia might not have enough of the *right* competition for him to make ends meet.[4] Moving on to New York City, a hotbed for the fight game was one option, but it too had issues. As the *Evening World,* a popular New York daily, noted under the headline "Colored Fighters Should Be Barred": "While Johnson is the legitimate Colored

Tom Kennedy (left), matchmaker, "White hope" boxer, and actor, poses with pugilist Joe Jeannette. Like McVey, Jeannette headed to France to capitalize on the lucrative purses offered there (*Library of Congress, LC-DIG-ggbain-10000*).

champion, no one wants to see him or any other Colored fighter in action. Colored fighters frequently are tricky persons, and when once two of them meet they usually frame up a bout before they enter the ring, and as a result the contest is an unsatisfactory one. In some of the clubs, the matchmakers will not let Colored pugilists box, which is a wise thing. If other matchmakers would follow suit it would be a good thing for the sport."[5]

The same periodical called Jeannette "another Colored 'pug' of little importance."[6] Yet his name in the press was never far from Jack Johnson. Also emerging, with over 50 recorded battles, was Sam Langford, the versatile fighter battling out of Boston.

The following year (1907) differed from its predecessor, as Jeannette fought less, but did not lose a single contest. Meeting a seasoned "Young" Peter Jackson, Sam McVey, and Morris Harris, each for the first time, widened his scope a bit. Despite meeting Jackson in Philly, or the six-round land of no-decisions, Jeannette still believed New York City was the place to be.

The *Evening Star* noted in the fall of 1907: "Joe Jeannette, the Colored fighter, is anxious to butt into the game on this [West] coast, and hurls a challenge at any of the big fellows now making this section their headquarters. Jeannette feels that he is entitled to recognition by Tommy Burns, Jack Johnson, [Mike] Schreck or any other prominent heavyweights. Jeannette is the only fighter who has been able to make Sam Langford quit, and during his three years in the ring has met some of the best fighters of the east, including Jack Johnson."[7]

Much of the same action followed Jeannette in 1908, and frankly speaking, he was getting bored with pool fighters.[8] The few White pugilists who would not draw the color line, like Jim Jeffords and John "Sandy" Ferguson, weren't challenging him. By May, newspaper articles convinced Jeannette that the Paris fight scene had the coin. If fighters like Willie Lewis were drawing a $10,000 house in France, then certainly he could. Or so he believed—granted Jeannette was picking up some extra cash by sparring with fighters like Billy Papke, but certainly France had a similar pool of contenders. Also, "In France," as Frederick Douglass once quipped, "the Negro was a man."[9] On December 31, 1908, Joe Jeannette and his White wife, Adelaide Atzinger, sailed for Paris. Having lined up six fights, for far more money than he would ever receive in America, he was convinced it was the correct career move.[10]

Jeannette, in his first fight in Paris on January 23, 1909, knocked out Ben Taylor, the English heavyweight, in the third round of a scheduled 20-round contest. Floored five times, Taylor finally caught a right to the jaw that sent him to dreamland. Following a victory over tomato can Charley Croxon, Jeannette was scheduled for two battles with Sam McVey.

Sam McVey v. Joe Jeannette—World Colored Heavyweight Championship

Outweighed by 16 pounds and dropped twice by his opponent, Joe Jeannette lost his February 20, 1909, skirmish against Sam McVey, "The Idol of Paris," via a 20-round decision. This fight, it was believed, was for the World Colored Heavyweight Championship relinquished by Jack Johnson—the "Galveston Giant" would later deny the action. While McVey didn't have the cleverness of his opponent, he had the power—Jeannette was clinching for his life in the 18th round. Newspaper accounts claimed the decision, which was reversed, actually belonged to Jeannette. To clear the air, a Paris rematch was scheduled for April 17, 1909.

Joe Jeannette v. Sam McVey—World Colored Heavyweight Championship

The Jeannette v. McVey rematch was one of the finest fights on French soil since the Battle of Castillon. However, the wire article, picked up by numerous sources, was likely

Joe Jeannette began fighting out of Philadelphia only a few months before this photograph was taken in 1905. This was a typical day along Chestnut Street (*Library of Congress, LC-DIG-det-4a12905*).

the worst account ever given to a professional fight. Clearly, the encounter was worthy of far greater accolades. Perhaps this subheadline sums it up best: *McVey's Seconds Throw Up Sponge to Avoid Knockout, Lasted Three and Half Hours, Californian Has Advantage Up to Fortieth—Nearly Put His Opponent Out in 21st and 22nd Rounds—Great Crowd Attends*[11]; and *Takes Joe Jeannette This Long to Make Sam McVey Throw Up Sponge.*[12] With the victory, Jeannette took possession of the World Colored Heavyweight Championship.

George Weedon, Young Corbett's former manager, upon his return from Europe, remarked about the affair. It appeared in the *Ogden Standard*: "Joe Jennette is one of the gamest fighters I ever saw in the ring. I never saw a man take more punishment and stand up under it than Jeannette took that night. McVey knocked him down and practically out no less than 45 times during the battle. Several times after one of those knockdowns I thought it would be utterly impossible for Jeannette to get up, but somehow he would manage to get on his feet before he was counted out."[13]

Naturally, Jeannette called out Jack Johnson (now Heavyweight Champion of the World), Sam Langford, and Al Kaufman. Confident he could whip them all, he had never looked better, and unfortunately, his targets knew it. Instead, Jeannette would finish his European trip with a first-round knockout of Jack Scales, a 20-round decision over White commoner John "Sandy" Ferguson, a second-round victory over Trooper Cooke, a fourth-round victory over Harry Shearing, and a couple of exhibitions.

On June 4, fresh off the *Lusitania*, Joe Jeannette was back in America. He split a pair of battles with the familiar face of John "Sandy" Ferguson, before drawing Al Kubiak.[14] But most newspaper accounts of the fight scene in Paris made him lonesome for the city. However, there were exceptions. The *Detroit Times* described the scene in this tasteless and racist view that began with McVey, followed by Jeannette:

> A first water dub on this side, he [Sam McVey] was a veritable king in the French capital, where the nobility lionized him to an extent that his head swelled like a waterlogged hardtack. Imagine a great, big, overgrown chunk of Black humanity, of the type that sometimes gives credence to Darwin's theory that we are creatures of evolution, with a small cone-like bean, powerful torso and ape-like arms, possessed with little intelligence and as ignorant as a freshly landed Slav immigrant, wined and dined by the so-called representatives of a nation's leisure class. Imagine pretty women, bearing names that trace back through generations of gentle blood, fussing over the big brute. That's what they did in La Belle France. McVey was a fad. He was admitted to the privacy of the boudoir and den without muzzle and chain, and lucky the count or countess who secured him for the nonce. Distinguished was the party he honored with his presence on the boulevards. Phew![15]

The article shifted to Jeannette, who was likely as appalled as McVey for being included in such a diatribe:

> But it's different now. Paris won't stand for a loser, and the popular song is "Le Roi est Mort! Vive le Roi," [The king is dead! Long live the king] which is apropos in this case. McVey is down and out and Joe Jeannette has stepped into his place. Not much difference, you say. On the face of it, no. Jeannette is of the same complexion as McVey, but he is a different breed. In the first place, Jeannette has something in his head beside bone. He has some education, quiet, unobtrusive and well behaved. You won't see him riding about Paris in an open carriage dressed in silk evening clothes and buried in flowers, as did the man he knocked out. He won't permit the Parisians to make a jackass of him as it did out of McVey. Jeannette is a fighter, not a monkey, and if his skin is Black, his head is full of common sense.[16]

This was just one example of the media cruelty and bigotry these fighters faced. And it originated in their home country. Jeannette looked back across the pond, and once again he packed his trunk.

Joe Jeannette v. Sam McVey—World Colored Heavyweight Championship

In the fall, it was back to Paris where Jeannette knocked out Al Kubiak in the tenth round in October, took a 15-round decision over Sid Russell in November, and drew Sam McVey over 30 rounds in December.[17] For the latter bout, the winner was offered $3,500 ($96,812 in 2019 dollars) and the loser $2,000.[18] In 1909, the average American worker made between $200 ($5,532 in 2019 dollars) and $400 annually. In other words, Jeannette was making a comfortable living.

Sam Langford v. Joe Jeannette—World Colored Heavyweight Championship

Johnson's victory over Jeffries was a clear indication that the color line was in a state of flux. Jeannette, like others, ignored the champion's position on Black opponents and considered it only temporary. Logging all his fights inside the United States, Jeannette opted for a few minor bouts before agreeing to meet Sam Langford in Boston on September 6, 1910. Following 15 grueling rounds, at the Armory Athletic Club, Langford took the uncontested decision—he would later claim the World Colored Heavyweight Championship, although there was no mention of the title prior to the engagement. The *Norwich Bulletin* noted the Boston fighter's dominance: "In only two rounds did Jeannette have an advantage. [sic] In the third round he had possibly a shade of advantage and in the ninth Jeannette landed repeatedly, but Langford came back stronger than ever in the tenth. In strength and skill Langford was Jeannette's superior and left the ring with scarcely a mark, while Jeannette's face was badly cut."[19]

Jeannette's weight advantage of 13 pounds proved useless as he often broke ground to avoid a beating. Langford was relentless with his crippling body punches. Following the tenth round, a session in which Jeannette was sorely beaten, he essentially was just trying to make the distance. The *Evening Star* reported the last minutes: "The final mix was a corker. Langford got both hands in play, and his gloves beat a steady tattoo on Jeannette's head and mid-section. From face to body they moved in lightning style, while the beaten man was doing his best to save himself from punishment. A second before the bell rang Langford smashed Jeannette once more on the jaw and the big fellow slowly tottered. But the bell clanged, his seconds jumped into the ring, and what looked to be a possible knockout was averted."[20]

Following the Langford battle, Jeannette essentially disposed of a few pool fighters while his manager, Dan McKetrick, tried valiantly—including a $20,000 offer to do battle in Paris—to make a match with Jack Johnson. True to form, Johnson met every offer with a higher, untenable counter-proposal—the champion had no intention of meeting a Black competitor.

Opening up a new year (1911) with another loss to Sam Langford was something Joe Jeannette hoped to avoid. However, economics and opportunity prevailed. Just going the distance with the "Boston Tar Baby," especially at this stage of his career, was an accomplishment. Granted, the 12-rounder on January 10 was one-sided—Langford had a decisive lead in every round but one. Yet it was against one of the most imposing figures in professional boxing and in his hometown. He would meet Langford again on September 5, as the pair fought to a 10-round no-decision in Jeannette's first appearance in Madison Square Garden.[21] During what proved to be an active and successful year, Jeannette even managed to sneak in a leisurely trip to Paris—he left in late March—and also trained "White Hope" Carl Morris.

> An article that appeared in the *Evening Times* in February 1911, summed up the current heavyweight picture: "When all is said, the Colored heavies present a big front, and if they were to form a union for the purpose of preserving the championship of the Negro race, the bravest of our 'hopes' would admit that the task of recapturing the title is not quite so easy as it might at first appear."[22]

As Jeannette fought, McKetrick continued his tireless pace of offers and side-bets to Jack Johnson. The seemingly endless proposals to the champion were routinely published in the newspapers. But not even an open letter to Johnson would draw him out. Often, when it looked like Johnson was on the hook, something would foil the effort. For the record, McKetrick's cut would be one-third.

Joe Jeannette opened 1912, in Utica, New York, dropping Griff Jones six times on the way to a third-round knockout. It was a good omen. In a prolific year that found the fighter participating in over 20 bouts, he would not "officially" lose a single contest.[23] Often his antagonist was a pool fighter—battlers like Morris Harris, "Black Bill" (Claude Brooks), "Battling" Jim Johnson and Jeff Clark—and while they were familiar to Jeannette, they kept him sharp.

In Newark, New Jersey, on August 20, Joe Jeannette, who had fought the previous evening across the river in New York, met two Black opponents separately, Bill Tate and Battling Brooks.[24] He sent each to dreamland in the second round. If that didn't send a clear message that he was on his game, nothing would. For the most part, Jeannette felt comfortable battling at around 200 pounds. As a heavyweight contender and prolific fighter, he was under constant scrutiny, especially by White critics. In a piece penned by former heavyweight champion James J. Corbett, Jeannette's demise and that of the Negro pugilist were once again predicted. The article was printed in the *El Paso Herald*: "Jeannette has not faced a first class fighter since his bout with Sam Langford last year. Not that it is his fault. No one in his class has shown a desire to mingle with him in the ring. Even the doughty Langford was accused of running out of a 20 round match scheduled for California last fall. The majority of Joe's matches during the past 12 months were more in the nature of workouts than anything else, but when he ran across Jeff Clark it was another story. Clark, a man 25 pounds lighter and of little reputation, made matters more than interesting for the ambitious Jeannette."[25]

Since his victory over Jim Jeffries, back on July 4, 1910, Jack Johnson had fought only Jim Flynn—a battle that took place exactly two years later. All of his other activities appeared to ride on his title as Heavyweight Champion of the World, a designation he was no rush to defend. The talented sportswriter T.S. Andrews noted in an article in the *El Paso Herald*:

> Now that the big boxing promoters of the country have decided to get together and bring forth a real White heavyweight champion, the interest among the big fellows becomes more noticeable. With Jack Johnson practically barred in all the big centers of the country there is no chance for a battle between the Negro champion and a White man, therefore, Johnson will have to be considered eliminated. It will be the same with all the Negro fighters. It may not be fair to Sam Langford and Sam McVey or Joe Jeannette, but the fact remains that the followers of boxing in this country, as well as the public generally, are about through with big matches between Whites and Blacks and in the future it will be Whites in their own sphere and Blacks by themselves.[26]

As unrealistic as the article sounded, it was a clear indication of the frustration many fight fans were experiencing: As there were no White fighters talented enough to defeat Jack Johnson, and the champion drew the color line against the only three boxers who had the slightest chance of beating him, the sport was at an impasse.

By January 1, 1913, there was a World White Heavyweight Champion, a World Colored Heavyweight Champion, and Jack Johnson, the Heavyweight Champion of the World. In boxing, the public demands that its champions face all contenders or forever have their reign footnoted. Was Jack Johnson *perceived* as heavyweight champion after his battle with Tommy Burns or following his fight against James J. Jeffries? Or was he even a champion if he refused to meet Sam Langford and Sam McVey or Joe Jeannette? Perception and its interpretation were often a function of power and not truth.[27]

During the year, Joe Jeannette once again tackled pool fighters "Battling" Jim Johnson, Jeff Clark, and Black Bill. It was redundant, but it was also reality as the New York Boxing Commission ban on mixed bouts was still in place. He also tackled "White Hope (less)" Al Benedict (in Missouri), Harry Wills (in New Orleans), and John Lester Johnson (in New York), to name a few. He finished the year in style with a pair of battles against Sam Langford.

In what was reported as the ninth time the pair had met, Sam Langford faced Joe Jeannette, over 10 rounds, on October 3 at Madison Square Garden. As a reminder: Jeannette had captured the first, Langford the next three, with the remainder all draws. Although Langford, who tipped at 199½, was favored, Joe Jeannette, who weighed 195 pounds, performed strongly enough to make it a draw.

As the *Rock Island Argus* reported: "Jeannette was in superb condition while his opponent did not appear as well trained. Langford's weight began to tell upon him in the latter part of the contest. Jeannette outboxed his man in the first three rounds, using a left jab to the face to good advantage. The men fought hard at close range at times and both suffered severe body punishment."[28]

In seven out of 10 rounds, Langford, who appeared out of shape, was outpointed. His performance was so out of character that many in the audience perceived him to be stalling. The fight, which attracted 10,000 spectators, had no knockdowns. The contest entered the record books as a 10-round no-decision.[29] Nine days later, Jeannette, along with McKetrick and a handful of other fighters, sailed for Europe.

Sam Langford v. Joe Jeannette—World Colored Heavyweight Championship

This fight, in accordance with the Parisian Boxing Association, saw Joe Jeannette face Sam Langford, on December 20, 1913, in Paris, France, to determine "who is entitled to the Colored Heavyweight Championship honors."[30] Luna Park Amphitheatre was crawling with members of Parisian society, including many women adorned in the finest evening attire. In contrast to his previous effort, Sam Langford took command of the 20-round fight and gained the points decision. In the 13th round, Jeannette, clearly scrambling to survive, hit the canvas three times for a count of nine. After the battle, French authorities, having stripped Jack Johnson of his title, tried to hand it to Langford. However the pugilist wouldn't accept it.[31] He wanted to fight Johnson, plain and simple.

As 1914 began, Jeannette, his White wife, and two children were still in Paris. On February 21, at the Wonderland, his first engagement of the year proved rather memorable: In the seventh round, his opponent, Langford (Alfred, not Sam), fell to the canvas during an attempted fight-ending blow. He remained there, motionless, and was counted out. Unsure of what had just transpired, the referee disqualified Langford.[32]

On March 21, Jeannette met his friend Georges Carpentier, the heavyweight champion of Europe, over 15 rounds at Luna Park. The French idol, far less experienced than his opponent, also conceded 20 pounds. Taking command of the fight, Jeannette moved quickly during a contest marked by continuous in-fighting. Exhibiting greater athletic prowess, Jeannette was given the decision. Following three more battles and three more victories, Jeannette sailed for America in May.

Upon his return home, Joe Jeannette fought a no-decision over 10 rounds against a dominant Harry Wills, engaged "Battling" Jim Johnson three times to a no decision and once to a draw, took a victory over Black Bill, and tangled with "Big" Bill Tate twice. He also picked up a couple of other easy wins. And, on October 1, he once again entered a ring against Sam Langford. Under mixed reviews, the pair fought to a 10-round, New York no-decision. To Jeannette, his list of opponents invited boredom and a sense of déjà vu.

A pair of New York battles, against pool fighters, began 1915 for Joe Jeannette. But by the end of February, and honestly a bit fatigued, he chose to head north to Montreal, Quebec, Canada. There he fought tomato can Larry Williams to a no-decision before grabbing victories over Black boxer Cleve Hawkins and former White Hope Arthur Pelkey, both seasoned veterans.

Joe Jeannette v. Sam Langford—World Colored Heavyweight Championship

When Jack Johnson lost the World Heavyweight Championship to Jess Willard on April 5, 1915, nobody was certain just how the fight game would play out. Feeling rather good about his chances to be in the mix, Jeannette headed south to Boston, where he was slated to meet Sam Langford on April 13. Just as a reminder, Joe Jeannette hadn't officially lost a fight since December 20, 1913. Despite the superfluity of Langford engagements—the "Boston Tar Baby" was the last fighter to defeat him—Jeannette took the 12-round verdict and Langford's Colored title.

As anticipated, Langford took the first four rounds of the contest, firing solid left hooks and short rights to his opponent's head. Meanwhile, Jeannette remained patient, working the jab while doing his best to tire his antagonist. In the fifth round, Langford's gloves dropped and he became a target for a solid right hand. Jeannette began striking at will and not only jarred Langford's equilibrium, but also closed his left eye. The decision went to Jeannette.[33]

Following a fourth-round knockout victory in New York over Jack Brooks, Jeannette returned to Boston to draw Sam McVey over 12 rounds. Now in the hands of veteran manager Billy Gibson, the fighter was optimistic about his future. Yet it was Gibson—naturally he had his own agenda—who persuaded Jeannette to assist him with his stable of fighters, including Irish boxer Jim Coffey. Three fights later, Joe Jeannette was thinking about retirement. The *Sun* printed this announcement on September 3, 1915: "[Jess] Willard has drawn the color line. In this he uses excellent judgment, and his decision will benefit the game. Willard can make himself popular by ignoring second raters and meeting only real contenders. I have boxed with them all, and Jim Coffey and Battling Levinsky are the only ones with class or promise…. With no one to box my fighting days are over, so I intend to devote all my time to business."[34]

Sam Langford v. Joe Jeannette—World Colored Heavyweight Championship

Was there hesitation in Jeannette's retirement claim? Of course, by February 1916, Joe Jeannette was talking comeback. Knocking out pugs Silas Green in Montreal, on February 26, and George "Kid" Cotton on March 24 in New York, it was time to head to Syracuse for a bout with his old nemesis, Sam Langford, on May 12 at the Ryan Athletic Club. Owners Tommy Ryan and Charlie Huck were just thrilled to host the event, even if it did end in controversy. Joe Jeannette, floored in the seventh round and being counted over by Referee Tom Cawley, was declared out even though he reached his feet. It seemed that everyone, even Langford, thought Jeannette had beat the count.[35]

From Syracuse Jeannette headed a short distance west to Rochester, where he fought Dan "Porky" Flynn to a 10-round no-decision. Four consecutive knockouts would close out the year for a semi-retired Jeannette. Part of the reason for Jeannette's return was his feeling that Willard was vulnerable to defeat. At the hands of a boxer like Georges Carpentier, and at a short distance, Willard could be made to look foolish. If a fighter like Carpentier took the title, he might opt to take on all comers. Just the thought of missing an opportunity to cross the color line for a championship shot would be devastating. Nevertheless, he also knew his skills were diminishing. Jeannette fought only five times in 1917, all five to a no-decision result. One of those battles was a 12-round newspaper loss against Sam Langford, and it was the final time Jeannette would work that distance and the last time he would meet his nemesis. Unfortunately, he also injured his right hand during the fracas.

Battling multiple times in 1918 and in 1919, and even once in 1922, Jeannette's ring contests were shorter (10 rounds or less), less decisive (nearly all no-decision results), and garnered little press. In November 1918, his name once again hit sports section across the country when Jack Dempsey refused to engage with the fighter at a United War Work Fund boxing carnival held in Madison Square Garden. Joe Bonds was scheduled to battle with Dempsey, but reported sick. Jeannette, who appeared on the program to meet Kid Norfolk, stepped up as a possible replacement. According to the Norwich Bulletin: "In one of the most dramatic scenes enacted in the history of the prize ring in this city, Jack Dempsey, conqueror of Fred Fulton and generally considered the foremost heavyweight in the world, with the exception of Jess Willard, took refuge behind the 'color line' in Madison Square Garden Saturday night, when Joe Jeannette, the veteran Negro heavyweight of West Hoboken, challenged him to fight before upward of 8,000 persons who filled the historic amphitheatre."[36]

Dempsey's manager, Jack Kearns, announced that his fighter would box any White man in the world, but would not meet a Negro. As pandemonium ensued, a stoic Joe Jeannette stood against the ropes, looking scornfully at his White rival. All this to the howls of "Stay there, Joe!" Living in a dream with no opening bell was never fun.

In retirement, Joe Jeannette was one of the few Black fighters who could live comfortably. He became a respected referee in New Jersey. However, most knew him as a proprietor of a boxing gymnasium (1924–1949) on 27th Street and Summit Avenue in West Hoboken

(Union City), New Jersey.[37] Jeannette eventually converted the gym into a garage and operated a fleet of Cadillac limousines. In 1923, he became the first African American referee and judge licensed by New York State. He died on July 2, 1958.[38]

The Color Line, 1909–1915[39]

In 1915, or halfway through the second decade of the 20th century, the *El Paso Herald* published some thoughts regarding the color line: "In other days the good old 'color line' was the barrier raised by the White boxers themselves, especially when some dangerous looking Black competitor loomed up against the horizon of the White man's chances, but they had no regular legislation anywhere on the subject. The 'color line' was a pretty hazy proposition, yet it sometimes served. It found few sympathizers among real sportsmen, but it served."[40]

The article continued: "Today, the blond biffers are protected by law, so to speak, here and elsewhere. Even if there were no definite rule in the premises, it is doubtful if any White walloper would have to dodge behind the 'color line.' There is no great demand now for meeting of any White man with a Black, and there has been no such demand for some time past."[41]

And, as for a champion's evaluation, the article noted:

In other times the clamor of the so called sporting public to see some White champion defend his title against some Black boxer who was showing exceptional class, usually developed the "color line"—or a fight—but not since John Arthur Johnson has clamor of that nature been clamming to any alarming extent. With the rise of Johnson came the decline of the Black fighter generally. In the Galveston dock walloper the Negro race produced a good fighter, but the author of the downfall of his kind.[42]

TEN

Boston Tar Baby

A brawny, compact and versatile gladiator, Samuel Edgar Langford stood a rock-hard five feet seven inches. With muscular development so extraordinary that he seemed to draw additional power at will, the pugilist was a dangerous package every time he entered a boxing ring. Langford's shoulders were so broad that they looked like he could support a doorframe and possibly a person standing in it. But his opponents had no time to admire his physique, or to doddle within range, as his 74-inch reach could be recalled at an instant. Fighting at multiple weight classes, Langford tangled from lightweight to heavyweight with unmatched skill and confidence. As a gifted teenager he climbed between the ropes to tackle Joe Gans, the legendary "Old Master." Intimidated by no man, Sam Langford was likely the greatest pound-for-pound fighter of his era.

Born in the hamlet of Weymouth Falls, Nova Scotia, on March 4, 1886, young Samuel inherited his father's fine genetics—Robert Langford stood over six feet on a muscular form.[1] His family, Samuel's great-grandfather to be specific, like many of the Black slaves still loyal to the British crown, fled their masters during the American Revolution—political asylum was found on the picturesque peninsula on the southeastern coast of Canada. Nearly the entire small community of Weymouth Falls was African-Canadian and dependent upon the lumber industry.

Following the death of his mother, Sam found life at home a bit challenging and decided to run away.[2] Still a teenager, he headed southwest to America. Eventually he landed in Boston, a city with a population exceeding 400,000, an environment conducive to his needs; the Canadian seemed to feed off the energy and opportunity. It was inside a small boxing club, operated by Joe Woodman, that Langford found solace. With the youngster, Woodman discovered a hard-working adolescent willing to do what it takes, be it mopping floors or even sparring, just to stay around the fight game. Langford was hooked and soon asked his boss and mentor if he could grab a spot on one of the club's fight cards. Since he was still raw, Woodman wisely steered Langford toward the amateur ranks. There he could develop and refine his skills. Success came quickly to the maturing teen, and it wasn't long before he considered turning professional. Seeing the promise of his protégé, Woodman became his full-time manager.

In his pro debut on April 11, 1902, Langford knocked out Jack McVicker, a local fighter he had met as an amateur. The following year his fight frequency increased, as did the caliber of his opponents.[3] Langford defeated Bob "Stonewall" Allen twice, then fought a quartet of battles with Andy Watson—both Black fighters and scrappy ring veterans. Langford also tackled Walter Burgo, Danny Duane, and Patsy Sweeney, all competitive White ring doyens. However, his final two fights of the year were far different: both were against pugilists of extraordinary skills.

A punishing Canadian boxer, Sam Langford was known as the "The Boston Terror," "The Boston Bonecrusher," and, infamously, "The Tar Baby." He was clearly deserving of the heavyweight championship of the world but denied the opportunity to win it (*Library of Congress, LC-DIG-ggbain-12254*).

On December 8, 1903, Langford grabbed a 15-round decision over lightweight champion Joe Gans, who also happened to be the first Black American to win a world championship. Although over the 135-pound lightweight limit, the youngster fought well and impressed many at the Criterion A.C. in Boston—he even picked up the support of the legendary fighter. As the *Evening Star* noted: "Langford assumed the aggressive and simply jabbed his opponent all over the ring, landing on the face, but occasionally he whipped his right hard to the face. Gans was worried, and what blows he did send home lacked steam. Several times he sent in hard body punches and a few rights to the face, but he was outclassed."[4]

With a knockout victory over Jack McVicker, Sam Langford began his professional boxing career in 1902 at the young age of nineteen. Pictured here is Bromfield Street in Boston, the city hosting that fight, at the turn of the century (*Library of Congress, LC-DIG-det-4a22598*).

Jack Blackburn was quick, and possessed both an outstanding jab and a powerful left hook. Although he weighed only 135 pounds, he often fought much larger men, including Sam Langford (*Library of Congress, LC-DIG-ggbain-15440*).

Thrilled by his performance, but having difficulty making weight, Langford stepped up to the welterweight division. On December 23, he faced Jack Blackburn, a clever young Philadelphia fighter with enormous potential. Both Black boxers put on a productive 12-round display, Blackburn in supreme command. The *Washington Times* noted: "Had the pair not made an agreement for a draw in case both were on their feet at the close of the bout, the Philadelphia boxer would have received the decision. Blackburn pummeled his opponent severely, and at the end of the tenth Langford was all in. He managed to last out the two last rounds by stalling."[5]

Like Langford, the Philly fighter was aggressively working his way through regional competition. Creating an impression with his targeted left jab and powerful left hook, Blackburn too had been in the ring with the great Gans.

Langford entered the ring over a dozen times in 1904. The highlight of the year came on September 5. At Lake Massabesic Coliseum in Manchester, New Hampshire, Langford drew Joe Walcott over 15 rounds. For a novice like Langford to be in a ring with the legendary welterweight was the thrill of a lifetime. According to the *Waterbury Evening Democrat*: "The referee, Owen Kinney, decided the bout a draw because Walcott carried the fight up to Langford in nearly every round.... Walcott played for the body.... Langford paid most attention to Walcott's head ... in the third round Langford caught Walcott, and tried hard to put his man out [he dropped him to a knee], but Walcott was too much for him. The crowd was not satisfied with the decision, and shouted for Langford."[6]

A year later, Langford met "Young" Peter Jackson, the experienced Black welterweight, in a trio of battles; taking the first two local contests, he drew Jackson in the third bout that was held in Baltimore (Jackson's hometown). Finishing the year on December 25, 1905, at the Unity Cycle Club in Lawrence, Langford met Joe Jeannette for the first time. Although Jeannette, who was 20 pounds heavier, had less experience, he frustrated the Boston boxer to no end. When a precision New England uppercut sent his antagonist to the canvas, Langford believed he had finally brought the bout under control. He was mistaken. Enduring far more than anticipated, Langford was forced to surrender in the eighth round.[7] It was only his second loss of the year.[8]

Avenging his loss to Jeannette with a 15-round points victory on April 5, 1906, was the infusion of confidence Langford needed. The fighter used the local victory as preparation for his next fray, against the daunting figure of Jack Johnson on April 26. Both bouts were held at the Lincoln Athletic Club in Chelsea, Massachusetts, a mere four miles, as the crow flies, from the center of Boston.

Johnson, the World Colored Heavyweight Champion, was rattling the cage of James J. Jeffries, the recognized White titleholder. At 156 pounds, or 29 pounds lighter than his opponent, Langford was simply dominated by his antagonist. His lack of experience against heavyweights was clear as he was trimmed like a Christmas tree. Dropped multiple times by Johnson, the Hub fighter was simply outclassed and lost the 15-round decision. Langford finished the year with a record of 6–2; every adversary he faced was Black.

Although Langford began 1907 with a draw against Joe Jeannette, he picked up eight consecutive victories to add to his total along with his first designation.[9] By knocking out southpaw James "Tiger" Smith in the fourth round of a scheduled 20-round encounter, Langford picked up the Commonwealth (British Empire) Middleweight Title. The fight was held on April 22, 1907, at the National Sporting Club in Covent Garden, London. Fighting magnificently at 155 pounds, every element of his game was improving.[10]

The following year (1908), Langford fought over 10 times, including White fighters

Jim Barry, John "Sandy" Ferguson, and "Fireman" Jim Flynn, along with Black fighters "Black Fitzsimmons" (Ulysses Cannon), Joe Jeannette, and Larry Temple.[11] He did not lose a single battle. The only crusade that eluded him was entering a ring with the new Heavyweight Champion of the World, Jack Johnson. As Johnson had shadowed Burns, Langford would now pursue Johnson—openly challenging him at every opportunity. From sipping a cocktail at a local watering hole to having his shoes shined, the champion was relentlessly stalked by Langford. Yet he never forced the issue, which begs the question: Why not?

Perhaps Langford never forgot the "terrible beating," as the *New York Police Gazette* called it, that he was given by Johnson. Never. The betting on the fight told the story: it wasn't whether Langford would be defeated, only when? After the bout he was taken to the hospital. When he saw his face in the mirror, he just couldn't believe it; he had never seen his countenance so badly beaten, his left eye swollen shut. In defense of his performance, he found consolation in the fact that he wasn't knocked out.

As boxing opportunities in the Northeast dwindled—for any number of reasons including police intervention—the fighter's manager, Joe Woodman, started looking elsewhere. Boxing wasn't confined to the shores of America—Langford had already boxed in London (1907). The year 1908 was also memorable for Langford, as he and his wife Martha welcomed their only child, Charlotte.

Taking about a dozen campaigns in 1909, Sam Langford did not lose a single contest. He skillfully battled pool fighters Morris Harris, Klondike, and Dixie Kid, along with White fighters Jim Barry, Al Kubiak, John "Sandy" Ferguson, William Ian Hague, and Mike Schreck—to name most.[12] His fourth-round knockout over "Iron" William Ian Hague on May 24 garnered him the National Sporting Club British Heavyweight Title, not to mention a $9,000 guaranteed purse.[13]

Langford was refining his skills and learning to instinctively counter an assault. He adopted a commonly taught strategy: Box a fighter and fight a boxer. And don't let your antagonist take control of the battle. His old method of chase and punch was traded in for stand and let your opponent come to you. If he decides not to, chase him out of the ring.

In the Championship Mix

Following the Hague fight, Langford, in a new twist, took to the stage in London, pulling down the pounds for his assessment of the current condition of the sport.[14] Naturally, a short speech calling out Johnson was befitting of the contemporary English heavyweight champion. The *Los Angeles Herald* noted Langford's West Coast stage appeal: "Langford is an excellent drawing card anywhere he is staged, and this is especially true as regards Los Angeles. The hefty Negro mauler has made himself popular with local fans by his unassuming and quiet manner and by his championship work in the ring. He outranks all other Negro fighters because of these facts."[15]

It wasn't until the end of January 1910 that many realized just how intense the relationship between Sam Langford and Jack Johnson had gotten. Following Langford's fight against Mike Schreck, at Old City Hall in Pittsburgh back on November 23, 1909, the Boston fighter ventured to a Negro club to catch up with an old friend. That acquaintance just happened to be Bob Armstrong, who was in town that evening as part of Jack Johnson's theater show. The *Morning Examiner* described the scene:

They were talking when Johnson came in and without speaking to Langford began to slur Armstrong about his company, until Langford became angry and opened up on Johnson, threatening to whip him then and there. There was a crowd of Langford sympathizers in the club, and both Johnson and George Little, his manager, are said to have made moves toward their pockets. Adam Mann, a giant Negro County detective, grappled with Johnson and took something away from Johnson, saying loud enough for all to hear: "It's good that gun is empty or I'd run you in." After this there was some difficulty in keeping Langford away from Johnson until the champion left the club with Little. Mann declines to admit or deny that the object he and some others took from Johnson was a revolver.[16]

Authorities didn't learn of the episode until after all parties left town. Since no harm had been done, there was no reason to pursue the matter any farther.

A pair of California battles against "Fireman" Jim Flynn highlighted 1910. On February 8, Flynn entered Naud Junction Pavilion in Los Angeles and held Sam Langford to a 10-round no-decision that resembled a wrestling contest. With Referee Charles Eyton doing his very best to sunder the gladiators, Flynn took command and managed to pick up the newspaper verdict.[17] Working from a crouch, "Fireman" wisely clinched when he felt the momentum shifting; his primary target after the third round was Langford's bleeding right eye. The pair moved over to Vernon, California, and Jeffries Arena on March 17. The *Evening Times* described the action:

A fight that was supposed to go 45 rounds, came to a sudden and unexpected conclusion in the last half of the eighth when Sam Langford, Boston's colored fighter did away with Jim Flynn, the Pueblo fireman. Flynn missed a right swing at Langford's jaw and lost his balance, and a left handed uppercut delivered by the Negro merely accelerated Flynn's fall, and he fell prone on the mat, with his arms extended, dislocating his jaw. Consequently the knockout is not considered as a clean one. Before Flynn's seconds were able to realize what happened, Referee Charles Eyton had counted the fireman out, and the badly punished fighter staggered to his feet, making feeble efforts to do away with his opponent, who by this time was imaginary.[18]

Finishing his West Coast swing that added five bouts to his resume, Langford headed back to Philadelphia. He met middleweight champion Stanley Ketchel on April 27, at the National Athletic Club. In one of those encounters where the hype was more stimulating than the battle, the headlines in the *Daily Arizona Silver Belt* said it all: "Langford Off Six Rounds; Colored Man Has Slightest Shade of Best of Battle Last Night; Not a Scratch on Either of Boxers; Ketchel Rushed the Fighting, But Was Clearly Outgeneraled."[19]

Many sources believed the six-round no-decision was a draw, including the newspaper above. There were no knockdowns. Langford fought five more times before the end of the year, a majority of the bouts against pool fighters. However, there was an exception: he met Joe Jeannette on September 6 in Boston.

Sam Langford v. Joe Jeannette—World Colored Heavyweight Championship

When Jack Johnson drew the color line against Sam Langford, the action was contrary to that of a true champion. Even if it was not inconsistent with his predecessors, most of his Colored peers viewed the heavyweight champion's behavior as an insult. Immediately, Sam Langford claimed the vacant World Colored Heavyweight Championship.[20] Few noticed, as that was not the heavyweight title most were interested in.[21] Naturally, Joe Jeannette challenged that claim with hopes of capturing the real prize: being matched against Jack Johnson. The *Norwich Bulletin* reported: "After 15 rounds of grueling fighting, Sam Langford of this city [Boston] defeated Joe Jeannette of New York, both Colored, before the Armory Athletic club tonight [September 6, 1910]. The decision of the referee was concurred by all as the Boston man maintained an advantage throughout."[22]

Team Langford had intended to sail to London in the beginning of January 1911, but the Armory Athletic Club of Boston persuaded them to postpone their trip by signing them to another battle against Joe Jeannette—this time over 12 rounds. Once again, the reward, or so it was believed, was a match with Jack Johnson. Langford, a two-to-one favorite in the January 10 contest, was one of many shocked at the lack of press interest. In Round One, Jeannette drew first blood. It was a bad idea. Catapulting a left hook to the side of Langford's face that dropped him for a count of eight left Langford enraged—he abhorred ring embarrassment. From that point on, minus the third round, it was all "Boston Tar Baby."[23]

Sam Langford v. Sam McVey—World Colored Heavyweight Championship

Following a brief stop (Fred Atwater TKO3) in Utica, New York, Langford headed to Europe to defeat Bill Lang in London, followed by a 20-round draw with Sam McVey in Paris. The latter occurred in Hugh McIntosh's new club (Cirque de Paris) in the French capital and carried a purse of $10,000 ($264,455 in 2019 dollars). Although Langford dominated the engagement on April 1, the referee called it even.[24]

Returning to North America, Langford made stops in Syracuse (Ralph Calloway, KO4) and Winnipeg, Manitoba, Canada (Tony Caponi, ND10), before settling back in New York in the fall. Six fights, and essentially six victories later, and it was off to Sydney, Australia to meet Sam McVey.

Sam McVey v. Sam Langford—World Colored Heavyweight Championship

With Jack Johnson's life in turmoil, title claims became plentiful—many were convinced of his inexorable retirement. The *Nashville Globe* noted: "Hugh D. McIntosh, who is promoting the McVey-Langford affair [December 26, 1911], is not advertising it as an out-and-out championship battle. In his posters and circulars, McIntosh describes the bout as the 'semi-final of the world's heavyweight championship.' This may be modesty on the promoter's part or it may be that Mc is not in a hurry to kill the goose that contributes the golden eggs. Where there is a semi-final, the inference is there will be a final and Mc probably is looking forward to another big gathering of sporting men, and, of course, another big 'gate.'"[25]

Others, like W.F. Corbett, the noted Australian boxing critic, emphatically stated, "Sam McVey is the heavyweight champion of the world and that he gained his title through default on Johnson's part."[26] However, most saw this engagement as nothing more than an elimination contest for the right to challenge Jack Johnson. So when Sam McVey secured the 20-round point decision at Rushcutters Bay (Sydney) Stadium, on "Boxing Day," he became Johnson's logical opponent.[27]

Sam Langford and company would spend all of 1912 in Australia. The pugilist clashed against Chicago heavy Jim Barry twice, stablemate Dan "Porky" Flynn once, and nemesis Sam McVey four times. He did not lose a single contest. The shift from France to Australia was due to public demand. According to media sources, including the *Tacoma Times*: "Fights between Black men are dead and gone in Paris, says one sporting publication. The Negroes are out for the coin, caring nothing about their reputations. One Negro will always lie down to the other. White pugilists are welcome and the sporting public will spend money to see them in action but never again for the Blacks."[28]

Sam Langford v. Sam McVey—Heavyweight Championship of Australia

Viewed as being for the Heavyweight Championship of Australia, the 20-round fight between Sam Langford and Sam McVey took place in front of a large crowd of enthusiastic spectators—estimated at about 15,000—in Sydney on April 8, 1912. To little surprise, it went the distance in a fairly even fight until the last few rounds.[29] Although Langford took the decision and was clearly the aggressor in the final 10 rounds, he did not have the strength to knock out McVey. Some saw the contest as for the World Colored Heavyweight Championship.

The pair met again in Sydney on August 3, 1912, Langford in defense of his Australian title. Again the "Boston Tar Baby" captured the 20-round decision. The aggressor throughout the contest, Langford capitalized on his discreet close quarters game and controlled the clinches. There were no knockdowns. McVey's cleverness simply could not overcome Langford's strength and stamina.

The pair's third battle of the year was moved to Perth, West Australia, on October 9. It proved far more controversial. In the 11th round, McVey declared he had been fouled and refused to continue. Langford, who was given the ambiguous decision, denied the California fighter's claim and urged his rival to proceed. McVey stood his ground.

In related news: Jack Johnson, a day after being arrested for violating the White Slave Traffic Act, finally agreed to meet both Langford and McVey in Australia. Cynicism came in the form of smiles that painted the faces of both fighters.

Finally, on December 26, the pair met for the fourth and final time of the year. In a fierce contest, Langford knocked out McVey in the 13th round of a battle held in Sydney. McVey was floored in the fourth round and from that point on looked in full defensive mode. In proof of what goes around, comes around, the *Evening Star* noted: "Conditions have changed since Langford left here [America]. He will learn that Johnson will not be able to fight until the federal authorities have finished with him. Incidentally he will learn that practically all the White heavyweights have drawn the color line for the good of the sport. The Palzer-McCarty fight at Vernon, California, New Year's Day will be for the White Championship of the World. To the winner will go a gold belt, with the stipulation that the holder cannot fight a Negro for the world's title."[30]

World White Heavyweight Championship

On the first day of 1913, the White Heavyweight Champion of the World was crowned in Vernon, California, as Luther "Luck" McCarty disposed of Al Palzer in the 18th round.[31]

The White race had their leverage should Johnson balk at a challenge. McCarty told the *Rock Island Argus*, "I have no doubt that I can beat Jack Johnson, Sam Langford or any other fighter in the world. I know I can win from any one of them or all of them, but I shall never try—excepting on one condition, and that is when the public demands the match."[32]

McCarty's appearance and claim to the White heavyweight crown confirmed the racial separation of the title. The *Washington Times* was quick to predict that "In time the White title will be considered the real thing."[33] This was precisely what many of the Black heavyweight contenders feared would happen, and why the World Colored Heavyweight Championship had not been exploited. Bifurcation does not lend itself to unification.

While some felt "White Hope" McCarty could have defeated Jack Johnson, he would never get the chance. The fighter collapsed and died in the ring on May 24, 1913, during a battle against Arthur Pelkey in Calgary, Alberta, Canada. He was only 21 years old. Following the tragedy, Pelkey lost to Ed "Gunboat" Smith on January 1, 1914. Then Smith, in his lone title defense, lost to Georges Carpentier on July 16, 1914. The title became defunct when Jess Willard defeated Jack Johnson for the world heavyweight crown on July 5, 1915.

Financially and legally strapped, a seemingly illiterate Sam Langford, who had turned into a bit of a spendthrift, began 1913 in Australia. He traveled to America in the summer before heading back to France at the end of the year. Meanwhile, his first major decision was outside the ring: a split with Hugh McIntosh. Demanding money he claimed he was owed from the manager, Langford hoped to rectify his situation in court. In a rare decision, "Boston Tar Baby" lost and was given 14 days to amend his complaint.

Back inside the ropes, Langford knocked out Jim Barry in the first round on March 15, 1913, drew Sam McVey over 20 rounds on March 24, and drew Colin Bell over 15 rounds on June 19, in a battle for the Heavyweight Championship of Australia.

Sam Langford v. John Lester Johnson—World Colored Heavyweight Championship

Returning to America on July 18, 1913, Sam Langford was matched for five battles. He knocked out stablemate Dan "Porky" Flynn in Boston on August 26 and John Lester Johnson in New York on September 9, the latter bout in defense of the World Colored Heavyweight Championship.[34]

Adding an interesting footnote to the year: Langford lost a 12-round decision to Ed "Gunboat" Smith in a bout held at the Atlas A.A. in Boston on November 17. Surprisingly, Smith's relentless jab was superb and kept Langford at bay. There were no knockdowns during the contest. According to the *Evening World*, Smith was only the second White man to defeat Langford, Danny Duane (June 26, 1903) being the other.[35] But there has always been an invisible fragrance to ring competitions.

The *San Francisco Call* spoke for many others: "Gunboat Smith is going to have a hard time convincing the world he beat Sam Langford on the level when they tangled up in Boston on Monday evening. The press dispatches say it was the gunner's fight nearly all the way, but they do not mention any agreement that might have been reached between the tar baby and the white hope before they stepped into the ring. Sam has been noted for his many peculiar tricks in the past, especially in important battles with white men whom the public was desirous of boosting to the front. Who knows but that history repeated itself back in Boston town?"[36]

Sam Langford v. Joe Jeannette—World Colored Heavyweight Championship

Langford's subsequent defense of the title came against Joe Jeannette, in Paris on December 20; the pair last met in a 10-round no-decision on October 3.[37] Parisian society, many of whom attended the previous night's affair (Jack Johnson v. "Battling" Jim Johnson), turned out in droves to watch Langford take a 20-round points victory. Dominating the affair, the hub fighter floored Jeannette three times in the 13th round.

In a prolific fight year (1914), Sam Langford battled at least 17 times—he fought Harry Wills twice and "Battling" Jim Johnson three times. Additionally, he battled Joe Jeannette to a 10-round no-decision and even absolved himself from his loss to Ed "Gunboat" Smith with a third-round knockout victory. Both battles against Wills were believed to be for the World Colored Heavyweight Championship.[38]

Sam Langford v. Harry Wills—World Colored Heavyweight Championship

On May 1, 1914, Sam Langford battled Harry Wills over 10 rounds at the National Baseball Park in New Orleans. Fighting in his hometown, Wills, a relatively new face, stood six feet, three inches and weighed between 210 and 230 pounds. Muscular, quick and confident, Wills had boxed Joe Jeannette to a 10-round no-decision only last year and was yet to lose a contest. The first four rounds favored Wills. Nevertheless, by the sixth round the 24-year-old began to tire. It was a close bout, very close. As both participants claimed victory and the title, the newspapers called it a draw.[39]

Sam Langford v. Harry Wills—World Colored Heavyweight Championship

In their second meeting of the year, about halfway through the 14th round, Sam Langford delivered a robust left to the jaw of Harry Wills that sent the New Orleans fighter to dreamland. The fight was scheduled for 20 rounds at the Vernon Arena, on November 26, but few believed it would go the distance. As the *Ogden Standard* reported: "Langford in the two opening rounds hurt his left ankle as he fell to the mat in a vicious breakaway. Twice in each of these rounds Langford to the benefit of the count of nine. Wills' effective straight arm drives gave him an apparent even break in most of the rounds."[40]

But, Langford gradually wore down his antagonist while accumulating rounds. After a barrage of right hooks and aggressive exchanges, the final blow was delivered with precision. As the *Ogden Standard* continued: "Early in the 14th Sam caught his man with a left swing as the boxers were in mid-ring. Wills staggered back and from the way his long, lean legs bent under him and his head sagged to his chest, it could easily be seen that the New Orleans boxer was hurt. Panther-like, Sam followed Wills toward the latter's corner. Another left to the jaw and Harry began to sink like a floundering [sic] ship. His body grazed the lower rope in falling and he stretched out at full length with his kinky head against the post."[41]

Unbeknownst to either fighter would be the frequency—believed to be between 17 and 22 times—with which they would enter a boxing ring together.[42]

Not taking a fight until April 6, 1915, Sam Langford fought 10 times before the year concluded. While half of the battles were against heavyweight championship contenders—Joe Jeannette, Sam McVey (three times) and Harry Wills—the rest, with the exception of Dan "Porky" Flynn, were Black pool fighters.[43] Not only finding it difficult to get matched, Langford was having trouble finding a venue—the State Boxing Commission of Wisconsin refused his match against Sam McVey in January at Kenosha. Meanwhile, White pugilist Jess Willard defeated World Heavyweight Champion Jack Johnson, on April 15, in Havana, Cuba. For Black heavyweight contenders, Willard represented either hope and a new beginning, or another roadblock on the path to the World Heavyweight Championship.

Joe Jeannette v. Sam Langford—World Colored Heavyweight Championship

This small article in the *Bridgeport Evening Farmer* surprised some:

Last night [April 13, 1915] for the second time in 10 years Joe Jeannette of New York, secured a decision over Sam Langford, the local heavyweight. This pair of tar babies have met often and usually Sam has had the better of the argument, even the no decision encounters, but Jeannette had a wide margin over his opponent at the Atlas A.A. last night in a 12 round go.

Langford forced the fighting in the early rounds and had considerably the best of it during the first four, but his opponent outscored him during the remaining sessions. Left hooks to the jaw and short rights to Jeannette's head gave Sam a nice lead, the New Yorker contenting himself with jabbing.[44]

Waiting patiently until the fifth round, Jeannette unleashed the jab and landed hard shots to his opponent's chin. Sam's left eye closed faster than a bar on Christmas Eve.

Sam McVey v. Sam Langford—World Colored Heavyweight Championship

At the end of 12 hard-fought rounds, at the Atlas A.A. in Boston, Sam McVey was given the decision over local favorite, Sam Langford. Whether or not the title was on the line during the June 29 bout was debatable—Jeannette, at least to some, still held the crown. To little surprise, the decision was met with disapproval. Many felt it was more of a draw than a decision victory. According to the *Washington Times*: "McVey used a left hook to advantage, and had Langford's [right] optic nearly closed at the end of the bout, while his left eye was out of commission early in the battle."[45]

A large crowd, estimated at 1,200 spectators, attended the conflict.

On September 30, the pair battled to a 20-round draw in Denver, Colorado. This decision wasn't contested, and the three-line review that appeared in most newspaper was uninspiring. Which raised the question: Why did some opponents last only one or two rounds against Langford, while others seemed to go the limit? The *Rogue River Courier* had the answer: "The answer is simple. At the beginning of each bout Sam counts the house. If it's a slim house Sam knows there's no chance for a return match, whereupon he finishes the other guy as quickly as possible. If it's a big house Sam lets the other guy stay the limit so that a return match will be a good drawing card."[46]

While some might think this a criticism of Langford, it was not—the technique had been used for years as a way to verify a fighter's draw, not to mention if he was being given a proper cut of the house.

On November 23, Sam McVey, who tipped at 212, outfought Sam Langford, who weighed in at 196, over a 10-round no-decision. It was the pair's third meeting of the year, and the reviews were mixed. According to most accounts, Langford took only the fourth and sixth rounds. All the other terms belonged to McVey. This was the first ever "no tickee-no washee" bout ever held in "no decision" New York. Or in other words, Referee Charley White would determine the fighters' cuts after the bout. Langford would finish the year on December 3 by tackling Harry Wills over 10-rounds to a no-decision. It wasn't pretty as Wills dominated every round.

Six Key Battles of 1916

Fighting Harry Wills four times, Sam McVey four times, and Joe Jeannette once, along with a plethora of pool fighters and one White Hope, Sam Langford conducted all but two battles inside the United States in 1916. As some believed Joe Jeannette still held the World Colored Heavyweight Championship, all of Langford's 1916 bouts prior to May 12 were subject to interpretation. [See Appendix.]

Harry Wills v. Sam Langford—World Colored Heavyweight Championship

On January 3, 1916, at the Tulane Athletic Club in New Orleans, Sam Langford took on local favorite Harry Wills. This was the three-sentence review of the fight that ran in most dailies, including the *Honolulu Star-Bulletin*: "Harry Wills of California was given the decision at the end of the 20th round in his boxing bout with Sam Langford last night. Wills showed an improvement in his work and Sam was unable to put over his celebrated body punch. The result of last night's bout gives Wills the best claim to the colored heavyweight title."[47]

The referee for the battle was none other than Tommy Burns. Jim Buckley, who managed Wills, was now wagering $25,000 that his fighter could defeat any man, bar none. As the bout was announced as being for the World Colored Heavyweight Championship, it marked a renewed interest in the crown.[48] However, sources varied in their acknowledgment of the designation. The *Evening Star* printed this analysis: "He [Wills] claimed the heavyweight Colored title after beating Langford, but to do that he will have to defeat Sam McVey, who is without doubt one of the greatest heavyweights living, but barred by the color line. If Wills wants to annex the Colored title he will have to meet and defeat McVey over the marathon course, and then he will have a clear title to the championship."[49]

Sam Langford had a different opinion.

Sam Langford v. Harry Wills—World Colored Heavyweight Championship

As turnabout was fair play, Sam Langford knocked out Harry Wills in the 19th round of a scheduled 20-round battle on February 11. Once again, the bout was held in New Orleans, only this time it was at Tommy Burns Arena. It was a close confrontation throughout, and many felt it was even before Langford's left hook found his adversary's chin.

Sam Langford v. Sam McVey—World Colored Heavyweight Championship

This confrontation, held on February 17 at Madison Square Garden in New York, was billed as for the title. Although the bout concluded as a 10-round no-decision, most press reports saw it in favor of Langford. It was believed to be the 11th meeting between the pair.[50]

Sam Langford v. Sam McVey—World Colored Heavyweight Championship

Less than a month later, on April 7, the pair conducted a rematch in upstate Syracuse, New York. Although fight details were limited, most newspaper reports saw the 10-round no-decision in favor of Langford.

Sam Langford v. Joe Jeannette—World Colored Heavyweight Championship

Some, including boxing historian Nat Fleischer, believed Langford's mastery of rival Joe Jeannette was never more evident than this encounter that took place at the Arena in upstate New York on May 12, 1916.[51] Battling tooth and nail over the first three rounds, Jeannette was lightning fast while utilizing his left jab to keep Langford in check. But it was only a matter of time before the "Boston Tar Baby" penetrated the defense of his antagonist—the fighters were far too familiar with each other not to anticipate counter-strategies. The fourth term saw Jeannette double up when a crushing right landed in his breadbox. Taking the wind out of sails, Jeannette attempted a recovery over the following rounds. Nevertheless, in the seventh session, Langford caught his opponent dropping his guard in response to a feint and let loose a solid left hook to the chin. Jeannette dropped to the canvas like a felled redwood in a clearing. Trying desperately to recover his footing, he was counted out. Later, Langford, clearly the World Colored Heavyweight Champion, would claim the wallop was more accidental than calculated.

Sam Langford v. Sam McVey—World Colored Heavyweight Championship

In June, Langford, along with a number of his peers, set sail for Buenos Aires to participate in a boxing carnival that was held in conjunction with the city's anniversary. Drawing Sam McVey over 20 lackluster rounds on August 12, 1916, was his recorded contribution to the festivities. Upon Langford's return from South America, three battles—"Big" Bill Tate, "Battling" Jim Johnson, and Bob Devere—completed his fistic year.[52]

As World War I continued to rage in Europe, the United States was making every effort to remain outside the political tensions. However, all that would change in 1917. Those White boxers who lent a hand during the war included: Johnny Coulon, bantamweight champion; Johnny Kilbane, featherweight champion; Benny Leonard, lightweight champion; William Rodenbach, amateur heavyweight champion; Bob McCusker; Mike Gibbons, "the St. Paul Phantom"; Tommy Gibbons, light heavyweight champion; and Johnny Griffiths, welterweight champion, to name only a few. Black fighters of equal patriotism included William "Battling" Gahee, Allentown Joe Gans, Lee Johnson, and Bob Scanlon, also to name only a few.

The year found Langford meeting "Big" Bill Tate twice and Harry Wills three times, along with his fair share of pool fighter engagements. He also met "White Hopes" Bob Devere, Fred Fulton, and Andre Anderson.

"Big" Bill Tate v. Sam Langford—World Colored Heavyweight Championship

Following a 12-round points victory over "Battling" Jim Johnson on New Year's Day, Sam Langford stayed in Kansas City, Missouri, where he met "Big" Bill Tate on January 25, 1917, at the Grand Opera House. The event was far from exciting but the small crowd enjoyed the effort. Although Langford took command and dominated the infighting, he could not avoid his adversary's targeted jab. The 12-round verdict was awarded to Tate.[53]

Sam Langford v. "Big" Bill Tate—World Colored Heavyweight Championship

On May 1, 1917, this time inside the Future City Athletic Club in St. Louis, Missouri, Sam Langford needed only five rounds, of a scheduled 12, before he knocked out "Big" Bill Tate. Despite the victory, Langford continued to take criticism in the press for his perceived diminishing skills. The *El Paso Herald* noted: "Whatever the age Samuel has attained, it cannot alter the fact that he is now in the decline of his fighting years. Sam moves like a battleship with a barnacled bottom. He has a large and permanent watermelon in the food belt, and when he is clipped a stout one it takes a long time to clear his head."[54]

For Sam Langford, the year was marked by physical tragedy—he lost the sight of one eye during a loss against Fred Fulton on June 19, 1917. Remarkably, he did not allow the handicap to impact his desire to box, figuring there was still plenty of fight inside his mitts. Langford carried on with the use of one eye for another nine years.

Another sign of Langford's fading skills came courtesy of Harry Wills: Back-to-back battles in Panama, at the Plaza de Toros Vista Alegre in Panama City, on April 14 and May 19, 1918, were decisively won by Wills and proof positive that the best of Sam Langford had come and gone.

The Final Rounds

From 1918 until 1922, Sam Langford added nearly 90 fights to his resume. Many of these—an estimated one-third—were against four outstanding Black fighters: Jeff Clark, "Big" Bill Tate, Jack Thompson, and Harry Wills. In his mid–30s, he was fighting only for a paycheck.[55]

Following an estimated 300 bouts, Sam Langford left the ring at the age of 43. In retirement his eye problems continued and eventually resulted in blindness. As time passed and fans became more cognizant of his career, his reputation grew. In 1932, the *Evening Star* took another look:

Blind in one eye, scarcely able to see out of the other, Sam Langford, ranked by many experts as one of the greatest Negro fighters of all time—Peter Jackson, Joe Walcott, Joe Gans and Jack Johnson being the others—is living in Chicago eking out a living as an instructor in a gymnasium. Handicapped as he is, he is unable to do much boxing himself, but he is found a most valuable aid in giving the novices pointers on the finer points of the game and his services are in demand. Until recently, Langford, the man who drove Jack Johnson all over the continent and out of America because Jack wouldn't meet him, lived in New York, where he was cared for by friends, and later he went into vaudeville in Boston with Joe Walcott as his partner, but their skit didn't go over and the partnership was dissolved, Now, while Walcott is in New York City, stone broke, Langford seconds and instructs boxers for a living.[56]

As for how Langford might fare today, the article continued:

Langford was one of the greatest fighting machines of all time. He would plough through the present crop of heavyweights with ease were he now in his prime. Sharkey, Schmeling, Poreda, Schaaf, Walker, Risko, Hamas—each would be hearing birdies sing in less than three rounds were the Sam Langford of 20 years ago in competition today.

Had "ol Tham's" skin been White instead of Black, he undoubtedly would have been Jim Jeffries' successor. He was a natural fighter who loved the sport for sport's sake and every time he fought gave the fans a million dollars' worth of entertainment. What a manger wouldn't give for a Sam Langford now![57]

Three years later, and totally blind, Langford found comfort in a third-floor hall room in Harlem. With barely a dime to his name, he was taking life day by day. In 1944, a newspaper column written by Al Laney and published by the *New York Herald Tribune* documented Langford's plight and generated $10,000 in assistance. Sam Langford died on January 12, 1956, in Cambridge, Massachusetts, where he had been living in a private nursing home. He was 72 years old.

The sheer frequency of battles between the colored title contenders in the heavyweight division, along with Jack Johnson's ascendency to the heavyweight throne and his drawing of the color line, created confusion around the World Colored Heavyweight Championship. Unsanctioned, unorganized and unfunded, the title was subject to interpretation. Sam McVey and Joe Jeannette exchanged the title in 1909. Then Langford took it from Jeannette on September 6, 1910. He would hold it periodically until 1917—a record five times by some accounts—before relinquishing it briefly to Bill Tate in 1917, then to Harry Wills in 1918.

From 1903 to 1918, Jack Johnson, Sam McVey, Joe Jeannette, and Sam Langford were arguably the four finest heavyweights in boxing.

The Color (Time) Line, 1910–1918[58]

As W.E.B. Du Bois stated in his "Address to the Nations of the World," at the First Pan-African Conference in London in July 1900, "The problem of the Twentieth Century is the problem of the colour-line." Look no further than the oldest sport in history to prove its existence. Contagious, racial discrimination was a disease that could not be contained. In the United States it would eventually spread to include intolerance beyond that of black versus white.

Nobody in the fight game, excluding Jack Johnson, had the color line ("fear meter") drawn like Sam Langford. So rather than viewing only a few examples of the enigma during the span of his believed title reign (1910–1918), let's prove it.

A Langford Color (Time) Line

Drawing the color line against Sam Langford was publicly evident by 1907.

On June 12, 1907, the *Waterbury Evening Democrat* noted, "Langford tried to get a battle with 'Gunner' Moir the English heavyweight champion, but Moir said he had drawn the color line" (p. 9); on August 15, 1908, the *Pacific Commercial* Advertiser said, "Ketchel has also failed to reply to Langford, and will probably draw the color line. We can't blame Ketchel for refusing to meet Langford; he is coming to the top fast, and by drawing the color line will remain for some time to come" (p. 3); on January 10, 1909, the *Sun* stated, "Langford has had the color line drawn on him repeatedly, probably because of his ring prowess" (p. 10); on November 27, 1909, Franklin's paper, the *Statesman* said, "Langford has taken the middleweight crown, because Papke refuses to fight on account of the color line, and Langford has defeated all of the other middleweights, so there is nothing for Langford to do but 'o wait and gather in the middleweight (coin) for Johnson can take care of the heavyweights" (p. 12); and on December 22, 1909, the *Norwich Bulletin* noted, "Memphis has drawn the color line on Sam Langford. That dark skinned gentleman is certainly having a hard time making a living. Practically all the boxers of his weight drew the line on him some time ago" (p. 3).

The definition of "The Color Line," continued to evolve.

On June 10, 1910, the *Ogden Standard* said, "The big affair is a contest between men, not races of men. Those fighters who have drawn the color line in the past have, almost without exception, done so because there happened to be a Negro of whom they feared. Take Billy Papke tabooing the Colored fighters, for instance. Without closing your eyes in thought for an instant you can conjure a picture of Sam Langford. Sam is Papke's color line reason" (p. 8); on June 19, 1913, the *Evening Star* proclaimed, "Sam Langford, the Colored pugilist, arrived here [San Francisco] yesterday from Australia after an absence of nearly two years. Matches were hard for him to find when he left and they look no more plentiful now. Arthur Pelkey, the last recruit among the White hopes, announced a few hours before the ship was in sight that he had drawn the color line" (p. 6); on March 6, 1914, the *El Paso Herald* announced, "Mixed fights will not be permitted in the state of Wisconsin. This is the ultimatum of the Badger State boxing commission, when Kenosha promoters applied for a license to promote a bout between Carl Morris and Sam Langford. A strict color line has been drawn, regardless of the wishes of the fans" (p. 11); on April 11, 1915, the *Omaha Daily Bee* stated, "Willard has drawn the color line. With Sam Langford, Sam McVey and Joe Jeannette enjoying perfect health, we don't blame him" (p. 4-S); and on June 24, 1917, the *Sun* agreed, "Langford would unquestionably have been the heavyweight champion of the world had he been able to get the titleholders into a match at the time he was in good form. Like Peter Jackson, Langford was the victim of the color line, which first was drawn by Tommy Burns" (p. 5).

On March 19, 1919, the *Daily Gate City and Constitution-Democrat* announced, "[Willie] Meehan, who is a local [San Francisco] man, was scheduled to meet Sam Langford, Boston Negro, at the [Soldier's] benefit. He suddenly announced his withdrawal, saying he has drawn the color line. Meehan shaded Langford in a recent bout here. Angry local fans accuse him of being afraid of the 'tar baby' and say they will have him barred from boxing anywhere in the country" (p. 6); and on October 29, 1922, the *New York Herald* declared, "[Tommy] Burns drew the color line, the objectionable person being Sam Langford. The Tar Baby would have made shorter work of Burns than Jack Johnson did, and the latter never would have held title had Langford succeeded in getting the match with Burns instead of Johnson. Had Johnson kept his engagement to meet Langford in London after defeating Burns, it is not unlikely that Langford would have taken the title. Johnson studiously drew the color line against Langford. In accepting a match with Johnson, Burns indicated a belief that Johnson was not so dangerous as Langford" (p. 7).

If this doesn't paint a clear picture of the effect of power on the powerless, nothing will. Decades later, the price Sam Langford had to pay for "The Color Line" became obvious. Sad is the fact that such a racist chronology could be compiled for each Black pugilist profiled inside this work.

ELEVEN

The Black Panther

It was the perfect solution. With his victory over Sam McVey on September 7, 1915, Harry Wills claimed the World Colored Heavyweight Championship from obscurity. Convinced that he needed a logical path to the Heavyweight Championship of the World, Wills, prompted by Jack Johnson's loss to Jess Willard, believed this assertion was the answer. It just made sense. In his mind Willard's victory extinguished the flames, or took away the leverage, of the dubious White Heavyweight Championship held by Georges Carpentier. Therefore, the heavyweight champion of the world was either Jess Willard or Harry Wills. Or so the logic concluded and the latter believed. Unfortunately, the pair would never resolve the argument in a boxing ring—uncertainty was as common to Wills' career as his knockout victims.

The road to the Heavyweight Championship of the World, during the 20th century, would be forever tormented with inconstancy thanks to Harry Wills. There, I said it. Unable to transform the obstacles he faced into opportunities, the gifted boxer resigned himself to a citation in ring history, alongside the greatest heavyweight champions of his era. Standing an unyielding six feet, three inches, and tipping on or about 220, Wills was chiseled like a Donatello carving. When he chose to crawl between the ropes, he considered it his calling.

Born in New Orleans on May 15, 1889, Wills was a jockey and stevedore before moving on to the sweet science.[1] Turning professional around 1910, he fought out of New Orleans and quickly progressed through the local ranks. As a knockout artist, it didn't take long for Wills to establish an intimidating reputation. By the end of 1913, he had picked up no-decisions against Jeff Clark (also spelled Clarke) and Joe Jeannette—both men already had over 75 career victories to their name. Wills even made the sports pages—two sentences better than none at all.[2]

Still in his mid–20s, Harry Wills engaged in over a dozen battles in 1914. The first half of the year was marked by two no-decisions or wake-up calls: He took a solid beating, over 10 rounds, against Sam Langford on May 1, and followed it with a better performance against Joe Jeannette on June 9.[3] Both events attracted over 2,000 spectators at the National Baseball Park in New Orleans. Improved competition had Wills fighting far more cautiously and fine-tuning his punches. Picking up six consecutive late-summer victories in San Francisco led to a rematch against formidable Sam Langford, the scheduled 20-round clash to take place in Vernon, California, on November 26. Naturally, the focus was placed on Langford, a fighter with more than 100 victories to his credit, as few had any idea who Harry Wills was. The *El Paso Herald* stated this about the rising star: "This fellow Wills is no boob by a whole lot. He has not been arousing a lot of enthusiasm in the past, but he has been working good [*sic*]. Joe Jeannette and Langford are among his victims, so he must have some sort of class. He does not figure with Langford in the matter of cleverness and generalship, and this may prove his undoing, but he certainly is game and has the punch. I look for an early ending to this fight because the Black boys are somewhat impatient when fighting each other and will not waste time."[4]

Wills' manager, Steve Corola, did an admirable job spinning the press in order to set the table for his fighter. He believed a distance (20 rounds) battle against Langford would thrust Wills into the spotlight—win, lose, or draw—and he was right. By the end of October, not only did Wills' photo appear in West Coast dailies, but he was touted as another Peter Jackson.

Thankfully, the battle lived up to all the hype, the *Harrisburg Telegraph* noting: "With a left swing to the jaw, Sam Langford of Boston, knocked out Harry Wills, the giant New Orleans Negro, in the 14th round of a scheduled 20-round fight, yesterday afternoon at Vernon. Both men were knocked down repeatedly, Langford himself taking the count four times in the first two rounds. Langford early in the fight hurt his left ankle as he fell to the mat in a vicious breakaway. Wills' effective straight arm drives gave him an apparent even break in most of the rounds, but Langford fought with a superior knowledge of the game that gradually wore out Wills."[5]

In defeat, Wills still impressed. His spectacular—many critics ringside felt he was just one punch away from a victory—performance in opposition to Langford gained him a 20-round match against Sam McVey on December 20.

More than anything, Wills, as crazy as it might sound, wanted to defeat McVey. But such was not the case. "Big Sam," who tipped at 217, overwhelmed his opponent, who weighed 206 pounds. A superior left hook and timely uppercuts saw to that. At the end of the 20 rounds, Referee Dick Burke awarded the fight to McVey. Spectators, some 3,000 at the West Side Athletic Club in New Orleans, approved the verdict. The *Rock Island Argus* saw it like this:

> Wills started like a winner. He won the third, fourth, fifth, sixth and seventh round easily. McVey seemed unable to fathom his infighting and the local Negro punished the "Parisian." The eighth round saw a change when McVey rushed and broke Wills' guard. McVey won the ninth and tenth, but Wills came back strongly and shaded him in the 11th.
>
> Outside the 17th and 18th rounds, which were even, the other rounds belonged to McVey. His slashing left and his right cross worried Wills. In the 13th, 14th and the 15th rounds he almost dropped the southerner with vicious left hooks to the jaw, which sent Wills reeling to the ropes.[6]

Wills could not overcome the aggressiveness of McVey, who constantly forced the action. As his second consecutive loss, it was hard to stomach. But to Wills' credit, he kept it in perspective. The fact that he was still standing at the end of the bout was more surprising than McVey's victory.

After 1914, Wills was not only considered a pool fighter, but on his way to becoming a serious contender for a title—yes, it was presumptuous but his skills were improving at an impressive rate.[7] More importantly, the youngster understood his place. If that meant being a no-decision punching bag for Langford or Jeannette, that was fine for now—certainly he could fill in, or so he believed, for other fighters like "Battling" Jim Johnson.

Wills took five noteworthy battles in 1915, highlighted by two with Sam McVey and one with Sam Langford. His claim to fame thus far, at least to some of the beat writers, was demonstrating that Langford could be felled with a punch to the jaw, having accomplished this back on November 26, 1914.[8] Or, perhaps better said, proof to White contenders that Langford was at least human and vulnerable to some type of assault, something fighters like Jess Willard didn't believe possible.

Harry Wills v. Sam McVey—World Colored Heavyweight Championship

Without fanfare and little press, Harry Wills took a lackluster 12-round decision over Sam McVey on September 7, 1915, at the Atlas Athletic Club in Boston. As some saw it, the bout ended McVey's claim to the World Colored Heavyweight Championship. Honestly speaking, McVey was only interested in Willard's title.

Closing out his year, Wills outpointed Langford on December 3, 1915, during a fight that would enter the record books as a 10-round no-decision.

Three consecutive battles against Sam Langford greeted Harry Wills at the beginning of 1916. Claiming the World Colored Heavyweight Championship, the New Orleans–born fighter was more than happy to defend it.

Harry Wills v. Sam Langford—World Colored Heavyweight Championship

In a fight billed for the Colored Heavyweight Championship of the World, Harry Wills was granted a 20-round decision over Sam Langford on January 3. The fight, held at the Tulane Athletic club, was even refereed by Tommy Burns. The *Evening World* saw it like this:

> The decision was popular and just. Langford had the better of the seventh round and even up in the eighth, ninth, 12th and 19th sessions. Wills gained the honors in all the other rounds. Langford's right eye was nearly closed, his nose skinned and his lips puffed. Wills did not show a mark. Wills scored the nearest approach to a knockdown in the first when he sent Langford crashing to the ropes with a stiff right to the chin. The 13th and 15th rounds were fast rallies, with Wills punching Langford all over the ring. Langford's best chance was in the seventh, when he caught Wills on the ropes with a hard left to the face.[9]

Managed by Jim Buckley, Harry Wills was now picking up many of the headlines Langford once had. A highlight of his skills, which was noted by the *Norwich Bulletin*, was his ability to utilize the "Fitzsimmons shift," a Bob Fitzsimmons trademark maneuver he used to knock out Jim Corbett in 1897. It begins with a straight blow from the lead hand, followed by a rear foot shift and an overhand or hook to the side of the jaw. Wills had mastered the movement, then inserted it into his fight arsenal.

Sam Langford v. Harry Wills—World Colored Heavyweight Championship

On February 11, Sam Langford knocked out Harry Wills in the 19th round of a scheduled 20-round clash held in New Orleans at the Tommy Burns Arena and refereed by Sammy Goldman. Until the fight-ending wallop by Langford, the fight looked rather even— this claim made despite the fact Wills had been knocked down three previous times.[10] The New Orleans fighter blamed himself for being in the wrong place at the wrong time. Langford thought he regained the title with the victory, even if Joe Jeannette, who had a valid claim, disputed it. (See Appendix.)

From New Orleans, the pair traveled to New York. On March 7, Wills, who tipped at 204, fought Sam Langford, who weighed 195 pounds, to a 10-round no-decision at the Broadway Sporting Club in Brooklyn. When the action stalled in the finals rounds, it cast a bit of uncertainty regarding the performance. However, the newspapers saw it easily in favor of Wills.

A month later, on April 7, Wills conducted another lackluster display during a 10-round no-decision against John Lester Johnson at the Harlem Sporting Club. Following a tough first two rounds, the local light heavyweight was just trying to last the distance.

Robert James Fitzsimmons, a.k.a. "Ruby Robert" and "The Freckled Wonder," loved boxing but hated training. Taught numerous boxing techniques from the great Jem Mace, he developed a reputation for being the hardest puncher in boxing (*Library of Congress, LC-USZ62-57869*).

On April 25, this time in St. Louis, Wills took an eight-round newspaper decision over Sam Langford. To say this match was a superfluous undertaking was an understatement. But bills don't pay themselves, and healthy appetites, whether inside or outside a boxing ring, don't just disappear. Harry Wills essentially finished out the year with a 20-round decision over Jeff Clark on May 19.[11] A fight frequency of about a half-dozen bouts per year seemed to suit the rising star's needs for the time being.

Two fights against "Battling" Jim Johnson (February 7 and June 1), one fight against pool fighter Jack Thompson (April 30), a single battle against William "Rough House" Ware (November 8), three fights against Sam Langford (May 11, September 20, and November 12), and a knockout of Jeff Clark (December 16) accounted for the year 1917 for Harry Wills.[12] He posted a record of 1–1–0, with six no-decisions. It wasn't a busy year, but it was an eventful one.

On February 7, in his first fight of the year, Wills broke his right wrist. It happened in the second round of his confrontation against "Battling" Jim Johnson in St. Louis. Clearly in pain, he had little choice but to absorb the loss. Convalescing from his injury over the next 82 days, Wills plotted his recovery.[13]

Beginning on April 30, against Jack Thompson, Wills tested his healing power. Taking the 10-round no-decision, he was satisfied with the results—little did he know that the injury would follow him the rest of his career. Tackling Langford over six lackluster rounds to a no-decision, he pushed himself four rounds further to the same result against "Battling" Jim Johnson.[14] Highlighting the second half of the year was a pair of battles against Sam Langford. The first, held in Brooklyn, was an uneventful 10-round newspaper decision in favor of Wills. But the second, a 12-round no-decision held out in Toledo, Ohio, didn't go over well. The Toledo boxing commission believed the fight was not on the square and barred both fighters. Disillusioned with everything from the lack of willing opponents to poor purses, Wills began searching for options.[15]

Working with "White Hope" Fred Fulton during 1917 was a highlight for Wills. Many believed the Minnesota giant—he stood six feet four inches and tipped at 225—deserved a title shot at Jess Willard. The powerful heavyweight possessed an impressive jab and held victories over Al Kaufman, "Fireman" Jim Flynn, and Al Reich. Wills believed that by working with Fulton, he could not only assist the fighter in defeating Willard, but perhaps be given a title shot as a reward. As the *Richmond Palladium and Sun-Telegram* saw it: "Wills is well thought of by lots of promoters and there's little doubt that he has quite a bulge on Fulton. Wills worked with Fulton when Fred was training for his last bout with Carl Morris. He showed footwork and feinting skill that was way ahead of anything Fulton had."[16]

As the Toledo ruling was a bit of an embarrassment, Wills joined others looking for a change of pace, and they found it Panama City, Panama. He closed out his year by knocking out pool fighter Jeff Clark at the Vista Allegre Bull Ring in the capital city.[17]

Taking just a handful of battles in 1918, Wills would not face defeat.[18] Still in Panama, he began the year on solid ground with a fifth-round knockout of Sam McVey—the latter tried to claim a foul blow but it was ignored.

Harry Wills v. Sam Langford—World Colored Heavyweight Championship

Harry Wills knocked out Sam Langford in the sixth round of their Panama contest on April 14, 1918, at the Vista Allegre Bull Ring. Although Wills was the aggressor for the first two rounds, Langford took the next two terms. Regrouping, Wills looked refreshed in the fifth round and made his opponent pay in the final session—Langford went horizontal in the sixth round for the full count. Clearly, Wills was the principal Black heavyweight contender. Just to confirm his position, he repeated his dominance over Langford on May 19, when the latter failed to answer the bell for round eight. Despite his impressive victories, a bulk of the fight reports focused on Wills being chosen once again as a sparring partner for Fred Fulton—the big White heavyweight was scheduled to meet fight sensation Jack Dempsey in July.[19]

So had the old Black quartet—Johnson, Jeannette, McVey, and Langford—finally come of age? Some thought so, however others still feared just the thought of meeting any of these great heavyweights. The *Norwich Bulletin* commented:

> Wills, who is now 26 years of age, has whipped all the men who cared to face him and only recently knocked out Sam McVey and Sam Langford in six and five rounds respectively at Panama. He trained Fred Fulton for his fight with Carl Morris at Canton, Ohio, and there were times when the two big fellows went at it hammer and tongs. Wills admitted at the time that Fulton had the best left hand of all the heavies and could hit harder with it than any of them. It was Harry's claim at the time that if Fred ever met Willard it would be a payday for Jess, with the title going over to Little Frederick. Fulton stands six feet four and a half inches and weighs 216 pounds; while Wills is six feet three inches and scales at 215. What a battle these two giants would put up if matched! There is little chance of their meeting, however, owing to the color line being drawn by practically all states these days. Fulton had great praise for Wills and said he was more scientific than any of the big men he had ever met. What a difference it would make to Mr. Wills if he were White![20]

Wills returned to America in July and finished out his year battling against pool fighters. He also took on new management. Under Paddy Mullins—the well-connected manager looked after Johnny Ertle and Mike O'Dowd (1917 middleweight champion)—Wills believed he could improve his championship pursuit.

I'm All right, Jack

Harry Wills officially issued the challenge to White pugilists Jess Willard and Jack Dempsey on September 12, 1918. The *Washington Times* published it: "I am willing to meet either [Jess] Willard [Current Champion] or [Jack] Dempsey for any number of rounds and let the entire receipts go to any war fund designated by a committee. That I shall carry out my end of the contract I stand ready to post $1,000."[21]

Skating away from the issue, Dempsey stated that he was more than willing to meet Wills or any Colored contender, but qualified the statement by insisting that the matter rested entirely with his manager. According to his manager, Jack Kearns, the *El Paso Herald* noted: "I was never in favor of mixed matches and I don't think I would make such a match for Jack unless I was convinced that the public deserved it. There are just as good White boxers as there are Colored, and if Jack licks them there will be no need of him meeting the Black boys to prove that he is the best in the class. Jess Willard squelched the Black peril when he knocked out Jack Johnson, so why resurrect it?"[22]

Many, including the *El Paso Herald*, saw it differently: "When a man lays claim to the championship of the world he should be prepared to defend that claim against any man, White, Black, Red, Brown or Yellow. For a champion to bar a man because of the color of his skin is to make himself look ridiculous. There is no room for argument on the point.

Harry Wills, standing alongside his wife in this undated photo from the Bain News Service, was ranked throughout the 1920s as one of the most talented heavyweight contenders. His lean, muscular physique was often attributed to his periodic fasting (Library of Congress, LC-DIG-ggbain-38626).

Various champions have drawn the color line in the past, but they succeeded in deluding no one but themselves."[23]

Dempsey's position confirmed, at least to Wills, that he was the most feared Black boxer in the world. From this point forward, the New Orleans boxer, who was at or near his fighting peak, would shadow Dempsey like a cat would a mouse.

Speaking of the "Manassa Mauler," Dempsey landed a July 4 title shot against Jess Willard. On February 6, 1919, it was further confirmed that Harry Wills had an offer to assist Dempsey in his training for the bout. However, Wills saw himself as an opponent, not a sparring partner. Having difficulty finding matches, Wills again looked to the pool in late spring of 1919. He took a no-decision over John Lester Johnson, two wins and a no-decision over Sam Langford, a knockout over Jeff Clark, and a no-decision over Joe Jeannette.

Harry Wills v. Sam Langford—World Colored Heavyweight Championship

On November 5, 1919, Harry Wills entered a Tulsa, Oklahoma, ring and took a 15-round decision over Sam Langford. He also, according to the *News Scimitar*, picked up the World Colored Heavyweight Championship, as Langford had won the title on October 20 by defeating Jack Thompson.[24] (See Appendix.)

Rumored to be fighting everyone from Fred Fulton to Jack Johnson, the only thing clear to Wills was that many of these so-called opportunities were not panning out. Packing up his things, he left Tulsa for the hills of San Francisco. Wills knocked out K.O. Kruvosky in the first round of their Coliseum match on November 20, then followed it up with a third-round knockout of Ole Anderson on December 5. Also finding West Coast matches a struggle, Wills obtained employment in the shipyards to pick up some extra cash.

If the first day of any given year was an omen, then Harry Wills was destined to have a challenging year. On January 1, 1920, the fighter was charged with stalling during a battle against Jack Thompson in San Francisco. According to the *Butte Daily Bulletin*: "Eddie Hanlon, referee of the bout between Harry Wills and Jack Thompson here [San Francisco] yesterday, quit the ring in the third round, charging that the fighters were 'stalling' and the fight was 'framed.' Managers of the fighters protested that their men were doing their best, but the crowd supported the referee and booed and jeered the fighters as hundreds of fans left the hall."[25]

With their San Francisco welcome worn out, both fighters headed back to Tulsa. In a rematch on January 12, Wills took the 15-round decision at Convention Hall. Despite having the advantage in 12 of the rounds, he had difficulty penetrating Thompson's defense. Following the battle, Wills was off to Saint Paul, Minnesota, to meet "Kid" Johnson in March. Still having difficulty making a match, Wills entered the ring against the Black heavyweight more to occupy his time than to polish his skills. The fight lasted 42 seconds. Greatly overpowered, Johnson dropped to the canvas, got up, then changed his mind and went down again.[26]

After some serious coaxing by Tom O'Rourke, Fred Fulton finally agreed to meet Harry Wills in Newark, New Jersey. The bout, originally planned for February, would not take place until July 26.

Wills was out in Denver to greet the familiar face of Sam Langford on April 23. After 15 rounds, at the stockyards stadium, the referee's decision went to Wills. "The Black Panther"—his cherished moniker—dominated his antagonist and even dropped Langford twice in the first round. Working his way east, Wills took a bout against Ray Bennett, a complete bust, at the Stratford Athletic Club in Connecticut. The *Bridgeport Times and Evening Farmer* detailed the June 1 fiasco:

> When the opening gong sounded, Bennett came out of his corner looking at Wills' [*sic*] giant frame with awe. He sparred and backed around the ring, with the Californian quickly following, with a grin on his face from ear to ear. Wills started to send that wicked right, for which he is known, and Bennett sank to the floor, to the surprise of everyone, without being struck. He refused to get up, and [Referee] McAuliffe began to count, yelling for him to get up between the count. At the stroke of nine Mack got disgusted at this ham acting, and pulled the frightened man to his feet. With resumed courage began to spar, but Wills only laughed and sent in a series of rights to the head.[27]

The process was repeated again and the fight was finally stopped. The debacle, which frankly was an insult, was not what Wills needed before meeting Fred Fulton. As that fight loomed, more details followed. Considered one of the first important boxing contests conducted under the Walker boxing law, which New York State passed in 1920, the 15-round decision bout was being closely watched. According to the *Washington Herald*: "The men will battle for a purse of $40,000, of which the winner will receive $30,000 and the loser $10,000. A referee and two judges will render the decision in the contest and, according to my informant, the bout will be conducted by the officials of the International Sporting Club and only 1,500 persons will be permitted to see the battle, they being the legitimate members of the club."[28]

The fight, originally scheduled for New York, was moved to Newark, New Jersey.[29] One week prior to the fight, Jack Dempsey announced that he was no longer averse to fighting a Negro boxer and was ready to make a match with Harry Wills. The *News Scimitar* provided Dempsey's view: "As for the Colored boxers you can say for me and make it as strong as you like, that I have absolutely no scruples about boxing them. After I won the championship, Jack Kearns, my manager, contended that mixed bouts are injurious to the sport and for that reason would not consider any for me. It is different now. If the press, public or promoters want me to box a Negro I'll gladly take the match. That goes for Harry Wills and the rest of his like. To be quite frank about it, I need the money."[30]

Only a few days later, Dempsey, whose contradictions were as common as sawdust in a lumber mill, denied that he would meet Wills. The *Washington Times* reported: "If Fulton wins, yes. But if Wills wins, no. Not that I'm not confident that Wills would be easy. That isn't the thing. It's simply the idea of boxing a Negro. We had one Colored champion—Johnson—and he almost killed the game. So I don't think the public wants me to put my crown in jeopardy in a bout with a Negro. As for Johnson wanting a bout with me, that is laughable. He is 43 years old, which is a sufficient reply to make to all his challenges. Johnson should consider himself lucky to get back in this country without being lynched, and keep quiet about being able to beat any man in the world."[31]

Fred Fulton, the big White Minnesota heavyweight, aka "The Rochester Plasterer," climbed between the ropes of the ring at the First Regiment Armory on July 26, not with a vision of Wills in his head, but that of Dempsey. You see, the plasterer had lost a roof's worth of ceiling tiles when Dempsey decked him in 18 seconds back in 1918. Understandably, it was a tough image to shake.

This fight, scheduled for 12 rounds, saw Wills, who scaled at 204, wasting little time. A hard right uppercut to the chin of Fulton, who tipped at 210, sent the fighter to the canvas in the third round—497 seconds later than Dempsey.[32] Aggressive from the beginning,

Wills was relentless with combinations to both the head and body. The former "White Hopeless" countered well in the second round and even managed to get to the body of Wills with combinations, but the effort was clearly inferior. When Wills broke well from a clinch in the third round, it set the stage for his knockout punch.

All eyes turned to Dempsey after the fight, but he was still seeing only what he wanted to see. Disheartened, Wills had no choice but to remain vigilant. Everyone had an opinion about the champion's position; Robert Edgren, the famed columnist, believed that scarcity of opponents could compel Dempsey to cross the color line. But nobody was certain.

Wills turned to Sam McVey on September 8, an event that was part of the opening of the Ice Palace of Philadelphia. Unfortunately, fan interest quickly faded, one session at a time. By the sixth round, the referee claimed that McVey was stalling, then stopped the fight and declared it a no-contest. Wills, who was simply dominating the encounter, once again had to deal with a ring embarrassment—both fighters were barred from ever appearing in local bouts.

Though Wills remained silent, the situation was tearing him up inside. Troubled by his lack of matches, distressed over his financial situation, and embarrassed by his current fight results, he seemed to have everything working against him. His daily dose of Dempsey denials made headlines, but only added to his frustration. At the end of September, he unloaded his feelings to the *Seattle Star*:

> Kearns knows that I can beat his meal ticket, so he is not going to take a chance. He pretends he is willing for Dempsey to meet me, but he doesn't mean what he says. He talks of making the match as soon as the public demands that Dempsey fight me. That's all bunk. He doesn't care anything about what the public thinks. I'm not going around challenging Dempsey when I know he doesn't want to fight. I'm just waiting until people get tired of seeing him knock over the setups. Then they are going to ask why he doesn't fight Harry Wills. It's so hard for me to get fights that I have to work at the docks sometimes, although I can beat any man in the world.[33]

In stark contrast to Wills' opinions, T.S. Andrews, the popular White ring columnist, penned a New Year's Day column with the bold headline "Boxing Experiences Banner Year, Two Champs Lose Titles and Game Much Advanced." The decade's first year, 1920, was the greatest in fistic history. Praising war veterans, increased fight purses, better boxing commissions, and enhanced worldwide popularity, Andrews felt that things couldn't get any better. The article shifted to Dempsey. Billy Miske, Bill Brennan, Georges Carpentier, Jess Willard, Fred Fulton, Frank Moran, and Battling Levinsky were all mentioned. He even noted British heavy Joe Beckett and Australia's Jim Tracey. But there was not a single mention of Harry Wills or any Black heavyweight.[34]

Such a racist ring evaluation from the muzzle of Andrews was an absolute insult.[35]

Averaging about a fight a month during 1921, Harry Wills faced Bill Tate three times, Jack Thompson twice, and also Denver Ed Martin. Pool fighters filled the gaps, with one exception: Ed "Gunboat" Smith.

Harry Wills v. "Big" Bill Tate—World Colored Heavyweight Championship

Wills started the year in Buffalo, New York. There he greeted "Big" Bill Tate, the six foot, six inch heavyweight, on January 17, 1921. Currently known for being the primary sparring partner of Jack Dempsey, Tate brought with him an 81-inch reach backed by considerable power—he was not the same fighter that greeted the New Orleans boxer back in 1916. Regardless, Wills was not intimidated. In a fight promoted as for the World Colored Heavyweight Championship, Wills knocked out Tate in the second round. None too happy with the expedient finish, the 10,000 fans—8,431 seats were sold at $1 each—inside the Buffalo Auditorium began shouting, "Fake!" It was Tate's unwillingness to engage that prompted the futile chant.

For the moment, Wills' name stayed on the sports pages. However, Dempsey versus Carpentier, scheduled for July 2, 1921, dominated the dailies; related articles focused on all aspects around the heavyweight contest. In March, the French fighter was asked about Wills in a piece that appeared in the *Bridgeport Times and Evening Farmer*: "Georges Carpentier will never draw the color line if he wins the world's championship and is challenged by a boxer of dusky hue. Carpentier made this stand known to friends here [Paris] recently it became known today [March 24], in discussing the scrapping merits of Harry Wills, the American Negro, touted as a contender for the world's title."[36]

These articles typically elicited a counter: Dempsey was quick to note his willingness to employ Black sparring partners—Kid Norfolk, Harry Wills, and Jamaica Kid were mentioned as potential targets. Few bought the dodge—target practice wasn't warfare. On May 25, the champion also stated a contingency: Should he defeat the giant Frenchman, his next opponent would be the man most worthy. As usual, stipulations were attached. Wills, who was rumored to be assisting Carpentier in his fight preparation, had no response to the champion's gibberish.[37] Speaking of rumors, Wills was mentioned as a possible opponent for Jack Johnson upon his release from Leavenworth penitentiary. As it turned out, the rumor gave Jack Kearns—who by the way confirmed that he had drawn no color line—another out: Johnson should meet Wills first before even being considered a Dempsey alternative. As usual, Dempsey, who knocked out Carpentier, changed his mind. He stated to the *Omaha Dispatch*, in remarks picked up by the *New York Tribune*: "I will never meet a colored man. There is nothing to this talk of me meeting Jack Johnson. I am confident that the public does not want this fight, and while I will govern myself to a large extent according to the wishes of the public, I can't see my way clear to fight Johnson or any other Colored man."[38]

As the press continued to print every word from Dempsey's mouth, Wills was preparing for battle against veteran Ed "Gunboat" Smith on October 10 in Havana, Cuba. The former White Heavyweight Champion (1914), who six months later lost the title to Georges Carpentier on an "ill-called" foul, was far removed from his prime. But he was still a man who withstood nine knockdowns at the hands of Jack Dempsey. Must hand it to the "Gunner" —getting in a ring against Wills at this stage of his career was like a death sentence. Smith lasted 67 seconds. According to the *Bisbee Daily Review*: "Six clean blows from Wills, among them a crushing right to the back of Smith's neck, dazed the former sailor and a left uppercut to the jaw sent him to the floor, where he was counted out. Smith did not land a blow. The fight was to have gone 20 rounds."[39]

Wills' devastation of Smith drew little attention. The reason was simple: Kearns, who was getting fed up with answering questions about Wills, reminded the beat writers that Jack Dempsey was their job security, not Harry Wills. When the champion spoke, the ink sold newspapers. By November, some dailies were insisting there was little demand for Dempsey v. Wills. Kearns was spinning again.[40] Under the subtitle "Public Does Not Want Wills," the *Great Falls Tribune* noted the words of Jack Kearns: "There is some talk of a match with Harry Wills, Negro heavyweight, but it does not seem that the public is clamoring for such a match now. We will be willing to sign with Wills any time the promoters and public think that he is a real contender in the heavyweight class."[41]

If Dempsey couldn't put the fire out, Kearns would, and he knew just how to do it.

On November 18, Wills took on Denver Ed Martin at Milwaukie, Oregon. Martin, now years past his salad days, was on the comeback trail and fighting in his hometown. In many ways the encounter was perfect: In his prime, Martin couldn't land a match with the great White heavyweights either. Was Wills looking across the ring at his future? The thought scared the young contender. In the first round, he sent a right to the back of the legendary fighter's ear. Martin, who had already tasted the canvas, dropped for the final time. Referee Louttit had little choice but to stop the fight.

Harry Wills v. "Big" Bill Tate—World Colored Heavyweight Championship

Finishing the year as it began, Wills took a decisive 12-round decision over "Big" Bill Tate in Denver on December 8. The fight, which garnered only about two lines of press coverage, was viewed by most as a successful title defense.[42] The pair would meet again in less than a month.

"Big" Bill Tate v. Harry Wills—World Colored Heavyweight Championship

The first fight of the year for Harry Wills, on January 2, 1922, in Portland, Oregon, had to conclude with a decisive victory. This was the conclusion of the fight media. No other result would guarantee the fighter a crack at Dempsey. Well, in the first round of the scheduled 10-round battle, Wills delivered what he believed to be the perfect punch, a crushing right to the jaw of his antagonist. Unfortunately, it happened while he was attempting to obey the referee's order to break from a clinch. With only 10 seconds left in the round, Tate was awarded the victory on a foul. The loss was heartbreaking for a fighter desperately trying to stay relevant.

Before the fight, comparisons between the fighters emerged. According to the *Omaha Daily Bee*:

There is quite a contrast between him [Tate] and his adversary [Wills] whom he has fought four times. Wills to begin with, is of a darker shade, Wills is of chocolate hue; Tate of lemon verbena. Wills is volatile, buoyant, a healthy fighting animal, "a Black panther." He is fond of hearing himself called that name. He is funny in his talk, and yet strangely enough his English is almost as good as that of Tate. He uses a little more slang, a few "hot dams," a rough toss jest now and then. But his grammar is as steady as his eye. Remarkable, eh? Two rugged rhetoricians, two Colored men whose speech puts to shame that of many a White schoolteacher. "Hot dam," says Wills, talking about his first fight.[43]

The piece was an absolute insult to both fighters. It was hard to believe that Harry Wills, at this stage of his brilliant career, had to endure such a toxic and racist comparison. No mention of his endless battles against Sam Langford, the one-round delivery of "Gunboat" Smith, or his having to work the docks to make ends meet because every White fighter on the planet wouldn't match with him. Four days later, perhaps things would be different.

"Big" Bill Tate v. Harry Wills—World Colored Heavyweight Championship

On January 6, in a Portland rematch, the pair fought to a 10-round draw. Both claimed the World Colored Heavyweight Championship after the bout, however according to the *Daytona Daily News*, the *Washington Times*, and others, Wills retained the title. The *South Bend News-Time*s stated that Tate retained the title. According to the *Great Falls Tribune*: "Paddy Mullins, Wills' manager, protested that the draw does not entitle Tate to the championship. Mullins asserted that Friday night's fight was a 'fight all over again' and that by fighting it, the two completely cancelled Monday's battle. Sporting writers, however, are inclined to the view that Tate is now technically the champion."[44]

The *Seattle Star* went so far as to say the draw eliminated Wills as a contender for Dempsey's heavyweight crown. Really? Wills could have killed Tate and that still would not have forced a Dempsey-Wills fight.

Meanwhile a new star was being touted, a White boxer by the name of Gene Tunney. By defeating Battling Levinsky on January 13, 1922, in Madison Square Garden, Tunney captured the World Light Heavyweight Championship.

Killing time in Portland, Wills met Sam Langford for the final time on January 17, 1922. "The Black Panther" prowled to an easy 10-round victory. Neither fighter expended much energy during the engagement. In an attempt to corner Dempsey, Wills took a 15-round match against Kid Norfolk in Madison Square Garden on March 2. As the *Capital Journal* reported:

> Norfolk, a Baltimore product, went to the canvas after 26 seconds of boxing in the second round with Wills last night. Several persons claimed to have seen the blow which sent the "Kid" down, but it escaped the notice of a majority of those ringside. After a tame first round Wills and Norfolk started and missed a few punches in the second round, then fell into a clinch. The referee made an effort to separate them when Norfolk toppled over backward. He arose and walked to his corner, apparently unhurt, after taking the count. Wills and the referee, "Kid" McPartland, said the knockout blow was a short inside right to the jaw.[45]

The fighters battled for 25 percent of the net receipts, which meant each received $11,964.77 ($178,925.30 in 2019 dollars).[46] About 14,000 spectators attended the event. Norfolk tipped at 176, while Wills scaled at 211¾ pounds. Paddy Mullins, Wills' manager, was nearly tipped over with the excessive offers that were thrown at his fighter to do battle with the champion: William A. Brady, the noted Broadway and boxing promoter, submitted an offer of $200,000; Harry H. Frazee, noted theatrical man and owner of the Boston Red Sox, stated he would guarantee Dempsey $350,000, and another syndicate offered Dempsey $500,000 … all the interest was beyond the imagination of Wills and everyone associated with the fighter.

Sorting through offers, Wills and his team waited for a positive response from Dempsey. Then they waited again, and then waited some more. Finally in June, Wills, more frustrated than ever, booked a pair of fights with Jeff Clark. They were followed by battles with Buddy Jackson, Tut Jackson and Clem Johnson—all in an attempt to escape the ring rust. He knocked out every opponent. The near-daily articles about the possibility of Dempsey-Wills produced nothing more than hope.

By January 1923, Kearns was once again spinning tales like a top, with common phrases such as: "Wills is not nearly the man he was a year and a half ago…. [He] cannot hit with the same old bone-crushing force…. His hands, fragile as a wine glass, will not stand the strain." Fact or fiction, the propaganda was slowly eroding public demand for the match. And Wills knew it. But his manager, Paddy Mullins, more of a clergyman than a ring jockey, was not doing anything about it—he was totally ineffective. The *Cordova Daily Times* even noted the problem: "No better proof of this is needed than the fact that Wills, a potential million-dollar asset as late as last summer, is now barely solvent, in a fistic sense. He has been allowed to depreciate beyond all reason just because Mullins thinks that modesty is a more seemly virtue than garrulous enterprise. He has never made a serious attempt to keep Wills' name before the public, and as a result the Negro's quest of the heavyweight title is now almost a dead issue…. Mullins, on the contrary, is a managerial oyster."[47]

Harry Wills fought twice in 1923, defeating Homer Smith over 10 rounds on October 11 and knocking out Jack Thompson in the fourth round on November 5. Now being shadowed by a large Colored protégé of Philadelphia fight manager Jimmy Dougherty, his situation looked all too familiar. Dougherty's discovery was a fellow by the name of George Godfrey. The way things were going for Wills, he would have gladly taken a battle with Godfrey had he found a color-blind promoter.

Lick and a Promise

The following year (1924) began with promise as promoter Tex Rickard offered $100,000 to Wills to match against Luis Angel Firpo. Should he win, a $200,000 guarantee would follow for a title fight with Dempsey in September. The famous promoter also desired to match Harry Wills with George Godfrey. Paddy Mullins, as hoped, was deep in negotiation with Rickard. According to the *Evening Star*: "Mullins was quoted tonight [January 12, 1924] as demanding $500,000 for Wills to fight Dempsey and from $250,000 to $300,000 to meet Firpo under Rickard's management, in addition to a share of the motion picture rights."[48]

On January 16, Harry Wills sustained a right hand injury that forced him to postpone four bouts. The best guess was that he would be out of commission for three weeks; moreover, Kearns had a new excuse. As fisherman say: a mackerel's bad luck is a tuna's good fortune.

Taking a 15-round decision over Bartley Madden on June 9, 1924, a recovered Wills was scrambling a bit to get back in the heavyweight picture. Naturally, some critics believed that he should have knocked out Madden. Born in Dublin, Ireland, on September 1, 1890, Bartley Madden was a West Side scrapper with an iron jaw.

A "Working Press" ticket stub from the Firpo v. Wills battle at Boyle's 30 Acres in New Jersey (author's collection).

Far from graceful in the ring, his strengths were his defensive skills and his ability to take a punch. Madden making the distance, as Rickard saw it, cost Wills in the pocketbook. Later, it was rumored that it may have cost Wills a tentative battle against Luis Firpo. Thankfully, that wasn't the case.

August found Harry Wills training at his camp in Peconic Bay in Suffolk County, New York, for his September 11 battle against Firpo, aka El Toro Salvaje de las Pampas. It would take place at Boyle's 30 Acres, over in Jersey City, and was the last bridge to the champion. The prize behind the Rickard promotion was a date with Jack Dempsey on Labor Day, or so he insisted.

Going the 12-round distance, Wills gave a command performance. By New Jersey law, a decision could not be given, but none was needed. Everyone knew who won the fight. Wills' first act was to drop the bull in the second round, which he did with a rigid right to the jaw. The fight crowd—estimated at 80,000 fans—roared in approval as Harry Wills displayed the skills of a heavyweight contender.[49] As the *Evening Star* saw it: "Wills won by a one-sided margin on points. He fought a cool, carefully planned battle. In superb condition and employing all his assets of speed and ring skill, the big Negro blocked the most furious of Firpo's rushes and at the same time delivered an attack at close range that steadily beat down even the staunch courage and endurance of the massive South American."[50]

Although New Jersey's boxing law did not permit decisions, Harry Wills dominated Luis Angel Firpo over 12 rounds at Boyle's 30 Acres, Jersey City, New Jersey. A popular handbill compared both pugilists (author's collection).

Following the fight, Wills headed to a relative's farm in Petersburg, Virginia, to await Rickard's response. A mere two days after the fight, the *Evening Star* disclosed, "Tex Rickard was not impressed by Wills' showing, and has made no plans for a match which would bring the Negro and Dempsey together."[51] You cannot be serious, Wills thought.

Critics were quick to point out that Wills gave so skillful a performance that there was no way Rickard would ever allow him to enter a ring against Dempsey. It appeared as if Wills was damned if he did, and damned if he didn't. Meanwhile, Kearns continued to dangle the carrot in front of Wills in the press, telling reporters that his fighter would likely meet Wills in the fall of 1925. The *Evening Star* reported in January: "Talking to Mullins it is plain to see, too, that he has not great faith that Kearns, Dempsey and company, will risk the valuable title against the Negro, who, while offering no assurance as to his ability to knock out the champion, must certainly be credited with boxing ability sufficient to make it a good bet that he would stand Dempsey off and perhaps outpoint him."[52]

The disappointment continued: It was reported that Wills injured his hands again. He was expected to be out for at least three months. Once healed, he mixed it up a bit during early summer. But with no inviting ring offers, he decided to head to Europe on July 8 with his wife. His goal abroad was to get stronger, stay healthy and not put on a glove.[53]

Rickard went to the press on July 16, claiming that Dempsey signed a contract to fight Wills, but left the date open—the reason for the postponement being Dempsey's long layoff and Wills' absence from the country. On that very same day, Dempsey stated he would likely fight Gene Tunney or Bartley Madden in the fall, and Wills next year. Countering claims was Billy Gibson, Tunney's manager, who stated emphatically in late July that Dempsey would never battle Harry Wills. Surprisingly, on August 1, Dempsey announced a split with Kearns—all negotiations were now up to the fighter.

A relatively inactive Harry Wills, back from Europe and still tired of the Dempsey nonsense, knocked out heavyweight Floyd Johnson, on October 26, 1925, inside the First Regiment Armory in Newark. It took him all of 120 seconds to accomplish the task. Johnson's second threw a towel into the ring when it was clear their fighter could no longer endure the punishment from Wills.

In his only meaningful battle of 1926, Harry Wills, scaling at 214½, lost to Jack Sharkey, who tipped at 188 pounds, by way of a 13th-round disqualification. The battle was held on October 12, at Ebbets Field in Brooklyn. In front of an estimated 45,000 spectators, Referee

A ticket from the Harry Wills v. Charley Weinert bout held on June 19, 1925 (author's collection).

Patsy Haley had to make the disappointing call. As Dempsey lost the title to Gene Tunney in Philadelphia, Pennsylvania, in September 1926, the worthless talk of a battle between Wills and the now-former champion finally came to an end. As the *Evening Star* reported: "Wills, 37, was a bleeding, almost helpless figure, stumbling about the ring in an effort to stem the two-fisted attack of a 24-year-old, when the referee, Patsy Haley, stepped between the fighters in the 13th round of the 15-round match and disqualified the Negro for illegal use of a backhand blow. Wills had been warned repeatedly by Haley for unfair tactics.... It was the first time Wills has met defeat at the hands of a White opponent in his 15 years in the ring."[54]

Afterwards, Wills claimed he had been sick only a few days before the battle—few bought the alibi. Naturally, he was thinking of a rematch with Sharkey. The *Evening Star* predicted: "The chances are Wills will have to pass into limbo of forgotten fighters and live in the memories of the days the great Jack Dempsey refused to fight him and people actually believed he was the real champion."[55]

The end essentially came during a bout held on July 13, 1927, at Ebbets Field in Brooklyn. Harry Wills was knocked out in the fourth round of a battle against Paulino Uzcudon. It took the greatest heavyweight Spain has ever produced to do the job.

Inactive in 1928, he later fought a pair of bouts against Andres Castano (1929). Following a couple of meaningless bouts, Harry Wills, "The Black Panther," retired in 1932. At the age of 43, he had seen and heard enough. Wisely investing his ring earnings in a Harlem real estate business, he finally felt secure. Handsome, articulate, and always sharply dressed, Wills was a successful businessman and was loved by his community. Folks recalled that he enjoyed an occasional good cigar (though he never drank or smoked cigarettes), dancing and going to the theater. He died at Jewish Memorial Hospital in New York City of complications from diabetes on December 21, 1958.

The Color Line, 1918–1922[56]

Forever remembered for the one fight he never had, Harry Wills, a top heavyweight contender in the early 1920s and a World Colored Heavyweight Champion, was denied a title shot because Jack Dempsey & Company couldn't look beyond his skin color. Even to this day, it's hard to believe that one party could have such a monumental influence on one sport.

But not even Dempsey, or Kearns for that matter, could stop the erosion of the color line outside boxing. Taking a look at the proof:

In his first statement after becoming world heavyweight champion, Jack Dempsey announced that he would draw the color line. And he did just that. His statement happened to coincide with Red Summer—a label given to 25 race riots that took place across the nation. Voices needed to be heard.

Almost a year after Dempsey's first title defense, the 19th Amendment to the Constitution was ratified, giving all women the right to vote. Nonetheless, African American women, not to mention African American men, were continually denied the franchise in most Southern states. Actions needed to be taken.

In 1921, the year in which Dempsey defended his title against his first foreign adversary, Georges Carpentier, three ladies become the first African American women to earn Ph.D. degrees. Voices were being heard.

By the time Dempsey lost his World Heavyweight Championship, on September 23, 1926, the Cotton Club opened in Harlem (1923), Rojo Jack became the first African American to participate in professional automobile racing (1923), and the National Bar Association, an organization of Black attorneys, was established in Des Moines, Iowa. Actions were yielding results.

Alexander Graham Bell once quipped, "When one door closes another door opens; but we so often look so long and so regretfully upon the closed door, that we do not see the ones which open for us."

While Harry Wills never had his door opened, thankfully others did.

TWELVE

"Big" Bill Tate

Thirty-two years before the birth of William G. Tate, the Confederate States of America chose Montgomery, Alabama, as its first capital. It remained so until the Confederate seat of government moved to Richmond, Virginia, in May of that year, 1861. As one of the seven original secessionist slave-holding states in the Confederacy, Alabama residents were secure in their beliefs. Heavily dependent upon agriculture, particularly cotton, and a plantation system that relied upon the labor of African American slaves, they had to be. As one could imagine, reestablishing race relations after the Civil War presented a challenge.

William George Tate was born in Montgomery on November 5, 1893. Like other Blacks born during the late 19th century, he developed the art of forbearance to deal with racially insensitive remarks and behaviors.[1] Fortunately for William, he had two pathways in which to focus his energy, education and pugilism. For education, he turned to Alabama's Normal School for Colored Students, a state-supported teacher's college for African Americans, and received his diploma in 1905. With his long face, bushy eyebrows, and captivating eyes, Tate was a handsome man with an impressive physique. Standing over six feet, six inches, he was tough to overlook. Soon, Tate met a gentleman named Dr. Caffrey, who convinced the youngster that prize fighting just might be a viable option. Tate, who had his heart set on becoming a doctor, wasn't so certain. Yet, encouraged by the optimism expressed by those around him, he packed his belongings and headed off for New Jersey.[2]

The City of Newark was undergoing tremendous population growth entering the 20th century. As a shipping and rail hub, only a stone's throw from Manhattan, it had a population of more than 350,000 when Bill Tate arrived. Boxing flourished, and if the youngster was looking for a place to refine his skills, this was it.

Tate emerged in the city thanks to a peculiar opportunity. Colored heavyweight contender Joe Jeannette was training in the area and needed some sacrificial lambs, or punching bags if you will. The reason: He was preparing for a tentative match against Jack Johnson. So on August 20, 1912, he tackled not one, but two fighters at Morris Park. The results were picked up by the *El Paso Herald* under the headline, "Jeannette Knocks Out Two Negro Opponents": "Joe Jeannette, who is matched to meet Jack Johnson, defeated two Negro opponents, Bill Tate, of Tennessee, and Battling Brooks, of Michigan, knocking each out in the second round."[3]

Tennessee was likely a stop along Tate's pugilistic journey as he made his way northeast. Naturally, Jeannette's name carried prestige suitable for the sports pages, so the news snippet was picked up by the dailies. That this was Tate's first professional battle was unlikely. But if it was, what a way it was to get his feet wet. Jeannette's other opponent, Jack Brooks, a middleweight punching bag from "The City," was familiar to many area pugs—he trained at the Sharkey Athletic Club.

Tate surfaced again in the fall of 1912, only across the river in New York City. According to the *Washington Herald*: "Bill Tate, the Tennessee heavy-weight, stopped "Chuck" Carlton, of New York, in five rounds at the Queensboro Athletic Club matinee today. Tate floored his adversary six times in the fateful round and the referee then halted the bout."[4]

As Carlton, also spelled Carleton, was a bit more than a tomato can, the win was a boost for Tate. As a young heavyweight, he was engaging in as many ring opportunities as he could. On December 7, he climbed into the ring with the big Canadian, Fred McKay, aka Fred McLaglen. Standing over six feet, five inches, with an 82-inch reach, McKay, like Tate, was trying to establish a reputation. A recap of their ring battle was printed in the *Salt Lake Tribune*: "Fred McKay, the Winnipeg giant, came a little closer into the limelight as a prominent White Hope last night by knocking out Bill Tate at the Queensboro A.C. The work was done in the eighth with a left to the body and a right to the jaw. This is the seventh knockout scored by McKay during a month."[5]

Questioning his commitment to the sport, Tate, who had lost four of his five ring battles, disappeared from the city boxing scene. It was believed that he headed to California.[6]

Resurfacing on August 11, 1914, at Rockaway Beach Athletic Club, Bill Tate greeted, of all people, Joe Jeannette. The seasoned veteran of more than 100 battles stopped the youngster in six rounds—more of a punching bag than an opponent, felt the referee, who was forced to conclude the contest. Tate would meet Jeannette again on December 14, at the Irving Athletic Club in Brooklyn. Although Tate outweighed his antagonist by 23 pounds, he was clearly no match for a talent like Jeannette. Tate lost the 10-round no-decision. However, Jeannette, well over a decade older than Tate, saw promise in the youngster and encouraged him to continue his training.

Tate began 1915 with a draw against John Lester Johnson on January 25 and a loss to Joe Jeannette on February 1. In the latter, Tate was forced to quit due to an injured hand. The

Living in Brooklyn (pictured here) in 1915, Tate often recalled the frustration brought about by the transit strike (Library of Congress, LC-DIG-ggbain—29002).

remainder of the year was rather lackluster, as the fighter noticeably stepped down in talent. Participating in Jim Clancy's first boxing show in the New Haven, Connecticut, rink, Tate met Dave Mills, the California heavyweight and protégé of Sam McVey. Although a great opportunity for both fighters, the battle was halted after seven rounds because of stalling and deemed a no-contest.

Unfortunately, some of Tate's ring hardship carried over the following year. He was disqualified for stalling during a bout against John Lester Johnson, his next recognized opponent, in Brooklyn on January 24, 1916. Feeling it was time for a change, he accepted an invitation to travel to Panama City, Panama, to display his ring prowess. Four consecutive knockout victories, including two on the same day, were enough to match him against Kid Norfolk on June 11. In a battle billed as the Heavyweight Championship of Panama, Norfolk, who was being touted (along with Harry Wills) as a candidate for the heavyweight championship, pummeled Tate over 20 rounds. Tate was in over his head and he knew it.

Returning home in October, Tate participated in the opener for the winter season of boxing at the Harlem Sporting Club, of Hammel's, Rockaway Beach. There he knocked out Rufus Cameron, the Canadian heavyweight, in the sixth round of the main event. The year ended with two solid and memorable contests: a 10-round no-decision against Harry Wills in Brooklyn and a 10-round no-decision against Sam Langford in Syracuse. While Wills clearly got the best of him in the former, Tate rebounded with a performance seen as a draw against Langford. Extolled as the "Black Jess Willard," Tate hoped to be given the same opportunities as the "Pottawatomie Giant." But hope, like life, was a four-letter word without obligation.

"Big" Bill Tate v. Sam Langford—World Colored Heavyweight Championship

For Bill Tate, 1917 was all about Sam Langford and Ed "Gunboat" Smith. On January 25, he was given a 12-round decision over Langford in a fight held at the Grand Opera House in Kansas City, Missouri. While the event results appeared in a few newspapers, it was given the typical two-sentence synopsis with no mention of the title. Satisfied with his victory—which any fighter would be after facing Sam Langford—Tate took a brief break. He faced Langford again, this time in St. Louis, Missouri, on May 1.

Sam Langford v. "Big" Bill Tate—World Colored Heavyweight Championship

If this fight was for the Colored Heavyweight Championship of the World, it certainly wasn't reported as such in most newspapers. The Lake County Times, one of the few periodicals which gave it more than a two-sentence review, stated: "Sam Langford of Chicago knocked out Bill Tate of New York in the sixth round of a scheduled 12 round bout. A right hook to the jaw, which Langford put over while Tate was holding, sent Tate down and out. It was Sam's bout all the way. Tate did a lot of holding and backed away most of the time. Langford kept after him all the time and inflicted severe punishment about the body."[7]

At this stage of his career, Langford, always mindful of the prize, expelled only the energy needed to conquer his rival. As for Tate, the highlight of his career thus far was his previous victory over the "Boston Tar Baby"—up to that point he had never defeated a fighter with over eight recorded wins.

Ed "Gunboat" Smith, who we are all too familiar with at this point, wasn't bashful about meeting the best competition he could find, even if it wasn't intended that way. According to the *Evening World*: "Bill Tate, substituting for Battling Levinsky at Brown's Far Rockaway Club, was outpointed by Gunboat Smith in 10 rounds last night (August 10). Tate hung on a great deal to avoid the Gunner's healthy lunges. Levinsky did not appear because of an injury to his foot suffered during training."[8]

Concurrently, Salt Lake City White heavyweight Jack Dempsey was putting forth a claim to battle Jess Willard for the title. According to the *El Paso Herald*: "Dempsey has a good record in the four round game on the Pacific coast. His most notable achievement was a victory over Carl Morris. Dempsey also claims a decision over Gunboat Smith. Dempsey is six feet two, and when in condition scales a few pounds more than 200. Most of his battles have been at San Francisco or in that vicinity."[9]

Getting away from New York in 1918, three of Bill Tate's four engagements occurred in Philadelphia. A couple of lackluster victories, along with sparring and exhibitions, occupied his time until spring. Two April battles, the first against Kid Norfolk and the next against Jack Thompson, would highlight his year.

On April 22, as part of a big all-star card the Pickwick Club conducted in Baltimore at the Lyric, Bill Tate was defeated by Kid Norfolk. Tate gave it his best effort over seven rounds, but simply could not sustain any more damage—it was a loss by technical knockout. A week later he was back in the ring, this time facing pool fighter Jack Thompson. The bout was held at the Olympia Athletic Club in Philadelphia and proved to be a controversial affair. The *Evening Public Ledger* described the affair:

> The first two rounds were slightly in Tate's favor, for it was the first time Thompson had fought a larger opponent than himself and he was at a loss as to how to meet his man. In the third Thompson appeared to have fathomed Tate's style and landed quite a few telling rights and lefts. Instead of directing his attack to Tate's stomach, as Kid Norfolk did with such success as to make Tate quit last week in Baltimore, Thompson tried to land a knockout punch on Tate's jaw. It was in this frame that the big New Yorker began to get the "razz" for his continual holding.[10]

Despite warnings from Referee Pop O'Brien, Tate continued to hold until the bout was stopped.[11] For a dejected Tate, it was his final recorded fight of the year. Just when he felt his career was on a downward slide, a door opened.[12]

A Burgeoning Friendship, Bill Tate and Jack Dempsey

In 1919, Jack Dempsey asked Bill Tate to assist him in pursuit of the World Heavyweight Championship. He accepted, a decision that would forever alter his life. Granted, Jess Willard was a half-inch taller, with a two-inch reach advantage, but Tate could be equally intimidating. Had Dempsey made the perfect choice?[13] Only time would tell.

Although not a household name like that of his employer, the name Tate would become familiar to many in the fistic world; consequently, he received three times the amount of publicity he had prior to his commitment.[14] In addition to Tate, Dempsey also employed Billy Miske, Dan Dailey, Denver Jack Dyer, the Jamaica Kid, and John Lester Johnson. The field of half–White and half–Black sparring partners was aimed at giving Dempsey all the skills he felt necessary to defeat Willard. However, just in case, Dempsey also employed wrestler "Strangler" Lewis. Hey, you never know.

Bill Tate quickly became an attraction at Dempsey's training quarters as throngs of fans paid a small fee to watch him spar with "The Manassa Mauler." He even signed a few autographs. The pair had their first workout on May 24, when they went two rounds in front of 400 visitors. Tate's size was a novelty, the contrast ever apparent in the 16mm black and white movie film of the pair sparring in the ring. Shuffling his big feet, while keeping his bobbing and crouching White nemesis at arm's length, Tate had the strength but not the speed of his adversary. Dempsey's spring-loaded assaults, featuring that roundhouse left, were punishing. Pushing head-first into Tate's chest, Dempsey diligently attempted to move the giant. But Tate's upper-body strength, anchored by his massive shoulders, proved difficult to overpower.

As Tate's responsibilities with Dempsey began to wind down, he took a bout in Minneapolis on June 19, against Sam Langford, the first in a pair of fights against his rival that year. The outdoor bout saw Dempsey's sparring partner disqualified in the fifth round for holding—the action was now tarnishing his reputation. Tate, having clinched relentlessly, refused instructions to break. This left Referee George Barton with little choice but to award the bout to Langford. The verdict was an embarrassment, yet somewhat understandable considering Tate's current role.

Sixty-five days later, on August 23, it was time for a rematch. In outstanding fighting form, Bill Tate once again faced the "Boston Tar Baby." The location this time was Grand Rapids, Michigan. Taking it hard to his rival early in the 10-round fracas, he managed to drop his adversary in the third term. Just the same, Langford took command over the bulk of the battle and was awarded the referee's decision. Those in attendance, a majority curious to witness Dempsey's primary target, were part of the largest crowd that ever paid to see a Grand Rapids boxing bout—neither fighter objecting to riding a pair of coattails all the way to the bank.

When Willard lost the Heavyweight Championship of the World to Dempsey on July 4, 1919, everything in and around boxing changed. The victory was awarded when the champion was unable to continue after the third round. Reigning atop the heavyweights from 1919 to 1926, Jack Dempsey was as alluring as he was dominant. His aggressive fighting style and exceptional punching power made him one of the most popular boxers in history and a cultural icon of the 1920s. Setting fi-

William G. Tate, pictured here in a passport photograph, was often called to mind as Jack Dempsey's favorite sparring partner (author's collection).

nancial and attendance records—the first million-dollar gate often recalled—was only part of his appeal. He was believable—that alone proved inspiring to many. If Jack Dempsey could do it, then so could they.

Forever tied to the champion, Tate was proud of the association. He had grown close to Dempsey and was considered a confidante. After the Willard fight, when the champion headed west to his posh rented Victorian home in Los Angeles, Tate was invited along. Dempsey, with his fierce good looks and swarthy brow, had turned Hollywood. Figuring every star had a butler, Tate assumed the task—the fictional role, not an insult, but evidence of an endearing friendship. Naturally, Bill knew Jack, and more importantly knew his place.

On February 25, 1920, Tate knocked out veteran Ed "Gunboat" Smith in the fourth round of their bout in Oakland, California. A mere dozen fights from the end of his career, Smith witnessed firsthand the renewed confidence in Tate—a byproduct of sparring with the champion.

Dempsey, to his credit, always backed his supporters. When Jack Johnson challenged the heavyweight champion in March, Dempsey stated that he would match the ex-champion with his sparring partner, and "bet Johnson all he wants that Tate will lick him."[15]

Bill Tate met Sam Langford once again, but this time as a six-round preliminary before the Dempsey-Miske fight held in Benton Harbor, Michigan. The close but uneventful bout saw Tate take command of the ring. He led with his effective left jab and maximized his 36-pound weight advantage. As the *Arizona Republican* noted: "Tate won by a shade, but not because Langford was not game, for the visitor from the East displayed an almost inhuman capacity for turning wicked rights by interposing his head as an obstacle."[16]

Obviously, being on a heavyweight championship card—Dempsey's first defense of the title, though the third time he had met Miske—wasn't a bad opportunity for any fighter, yet alone a Black pugilist. The exposure for both Tate and Langford was invaluable. Attendance at Floyd Fitzsimmons Arena, on September 6, 1920, was reported to be 11,346. This was also the first bout broadcast on radio. Incidentally, Tate had his boss in fine condition as Dempsey took the knockout victory at the 1:13 mark of the third round.

Dempsey had one more defense before finishing the year: Bill Brennan was knocked out by the heavyweight champion of the world at the 1:57 mark of the 12th round. The scheduled 15-round bout was held in Madison Square Garden on December 14. In a nice twist to the event, Bill Tate, Dempsey's primary sparring partner, met "Kid" Norfolk, Brennan's primary target, in a 10-round preliminary. The latter was assisting Brennan at the Thomas farm, just outside of Providence, and locally at Billy Grupp's gymnasium. While training in the city, Dempsey found two sites accommodating, Central Park and aboard the United Sates training ship USS *Granite State*, formerly the USS *New Hampshire*, which was anchored in the Hudson off Ninety-Sixth Street. The champion brought with him six sparring partners, including Tate.

Tate, who scaled at 234¾, towered over his Black opponent. Norfolk, who tipped at 182¼, looked like David facing Goliath. But the Baltimore boxer, with his spring-loaded, crouching assaults and targeted rights, was not the least bit intimidated. Norfolk was also quicker and ducked far more punches. By the fifth round, Kearns, who was in Tate's corner, reprimanded him for not being aggressive enough. It was Norfolk's fight from the seventh round forward, and thus he was awarded the decision.

A diamond belt was also put on the line during the contest. The belt, which belonged to promoter Tex Rickard, had to be defended and won three times (the promoter's rules) before a fighter could take ownership. Norfolk, with one victory to his credit, was on his way.

Not so fast, declared Jack Johnson from Leavenworth Prison in Kansas. Some Black fighters believed Johnson was still the World Colored Heavyweight Champion—as title-holder he was never defeated by a Black man. "Therefore, they say," according to Damon Runyon, "if there is such a thing as a Colored title, Johnson is the title holder." The famed columnist continued, "Even if Johnson is automatically legislated out of the running by not being given any matches, there is still Harry Wills. To call a man who has not met Wills, the colored champion, would be ridiculous."[17]

Harry Wills v. "Big" Bill Tate—World Colored Heavyweight Championship

On January 17, 1921, Bill Tate, in his first fight of the year, was knocked out by Harry Wills. It happened in the second round of a scheduled 15-round contest. It was also the first of five battles between the pair. With the victory, inside the Broadway Auditorium in Buffalo, New York, Harry Wills retained the World Colored Heavyweight. The intriguing encounter picked up some media attention. The *Evening Star* noted:

> Tate, whose job has been to stall off Dempsey's wallops the past two years, has developed a defensive attitude in his fights, and thus in recent bouts has not shown as well as he should. For he has a wallop and, for a big man, is very fast. Anyway, in the first round of the Wills match he clipped the New Orleans fighter on the jaw and sent him against the ropes. Rushing in, he landed again as Wills was recovering. Wills almost went out of the ring and was plainly groggy. Tate let drive what was intended to be—and would have been—the finishing blow. But in his eagerness his aim was not good. The punch glanced off the side of Wills' head. The bell rang and Wills recovered from the effects of his punching. In the second round, he applied his well-known hitting ability to Tate's jaw and the Kearns fighter went to sleep.[18]

Feeling pressure from manager Jack "Doc" Kearns and his assistant, Dan McKetrick, Tate resigned his position as a sparring partner for Jack Dempsey the first week of February. Unfortunately, the fighter had to take Kearns to court in order to collect his overdue payments. According to a report published in the *New York Herald*: "The Negro claimed there was due to him $1,000 for training Jack Dempsey to meet Brennan, and another $800 for his service in stopping the champ's punches when Dempsey trained for his fight with Miske."[19]

To little surprise, sparring services of "Kid" Norfolk were contracted by Kearns. Tate, for all intents and purposes, fell from the sports pages until his 15-round battle against Harry Wills, on July 2, 1921. The event was conducted at Queensboro Stadium in Long Island City. In that contest, Wills, tipping at 214, knocked out Tate, who scaled at 243, in the sixth round. According to the *Evening Star*: "The bell saved Tate in the fifth round, when he was knocked down twice, and he took a count of nine in the sixth before the full count. Later, on July 14, it was learned, without explanation, that Tate's New York State boxing license had been revoked."[20]

Harry Wills v. "Big" Bill Tate—World Colored Heavyweight Championship

On December 8, 1921, at Stockyards Stadium in Denver, Harry Wills captured a 12-round decision over Bill Tate. It was the third time the pair had met. Promoted as for the

World Colored Heavyweight Championship, the match drew little fanfare surrounding the designation. The typical two-line summary of the conflict stated the result and an acknowledgment of Tate's ability to withstand punishment.

Now making his home in Chicago, Bill Tate left for Portland, Oregon, on December 24, to prepare for a new year. Out from underneath the Dempsey umbrella, Tate believed it was his time to shine. Heartened by his new manager, Howard Carr, who believed strongly in the fighter's ability, he had never felt better.

"Big" Bill Tate v. Harry Wills—World Colored Heavyweight Championship

British writer C.S. Lewis once quipped, "You can't go back and change the beginning, but you can start where you are and change the ending." Perhaps Tate was doing just that as he once again met Harry Wills. Having every intention to start off the year with a solid performance, Tate was confident and certainly not intimidated by his rival. After all, Wills wanted what he wanted: a championship date with Jack Dempsey. Even so, following the fallout with Kearns, Tate understood his chances were dramatically diminished.

On January 2, 1922, in Milwaukie, Oregon, in a bout for the World Colored heavyweight Championship, Bill Tate won on a foul over Harry Wills in the very first round. When the opening gong sounded, the battle, scheduled for 10 rounds, appeared routine. Targeting his range with his extended left hand, Tate moved about the ring with that customary shuffle of his. Wills, however, appeared like a man on a mission. The *Bisbee Daily Review* noted the action: "Wills smashed Tate with a right to the jaw when Tate was attempting to obey the referee's order to break from a clinch. The round had about 10 seconds to go."[21]

For both fighters, it was a disappointing ending. After witnessing Tate drop to the floor, Referee Louttit made the proper call—he had instructed both fighters to break clean. After Tate pulled himself up, he quickly left the ring. Meanwhile, Wills had no idea what had just happened. Noticing that Tate was gone, Wills headed to his opponent's dressing room to demand an explanation. Immediately, the crowd aired their dissatisfaction—they wanted Tate to finish the contest. Tate's manager, however, stated that they would stand on the referee's award. Perhaps the *Seattle Star* said it best: "The result of what had been hailed as a fight of first class proportions today was regarded as the smelliest fiasco ever staged in a Western ring."[22] Later, many sportswriters claimed that it was this fight that killed all talk about a possible Wills-Dempsey match.[23]

Harry Wills v. "Big" Bill Tate—World Colored Heavyweight Championship

Following the previous fiasco, both parties agreed to meet in the same ring, in front of the same crowd. It would also be the final time the pair would meet. According to the *Richmond Palladium and Sun-Telegram*: "With everybody connected with the show and the fans all "het up," the Milwaukie (Oregon) commission met, and the fighters demanding their money were told they would not receive it until the fight was finished. The managers agreed on another clash."[24]

Harry Wills validated his claim to the World Colored Heavyweight crown by battling

Bill Tate to a 10-round draw on January 6, 1922. According to the *Washington Times*: "Tate was on the defensive most of the time, but managed to land repeatedly on Wills with blows that hurt the New Orleans battler. In the ninth round Tate caught Wills with an uppercut that sent one knee to the canvas and had him groggy for a time. Wills punished Tate badly with smashing blows to the kidneys."[25]

Paddy Mullins, Wills' manager, confirmed his fighter's title: It was his belief that, by fighting again, the previous fight was cancelled.[26] Many sportswriters, however, disagreed; they were convinced that Tate was technically the champion.

Gospel According to Bill

If anyone could give an accurate assessment regarding a match between Jack Dempsey and Harry Wills, it would certainly be Bill Tate. Granted that to do so would require the former sparring partner to separate himself from all hard feelings regarding both fighters, but let's give him the benefit of the doubt. The *Washington Times* noted: "Tate's prediction: Dempsey would knock out Wills within six or seven rounds. The big fighter admitted that Dempsey could take Wills out in the first if his left hook caught Harry's jaw. According to Tate, 'When Jack hits you with that left swinger the show's over.' Tate also insisted that he was not a candidate for Jack's title. 'Dempsey is one of my best friends,' he remarked. 'If the public insist upon the match just lay your ticket at the window that Bill will take second place money.'"[27]

Following the Wills debacle, Bill Tate sporadically fought—he broke a bone in his hand in late March—and finished 1922 with two major loses: a 15-round defeat to Jack Thompson on June 21, in New Orleans, and a 12-round loss to Sam Langford on August 4 in Tulsa.

As Tate's stock fell, the fighter found consolation with only about a handful of battles per year until retirement in 1927. He picked up some pocket cash assisting Luis Angel Firpo in training for his battle against Jess Willard. There was an offer, made by Tex Rickard, to match him against Harry Wills in Madison Square Garden, but Paddy Mullins refused to accept it. However, on November 2, Tate did land a nice Garden 10-round semi-final—on the Renault-Johnson card—against George Godfrey. In a bout that didn't smell good according to some fans, Godfrey knocked Tate out in the seventh round.

William George Tate died on August 10, 1953, at the age of 59.

The Color Line, 1917–1922

For every worthy Black heavyweight, and there were a few, having Jack Dempsey draw the color line was the greatest frustration of their career. To look in a mirror and realize that you have all the prerequisites of being a champion except skin color, yet weren't given an opportunity, was simply inexcusable. And yet, that was William George Tate. Even if he wasn't alone, the situation was simply heartbreaking. What value a dream unfulfilled?

In retrospect, and attempting to look at it in a positive light, being forever known as the premier sparring partner to the greatest fistic box-office attraction of all time was at least being recognized. There were many men, of all ethnic origins, who would have given their right arm to be in Tate's position. But even Jack Dempsey, considered by some the apotheosis of the professional fighter, wasn't perfect.

There were instances where Dempsey was embarrassed to draw the color line. While he listened to Kearns, he respected Rickard. For four years, Wills and Mullins hounded Dempsey for a fight. It got to a point where Dempsey was sick and tired of hearing it, and he let it be known that he was fine with the idea. Rickard, who oversaw the Johnson-Jeffries battle, wanted nothing to do with a mixed promotion. In other words, he didn't want to have to search for another "White Hope," should Wills be victorious.

As for Kearns, well, he wanted no part of "a mixed bout on general principles."[28] Letting Black heavyweight contenders fight amongst themselves was perfectly fine for the crafty manager. Kearns masterfully played each situation, always certain to keep his fighter one hurdle, or bout ahead. His classic, overused quip was: If [blank] defeated [blank], then he would be in contention for a shot at Dempsey. If, of course, they found a promoter to meet their terms and conditions.

Turning to the *Evening World* and what boxing fans think:

> There's no shame to be beaten by any one, but there's lots of shame being called "afraid" or "yellow."
>
> Democratic as we all may be, we must nonetheless recognize the fact that the lowest instincts of man is aroused if a Negro should ever become champion.
>
> A well-known expert of boxing said a Negro champion would kill the sport. I, for one, think he is wrong. If anything, it will increase interest in boxing.[29]

Jack Dempsey noted many times that he felt Tate and the Jamaica Kid were the finest sparring partners he ever had. He said so with every ounce of sincerity. Dempsey and Tate developed a strong bond and one that became evident as time passed. Tate wasn't only in his corner while he battled Willard, he was always there.

Tate's time with Dempsey not only brought him some needed publicity, it also landed him on championship cards. Not to drag the whole psychology factor into play, but there were times when Tate represented more than just himself to the champion. He represented his race—he was Jack Johnson, Harry Wills, and every Black contender Dempsey was accused of ducking. Having Tate on his ticket was not only paying back a good friend, it helped dampen the racial criticism. "Big" Bill Tate may never have crossed, or even broken the color line, but he certainly lowered the bar.

Thirteen

The Leiperville Shadow

When somebody like Sam Langford tells you to look him up when you're in Chicago, you don't waste time. After resigning from military service, Feab Williams relocated to the "Windy City" and was taken under the tutelage of Langford, Bobby Dobbs, and Jack Blackburn. Williams, who stood an intimidating six feet, three-and-a-half inches and scaled at 205 pounds, needed a fight moniker, a name that set fear in the heart of his opponent. So he adopted the moniker George Godfrey as a tribute to the great Black Canadian heavyweight pioneer.

Born on February 27, 1896, in Mobile, Alabama, Feab Sylvestor (Smith) Williams spent his youth in Chicago—his family moved there when he was only two.[1] At about the age of 15, and growing like a weed, Williams headed south to New Orleans.[2] There the youngster, already about six feet tall, picked up odd jobs at the bustling port. To supplement his income, he began fighting at some of the smaller clubs. Like others his age, he was trying to find his calling. When the situation no longer suited his needs, he headed back to his roots, back to Mobile, Alabama. Finding employment at the boiler shop of a Mobile shipyard (Alabama Dry Dock and Ship Company), Williams worked hard until the United States entered World War I in 1917.[3] Enlisting, he became part of the 131st Infantry before being transferred to the 421st Labor Battalion stationed at Camp Sheridan, Montgomery, Alabama. Sparring in his spare time, Williams became rather proficient with the mitts. As fate might have it, Sam Langford, while giving a boxing exhibition in camp, happened to witness the youngster conducting a clinic against his opponent. The "Boston Tar Baby," who was impressed by few, liked what he saw in Williams. Handing the youth his business card, Langford told Williams to look him up in Chicago after the war.[4]

Turning pro in 1919, Godfrey picked up his fair share of recorded and unrecorded battles as he refined his skills. His hand speed was noticeably improving, as was his footwork. Working primarily out of the Southern Athletic Club in Memphis, he engaged—likely more confidence builders than anything else—with many of the Colored boxers including Sam Langford and Battling Gahee. When he fought Langford in Hot Springs on November 17, 1920, his name was picked up in the press, even if it was in a losing effort, Godfrey still got a kick out of the plug.[5] Later, by the fall of 1921, he was beginning to attract attention on his own. The *Washington Times* reported: "Down in Mobile they have unearthed a big fellow who shows signs of promise. He is George Godfrey, a giant scaling 215 pounds, standing six feet three and a half inches. Like so many Negro boxers, he possesses a marvelous physique, and on looks he should go far. At present he has not had much experience, although he has met a few of the tough ones, among them Sam Langford. Godfrey has been boxing with Jack Johnson as his sparring partner and is said to be learning fast."[6]

On July 9, 1921, Jack Johnson was released from Leavenworth Prison. Knowing that being Jack Johnson wasn't so easy before incarceration, the uncertainty of his release, or how society would greet the former champion, weighed on the fighter's mind. The ring was his stage, the vehicle that gave his life meaning. Without a spotlight, a star was no more than an extra. Johnson abhorred the thought of being yesterday's news, so he decided on a vaudeville tour. For that he needed a sparring partner, someone who looked impressive but wasn't skillful enough to do any damage. Godfrey auditioned for the part but proved too clever. The experience proved fruitful, however, as he landed a few local exhibitions with the former champion. It was Johnson who contacted his friend Jimmy Dougherty and suggested he buy out his contract, thus taking the fighter under his managerial wing.[7] With that, "The Leiperville Shadow" was born—the origin of the sobriquet soon to come to light.

Working him up in competition, Godfrey's handler matched him with the likes of George "Jack" Ward and Jack Thompson in 1922.[8] Other than Langford, Thompson, whom he lost to last year, was the most experienced fighter Godfrey had faced. Meeting over at the Pioneer Sporting Club in New York, the pair squared off in the main event on December 5. Thompson, suffering from an injured left mitt, tried hard to dispose of Godfrey early, but his strategy failed. Once he was taking a rather healthy beating, his seconds tossed up the towel to give Godfrey the fifth-round verdict. "The Leiperville Shadow" was quickly becoming noted for his cleverness, sharp left jab and powerful right hand.

In an indication of just how quickly Godfrey was maturing as a boxer, in February 1923, this piece appeared in the *Evening Star*: "Why, only today Jim Dougherty of Leiperville apologetically offered Harry Wills $5,000 to fight eight rounds with George Godfrey, in Philadelphia. Imagine being timid about offering a Negro roustabout what is two or three years' salary for most of us to fight eight rounds with an unknown ham. Ye gads! It's time to handle the fight game without gloves."[9]

James F. Dougherty, a flamboyant figure who had spent 25 years in and around the ring, saw promise in Godfrey.[10] "The Baron of Leiperville," as he was known, was recognized as a talented boxing promoter who helped establish Chester and Leiperville (which is now known as Crum Lynne, Pennsylvania, just outside Philadelphia) as hotspots for pugilism. If anyone in Philly could push Godfrey into the forefront, it was Dougherty. So, just as Harry Wills pestered Jack Dempsey, George Godfrey, via "The Baron," would shadow "The Black Panther." As the *Evening Star* noted: "The only thing that prevents Godfrey from looming as a serious annoyance to Wills is the fact that, both men being Colored, no promoter will offer much money for the bout. If some one should promise a purse of impressive dimensions Wills would probably be forced to fight, although it looks as though he doesn't care about the idea."[11]

Also in 1923, George Godfrey landed his first two dates inside Madison Square Garden: On February 21, he kayoed tomato can Jim Pearson in the first round, and later, on November 2, he knocked out "Big" Bill Tate.[12] The fighter's only losses for the year, thankfully, came at smaller venues. Godfrey was sent to dreamland by the clever Canadian heavyweight Jack Renault on March 9 (Pioneer Sporting Club) and lost on a disqualification on December 13 against punching bag Battling Owens (Oak Hill Auditorium).[13] With Godfrey erratic, yet still maturing, Dougherty needed to bring his fighter under control.

In May, Godfrey even found himself assisting one of his manager's friends, Jack Dempsey. It seems Dougherty convinced the champion that his fighter was the perfect sparring partner. Dempsey, who was preparing to meet Tommy Gibbons, invited Godfrey to join his training camp.[14] The experience—or instant credibility, if you will—garnered Godfrey some outstanding press, until he suffered a fractured rib at the end of June. Talk about punching power, Dempsey did the sparring damage with 16-ounce gloves! Later, in August, Godfrey caught up to the champion again during his preparation against Luis Angel Firpo. Dempsey's training camp was held at Saratoga Springs, New York.

Fighting out of Philadelphia in 1924, Godfrey had just a handful of battles. It was one of those years where his losses, which were against White fighters Tom Cowler and Jack Renault, were more impressive than his victories—he defeated Jack Thompson, Walter "Farmer" Lodge, and Joe White.[15] Meanwhile, Jimmy Dougherty, always a step away from a goldmine, was trying to persuade Tex Rickard to assist him in conducting a real Colored heavyweight championship—the winner to receive the title as champion of a new class, the Colored heavyweight class. Of course, Rickard would then pit the Black and White champions against each other. "The Baron" was also working hard to lure Harry Wills into a ring with Godfrey, but "The Black Panther" wasn't biting.[16]

By early 1925, a bit disillusioned by the Philly fight scene, Godfrey headed west to Los Angeles.[17] It was the Roaring Twenties, and Americans fell in love with the cinema and Southern California. Just the name "Hollywood," which became synonymous with the U.S. film industry, evoked exhilaration and opportunity. It was from this beautiful vista that manager Dougherty hoped to land bigger fish. On March 26, "The Baron" fired off a telegram to the New York State Athletic Commission (NYSAC) that challenged Harry Wills, Tommy Gibbons, and Jack Dempsey, and any other contender for that matter, to fight against Godfrey. While "The Baron" trolled, his premier fighter disposed of the catch of the day, or the seasoned local pugs. Six California bouts, along with a handful of one-offs, set up the year for "The Leiperville Shadow." A decision over Canadian favorite Jack Renault, two victories over White heavy Martin Burke, also a Dempsey sparring partner, and a fifth-round knockout of "White Hope" Fred Fulton catapulted Godfrey into the forefront. Compiling 11 consecutive victories, he finished the year in style.

On a sad and different note: During a year that looked promising for the Black heavyweight contender, White California residents, who objected to encroachment by the pugilist, attacked his home on October 9, 1925. The *Evening Star* described the event: "A mob of indignant White residents stormed the Los Angeles home of George Godfrey, Negro boxer, of Philadelphia last night [October 9]. They were driven away after they had smashed windows and destroyed furniture. Godfrey and other occupants were not at home. The mob's rage apparently was not directed at Godfrey personally, but against what residents declared was Negro encroachment on a White residence district."[18]

It was a pathetic reminder that ignorance has no boundaries. Following the incident, George Godfrey would battle in New Orleans, Minneapolis, and New York City, the latter bout part of a Christmas charity event held inside Madison Square Garden.

Nine battles comprised 1926 for George Godfrey—four on the West Coast, one in the Midwest, and four in the East. Posting a record of 6–2, with one no-contest, he never looked better. While on the West Coast, Godfrey also appeared in the battle scenes for *Old Ironsides*, a motion picture being filmed off Catalina Island. The silent film, distributed by Paramount Pictures, starred Charles Farrell, Esther Ralston, Wallace Beery, and George Bancroft. Godfrey was cast as the cook aboard the USS *Constitution*. As if the movie wasn't exciting enough, Godfrey also met White heavyweight Jack Sharkey on September 21. A rising star in his hometown of Boston, Sharkey was an unpredictable and dirty fighter. To little surprise, the "Boston Gob," battling in the hub, took the 10-round decision victory.

The year in pugilism was all about two men, Jack Dempsey and Gene Tunney. When Godfrey learned he had been given a spot on perhaps the most popular fight card of the decade, he was thrilled. With a 43-pound weight advantage over "Fighting" Bob Lawson, Godfrey took a six-round decision as part of the undercard of the historic battle held at Sesquicentennial Stadium in Philadelphia on September 23.

George Godfrey v. Larry Gains—World Colored Heavyweight Championship

On November 8, 1926, at the Broadway Auditorium in Buffalo, George Godfrey met a Black Canadian fighter, Larry Gains. "The Toronto Terror," who already had about 40 bouts under his belt, was making quite an impression, having defeated German pugilist Max Schmeling, Colored welter Dixie Kid, and White heavyweight Bud Gorman. While Godfrey certainly got the best of him, along with the six-round victory, the young man showed considerable heart. A majority of the media coverage around the event made no mention of it being for the vacated Colored Heavyweight Championship of the World—the designation became available, or so it was believed but not explained, following the loss by Harry Wills to Jack Sharkey on October 12, 1926.[19]

Without losing a single contest, George Godfrey participated in over 15 battles in 1927, and he won nearly all by knockout.[20] Yet he was old news in the media. According to the *Evening Star*: "Godfrey has not lived up to all the nice things Jimmy (Dougherty) mapped out for him. He is far from being a champion timber. One rather suspects that George got tired of being passed up by the big White fellows and has not tended strictly to business. The fat on him does not look well for one who has championship aspirations."[21]

The media's contemptible view was in stark contrast to the opinion of heavyweight contender Jack Sharkey, who undeniably stated this to the *Evening Star*:

> With no disrespect for any of the big boys, when John [John Buckley, Sharkey's manager] and I were asked who we thought was the most dangerous heavyweight with Tunney and Dempsey out of the argument, we both answered George Godfrey. That particular Negro heavyweight has developed one of the hardest left hooks to the body that anyone can show. Believe me, he drove plenty of them to my body when we fought. Still I was able to stay right with him and come to him so strong at the finish I captured the decision. I know Jack [Dempsey] can hit and I expect to be nailed plenty, but I don't think he will hit me any harder than big George did, or with any better results. Say, I was smacked so hard in the Godfrey row, that I had bumps on my head like eggs.[22]

While Godfrey had numerous impressive victories during the year, including Tony Fuente, Jack Roper, and Jim Maloney, none created more of an impression than his victories over the touted White heavyweight Monte Munn of Lincoln, Nebraska, and hub fighter Jim Maloney.

Munn, the former legislator and football star, with his handsome countenance and muscular physique, had developed quite a following, not to mention an impressive 18–1 record. At Ebbets Field in Brooklyn, on September 14, the pair squared off for a scheduled 12-round confrontation. As the *Evening Star* reported: "The giant Leiperville, Pennsylvania Negro started slowly, but after getting the range he started in to deal out severe body punishment. In the third round Godfrey put Munn to the floor for a count of nine with a series of smashing rights to the head and body. Munn was forced to clinch to save himself after getting up. Munn was so battered in the fourth that the referee stopped the bout. The Nebraskan was groggy and on the ropes. He gave away 17 pounds in weight to Godfrey, who scaled at 228½."[23]

Jim Maloney, a popular Boston fighter with an impressive record, was making a comeback and was the odds-on favorite to dispose of Godfrey. The bout was held at Shibe Park in Philadelphia and was covered by the *New Britain Herald*: "Godfrey dropped the Boston strong boy for the fatal count after one minute and 25 seconds of fighting last night (August 15, 1927). Maloney landed several blows to the head and body, but they did not stop the 223-pound Godfrey as he waded in with fists flying. Jim was driven to the ropes and as Godfrey shifted he sent a crushing left hook to the Boston man's jaw. Maloney pitched headlong to the canvas and was still unconscious several minutes after he had been counted out."[24]

Having defeated Jack Dempsey, not once but twice, Gene Tunney, the current World Heavyweight Champion, was calling the shots and drawing the color line. Promoter Tex Rickard was interviewed in the *Evening Star*: "Rickard said that there was no place in the elimination ranks for George Godfrey, latest 'black menace,' who boasts a formidable string of knockout victories. 'He's one of the worst fighters I ever saw,' the promoter declared. 'Fought three times here in the Garden and never showed anything. Besides Tunney wouldn't meet a Negro, even if Godfrey knocked out a few more set-ups.'"[25]

Obviously, these defamatory comments did nothing to boost the aspirations of a contender like George Godfrey. But by this stage of his career, he had heard plenty of criticism and wasn't about to let it ruin his performance. Taking 10 fights in 1928, he won eight, including victories over Paulino Uzcudon, Tut Jackson, and Bud Gorman, while losing only two—the first against Johnny Risko, the next against Larry Gains. Godfrey's victory (W10) over Paulino Uzcudon was in front of an estimated 40,000 spectators—it was Standing Room Only in Wrigley Field (Los Angeles). Godfrey's take for the evening was $21,623 ($317,695 in 2019 dollars).

Larry Gains v. George Godfrey—World Colored Heavyweight Championship

It was not the way he wanted to lose a title, but George Godfrey's third-round foul of Larry Gains, on August 15, 1928, in Toronto's Maple Leaf Stadium cost him claim to the Colored Heavyweight Championship of the World. It also cost him a $2,000 fine. Despite that, there was even more: the Ontario Athletic Commission suspended the fighter for 30 days.

Taking two handfuls of bouts in 1929, Godfrey posted a record of 7–2, with one no-contest. Looking at the high points: Following a January disqualification and three consecutive knockout victories, Godfrey had southpaw Jimmy Byrne out on his feet in round seven on June 3, followed by dropping Chuck Wiggins twice before grabbing a TKO victory in the seventh on June 26. With Tunney retired and Dempsey's plans uncertain, Godfrey, like many heavyweights, wasn't sure just where he fit in the mix. So keeping busy was to stay relevant.

On June 13, Joseph Kennedy, a Philadelphia boxing promoter, stated that he was prepared to offer Dempsey $500,000 to meet Godfrey for 10 rounds inside Municipal Stadium—the bout to be held in late September or early October. Although Dempsey fight offers of this nature seemed to occur almost daily, "The Leiperville Shadow" was flattered that his name was attached to the proposal. Needless to state, there was no response from Dempsey.

Not flattering was Godfrey's propensity to exchange questionable blows against his competition. The California State Athletic Commission withheld his $7,500 purse the fighter earned in his battle against "Long Tom" Hawkins on August 13, 1929. Godfrey was also suspended for 30 days for fouling the San Diego heavyweight. For three rounds, the pair tossed artillery south of the border—this was the second time this year that Godfrey had been disqualified. Hawkins, himself a misdirected and carefree puncher, did little to polish his reputation.

On October 29, 1929, Black Tuesday hit Wall Street as investors traded 16.4 million shares on the New York Stock Exchange in a single day. It was the fourth and last day of the stock market crash of 1929. Billions of dollars were lost, wiping out thousands of investors. As a result, America and the rest of the industrialized world spiraled downward into the Great Depression (1929–1939), the deepest and longest-lasting economic downturn in the history of the Western industrialized world up to that time.

On November 20, the NYSAC suspended George Godfrey—action in concurrence with the Massachusetts Boxing Fathers—due to an unsatisfactory bout against Louisville's Jimmy Byrne on November 7. The fight was declared a no contest due to lack of action. When it rains, it pours.

Now back east, George Godfrey remained competitive in 1930. He was still considered a contender along with Tuffy Griffiths, mentioned as possible opponents for the German sensation, Max Schmeling.[26] Impressive victories over Jack Gross, a competitive White southpaw out of Philly, along with Arthur De Kuh, an Italian heavy out of Boston, sustained his reputation. However, a misfire against Italian giant Primo Carnera at Shibe Park in Philadelphia on June 23, 1930, painted the picture of a different fighter and a dirty fight game.

The Baker Bowl, aka National League Park, Philadelphia Park, and Philadelphia Base Ball Grounds, was located on a small city block bounded by N. Broad St., W. Huntingdon St., N. 15th St. and W. Lehigh Avenue. As the crowd indicates, Philadelphia had more than its fair share of sports fans (Library of Congress, LC-DIG-ggbain—20092).

Since leaving for America, Primo Carnera had disposed of 17 consecutive opponents. When he entered the ring against George Godfrey, he was seven years younger than his opponent, 18 pounds heavier, five inches taller, and had a two-inch reach advantage. Everything else about the Italian was larger, with the exception of his waist and ankles. He devoured opponents like a traditional Easter meal.

The *Evening Star* summed up the altercation like this:

> The Carnera-Godfrey bout in Baker Bowl here [Philadelphia] Monday night went "the way of all fights." After 1 minute 13 seconds of the fifth round George Godfrey drove a sweeping left into foul territory, six inches below Primo Carnera's belt line, and the Italian mountain slumped to the canvas, writhing in pain. The verdict of the referee, Tommy Reilly, was that Godfrey had committed a deliberate foul. The result, coming so closely on the heels of Sharkey's disqualification, is regarded by some as a blow that will hasten the demise of professional boxing. Others take the optimistic stand that if the Queensberry sport were doomed to die, it already would have passed out of existence, in view of the abuses to which it has been subjected in recent years.[27]

Seemingly overnight, the fight game had gone from the color line to the belt line. Godfrey's license was revoked, his payment for the bout was cut in half to $5,000, and his status as a heavyweight contender was withdrawn. All of these actions were undertaken by the Pennsylvania Athletic Commission, which oversaw the event. To his dying day, Nat Fleischer of *Ring* magazine fame insisted that the fight between Carnera and Godfrey was fixed. There was no way, he believed, that Carnera's handlers would allow him to enter a ring against a conditioned Godfrey. Upon viewing "The Leiperville Shadow" and his behavior, Fleischer believed he pulled punches, clinched too often, and was deliberate in fouling.[28] Fighting out of state for the remainder of 1930, Godfrey essentially turned his focus to pool fighters like Cecil "Seal" Harris, Edward "Bearcat" Wright, Roy "Ace" Clark, and "Tiger" Jack Fox.[29] He was fouling his way out of contention and he knew it.

By the summer of 1931, Godfrey had temporarily quit the boxing business in favor of wrestling. Meanwhile the fight game, and William Muldoon of the NYSAC, attempted to create a weight class above heavyweight. The dreadnaught class would include fighters weighing around 230 pounds. Boxers such as Primo Carnera, Victorio Campolo, Walter

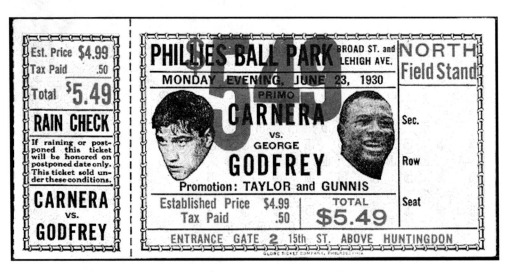

A ticket from the Primo Carnera vs. George Godfrey bout held at Phillies Ball Park on June 23, 1930 (author's collection).

Cobb, Ray Impellittiere, Jose Santa, and Godfrey would be eligible. Posting a record of 4–1 in 1931, Godfrey fought all but one of his bouts outside the United States.

George Godfrey v. Seal Harris—World Colored Heavyweight Championship

On August 24, 1931, in Toronto, Ontario, at Arena Gardens, George Godfrey knocked out Cecil "Seal" Harris in the second round. Having defeated Harris twice last year, he was clearly in complete command. It would be the pair's final meeting.

Harris, having drawn Bill Tate in 1927, then fought Larry Gains to a 10-round no-decision on December 20, 1928, and felt he had claim to the title after his bout with the latter—an assertion supported when Gains apparently relinquished the designation. However, Harris, as a competitive fighter, was not the caliber of Godfrey. Despite the fight drawing little media attention—the Colored Heavyweight Championship of the World was not a topic of conversation—some historians viewed it as a title fight.

Notwithstanding his victory over Harris, Godfrey was fading from the sports pages. By 1932, the caliber of the competition he was facing had fallen off. Yet it was less of a concern to him than just staying active.

Following his two-year suspension in Pennsylvania (as a result of the June 1930 bout against Carnera), Godfrey was reinstated late in 1932. He would finish out his year in Philly, posting an impressive string of knockout victories over lackluster competition.[30] In September, Godfrey knocked out pool fighter Roy "Ace" Clark in the third round of a bout held in Nuevo Laredo, Mexico. Although the fight was billed as for the Negro Heavyweight Championship of the World, it drew virtually no attention in the United States.

In 1933, Godfrey posted a record of 1–1, and one no-contest.

Obie Walker v. George Godfrey—World Colored Heavyweight Championship

In Philadelphia, on October 9, 1933, Obie "Bearcat" Walker, who scaled at 219, outpointed George Godfrey, who tipped at 251, in a 10-round battle held at the Arena. Walker hailed from Atlanta, Georgia, and held victories over Mickey Taylor (1933), Tony Galento (1933), and Bob Lawson (1931). The fight drew mention in some newspapers and was considered to be for Colored Heavyweight Championship of the World.

Having fought in Belgium in 1934, George Godfrey traveled back to Western Europe once again in 1935. The country on the South shore of the North Sea and English Channel was hosting the International Boxing Union World (1913–1946) Heavyweight Championship at the Palais des Sports. In late 1934, the IBU had ordered world champion Max Baer to defend his title against the reigning European champion, Pierre Charles of Belgium. When Baer opted to fight James J. Braddock instead, the organization withdrew recognition of him as champion. Subsequently, the IBU matched Charles with Godfrey.

George Godfrey outpointed Pierre Charles over 15 rounds on October 2, 1935. Charles, who hailed from Charleroi, Hainaut, Belgium, had been in the ring with some good fighters like Paulino Uzcudun, Young Stribling, and Primo Carnera, but was no match for "The Leiperville Shadow." Godfrey did not press any claim to the championship.

George Godfrey died on August 13, 1947.[31] The man who took a half a million dollars out of the ring died in a squalid room in Los Angeles. Godfrey had been under treatment for a heart inflammation, complicated by kidney trouble. A fixture along Los Angeles' Central Avenue, the former heavyweight contender was working as a cafe bouncer. Learning of his death, Jack Dempsey not only attended Godfrey's funeral service, he paid for it.

The Color Line, 1926–1933[32]

George Godfrey never challenged for the Heavyweight Championship of the World. Jack Dempsey drew the color line, as did Gene Tunney. Max Schmeling fought only Young Stribling and Jack Sharkey while holding the crown. And Sharkey lost the title to Primo Carnera. To think that a man who had been between the ropes with Sam Langford, "Big" Bill Tate, Jack Sharkey, Larry Gains, and Primo Carnera, and even sparred with both Jack Johnson and Jack Dempsey didn't get a title shot was inexcusable. Jimmy Dougherty, to his credit, tried hard, very hard, but he just couldn't budge the White champions. Thankfully, Godfrey lived long enough to witness the heavyweight reign of Joe Louis.

The *Worcester Democrat and The Ledger-Enterprise* stated firmly in 1926: "The sporting world does not want to see another grueling campaign for a White hope. The lull of Jack Johnson as King of the fistic world was enough for a while, and it should be good news to hear that Jack had drawn the color line and that all his successors had sworn to do likewise."[33]

The *New Britain Herald* clearly stated Gene Tunney's opinion: "The champion told Buck that even if George Godfrey, the Negro heavyweight who stopped Jimmy Maloney and Monte Munn in short order, were to win his way through an elimination tournament there would be no chance of a Tunney-Godfrey bout. I have drawn the color line."[34]

Drawing the color line bothered Godfrey, and more so out of the ring than in. He was forever disappointed that he was not permitted to view the Jack Sharkey versus Young Stribling fight in Miami on February 27, 1929, due to a law that prohibited Blacks from being within certain boundaries after dark. Imagine, a Black man, who had even been inside a boxing ring with one of the White participants, was not allowed to attend the event as a spectator. A Black man many believe held the World Colored Heavyweight Championship could not cross the color line in his own occupation. A Black man, not only confused by the state of the fight game, but a state in his own country.

It's difficult to believe now, but in the first half of the 20th century, Florida led the nation with the highest number of lynchings per capita. Folks often forget that Florida's Black communities—Ocoee on November 2, 1920, and Rosewood in January of 1923—were attacked by racially motivated White men.[35]

FOURTEEN

The Toronto Terror

Alice Gains always hoped that her son would turn to the pulpit rather than the ring. However, Larry, who sang in the church choir when he was 15, had other ideas. Gains soon embarked on a short amateur boxing career. He fought out of Toronto's Praestamus Athletic Club, an organization that prided itself on catering to Black boxers. Progressing quickly through the local ranks, his success led him to manager Louis Anastasie, who persuaded the youngster to turn pro and follow the coin. So it was off to Europe, with a brief stop in London before heading to Paris.

Lawrence Samuel "Larry" Gains was born on December 12, 1901, on Sumach Street in the Cabbagetown area of Toronto.[1] Athletic as a youth, he often played sports in the nearby parks or found solace at the Riverdale Zoo—its original location not far from his home. Living in a tough neighborhood prompted the youngster to join a Black boxing club. At 12 years old, Larry saw the great Jack Johnson, and the experience altered his ambitions. Mesmerized by the Black Adonis and his graceful ring presence, Gains believed he had found his calling.

However, his professional career began with a dose of reality: a fifth-round technical knockout loss to veteran Welsh middleweight Frank Moody. The bout took place in London on June 23, 1923. Following the engagement, Larry and his manager headed to Paris, where they took up residence. Just six fights into his career, Gains grabbed some attention in the *Evening Star*: "Quinten Rumo, a Chilean heavyweight fighter, last night [September 5, 1923] knocked out Larry Gains, former heavyweight amateur champion of Ontario [Canada], in the tenth round. Rumo was cautious, letting Gains do all the leading in the first rounds, but always watching carefully for a chance to put over a finishing blow."[2]

Embarrassed by the loss, Gains responded appropriately by knocking out Pierre Charles of Belgium in the first round. Just two fights later, the *Evening Star*, under the headline "Gains Whips Mahieu" noted, "Larry Gains, Canadian heavyweight, knocked out [Laurent] Mahieu, French army champion, in the second round last night [December 5]."[3]

Gains finished the year with a record of 7–3. It was a promising start to what would become a brilliant career. While battling in Paris, in 1923, Gains impressed many onlookers including two newspaper reporters, Morley Callahan and Ernest Hemingway. They had met through the *Toronto Daily Star* and shared a passion for the sweet science.

Gains and Hemingway

Hemingway, who understood boxing, took a liking to Gains. When the fighter arrived in France, he couldn't understand a lick of French. But that didn't stop him from signing a three-year exclusive agreement with his fight manager, Louis Anastasie. Also a boxing promoter and owner of the Stade Anastasie restaurant and sports facility, Anastasie was crafty, and Hemingway knew it. The writer also understood that some of the twists and turns in the fighter's contract might not favor Gains. In 1923, Hemingway told Gains he would write his attorney, Auguste Fabiani, in reference to the matter. That he did, prior to twisting the arm a bit, or as much as necessary, of Anastasie; consequently, Gains had a new manager the following year.[4]

The friendship between Ernest Hemingway and Larry Gains grew during the fighter's time in Paris. They laughed, joked, and even sparred together. The pair often attended boxing matches at

The friendship between Ernest Hemingway, pictured here on a passport photograph, and Larry Gains grew during the fighter's time in Paris. They laughed, joked, and even sparred together (author's collection).

This is Hemingway's soon-to-be home in Key West, Florida. The property would include a makeshift boxing ring located near his saltwater pool (Library of Congress, HABS FLA, 44-KEY).

venues such as the Cirque d'Hiver, or Winter Circus—a circular venue that catered to boxing, circuses, and musical events. The writer loved the fact that Gains would often provide him with the inside dope on the boxers, should the author of *Three Stories and Ten Poems* just happen to drop a wager or two.

The two would slowly drift apart, though Gains would resurface as the subject of Hemingway's sketch, "A Strange Fight Club" in *A Moveable Feast: The Restored Edition*.

The following year (1924), Gains posted a record of 9–4–1, having moved his base from Paris to Germany.[5] In 1925, one of the fistic idols of Europe was German Max Schmeling. When Gains scored a second-round knockout over the future heavyweight champion on September 1, 1925, you could hear the cheers all across Canada—it was a victory that would follow him for life. Gains would finish the year undefeated with one draw.[6]

George Godfrey v. Larry Gains—World Colored Heavyweight Championship

After winning his first two bouts in Germany in 1926, Gains headed home to Canada. Wanting to impress his hometown Toronto fans, the fighter did exactly that. Gains knocked out "Panama" Dixie Kid in the second round of their April 12 battle, then took a close 10-round decision over Earl M. Lovejoy, aka Bud Gorman, on May 14.[7] Crossing into the United States on June 21, he took a 10-round decision over Tony Stabenau in Buffalo, before losing to George Godfrey on November 8, 1926.[8] As Godfrey believed the World Colored Heavyweight championship was vacant, he claimed it. Gains finished the year with a record of 5–1, with his only loss to "The Leiperville Shadow." He also took on a new manager, Dan Rogers.

Minus a single battle, Gains would spend all of 1927 fighting in his hometown. Following a third-round knockout of tomato can Joe Burke on January 24, it was time to prepare for his next battle against the hard-hitting Horace "Soldier" Jones on February 28. At stake was the vacant Heavyweight Championship of Canada. Thanks to Rogers, Gains was learning to be far more patient in the ring, letting the fight come to him. Sporting a new moniker, "The Toronto Terror" exuded confidence. And it was working. The *Evening Star* noted the results: "Larry Gains of Toronto became the recognized heavyweight champion of Canada last night [February 28, 1927] by virtue of his fifth-round knockout of Solider Jones, also of Toronto, leading contender. Gains weighed 186½, while Jones tipped one pound less."[9]

During this period, the Canadian and American fight scenes were dynamic. All sorts of factors played into a fighter's willingness to do battle—from legislation to regulation, a boxer had to find the right market to meet his needs. Popular markets included: Baltimore, Maryland; Birmingham, Alabama; Buffalo, New York; Chicago, Illinois; Denver, Colorado; Cincinnati, Ohio; Detroit, Michigan; Erie, Pennsylvania; Hartford, Connecticut; Hot Springs, Arkansas; Hollywood, California; Indianapolis, Indiana; New York City; Milwaukee, Wisconsin; New Haven, Connecticut; Philadelphia, Pennsylvania; Phoenix, Arizona; Pittsburgh, Pennsylvania; Rochester, New York; Sacramento, California; San Francisco, California; Sioux City, Iowa; Spokane, Washington; Syracuse, New York; Tampa, Florida; Toledo, Ohio; Toronto, Ontario, Canada; Trenton, New Jersey; Winnipeg, Manitoba, Canada; and Youngstown, Ohio. If a fighter needed a break, these were the places where he could find it.

Mike McTigue, recognized as the light heavyweight champion by the NYSAC, after Jack Delaney relinquished the title, was supposed to meet Gains on May 16 in Toronto, but backed out—as a result, he was suspended.[10] Delaney too was offered fights with Gains but refused—White fighters always feeling free, if needed, to drop the color line excuse. Having established an impressive reputation, Larry Gains, with a record of 8–1–1 in 1927, seemed to improve with each passing year.[11]

In July 1927, Gains was greeted with an extraordinary opportunity: He traveled to up-state New York to assist Jack Dempsey in his preparation for his bout against with Jack Sharkey on July 21. To say it was a thrill just to be there would be an underestimation. In addition to the excitement created by the celebrities that would routinely drop by the camp, Gains enjoyed the camaraderie of his fellow fighters: Petro Corri, Jack Herman, Jack Hildebrand, Jack Ratti, and Dave Shade. Naturally, given an opportunity to impress Tex Rickard, he would certainly do so.

Realizing that competition was no longer going to come to him, Gains took only four of his 11 battles the following year (1928) in Toronto. His first four victories of the year, all by way of decision, were over seasoned opponents with winning records—Jack Humbeeck, Pat McCarthy, Art Weigand, and Clayton "Big Boy" Peterson. All four of these antagonists had over 35 victories. Gains took his only loss of the year—a sixth-round knockout—against pool fighter "Big" Bill Hartwell in Kansas City on June 8; incidentally, Hartwell hailed from the largest city in Missouri.

Larry Gains v. George Godfrey—World Colored Heavyweight Championship

Following a 10-round decision over Jack Gagnon on June 18, Gains met the formidable George Godfrey. On August 15, at Maple Leaf Stadium in Toronto, Gains won the battle on a third-round foul.[12] The fight, for the World Colored Heavyweight Championship, wasn't pretty, but Gains was happy nonetheless. A few weeks later, he crossed the border again to grab a 10-round victory over Pat McCarthy.

Larry Gains v. Cecil "Seal" Harris—World Colored Heavyweight Championship

On December 20, 1928, at the Cadle Tabernacle in Indianapolis, Indiana, Larry Gains closed out his year by meeting Cecil "Seal" Harris, a strong young fighter battling out of Chicago. Although most sources viewed the 10-round no-decision differently, a few viewed it as a title fight. Nevertheless, Harris claimed the World Colored Heavyweight Championship in spite of at least three sources favoring Gains.[13] Larry Gains finished the year with a record of 7–1–0, with one no-contest and one no-decision.

Beginning 1929 with a successful defense of his Heavyweight Championship of Canada, Gains started out on the right foot. The 10-round hometown decision, on January 25, was over Charley Belanger, a thriving Manitoba light heavyweight—not only did Belanger have over 30 wins to his credit, but he would later capture his division crown.

Crossing over the border to Buffalo, New York, Gains grabbed an impressive first-round knockout of Nick Newman on February 25, followed by a disappointing 10-round loss to veteran Chuck Wiggins, aka "Hoosier Playboy," on March 11. His fight with Wiggins—notorious for his unscrupulous prestidigitation—was his last ever conducted in the United States. Both fights were held inside the famed Broadway Auditorium. From Buffalo, it was home to Canada before heading to Europe for his final four bouts of the year. Gains would finish the term 8–1.

Somewhat bored of having the color line drawn on him, not to mention being viewed as a "third-rater," which was how he was portrayed in a June article of the *Sunday Star*, Gains found solace in Europe, in particular Leicester, England.[14] Posting a record of at least 11–0 in 1930, Gains fought in England, Italy, and Germany.[15] His two most challenging contests were against Italian Roberto Roberti on the latter's home soil. Although Gains took both 10-round decisions, they were much closer than he anticipated.

Taking nine fights in 1931, Gains went undefeated. All but one fight, which took place in Toronto, occurred in the United Kingdom. Although Charlie Smith battled him for nine rounds, Gains' first *real* challenge came from Phil Scott. The British heavyweight, finding retirement a bit boring, decided to make a comeback. He accepted a 15-round bout with Gains, on June 13, for the Heavyweight Championship of the British Empire.[16]

Scott came out quickly for Round One, measuring cautiously with his left jab. His first solid overhand right fell short, but the second did not and stunned Gains. Yet Gains responded with a solid left that sent the Brit to the canvas for a count of nine. Arising, Scott wisely kept his distance and managed to last the round. The Brit worked his left jab early in Round Two, but the Canadian was far too fast and ducked most. When Gains spotted his adversary dropping his left, he fired a roundhouse right that missed, followed by another that hit its target. Scott dropped backwards to the ropes, then down to the canvas. Falling on his port side, he rolled back to use the ropes to assist him in rising, but it was too late. His legs were gone, and he fell backward into the ropes as the referee waved it off.

Everyone—there were some 30,000 spectators at Welford Road Stadium—was shocked by the second-round knockout—understandably so, as the fighter had only taken a dozen losses during his career. Nevertheless, nobody appeared disappointed as they cheered for the victor. The next mountain Gains had to climb was Jack Renault, who made it 10 rounds before losing the decision, another successful defense of his Canadian heavyweight title.

In 1932, eight fights would define perhaps the most challenging year of the fighter's career. Posting a record of 6–1–1, Larry Gains began with back-to-back successful title defenses, followed shortly by a 10-round decision over Italian giant Primo Carnera. To add to his anxiety, he took his first loss since 1929, to an undefeated Walter Neusel.

As for the highlights: Gains fought Dan McCorkindale, the South African Champion, to a draw on January 28. With the Heavyweight Championship of the British Empire on the line, McCorkindale had to rally in the final rounds to stave off defeat. The South African light heavyweight had represented his country in the 1928 Amsterdam Olympic Games and also won the 1926 ABA light heavyweight title while battling in Great Britain. Familiar to fans, McCorkindale was also very popular. The pair matched up once again on March 3, in the same place, Royal Albert Hall in Kensington, and this time Gains took the 15-round decision victory. By the way, Larry Gains was the first Black boxer to fight at the prestigious venue.[17] The British Boxing Association was quick to point out that the heavyweight champion of the British Empire was not the same as the heavyweight champion of Great Britain. A boxer qualified for the latter only if both his parents had been born in Europe. So the British Empire title was essentially established for Larry Gains.

Gains understood that facing Primo Carnera was not merely challenging, but dan-

On January 28, 1932, Larry Gains fought Don McCorkindale, aka Dan McCorkindale, the South African Champion, to a 15-round draw inside Royal Albert Hall (pictured here). The fight was to decide the Heavyweight Championship of the British Empire (Library of Congress, LC-USZ6—33252).

gerous. However, he felt strongly that he could last 10 rounds on May 30, but no more. Scrapping in front of 70,000 fans provided plenty of encouragement—a British boxing attendance record. That was a good thing, as he was outweighed by more than 50 pounds. Gains actually landed some solid shots against the giant. As for Carnera, he was constantly tying up Gains and not countering in the clinch. Of course, this brought the skeptics out of the woodwork. The battle took place at White City stadium.

Walter Neusel, aka "Der Blond Tiger," was an over-six-feet heavyweight whose antagonistic style made him in vogue with fans. When he entered the Palais des Sports in Paris on October 17, to battle Larry Gains over 15 rounds, he was undefeated. Neusel left in the same condition, having taken his record to 29–0–2. His scrappy infighting just overwhelmed Gains. The following year, the German would defeat King Levinsky and Tommy Loughran, before losing to Max Schmeling and drawing Len Harvey. Neusel was that good.

The English experience was working well for Gains, and the money was outstanding. He was convinced that had he been in America, he would be facing only pool fighters, and he wasn't alone in his satisfaction. A slice of Harlem could be found in London, as Black performers found a home in Soho, next to the fashionable West End. Popular Jazz clubs, bottle parties, and dining clubs brought intrigue and excitement to the cosmopolitan and bohemian area.

Gains would fight in just a handful of bouts in 1933, all but one in England (the other being in Ireland). Believing he found a home in England, he held a 6–1 record which certainly supported his comfort level. While he had the support of his local press, newspapers across the pond typically carried few details of his engagements. His 1925 victory over Max Schmeling, who was contending for Jack Sharkey's heavyweight crown at this point, was the most frequent reference to the Toronto pugilist. After posting three consecutive victories on the year, Gains once again squared off against Don McCorkindale. On April 13, at Royal Albert Hall, the pair completed their trilogy. For nine solid rounds, the South African administered a severe beating to his opponent. Defeat was in the air, and Gains inhaled. From the seventh round forward, McCorkindale was unrelenting. It was Gains' only loss of the year, and thankfully it was a 10-round, non-title bout. His only defense of the Heavyweight Championship of the British Empire came against George Cook on May 18 at the Olympia in Kensington. Cook, a seasoned veteran with over 100 bouts, hoped to steal the crown from Gains. However, the champion thought differently and took the 15-round decision victory.

Taking only six fights in 1934 and losing two of them was an indication to some that Gains had topped out. On February 6, the champion lost his British Empire title to vet-

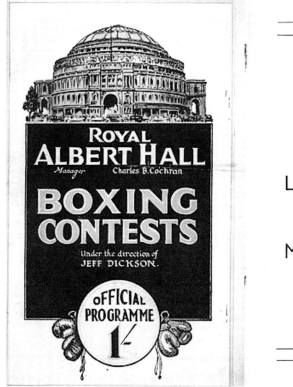
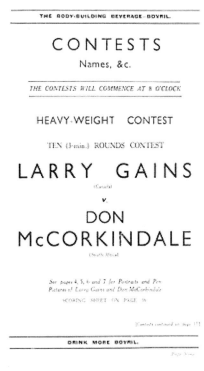

The fight program for the Larry Gains v. Don McCorkindale heavyweight boxing contest held at Royal Albert Hall on April 13, 1933. The battle saw McCorkindale capture a 10th-round, controversial knockout victory (author's collection).

eran Len Harvey in a 15-round decision. The versatile Cornish boxer, who had fought at every weight division, held victories over Marcel Thil, Frank Moody, Dave Shade, and Jock McAvoy. In his battle against Gains, you could see the benefit of his experience as he made few mistakes. Harvey's title and his Lonsdale belt were not at risk, as rules prohibited Colored pugilists from fighting for them.[18]

Gains bounced back strong and won his next four fights, three by knockout. Promoter Jeff Dickson, the Tex Rickard of Paris, matched Gains against Welsh boxer Jack Petersen on September 10. Petersen defended his British Empire title against the Canadian boxer by way of a technical knockout in the 13th round. Gains looked strong for seven rounds but faded. The bout was held at White City Stadium, in front of an estimated 70,000 spectators, with the winner expected to meet Primo Carnera. In addition to Petersen, Dickson was working with a Black fighter from Texas, Obie Walker.

Larry Gains took only a handful battles in 1935, posting a record of 4–1. His only loss came at the hands

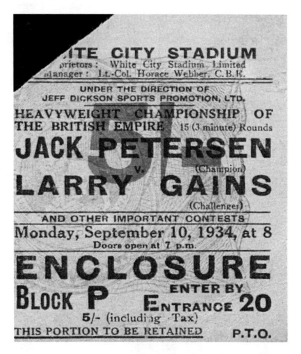

Here is a ticket stub from Jack Petersen's successful defense of his British Empire Heavyweight boxing title. "The Welsh Windmill" scored a 13th-round technical knockout over Larry Gains on September 10, 1934 (author's collection).

of Ben Foord. Following three consecutive victories, Gains had an opportunity to battle Obie Walker, the fighter Dickson had raved about. Walker also held the Colored Heavyweight Championship of the World, thanks to his defeat of George Godfrey in 1933.

Larry Gains v. Obie Walker—World Colored Heavyweight Championship

Honestly, Gains, who had held and defended regional titles, wasn't thinking about the World Colored Heavyweight Championship on July 20, 1935. He only wanted the belt worn by James J. Braddock. After defeating Walker (W15), his thoughts turned to the heavyweight title. Would Braddock draw the color line if challenged by Gains?

Gains compiled a record of 7–1, with one no-contest in 1936.[19] But his income was fading fast and he was forced to declare bankruptcy the following year. Like some successful fighters, he never adjusted his spending to match his ring earnings.

Winding down a brilliant career, in 1937, he went undefeated at 8–0, in a year that saw him knock out Charles Rutz, the French Heavyweight Champion, in the first round. The following year, he tallied a 6–0–1 mark, and although he wasn't doing business with tomato cans, the talent he faced wasn't overwhelming. Fighting purely for the economic benefit, the 37-year-old fighter took only two fights in 1939, and lost both.[20]

On September 3, 1939, Great Britain declared war on Germany. Gains would spend most of his time as a physical training instructor for the British Army. Five fights (1940–1942), most of which were RAF Benevolent Fundraisers, closed out his career. World War II was in his backyard, and everyone needed to pitch in.

Working odd jobs after the war, Gains did what he had to do to make ends meet for his family—his wife, Lisa, and their four children. In 1976, his autobiography, *The Impossible Dream*, was published, and it included—time heals all wounds—a foreword from former world champion Max Schmeling. All Larry Gains ever wanted was a shot at the World Championship.

On July 26, 1983, Larry Gains died from a heart attack while visiting friends in Cologne, Germany.

The Color Line, 1928–1935

America would have loved to claim Larry Gains as a fighter, but the Canadian truly was an international boxer. He loved the British Empire and they loved him.

In 1923, under the title "Would Not Draw Color Line in Olympic Games," the *Evening Star* noted: "Charles H. Sherwood of the American Olympic Committee said today [April 7, Paris, France] he believed it likely that such countries as Algeria and Morocco might be invited to participate in the next Olympic games. 'I see no reason why we should draw the color line,' he said. 'In fact, some of our best college athletes in American colleges have been Negroes and there has never been serious objection to them competing on teams with White men.'"[21]

Although Gains empathized with Wills and the pursuit of the heavyweight championship, the color line in Europe was not a daily distraction, nor was Dempsey. On July 6, 1923, the *Evening Star* noted: "'We want to box Wills if for nothing more than to convince the public that Dempsey does not draw the color line and has no fear of him,' Kearns said. 'The match was red hot a few months ago, but for some reason it was sidetracked. It is my opinion that it will draw better than a return match with Willard. Dempsey knocked him over seven times in one round and could do it again, so I don't see much object in fighting him.'"[22]

When Gains learned of this, he just shook his head and insisted that Wills would never get the opportunity. He was right, and in his heart he didn't want to be.

So 1,463 days—or four years, two days excluding the end date—after Jack Dempsey won the Heavyweight Championship of the World, the champion's manager wanted to convince the public that his fighter did not draw the color line. Dempsey had already defended the title multiple times without failure. Harry Wills, who began his career in 1911, before Dempsey was even riding the rails, had fought a little more than a handful of battles since 1922. This word came 79 days before Dempsey lost his title to Gene Tunney.

Ironically, it was just over a month after Larry Gains defeated Obie Walker that Joe Gould, James J. Braddock's manager, stated firmly that his fighter would NOT draw the color line.

FIFTEEN

Bearcat Obie

On the morning of September 19, 1911, the *Tacoma Times* reported: "There was a riot at a lecture in a New York Negro church when an address on Johnson proved to be about Dr. Samuel Johnson instead of Jack."[1]

On that same morning, in Cochran, Georgia, a mere 2,285.86 miles from Tacoma, Washington, a child named Obie Dia Walker was born. By the age of nine, the youngster, who was growing as fast as a summer garden, was living with his maternal grandparents, Frank and Elizabeth Powell. Like all grandparents, their patience varied like the direction of the wind. When the growing youngster, who was eating them out of house and home, expressed an interest in boxing, they weren't sure what to think.

Obie Walker made his professional debut on February 15, 1929.[2] It took place in Atlanta, Georgia, exactly one month after the birth of Martin Luther King, Jr., who was born over at 501 Auburn Avenue. The distance from where Walker was fighting, the Municipal Auditorium, to the King residence was less than one mile. King, who became a Baptist minister and activist, was the leader of the civil rights movement from 1954 until his death in 1968. Parrying with words, not punches, he was a visible spokesperson during his crusade against drawing the color line. Recognized for advancing civil rights through nonviolence and civil disobedience, King's canvas was his Christian beliefs. Peaceful and vigorous campaigning lay in stark contrast to the sweet science, even if the pursuit of acceptance bound them both together.

Walker's first battles were against local fighters, many of whom were still uncertain if they had found a profession. However, that would quickly change for some like Walker. Traveling from Georgia to Florida, the latter another hotbed of pugilism, Walker increased both his media exposure and the level of talent he would face. In 1931, he twice faced "Fighting" Bob Lawson, a tough Alabama-born boxer who called Atlanta his home. He beat him both times. The victories bolstered his image and confidence. Walker fought nearly 20 times in 1931, a marked increase from the handful of times he fought in both 1929 and 1930.

In 1932, Obie Dia Walker, who stood five feet, eight inches, was packing on the pounds, and the youngster was noticeably getting stronger. Tackling Big Boy Burlap, a heavyweight out of Rhode Island, twice; Willie Bush, the pride and joy of Tallahassee, three times; and Edward "Bearcat" Wright, the seasoned Nebraska heavyweight, three times, he found his fair share of challenges during the year. This, he believed, was serious ring competition. Take Wright, for example. He had been in the ring with Sam Langford, Dan "Porky" Flynn, James "Tut" Jackson and George Godfrey, to name only a few. Yet Walker remained focused on the war and not just the battles. Undefeated on the year with two draws, he was ready to head north to Pennsylvania, another popular market for boxing thanks to entrepreneurs like Jimmy Dougherty.

Obie Dia Walker, a.k.a. "Bearcat Obie," often had this view of Champ de Mars and the Eiffel Tower from the Trocadero Palace in Paris. From 1934 until 1936, Walker enjoyed Europe and its hospitality (*Library of Congress, LC-USZ62-59578*).

In 1933, Walker greeted, then defeated, 10 fighters, including: "KO" Christner, a tough heavy out of Akron, Ohio; "Two Ton" Tony Galento, the scrappy fighter from Orange, New Jersey; and Mickey Taylor, another Jersey pug. Entering the Arena in Philadelphia to battle against George Godfrey, Walker felt and looked great.

Obie Walker v. George Godfrey—World Colored Heavyweight Championship

Walker had heard enough stories about Godfrey to fill a book. Cautious? Yes, he was giving up 32 pounds to a seasoned veteran with more than 100 fights under his belt. Confident? Yes, he too had shared a ring with heavy hitters. The veteran, and Colored Heavyweight Championship of the World, had only fought in two recorded fights during the year and looked rusty. Godfrey was in Dougherty's stable, and the boxing impresario felt the match would polish Walker's resume. And it did. On October 9, 1933, Walker took the

10-round decision. If the title passed hands, as some believe, there was no fanfare—hard to believe considering the promoting prowess of "The Baron of Leiperville."

Bolstered by his victory, Walker had no intention on letting his guard down, but he did just that. On November 27, at the Arena in Philadelphia, Walker lost a 10-round verdict to Don "Red" Barry. It was a rebirth of sorts for Barry, who at one time looked like a heavyweight hopeful. The popular Washington fighter gave away 31 pounds against Walker and danced around him like he was standing still. As for a stunned Walker—his last defeat was back on April 30, 1931—he did his best to put the loss out of his mind. Finishing the year with a record of 11–1, Obie Walker was ready for a change. That adjustment was right around the corner.

What About Paris?

Parisians loved the sport of boxing during the early 20th century, and especially its participants. To drop a talented, handsome, and chiseled 23-year-old Black boxer into this rousing environment was like, well, a dream come true. The men cheered you, the women—yes, they were there too—threw themselves at you, and sometimes, depending upon the level of sobriety, the situation was reversed. By the time Obie Walker arrived, names like Sam McVey, Joe Jeannette, and Sam Langford rolled off the tongues of the Frenchman as fast as an anti-parliament slur. Obie had heard about France from his half-brother, John D. Rogers, aka Jimmy Tarante, aka "The Black Thunderbolt," who was a cruiserweight battler. It was Jimmy who was responsible for arranging Obie's ticket to Europe—the journey courtesy of promoter Jeff Dickson, aka the "Tex Rickard of Paris."[3]

Granted, Dickson wasn't overly impressed by the sight of Walker. But after witnessing the speed with which he knocked out Louis Verbeeren in the first round, everything changed. Everyone at the fight, held at the Salle Wagram on February 2, 1934, was dazzled by his performance against the Belgian giant.

Dickson, who was billing Walker as "Bebe Goudron" (Tar Baby), next matched him against Casmir Beszterda, an average fighter who thought more of himself than he was. Walker catapulted him through the ropes in the second round. Elevating the competition, Dickson matched his Parisian prospect against veteran Maurice Griselle on March 2. The seasoned veteran of nearly 100 battles was pummeled until he could no longer answer the bell, his seconds threw up the sponge in the seventh round. Thunderstruck, Dickson, along with most of the press for that matter, were sold on "Bearcat Obie" Walker.

None of Walker's next three opponents lasted more than three rounds. On September 3, he met Emil Scholz, a tough German scrapper whom some considered equal in ability to Max Schmeling. Scholz, who possessed an iron right hand, couldn't get beyond Walker's speed. Although accounts differ, all agreed that Scholz was out on his feet at the end of the bout and that Walker gamely assisted the German to his corner.

Walker's ring devastation continued. After taking victories over his next two opponents in five rounds or less, Walker was matched against Gustave Limousin.[4] The Belgian fighter's losing record was deceptive. Limousin, who stood 5 feet, 10 inches, had endless endurance. Although most saw the fight as belonging to Walker, Limousin took the eight-round decision. Few at the Palais des Sports, including the popular periodical *Paris-Match*, believed it a correct verdict.

Finishing the year by taking a 10-round unanimous decision over Otto von Porat in

Geneva, Obie Walker was feeling good about himself and his ring prowess. In 1935, Walker took four fights in France and three in Great Britain, while posting a record of 6–1, that included victories over Australian champ George Cook (May 8) and Don McCorkindale (November 11). In his first fight of the year, on February 15, he kayoed *boîte de tomates* Arthur Meurant in 45 seconds. His only loss of the year was to Larry Gains.

Larry Gains v. Obie Walker—World Colored Heavyweight Championship

On July 20, 1935, at Welford Road Stadium in Leicester, Obie Walker lost his claim to the Colored Heavyweight Championship of the World. However, it took 15 rounds—it was even a challenge to Referee Jack Smith, who had his hands full separating the fighter. In the end the decision went to Larry Gains. Later, promoter Dickson tried to lure George Godfrey back into the ring with Walker, but the wise former Colored champion wanted nothing more to do with the Georgia heavyweight.

Walker, a gentleman, took a few licks in the press but nothing he couldn't handle. He was reserved, not to mention polite, so attempts at painting him with the usual racial stereotypes failed.

Taking four fights in Europe, and winning three of them, Walker chose to return to America in the fall of 1936. A loss in Philadelphia to Willie Reddish on September 22, 1936, was his last fight of the year.

Beyond Comprehension

In Germany, transition was looming. As head of state, Adolf Hitler became commander-in-chief of the armed forces. Immediately after Paul von Hindenberg's death on August 2, 1934, and at the instigation of the leadership of the Reichswehr, the traditional loyalty oath of soldiers was altered to affirm loyalty to Hitler personally, by name, rather than to the office of commander-in-chief

A wartime poster in which boxing's heavyweight champion provides incentive for victory: "Pvt. Joe Louis says—'We're going to do our part ... and we'll win because we're on God's side'" (*Library of Congress, LC-USZ62-67814*).

(which was later renamed to supreme commander) or the state. On August 19, the merger of the presidency with the chancellorship was approved.

On June 19, 1936, and in the shadow of the increasing tension in Europe, German Max Schmeling faced undefeated boxing sensation Joe Louis, inside Yankee Stadium in the Bronx. It was the German's first fight on American soil in more than two years, and he was ill at ease. Schmeling was not just a betting underdog and a prime heavyweight contender but a symbol of the Nazi Party, a reflection of its pro–Aryan, anti–Jewish ideology. Prior to the match, he carefully analyzed films of Louis's prior fights, dissecting noticeable flaws in the Detroit fighter's technique. One such weakness emerged: Schmeling noticed that Louis lowered his left hand after throwing a left jab. Schmeling exploited this subtle flaw to his own advantage in the ring. The German countered nearly every Louis jab with a solid right cross. Schmeling's strategy paid dividends in the fourth round when a counter-punch by the German dropped Louis for the first time in his career. Dazed, Louis managed to make it to the 12th round. It was in this session that the German sent the American tumbling to the floor once more, and this time Louis could not recover. He was counted out on the canvas. After the fight, Adolf Hitler ordered the *Hindenburg*, a German passenger airship, to retrieve Schmeling and bring him back to his native soil. "The Black Uhlan of the Rhine" was now a national treasure and a symbol of Aryan superiority.

Germany, even before World War I, struggled with the interrelationship between gender, ethnicity and class. The idea of interracial marriage and the possibility of mixed-race children complicated matters. Such children would have German citizenship, and like

While the destruction of the color line didn't eliminate racism, nationalism at least catapulted out of the ring. Pictured here: Joe Louis (left) and Max Schmeling (right). The pair met twice. Schmeling was the winner in 1936, while Louis took the victory two years later (Library of Congress, LC-USZ6—14335).

White Germans could therefore return to the fatherland with the same rights to vote, serve in the military, and hold public office.

French occupation forces in the Rhineland, after World War I, included African colonial troops, some of whom fathered children with German women. Propaganda, primarily through newspapers, dubbed these children as "Rhineland bastards," then attached false stories of uncivilized African soldiers raping innocent German women, the so-called "Black Horror on the Rhine"—the region of western Germany through which the Rhine River flowed, especially the part west of the river, was called Rheinland. Adolf Hitler, in his manifesto *Mein Kampf*, viewed interracial marriage as a contamination of the White race and blamed Jews for bringing Negroes into the Rhineland—he even implied it was a French plot. Later, he would approve heinous programs aimed at remedying the situation.

Blacks were considered by the Nazis to be an inferior race and, along with Romani people, were subject to the Nuremberg Laws, or anti–Semitic and racial laws in Nazi Germany—they were also covered under a supplementary decree.[5]

Homecoming

Obie Walker returned to the United States in the fall of 1936. The tense boxing environment that greeted the fighter in Philadelphia was different from what he remembered. In 1937, it was off to Miami and the comfort of the Florida sun. Nine fights into 1937 found Walker with a record of 6–0-2, with one no contest. He had fought nothing but tomato cans—novice fighters hoping, okay praying, that a rogue punch might catch Walker off-guard.

On the night of June 22, 1937, at Comiskey Park in Chicago, the Heavyweight Championship of the World was exchanged. Challenger Joe Louis, a Black fighter who captured the hopes and dreams of so many of his own race, defeated champion James J. Braddock, a White fighter who captured the hearts of nearly every working-class American—the symbolism of this fight only to be eclipsed by the new American champion's fourth title defense against German Max Schmeling on June 22, 1938. Louis, having been sent down in round one, defeated James J. Braddock in round eight. Knocked out cold with a massive right hand that broke his teeth through his gum shield and lip, Braddock hit the canvas quicker than an anchor in shallow water—it was the first and only time that he was knocked out.[6]

By traversing the color line, the door to the Heavyweight Championship of the World was now open. Delighted for Louis, an energized Obie Walker went to work. He knocked out his next seven consecutive opponents in four rounds or less. Granted, "opponents" might be stretching the definition of the word, as only one antagonist had a winning record. But Walker was making a statement.

In 1938, however, the wheels started coming off Obie Walker's wagon. The fighter posted a record of 10–4-1, with the highlight of the year being his trilogy (2–0-1) against "Unknown" Winston. On July 13, 1938, Walker defeated Oscar Jenkins in a tenth-round knockout. The novice fighter, who was substituting for Oscar Matthews, died five days later from injuries sustained in their battle. Needless to say, the news hurt, but what seemed to bother Walker even more was that his world had been reduced to battling a novice fighter making his debut. In his final fight of the year, Walker knocked out Tiger Jack Wright in the fifth round of their November 30 bout. The fight, held at the City Auditorium in Galveston, was billed as for the Colored Texas State Heavyweight title.

From 1939 until 1946, Walker fought sporadically. World War II was raging for a large portion of the period. He posted a record of 5–6 to close out an amazing career. Participating in well over 100 fights, Obie Dia Walker was never knocked out.

On May 23, 1989, the fighter died at the age of 77. Obie Walker was the last living World Colored Heavyweight Champion.

The Color Line, 1933–1935

It was a world surviving in the shadow of the Great Depression. People were desperate—the only line they were concerned about was the one they encountered at the bread line or labor office. People were worried. The Versailles Treaty that had ended World War I was being encroached upon daily, Japanese troops invaded Manchuria in 1931, German, Italy and Japan were invading and occupying nearby nations, and the Spanish Civil War broke out in 1936.

Hitler's invasion of Poland in September 1939 led Great Britain and France to declare war on Germany. They had little choice. The following year, Germany defeated and occupied France before overrunning much of Europe. In 1940, Italy joined the war. The U.S. and Japan entered following the latter's attack on the U.S. fleet at Pearl Harbor—a surprise attack, on December 7, 1941, by Japanese carrier-borne aircraft inflicted heavy damage and brought the U.S. into World War II.

Soon, everyone understood that there were no color lines on a battlefield.

Sixteen

Driving the Last Spike

Despite every obstacle, legal and otherwise, that could be thrown into the pugilistic mix, World Heavyweight Champion James J. Braddock met Joe Louis on June 22, 1937. Yet a closer examination reveals how it almost didn't happen.

James J. Braddock won the World Heavyweight Championship from Max Baer, a charismatic yet lethal puncher, on June 13, 1935.[1] Afterwards, Braddock signed a contract to fight Max Schmeling, who had defeated Joe Louis and was the number one contender in 1936. However, arthritis in Braddock's right hand forced a postponement of that bout until 1937. With conditions in Europe changing on a daily basis, Max Schmeling and his management grew extremely concerned.

On January 9, 1937, came word that the Anti-Nazi League planned to boycott the June title fight between champion James J. Braddock and Max Schmeling. Promoter Mike Jacobs, of the Twentieth Century Club, who had Schmeling's services under contract, felt powerless to counter the action. But Jacobs also had Joe Louis in his pocket and suggested a Louis-Braddock exhibition in Chicago. Naturally, this did not bode well for Schmeling, who hastily sailed to New York to argue his case in front of the New York State Athletic Commission (NYSAC). Both fighters were forced to put up $5,000 bonds, which they would forfeit if either decided to fight Joe Louis before their scheduled bout on June 3, 1937. You could hear the German's sigh of relief in London. Adding a degree of complexity to the issue, Joe Gould, Braddock's manager, signed a second contract with Madison Square Garden—at that time the venue was still not comfortable with their relationship with Jacobs—agreeing on a Schmeling versus Braddock fight before any Louis versus Braddock confrontation.[2] A fail-safe for the forfeit was now in place.

By February, Braddock and Company turned their back on Schmeling. Promoter "Uncle" Mike Jacobs convinced Joe Gould, Braddock's manager, to fight Louis instead of Schmeling by dangling a carrot so large that even if Gould abhorred vegetables, he would have to consider it. The carrot, or "Pot of Gould" at the end of the rainbow: A tenth of Jacobs's profits from every Joe Louis world heavyweight title battle he would promote over the next 10 years, should Louis win, and payment of $500,000 or half the live gate and radio revenue for the fight.[3] The offer was too good to refuse. Regardless of the legal ramifications, Braddock's team consented to meet Louis.[4]

In Gould's mind, he had Jacobs over a barrel. If he gave Schmeling the title shot and the German defeated Braddock, there was a good chance that the Nazi government would forbid Schmeling any future ring opportunities. Joe Louis would never get a title shot. Like a hungry cat outside the last refuge of a mouse, Jacobs understood this. The situation was as delicate as spring ice on a pond.[5]

Born in rural Chambers County, Alabama, Joe Louis was the seventh of eight children of Munroe Barrow and Lillie (Reese) Barrow—his mother was half–Cherokee. Both of his parents were sharecroppers and children of former slaves. As a child he almost routinely overcame barriers, never allowing himself to wallow in self-pity. By the end of his amateur boxing career, Louis, fighting as a light heavyweight (175 pounds), compiled a record of 50–3, with 43 knockouts. He had also won the 1934 United States Amateur Champion National AAU tournament in St. Louis, Missouri.[6] Groomed by John Roxborough, Julian Black, and Jack "Chappy" Blackburn, Louis appeared to be everything Jack Johnson wasn't. Countering Jack Johnson's excesses, Roxborough transformed Louis outside the ring, while Blackburn concentrated between the ropes. It was Roxborough who told Louis never to have his photograph taken alone with a White woman. Blackburn taught him to how to modify his jab into a deadly left hook.[7] As the most popular Black man in America, Louis—who unlike Jack Johnson listened to advice—was undeniable as a professional fighter. With only one loss (to Max Schmeling) entering his fight against Braddock, he seemed destined for the world title.[8]

The Death of the World Colored Heavyweight Championship

The first nail driven into the coffin of the World Colored Heavyweight Championship was courtesy of Joseph Louis Barrow on June 22, 1937.[9]

One minute into the first round, of James J. Braddock's only defense of the Heavyweight Championship of the World, the champion was exchanging punches with Joe Louis. Suddenly, the White champion sent a right uppercut to the chin of his Black rival and dropped him to the floor. The echoes of "I told you so," from the mouths of nearly every White man in the audience, could be heard from every corner of Comiskey Park. But Louis quickly arose and the fight progressed.

In the eighth round, the worried look on Braddock's swollen face painted great concern. Cautiously leaving his corner, he stared over his mitts and commenced boxing. But it wasn't long before Louis threw a left to the body, followed by a hard right to the chin. Down went the "Pride of the Irish." A gasping Braddock sank to the floor and rolled over on his right side. Screaming "Jimmy" at the top of his lungs, Joe Gould, Braddock's manager, panicked—he wanted to stop the fight between rounds seven and eight, but Braddock would hear nothing of it. While "Cinderella Man" lay motionless on the canvas, the referee counted him out at 1:10 of the round.

The racial criticism that Joe Louis endured while becoming a contender for the heavyweight championship hit a pinnacle the moment Referee Tommy Thomas shouted "Ten" over the conquered James J. Braddock. A magnificent accomplishment was reduced to disapproval, instead of acceptance. Some newspaper columns had the audacity to note that more than a generation (20 years) had passed since fistiana had to deal with a Black man as champion. Phrases like "had to deal with" were nauseating and insulting. It got worse: Those who recalled Jack Johnson were quick to note that the pinnacle of hatred for him did not occur until after he captured the championship. Really? Our society was noting the degree of hostility for one of its own members? The most popular phrase spoken after Braddock was counted out wasn't "Did you see that punch?" It wasn't "Wow, what a spectacular left-right combination." It was "Now, what?"

Many, particularly those who were White, adopted a wait and see attitude. Just what type of man was atop the heavyweight pedestal? When the manner in which Louis handled his affairs was not only different from Johnson, but in stark contrast to the abnormality of Carnera, hijinks of Baer, and indolence of Braddock—the three previous heavyweight champions—some couldn't believe it, while others couldn't accept it. That was until his sincerity surfaced. The pugilist sought to be the people's champion and became just that. At a time when America needed him most, Joe Louis stepped up like no other man.

At the age of 23 years, one month, and 10 days, the Heavyweight Champion of the World was once again a Black man. Over 266 months had passed since the heavyweight division had a Black champion, and Joe Louis Barrow would see to it that a color reference was no longer needed.

It was still hard to believe that over 60 years had passed since Charles C. Smith made the first claim to the World Colored Heavyweight title. Adding further insight: over 650 months had passed since George Godfrey defeated Charles Hadley to stake his claim, and over 7,950 days had come, and gone, since Harry Wills claimed the World Colored Heavyweight Championship from obscurity. Born only a couple of weeks after Sam Langford defended his claim to the designation against Harry Wills, Joe Louis would never hold the World Colored Heavyweight title. Nor would he ever do battle against someone who did. He would, however, understand and appreciate the role it played in the sport.

The next nail into the title's coffin came on June 22, 1938—one year from the day Louis had won the world Heavyweight title—as the champion was matched once again with Schmeling. Paramount to Louis was vindicating his loss to the talented heavyweight—he refused to recognize himself as world champion until he defeated the German. Compounding the economic instability felt by Americans recovering from the Great Depression was a heated political conflict between Nazi Germany and the United States. People need an outlet for their anxiety and found it in the sweet science. After 41 punches and three falls on the part of Schmeling, Louis was declared the winner. The strongest man in the world was an American hero.[10]

The third nail driven into the coffin of the World Colored Heavyweight Championship came when Joe Louis knocked out his good friend John Henry Lewis in the first round of a Madison Square Garden battle on January 25, 1939. As the second World Heavyweight Championship fight between two Black boxers, it was more symbolic than anything else. Lewis, in his final fight and only career knockout loss, hit the canvas three times.

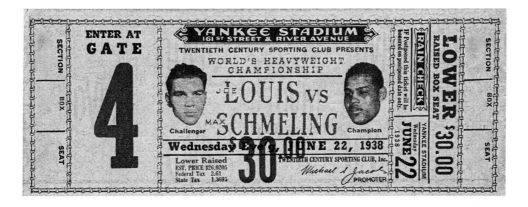

One of the most sought-after World Heavyweight Championship tickets was from this battle held in Yankee Stadium on June 22, 1938. The champion, Joe Louis, and the challenger, Max Schmeling, are pictured prominently on the souvenir (author's collection).

Driving the last spike, or final nail in the coffin, Louis held the title for an incomparable 12 years while defending it 25 times.

Promoting Inclusion

Exclusion, in the form of discrimination, may require a creative solution or leverage. Passive or aggressive, expensive or inexpensive, organized or unorganized, it can still be effective. Not only has boxing used tools, but so too have other sports. The first Black professional baseball team, the Cuban Giants, was formed nine years after C.C. Smith claimed the World Colored Heavyweight Championship.

Tools are successful when they erode the barriers of entry into a market. For example, calling out a fighter once required a stake (financial backing), cost being an economic barrier. Communication, in the form of newspaper coverage, an ancillary barrier to entry, was critical to increasing the awareness of the Colored designation. Transforming a barrier into a thoroughfare, followed by its proficient use, was an excellent first step, as attested by many a Black boxer.

Although these tasks were not simple, tangible barriers were easier to overcome than intangible barriers, such as the color line. While racial segregation in professional baseball was more of a gentlemen's agreement, boxing was never bashful about drawing the color line, or utilizing the fail-safe excuse. (Please excuse the word "gentlemen" in reference to racist behavior.) Discrimination occurs when people in the same situation are treated differently for no objective reason. Determining what triggers this behavior, and addressing it, has always been the key. Even so, it shouldn't have taken a patriotic principle to overcome an ignorant and injudicious belief.

Nationalism Trumps Racism

Drawing the color line was a social element, driven by fear and ignorance, and used as a technique of repression and control. Like every collective component, there were winners and there were losers. The World Colored Heavyweight Championship was a leverage mechanism, or tool, used as a technique to counter this social element. As a progressive instrument, its existence was far more important than its logical succession of titleholders. While it certainly proved useful, it took some extraordinary individuals, both Black and White, to step into the limelight and challenge the existence of the color line. While the destruction of the color line didn't eliminate racism, nationalism at least catapulted it out of the ring.

APPENDIX A

Roster of Pool Fighters

Drawing the color line forced Black boxers to consider alternatives. Hoping not only to battle their way into championship contention but also to garner a lucrative living, they turned to what they had, each other. Supporting their peers, not to mention the evolution of the World Colored Heavyweight Championship, were a pool of very talented gladiators. Although many realized they would never be household names, they remained undeterred in their affection for the fight game.

Not all states, cities, venues and clubs welcomed Black pugilists. Thus many traveled to locations where they could supplement their income. Philadelphia for example, despite decision and round restrictions (or perhaps because of it), welcomed Black combatants and provided them with opportunities. The following Philadelphia Athletic Clubs were good examples: 20th Century A.C. (Athletic Club), American A.C., Ariel A.C., Broadway A.C., Douglas A.C., East Side A.C., Golden Gate A.C., Industrial A.C., Keystone A.C., Knickerbocker A.C., Lenox A.C., Manhattan A.C., National A.C., Nonpareil A.C., Olympia A.C., Spring Garden A.C., Southern A.C., Southwark A.C., and Quaker City A.C.

As Black pugilists improved, many boxing managers (their pool fighter's name[s] in parentheses) took notice. Barney Abel (Cecil Harris), George Bishop ("Young" Peter Jackson), Jimmy Bronson (Jeff Clark), Jimmy Dougherty (Edward Wright), Leo P. Flynn (Kid Norfolk), Max "Boo Boo" Hoff (Roy Clark), "Uncle" Tom McCarey (Hank Griffin), Billy McCarney (George Cole, Dave Holly), James McMahan (John Lester Johnson), George Moore (Jamaica Kid), Billy Nelson (Jack Fox), Doc Nolte (Dave Holly), Tom O'Rourke (Larry Temple), Saint Saxon (William Gahee), Jack Skelly (Bobby Dobbs), Jack Waldron (George Cole), Sam Whitlock (Brad Simmons), and Joe Woodman ("Young" Peter Jackson) were a few who recognized the quality and value of Black fighters. Being part of a stable filled with talented boxers could assist a pool fighter in numerous ways, from refined training to landing a prominent position on a fight card. [See Jeff Clark.]

Payment for pool fighters varied dramatically—match, market,and card dependent. For instance, in 1903, when Professor Andy Watson met Frank Dunn in Montpelier, Vermont, the fighters split a purse of $150 ($4,290 in 2019 dollars), 60 percent going to Dunn (winner) and 40 to Watson (loser by foul). Naturally, Dunn wasn't Dempsey, and Montpelier wasn't Madison Square Garden.

For ease of reference a selection of popular fighters is included here. Pertinent information, such as birth and death dates, is provided whenever possible. Fighter records during this era are incomplete and can vary from source to source. Names, spelling, venues, and even identities can be confusing. For example, over a dozen fighters fought under the name Joe Walcott. Some also fought under variations of the name, such as Baby Joe Walcott, Jersey Joe Walcott, and Young Joe Walcott.

Although this is a humorous photograph depicting a ring casualty, many pool fighters could relate to the situation. Their role was to give their opponent a competitive battle. Paramount to them was a paycheck, and often a healthy one at that (Library of Congress, LC-USZ6—0542).

Jeff Clark (1886–1952). The "Fighting Ghost," or "Joplin Ghost," was no stranger to those competing for the World Colored Heavyweight Championship, as he met Sam Langford (1910, 1914, 1916, 1918, 1920), Joe Jeannette (1910, 1912–1913), Sam McVey (1915, 1917, 1921), and Harry Wills (1913, 1917–1922) on multiple occasions. The lanky fighter, who stood a reported five feet, 10 inches and maintained about 180 pounds, was quick and clever. Winlock Jefferson Clarke began his professional career in 1908, fighting out of Philadelphia. In a career that would last until the early 1920s, he also battled some talented White boxers, including Peter Maher (1908–1909) and Battling Levinsky (1911). Speaking of Maher, if anyone could attest to Clark's magnificent jab, it was he. The *El Paso Herald*, on November 18, 1914, noted the fighter's comments: "Clark is one of the greatest light heavyweight fighters that ever stepped into a roped arena and is a popular local favorite…. He is one of the fastest fighters of his weight in the game." In 1918, Jeff Clark fought Sam Langford in the semi-wind-up to the Jack Dempsey v. Billy Miske main event. He was a popular distance opponent for many Black fighters because he was responsible, competitive, and unlikely to overshadow his antagonist. Clark also happened to be the uncle of former World Heavyweight Champion Jersey Joe Walcott (Arnold Raymond Cream).

Roy Clark (c. 1908–N/A). Lashae Clarkwell, believed born in 1908, surfaced as Roy Clark in 1927, when Walk Miller, manager of Tiger Flowers and Young Stribling, claimed his discovery. The *Evening Star* noted on January 7, 1927: "The young giant is a Tampa Negro longshoreman named Roy Clark, 19 years old and weighing 245 pounds. Clark wears 15½ shoes and his huge arms extended stretch over 87 inches. Miller said he had never been able to get a pair of padded mitts big enough to permit the fighter to close his fists. Due to his size, Clark has had but a few matches, but has won them all by knockout."

Roy "Ace" Clark, a novelty due to his proportions, never really panned out as a dominant heavyweight, but he did engage with a few pool fighters, along with Primo Carnera (1930) and George Godfrey (1930, 1932). One of the bouts with the latter was for the

World Colored Heavyweight Championship. That engagement was held on September 1, 1932, in Nuevo Laredo, Mexico, and a far more talented Godfrey stopped Clark in the third term.

George Cole (1879–1923). "Pennsylvania's Terror" was the moniker George Cole earned thanks to his adept ring skills. Standing five feet, seven inches tall and tipping at 145, he was quick and versatile. Born in Bordentown, New Jersey, he began his professional career in 1894 and fought out of Trenton and Philadelphia. At first Cole wasn't all that serious about the pursuit, but that changed due to promise and profit. As a prolific no-decision era fighter, he wasn't hesitant about taking an out-of-town fight to improve his skills. A lengthy victory over his nemesis Charley Johnson, at Coney Island on September 25, 1899, was an excellent example. A solid defensive fighter, Cole became a tireless warrior and a dependable opponent. During a career that lasted until about 1916, he faced "Philadelphia" Jack O' Brien (1899, 1900, 1902, 1904, 1908), Joe Walcott (1902–1903, 1907–1908), Dixie Kid (1905, 1908, 1910), Sam Langford (1905), Jack Blackburn (1905, 1907) and Joe Jeannette (1905, 1908).

Frank Craig (1868–1943). A lanky fighter, Craig, aka "Harlem Coffee Cooler," stood a firm five feet, 10 inches. Likely beginning his career in the early 1890s, he fought primarily out of New York City. Making his mark first as a middleweight, Craig captured the World Colored Middleweight Championship by defeating his nemesis Joe Butler. Gradually working his way up in weight, he seemed never to ignore a challenge. During a career that lasted into the 1920s, Craig entered the roped circle against some great warriors. Black fighters he did battle with included: C.A.C. Smith (1892), Joe Butler (1893, 1894), "Denver" Ed Martin (1902), and Sam McVey (1907). He also fought White pugilists Peter Maher (1894), Frank "Paddy" Slavin (1895), Tommy Ryan (1899), Jack Root (1899), and George Gardner (1900). By the way, he earned his creative moniker when ring master of ceremonies Denny Butler said, "Now gentlemen, I want you to look at out next heavyweight champion of color, the 'Harlem Coffee Cooler.'" The event (1893/1894) took place at Professor John Clark's Academy at Eighth and Vine Streets in Philadelphia.

Bobby Dobbs (1868–1930). As quick as he was clever, Robert W. Dobbs, aka "Bobby" Dobbs, was a cagey grappler. Age-resistant, he was also a hustler who seldom met a business opportunity he didn't like. Dobbs' outstanding hand use and aggressive style were attributed to an earlier career as a wrestler. Odds-on his prolific boxing career began in the late 1880s, though records are scarce during this period. Dobbs was born in the southern United States, likely in Cartersville, Georgia. Most historians catch up to the lanky fighter, who stood five feet, eight inches, in the 1890s, fighting out of Utah and Colorado. Landing at California in 1892, the prolific fighter began boxing much stiffer competition. He held victories over "Philadelphia" Jack O'Brien (1897), Joe Gans (1897), and "Young" Peter Jackson (1901). In 1902, Dobbs took his talent to Europe, fighting primarily out of England—some sources claim he fought close to 200 battles over two decades. There, along with Frank Craig, he became one of the most beloved fighters of his era. Following a career that lasted until 1914, he later became known as a respected trainer and gym owner. On April 15, 1910, he commented on his longevity in the sport to the *Nashville Globe*: "The reason Black fighters last is they don't as a rule, dissipate and indulge in liquors as most of the White fighters, and they are continually at the game, and therefore never get stale. You will see on July 4 that Jeffries will never be able to reach the 28th round of his battle.

He is stale, and his early training will make him much worse. Two months would be just enough for him; over that will cause him to use too much energy which could be used to advantage at ringside."

As charming as he was creative, Dobbs, the ageless warrior, was a unique boxing figure.

Jack Fox (1907–1954). John Linwood Fox, aka "Tiger" Jack Fox, was born in Indianapolis, Indiana. Eventually rising to a height of 5 feet, 11 inches tall, and scaling at over 175 pounds, the youngster, with his muscular physique, presented an imposing image. Fox began toying with the idea of becoming a professional pugilist in the early 1920s. However, his records didn't catch up with him until 1928, when he was out west. When he returned to his home state of Indiana four years later, folks began to take notice. Considered a knockout artist, he captured the Heavyweight Championship of Indiana in 1932 and the USA Washington State Light Heavyweight title in 1935. He then looked to higher ground. Losses to Maxie Rosenbloom (1932) and George Godfrey (1933), would be the wake-up call he needed. Refocusing his efforts, Fox defeated Rosenbloom (1935), Bob Olin (1937), Jersey Joe Walcott (1937–1938), and Lou Brouillard (1938) before capturing the Light Heavyweight Championship of the World (recognized by New York State)

Robert Bobby Dobbs, pictured here (left) in a clinch with Danish boxer Holger Hansen, was reported to have had more than 1,000 ring battles. A scientific fighter, Dobbs often relied on his experience as a wrestler to extract himself from a difficult situation (Library of Congress, LC-DIG-ggbain—11547).

with a victory over Al Gainer on November 29, 1938. Losing the title the following year to Melio Bettina set Fox back a bit, as did a somewhat precarious lifestyle, and he slowly faded from the sports pages.

William Gahee (1895–1946). Born in Memphis, Tennessee, William "Battling" Gahee grew to a height of 5 feet, 10 inches and tipped between 155 to 180 pounds. Known for being the world's largest spot cotton market and the world's largest hardwood lumber market, Memphis had a large and growing immigrant population at the time and could be a bit challenging. Learning to defend himself early in life, Gahee turned to battling professionally and did so out of St. Louis, Missouri. Like many of his age, he heard the call to serve his country. Following World War I, he returned home and set up his base in Memphis. Working out of the Southern Athletic Club, most records find the fighter by 1919. On February 23, 1920, a second-round loss to Sam Langford quickly brought his aspirations into perspective—as did sparring with Jack Dempsey the following year. If Gahee had a nemesis, it was certainly Theodore "Tiger" Flowers, whom he lost to twice in 1921 and once in 1922. The pair met four times in 1924, Gahee losing two and taking two no-decisions. By the early 1920s, he was using boxing to pick up pocket cash both as a fighter and instructor. Gahee would later find employment with the Champion Spark Plug Company.

Hank Griffin (c. 1870–1911). A fighter with promise, Hank Griffin was never given the opportunity to fulfill his potential. He fought the greatest boxers of his era, including: Harris "The Black Pearl" Martin (1892), World Colored Middleweight Champion; Frank Childs (1893), World Colored Heavyweight Champion; and two Heavyweight Champions of the World, Jack Johnson (1901, 1902) and James J. Jeffries (1895). Born about 1870, Griffin was the son of an ex-slave. Blessed by good genetics, his muscular development was enhanced by his work as a railroad laborer. Standing over six feet tall, he had an intimidating and commanding presence. Fighting a bulk of his career out of Southern California, Griffin drew the gifted Frank Childs over 20 rounds in 1893, and battled the skillful Jack Johnson a recorded four times without a loss. Just how tough was Hank Griffin? James J. Jeffries forfeited $100 to him after he failed to knock him out in a four-round contest. Speaking of "The Boilermaker," Griffin was Bob Fitzsimmons' chief sparring partner prior to "Ruby" Robert's title loss to Jeffries in 1899. Some even called him the "Black Fitzsimmons."

Griffin was also a family man who wasn't hesitant about having his wife and children accompany him during his travels. Turning professional in the 1890s, his talent, not to mention management by "Uncle" Tom McCarey, carried him into the next century. Later, Griffin tended to his business endeavors, including a boarding house, hotel and boxing school in Ann Arbor, Michigan. Well-liked and respected in his community, Griffin, like many pool fighters, enhanced the image of the Black pugilist.

George Gunther (1881–1959). Some sources, such as the *Duluth Evening Herald*, claimed George Gunther was an Australian fighter. Yet other sources disputed it, in favor of a past as an American sailor. What was certain, however, was his tremendous speed and lack of intimidation. He fought against Sam Langford (1905), Jack Blackburn (1906–1908), Charles "Kid" McCoy (1912), Dixie Kid (1912), and Georges Carpentier (1912–1913). Eventually calling Newark, New Jersey, his home, Gunther stood five feet, seven inches and scaled at about 160 pounds. In a professional career that began around the turn of the century and ended in 1917, his superior defensive skills carried him through many a distance encounter—often against larger adversaries. Working out of Massachusetts (1904–1905) and Pennsylvania (1905–1909) early in his career, he headed to Europe in the fall of 1909 and stayed there until 1916, the latter term including a stint in the French foreign legion. His magnificent physique attracted the attention of many European photographers who asked him to model, including Maurice Branger studios of Paris, France.

Cecil Harris (c. 1906–1955). Born in Union Springs, Alabama, at the turn of the 20th century, Cecil "Seal" Harris, with his broad-shouldered, muscular physique, grew to a height of six feet, three-and-a-half inches and tipped a trim 230 pounds. At that time, Union Springs, situated in southeastern Alabama, had a population of about 3,300. Originally the epicenter of the cotton region, the arrival of the railroad spurred further economic growth after the Civil War. At the time of Harris' birth, many of the old cotton plantations had become hunting preserves. In the mid–1920s, Harris, in pursuit of a better life, headed north to Chicago to become a professional pugilist. During his first dozen recorded bouts, he met Ed "Bearcat" Wright (1926), Roy "Ace" Clark (1927), "Big" Bill Hartwell (1927), and "Big" Bill Tate (1927)—the latter being the most experienced of the Colored boxers. On December 20, 1928, Harris battled Larry Gains to a 10-round no-decision bout for the World Colored Heavyweight Championship. Since some of the newspapers saw it in favor of Harris, the fighter claimed the designation—Gains, however, thought otherwise. Heading to the West Coast in 1929, Harris fell into his role as a pool fighter. Following a nice series of engagements against Long Tom Hawkins, he faced defeat three times at the hands of George Godfrey (1930–1931)—the final time in Toronto, Canada, for the World Colored Heavyweight Championship. During the 1930s, the fighter gained a level of notoriety by sparring with James J. Braddock, Max Baer, King Levinsky, Primo Carnera (whom he also lost to on January 13, 1935), and Joe Louis. For a fighter who wasn't quick, or scientific as they say, he had a fairly impressive career.

Morris Harris (1886–N/A). Hailing from Philadelphia, Pennsylvania, Morris Harris seldom ventured far from home. He began his professional career in 1903, took his first loss in March of 1904, and by the end of the year was in a ring against Philadelphia Jack O'Brien. But Harris was recognized most often as the fighter who faced a debuting Jersey boxer by the name of Joe Jeannette on November 11, 1904. Fighting during the no-decision era was rarely rewarding, yet Harris, like many pool fighters, understood it put food on the table. During a career that lasted until 1914, Harris picked up victories over Bob Long (1904), Black Bill (1904), and George Gunther (1908). He also faced defeat at the hands of Jack Johnson (1905), Peter Maher (1905), and Sam Langford (1909, 1910). Standing nearly six feet tall, he had powerful shoulders and large upper arms that created a daunting defense, a good thing as Harris, a bit slow on his feet, often endured a tremendous amount of punishment.

Cleve Hawkins (c. 1884–c. 1937). Facts about Cleveland Hawkins are vague. Most accounts link him to Montreal, Quebec, Canada, and North Adams, Massachusetts. By 1915, his name was associated with other pool fighters including Jack Blackburn (1906), Joe Butler (1909), and George Cole (1910). Although records are incomplete, his breakout year came in 1916, when he engaged with John Lester Johnson, Sam Langford (a fighter he trained with), and Ed "Gunboat" Smith. White press, such as the *Bridgeport Evening Farmer*, noted his bout against Ed "Gunboat" Smith, former White Heavyweight Champion of the World, on September 19, 1916: "The Gunboat faced Cleve Hawkins, the Negro heavyweight from Montreal, at the Clermont A.C. in Brooklyn last night and Hawkins was forced to retire in the third round with several fractured ribs." Hawkins had been residing in Montreal at the time. Later in his career, he fought Kid Norfolk (1919, 1920), "White Hope" Arthur Pelkey (1919, 1920), and Theodore "Tiger" Flowers (1924).

Long Tom Hawkins (1905–1964). In 1924, there were over 700 boats in Southern California engaged in the tuna industry, and over 10 canneries in San Diego. That was the year "Long" Tom Hawkins, who stood six feet five inches, turned away from his odd jobs harborside and toward a career as a professional pugilist. Fighting out of local venues like the Coliseum and Dreamland Arena, Hawkins, who presented a large target, met numerous area fighters and even George Godfrey (1927, 1929). "The Leiperville Shadow," who fought Hawkins on multiple occasions, dropped the slower San Diego boxer a reported (*San Diego Tribune*) 11 times during his knockout victory on May 13, 1927. Relegated to a role as a pool fighter by 1928, he became all too familiar with the likes of John Lester Johnson (1928), Neil Clisby (1927, 1928), and Ed "Bearcat" Wright (1929, 1930). Of all the knockdowns in the fighter's career, it was his five-count accidental drop of Referee William Lovejoy, on November 10, 1927, that garnered him the greatest publicity. Lovejoy was trying to break up a clinch between Hawkins and Chuck Wiggins, during a very close, 10-round contest when he caught a Hawkins left hook. As Lovejoy was laid out on the canvas, the spectators stood and tolled off a five-count before the referee recovered. Believed retired from the ring by the end of 1930, Hawkins was always a challenging opponent.

Dave Holly (1881–1912). Born in West Chester, Pennsylvania, Dave Holly began his professional career before his 19th birthday in 1900. Battling out of nearby Philadelphia, the youngster excelled as both a featherweight and lightweight during the no-decision era. Standing a mere five feet, eight inches, Holly was never intimidated by an opponent and often welcomed a catch weight contest. Gradually increasing his level of competition, he found himself facing Joe Gans by 1902, Jack Blackburn by 1903, and both Sam Langford and Joe Walcott by 1904. "The Big Boys" liked matching with him because he was quite popular and typically drew a huge crowd. For years, however, Holly would be recalled for faking a fight with Joe Walcott at the Long Acre Athletic Club in New York. It happened during a 1906 comeback fight for the recently retired welterweight champion. The suspicious-looking encounter included passing remarks between opponents along with pulling and missing punches. Having seen enough, the referee ordered both fighters into their corners, then out of the ring. As the *Evening World* noted on January 25, 1906: "Walcott and Holly made an awful howl against being put out of the ring, and when they saw their bluff did not work they left the arena and let out a lot of oaths against the referee and the club officials that, if made while leaving a ring in some cities, would have got them something worse."

When Holly, with his ageless looks, retired from the ring he became a sign painter.

"Young" Peter Jackson (1877–1923). Baltimore-born "Young" Peter Jackson, aka Slim Tompkins (Sim Thompkins) or the "Baltimore Demon," stood a muscular five feet, six inches and fought at or around 150 pounds. In 1895, he began scrapping professionally in Colorado, before heading further west to California. Between 1900 and 1906, Jackson knocked out four elite fighters: Philadelphia Jack O'Brien (1900), Mysterious Billy Smith

(1901), Barbados Joe Walcott (1904), and Sam Langford (1906). Jackson claimed the Welterweight Championship of the World when he defeated Walcott on June 10, 1904. Quick, strong and determined, Jackson was managed by Joe Woodman (Sam Langford) and George William "Biddy" Bishop. His career, which included a stint as Joe Gans' sparring partner, lasted until 1914. Jackson, who later owned and operated a gym in Salt Lake City, employed, trained, and discovered Jack Dempsey—this according to Dempsey biographer Randy Roberts.

James Jackson (1900–1960). James Johnson "Tut" Jackson, aka "The Ohio Thunderbolt," was born at Washington Court House, Ohio. The city, located between Cincinnati and Columbus, is perhaps known best for a racial incident that took place in 1894. When Mary Catherine Parrott Boyd—a 53-year-old widow—was physically and sexually attacked, chaos erupted. Mary was white; her alleged assailant—William "Jasper" Dolby—was a 19-year-old Black man. During his trial a lynch mob was repelled by National Guard troops, and five of the would-be vigilantes were shot dead. Born six years after the event, Jackson, who felt safe in his surroundings, began a professional boxing career in 1921—this after participating in his fair share of bootleg, or unrecorded, battles. Standing an advertised six feet, two inches (he was actually five feet, 10 inches) and tipping about 190

Forever smiling, James "Tut" Jackson (left) is pictured here shaking hands with the legendary Jack Johnson (right) (Library of Congress, LC-USZ6—8695).

Standing only about 5 feet, 11 inches, James Johnson "Tut" Jackson had an impressive reach of 80 inches. Hailing from Washington Court House, Ohio, Jackson entered the ring against many outstanding boxers, including Harry Wills, Bill Tate, Jamaica Kid, Tiger Flowers, Kid Norfolk and George Godfrey (Library of Congress, LC-USZ6—05319).

pounds, Jackson had a miraculous reach of 80 inches (likely a bit less). Like some, Jackson, according to reports by Robert Edgren, padded his resume a bit—not uncommon for the era. Nonetheless, by 1922, the lack of local competition forced him to seek matches in the larger cities, such as Cincinnati, and even into Indiana. Over the next two years, Jackson would meet Harry Wills (1922), Bill Tate (1922), Tiger Flowers (1923–1924, 1927), Kid Norfolk (1923–1924), George Godfrey (1925, 1928), and many others. A capable and prolific boxer, his skills faded by the 1930s.

Jamaica Kid (c. 1896–1938). Robert Buckley was born in Belize, British Honduras. Lanky, with a muscular build, he began fighting professionally in 1916. Standing five feet, eight inches, he tackled middleweights first before moving up weight classes. Working out of New Orleans early in his career, he claimed to have won the Colored Middleweight Championship of the World by defeating Eddie Palmer (1916), and he badly beat Jack Blackburn. After he posted a record of 9–1–2 in his first dozen fights, few disputed his quip.

It didn't take long for the fighter to realize that his odds of success were better in New York City. Training at the Military Athletic Club in Brooklyn, he quickly honed his skills. By February 1917, his fight results were being picked up by the dailies. In 1918, the Kid began traveling out of town to increase the competition—not far, just up to Boston, or over to Syracuse or Philadelphia. Taking only a handful of fights that year, the Jamaica Kid spent considerable time doing exhibitions and assisting heavyweight Fred Fulton for his fight against Jack Dempsey on July 27. The Kid's manager, "Sunny" Banks, believed in his fighter and began increasing the level of his competition. In 1919, he confronted "Panama" Joe Gans, Jeff Smith (at least twice), and Kid Norfolk (four times). In March of that same year, word came that the Jamaica Kid would serve as a sparring partner for Jack Dempsey—the heavyweight contender was in preparation for his battle with Jess Willard.

Falling into his role as a pool fighter in 1920, Jamaica Kid battled for another eight years. During that period, he met standouts: Sam Langford (1920), Kid Norfolk (1920–1921, 1923) Theodore "Tiger" Flowers (1922–1925), and Maxie Rosenbloom (1926). On December 10, 1926, at the State Armory in Waterbury, Connecticut, Jamaica Kid suffered a third round technical knockout to Jack Delaney, the world light heavyweight champion. Title shots were rare for pool fighters, and had it been five years earlier, the result may have been different.

"Battling" Jim Johnson (c. 1886/87–1918). Forever known as Jack Johnson's opponent when they fought in Paris on December 19, 1913, "Battling" Jim Johnson stood six feet, three inches tall and weighed between 220 and 240 pounds. While his appearance alone was intimidating, his boxing skill was not. Yet he was the only Black fighter Jack Johnson faced during his reign as heavyweight champ from 1908 to 1915, and the pair's engagement was the first time that two Black boxers fought for the Heavyweight Championship of the World.

Believed born in East Orange, New Jersey, Johnson likely made his professional debut about 1908 in Memphis, Tennessee. By 1910, he was fighting primarily out of Philadelphia and welcoming the likes of Jeff Clark and Sam Langford. Heading to Europe in the fall of that year, Johnson hoped to take advantage of growing interest in Black pugilists; consequently, he attracted significant attention when he met the *toujours populaire* Sam McVey. Returning to America in the spring of 1912, he tackled Joe Jeannette four times before realizing the fight scene wasn't what he hoped. So Johnson returned to Europe in 1913.

After drawing Jack Johnson, during the champion's seventh defense of the title on December 19, 1913, "Battling" Jim returned to New York to benefit—and he truly believed this was going to be the case—from his new-found celebrity. Yet little had changed. In 1914, he fought Sam Langford three times, Joe Jeannette four times, and Sam McVey. All of the fight results were either no-decisions (newspaper losses in most cases) or draws. Johnson's lone loss of the year was a 12-rounder to Dan "Porky" Flynn in Boston.

A year later (1915), Johnson faced the formidable figure of Harry Wills, who took their first battle (a newspaper victory). In 1917, during the pair's third battle, Johnson broke the left wrist of Wills—it was his only apparent victory over "The Black Panther." The pair's final meeting, that same year, ended in a no-decision (a newspaper loss for Johnson).

John Lester Johnson (1893–1968). On July 14, 1916, John Lester Johnson, scaling at 170 pounds, met Jack Dempsey, who tipped at 181, at the Harlem Sporting Club in New York. The pair battled to a 10-round no-decision that a New York City newspaper saw as a draw—it was the first "mixed" bout allowed since the ban had been lifted, according to the *New York Sun*. Johnson, who broke three of Dempsey's ribs during the contest, was the last Black fighter "The Manassa Mauler" would face during his career.

John Lester Johnson was born on August 13, 1893, in Suffolk, Virginia. Beginning his professional career about 1912, as the years passed he would find himself in a ring against Joe Jeannette (1913), "Big" Bill Tate, (1914–1916), Harry Wills (1915–1916, 1919), Fred Fulton (1920), Kid Norfolk (1919–1922), Jamaica Kid (1922), and Dempsey, to name a few. Granted,

Dempsey wasn't DEMPSEY then—he slept in Central Park the night before the fight—but he was smart enough to hire Johnson later as a sparring partner. After his boxing career, Johnson headed to Hollywood to become an accomplished actor. He died on March 27, 1968, and as his gravestone notes, "Gone but not forgotten."

"Klondike" John W. Haynes (c. 1878–1949). Haynes, also spelled Haines, aka "Klondike," "Klondyke," or "Black Hercules," began boxing professionally in 1898. Something few would believe actually inspired the pugilist: facing Frank Childs, who was about to become the World Colored Heavyweight Champion, Haynes suffered back-to-back losses—the latter of which was billed as for the title according to the *Chicago Daily Tribune*. Victorious in a series of subsequent battles, "Klondike" sought to avenge his defeats to the "Crafty Texan." But Frank Childs, the only boxer to defeat "Klondike" prior to 1900, did so again—in fact he accomplished the task four times.

In 1900, Haynes, fought Denver Ed Martin to a no-decision, drew and lost to Jack Johnson, and lost to Peter Maher. Then he essentially disappeared or as some believed, headed off to Canada. Resurfacing in Chicago by 1902, he managed to bring himself into fight form, or at least enough to tackle John "Sandy" Ferguson (1903), Frank Childs (1904), Black Bill (1906), and Sam Langford (1909) before hanging up the gloves. "Klondike," who stood six feet tall and weighed around 200 pounds, died at the age of 71.

"Kid" Norfolk (1893–1953). William Ward, born on July 10, 1893, in Belmont, Virginia, created a name for himself as an adolescent by participating in battle royals in Baltimore. Growing to the height of five feet, eight inches, and tipping at 170, he was fast afoot and not intimidated by anyone. Catching the eye of an engineer working on the Canal Project in Panama, Ward was persuaded to travel to the region in pursuit of pugilistic riches. Turning professional in 1914, the youngster developed his skills—this while working construction on the 50-mile waterway. Entering the ring against heavyweights, he performed magnificently. However, it wasn't long before Ward, aka "Kid" Norfolk, ran out of fight options. Hooking up with Leo P. Flynn in 1917, it was back to America.

Defeating Bill Miske on October 16, 1917, Norfolk claimed the Light Heavyweight Championship. Following his battle with Miske, he would meet Sam Langford (1917), "Big" Bill Tate (1918), Joe Jeannette (twice in 1918), and the Jamaica Kid (1919) before defeating (a newspaper decision) Miske for a final time. Before retiring in 1926, he would also meet Harry Greb (1921, 1924), "Tiger" Flowers (1922, 1923), Harry Wills (1922), Battling Siki (1923), and Tommy Gibbons (1924). Norfolk, like many heavyweight challengers of his era, had visions of Dempsey dancing in his head. When a second-round, right uppercut by Harry Wills dropped him to a Madison Square Garden canvas on March 2, 1922, those dreams faded.

Boxing until 1926, Norfolk was regarded as one of the standout light heavyweights of his era. Failing vision in his right eye prompted an early retirement. While living in Harlem, he also worked as a porter at Yankee Stadium. His date of death has been disputed.

Brad Simmons (c. 1900–1961). Texas-born and Oklahoma raised, Bradford Simmons caught his first press coverage in his second professional fight. According to the *Morning Tulsa World*, on November 13, 1921, "Bradford Simmons of Drumright [OK] last night [November 11, 1921] knocked out Battling Thompson of Sapulpa in :59 of the first round of what was billed as a 10-round fight." Oklahoma fight fans had high hopes for Simmons, until fighters like "Battling" Gahee started taking him apart in the ring. A bit disillusioned by his failure, he fought less frequently. Then, on August 2, 1926, Simmons, battling in his hometown, ended the prolific career of Sam Langford: Near-blind, the 46-year-old boxing legend was knocked out in the first round. The following month, Simmons took a 10-round decision over Jack Johnson—the two would later become friends, even barnstorming together in 1931. No other fighter can say they beat both Sam Langford and Jack Johnson in a span of 35 days.

Larry Temple (c. 1882–1943). Lawrence Temple, aka "Quaker City Terror," began fighting professionally by the turn of the century. Battling primarily out of Chicago, he turned some heads on November 14, 1902, when as a middleweight he dropped local Billy Stift (often misspelled as Swift) six times on the way to a second-round knockout victory. Increasing his level of competition in 1903, Temple met "Young" Peter Jackson, Black Bill, and Joe Walcott. He gave the latter a run for his money, as reported on December 30, 1903, by the *Daily Morning Journal*: "After a 15 round bout, during seven rounds of which his opponent landed almost at will, Joe Walcott, the Colored pugilist of Malden, was given the decision over Larry Temple.… Close work on the part of both boxers marked the boxing contest from the first round, Walcott rushing in at every opportunity, only to be heavily countered and to find himself outclassed at infighting."

From 1904 until 1908, Larry Temple climbed inside a ring to fight against: Jack Blackburn (1905 twice), Dixie Kid (1904, 1905), Sam Langford (1905 twice, 1906–1908), "Philadelphia" Jack O'Brien (1904, 1908), and Joe Walcott (1904, 1907–1908), to name only a few.

Quiet, yet capable, Temple was rather private. Noted as being methodical and health-conscious—his favorite beverage was milk—the fighter's career faded after 1916.

Jack Thompson (N/A–N/A). Standing over six feet and tipping over 200 pounds, Jack Thompson understood that he was big and strong. Believed to have roots in Denver, Colorado, he picked up some pocket cash by sparring with heavyweights, good ones as a matter of fact. From 1913 until 1917, he entered the ring professionally against: Joe Jeannette (1913), Sam Langford (1915, 1917), "Battling" Jim Johnson (1915), Jeff Clark (1916), Sam McVey (1916), and Harry Wills (1916). It wasn't always pretty—Thompson didn't rack up the victories—yet the determined youngster survived. His confidence and contacts sent him to New York in the fall of 1916, then on to Philadelphia two years later. Talk about opportunities, Thompson fought Jamaica Kid in the semi-wind-up to the Jack Dempsey v. Billy Miske fight on November 28, 1918. His speed and punching power quickly enhanced his reputation—more than one fighter happily drew the color line against him.

In 1920, Thompson fought Harry Wills twice and split a pair of battles against Sam Langford. He was on his game and he knew it. While he even managed to draw out Fred Fulton—the longest chin in boxing and a brief Dempsey opponent—Thompson broke his jaw and lost the six-round affair. Like many solid pool fighters, when his reputation eventually preceded him, the competition wisely turned away. Conducting exhibitions with Jack Dempsey (1922), losing to Jack Johnson in Havana (1923), and sparring with numerous heavyweight contenders rounded out a ring career that drew to a conclusion in the mid-1920s.

"Professor" Andy Watson (1871–1935). Always up for a fight, Andy Watson was a scientific boxer, as they used to say, his cleverness earning him the sobriquet "Professor." Turning professional in the early 1890s, Watson would battle until 1905. As a distance fighter, he appeared to battle to the level of the competition, often to a draw. Watson always made for a suitable match; consequently, Sam Langford fought him at least a half-dozen times. He held victories over Black Pearl (Harris Martin, 1897), Belfield Walcott (1902), and Arthur Cote (1902).

Edward Bearcat Wright (1897–1975). Ed "Bearcat" Wright was born in Brazoria, Texas, and when it came to boxing, everything about the fighter was just right. Standing six feet, one inch, and scaling at 220 pounds, his arms and shoulders appeared twice as large as the average man. He had that mental toughness that seemed innate in every Texan. He started his professional career in 1919, fighting primarily out of Omaha, Nebraska. The *Bisbee Daily Review* noted on August 23, 1919, "Captain Snyder, athletic officer at Douglas, announced a match on Labor Day, ten rounds, between 'Bearcat' Wright of the Tenth cavalry and Rufus Langford of the Twenty-fifth infantry, Colored heavyweights." The 10th Cavalry Regiment was a unit of the United States Army. Formed as a segregated African American unit, the 10th Cavalry was one of the original "Buffalo Soldier" regiments in the post–Civil War Regular Army. Meeting the great Sam Langford once each in 1920 and 1921, and twice in 1922, put him in the press, but it also put him in a hospital with a broken hand in July 1922. While convalescing, he pondered retirement, but gradually returned to the ring over the next couple of years. By 1926, Wright was back in full swing. He captured victories over James "Tut" Jackson, Brad Simmons, Roy "Ace" Clark, and Cecil "Seal" Harris. On April 16, 1928, in Topeka, Kansas, Wright, tipping at 211, knocked out 50-year-old Jack Johnson, who scaled at 235, in the fifth round of a scheduled 10-round contest. Later, he met standouts Primo Carnera (1930), George Godfrey (1930, 1933), Mickey Walker (1931), and Max Baer (1936), to cite a few.

World Colored Heavyweight Championship and Timeline—Selected Entries

A claim was just an assertion of a boxer's championship status, typically without providing evidence or proof. Without rules and regulations or a governing body, not to mention White boxers drawing the color line and refusing to defend the Heavyweight Championship of the World against Black boxers, pugilists made claims. In reality, they made numerous claims, as did fight promoters. After all, if opportunity doesn't knock, build a door.

The World Colored Heavyweight Championship, not to mention the World White Heavyweight Championship, was created out of need—to enhance employment opportunities, sell tickets, and make a clear and definitive racial statement. Other titles, with similar intent, were also created. As all titles were not born with progression in mind, some defy logic. The pieces don't always fit.

The World Colored Heavyweight title can be viewed in three phases: Phase I—from Creation to Jack Johnson capturing the Heavyweight Championship of the World (December 26, 1908); Phase II—from December 26, 1908, until September 7, 1915, the obscured title was exchanged between Sam McVey, Joe Jeannette, and Sam Langford; and finally, Phase III—prompted by Jack Johnson's loss to Jess Willard, on April 5, 1915, Harry Wills claimed the World Colored Heavyweight Championship from obscurity on September 7, 1915. The final phase of its existence lasted until Joe Louis made it clear that the designation was no longer needed.

When Jack Johnson defeated Tommy Burns to capture the Heavyweight Championship of the World, it sent the World Colored Heavyweight Championship into a state of oblivion. As Johnson's new prize was what every Black contender sought, there was debate as to whether the World Colored Heavyweight Championship should even be recognized.

Things to remember: not all fights were recorded or reported; bootleg battles were common; record keeping was poor; not all newspapers reported details of contests featuring Black fighters; the concluding round may vary due to rules; newspaper fight reports were inconsistent, particularly during the no-decision era; some fight results were agreed upon in advance; the quality of officiating varied; the legality of prizefighting varied by period, state, and even country; some markets had round limitations; and a championship fight was not defined. Finally, since there was no definitive progression to the World Colored Heavyweight Championship, all interpretations are welcome.

This timeline takes into account numerous sources and historical viewpoints.

Key: Bold indicates a champion as recognized by some sources (typically opposite a title transfer); an indented line indicates a likely title defense; (*) indicates a point of information that may be relevant to a claim; DNDT = Did Not Defend Title; TD = Title Defense; WT = Win by Technical Knockout; RD = Result Disputed; WCHC = World Colored Heavyweight Championship; WF = Won via Foul/Disqualification.

Champion	Date	Opponent	Results/Notes
* Tom Cribb, a popular White English bare-knuckle boxer, defeated Tom Molineaux, a Black American bare-knuckle boxer, in the 35th round of a controversial ring battle held in December 1810. Cribb defended his position in a rematch the following year. Despite his two losses, Molineaux was America's first boxing star.			
1. **Charles C. Smith**	1876	Claimed title	
2. **Morris Grant**	1878		
3. **Charles Hadley**	1/14/1881	Morris Grant	W3, New York, NY
	4/6/1882	Morris Grant	W, New York, NY
Additional Notes: "Grant was knocked out of time and the championship medal was given to Hadley" ["Heavy-weight Colored Boxer," *Daily Republican*, April 7, 1882, 4].			
	12/7/1882	Morris Grant	W2, New York, NY, TD
Additional Notes: Both participants were labeled colored light-weight (period spelling) champions; The *Police Gazette* medal was then presented to Charles Hadley for the fourth time (appears to be an error). [See "The Ring," *Lancaster Daily Intelligencer*, December 8, 1882, 2.] Another source stated, "Hadley had won the Police Gazette medal, twice, and it was his to keep if he won it again" ["Mr. Grant Knocked Entirely Out," *Sun*, December 8, 1882, 3]. This was a title transfer.			
	1/10/1883	Harry Woodson	KO2, New York, NY, TD
Additional Notes: A rematch was given and won by Woodson. No details were provided. [See "Two Slashing Ring Fights," *Sun*, April 7, 1883, 41.] Other WCHC defenses by Hadley may exist during this period.			
	1/18/1883	George Godfrey	D6, New York, NY, TD
4. **George Godfrey**	2/23/1883	Charles Hadley	WT5, Boston, MA
Additional Notes: Some sources record Godfrey's opponent as Frank Hadley of New York. Also, some historians view this bout as the birth of the World Colored Heavyweight Championship title. John L. Sullivan refereed the bout. Sources vary on purse size.			
*On April 6, 1883, Harry Woodson knocked out White pugilist Jim McLoughlin in the seventh round. With the victory, Woodson declared himself the Colored Heavyweight Champion. [See "Two Slashing Ring Fights," *Sun*, April 7, 1883, 41.]			
	5/10/1884	McHenry Johnson	D4, Boston, MA, TD, RD
*On June 28, 1884, McHenry Johnson, of New York, fought William Wilson, of Boston, to a draw—the fight was stopped by police at the end of the second round. The fight, scheduled for six rounds, was for the heavyweight colored championship. [See "Brief Telegrams," *Salt Lake Herald*, June 29, 1884, 4.]			
*On May 22, 1887, Billy Wilson, aka "The Black Diamond," defeated Harry Woodson, aka "Black Diamond," 15 miles outside Minneapolis and claimed the national Colored pugilist championship. [See "Minnesota News," *New Ulm Weekly Review*, June 1, 1887, 2.]			

Champion	Date	Opponent	Results/Notes
	1/25/1888	McHenry Johnson	LF; Decision reversed (KO4), TD

Additional Notes: Many periodicals, including the *Denver Times*, noted this battle, which was held in Bloomfield, Colorado, as the first significant contest between two Black fighters in America; Godfrey retained the title.

| 5. **Peter Jackson** | 8/24/1888 | George Godfrey | WT19; San Francisco, CA, DNDT |

Additional Notes: With a purse of $1,600, this bout represented one of the largest coffers offered for a bout between two Black fighters; the fighters wore two-ounce gloves. It is believed that the fighter relinquished the title in 1897.

*On December 28, 1888, Peter Jackson defeated Joe McAulliffe (KO24) for the Heavyweight Championship of the Pacific Coast.

| 6. **Robert Armstrong** | 12/21/1896 | Charley Strong | KO19, New York, NY |

Additional Notes: After Peter Jackson relinquished the designation, Bob Armstrong defeated Charley Strong and claimed the vacant title. Parsons Davies, who managed both Jackson and Armstrong, approved—it was his idea. The fight was billed as for Colored Heavyweight title. But many newspapers, including the *Wilmington Daily Republican*, *Salt Lake Herald*, and *Scranton Tribune*, did not recognize the billing.

| | 3/6/1897 | Joe Butler | WT6, Brooklyn, NY, TD |

*Robert Armstrong defeated Black pugilist Sam Pruitt (WT1), in San Francisco on April 23, 1897, during a fight some claim was billed for the title. However, coverage by the *Topeka State Journal* summed it up best: "The exhibition which lasted about five seconds was of such a comical nature that the spectators roared with laughter."

| 7. **Frank Childs** | 1/29/1898 | Robert Armstrong | KO2, Chicago, IL, RD |

Additional Notes: Some sources believe the World Colored Heavyweight title transferred after this battle. Childs was Armstrong's sparring partner, and frankly speaking, was getting fed up with his role—his duties included losing. The fight, which was prearranged according to Armstrong, saw Childs double-cross his opponent; following the pair's encounter on March 4, 1899, the WCHC belonged to Frank Childs; Armstrong lost to Frank Childs in 1897, 1898 (twice), and 1899.

| | 2/26/1898 | Klondike (John Haines) | WT4, Chicago, IL |

Additional Notes: This was a limited round boxing carnival held before the Chicago Athletic Club.

| | 2/28/1898 | Robert Armstrong | KO10, Chicago, IL |
| | 3/4/1899 | Robert Armstrong | WT6, Cincinnati, OH, TD |

Additional Notes: If the title did not transfer on 1/29/1898, as some believe including the author, then Childs didn't have a title to lose to George Byers. This fight was a WCHC title exchange.

| 7a. **George Byers** | 9/14/1898 | Frank Childs | W20, New York, NY |

Additional Notes: Sources differ with regard to a title transfer following this fight. However, the efforts made by the Lenox Athletic Club, including the attempt to have the fight increased to 25 rounds [see *Sun*, September 12, 1898, 5] exhibit signs of a title bout. But, Tom O'Rourke, who managed Byers and the Lenox Athletic Club, did not confirm a title transfer, and he had every opportunity to do so. Those who believe Childs kept the title stated that he defended it at least twice. George Byers, regardless of whom he fought, viewed himself as a middleweight.

Champion	Date	Opponent	Results/Notes
*On May 6, 1899, Klondike (John Haines, or Haynes) wore down Jack Johnson to capture a fifth-round victory. In doing so, Haines claimed the "Black Heavyweight" title—the only title Johnson held was the Texas State Middleweight title.			
8. **Frank Childs**	3/4/1899	Bob Armstrong	WT6, Cincinnati, OH
Additional Notes: Those who believe Bob Armstrong didn't lose the title on January 29, 1898, to Frank Childs can be assured that he lost it here. The fight below was likely a title defense. [See "Jeffries to Train at Baden," *Topeka State Journal*, December 21, 1900, 4.]			
	3/16/1901	George Byers	KO17, Hot Springs, AR, TD
Additional Notes: Childs clearly dominated Byers and afterwards was again acknowledged as the World Colored Heavyweight Champion.			
* On October 2, 1901, Denver Ed Martin knocked out Hank Griffin in the seventh round at Hazard's Pavilion in Los Angeles. The fight was billed as for the World Colored Heavyweight Championship [see "Madden's Ambition Is Now Realized," *Evening World*, October 3, 1901, 8]. Fred Fox, Martin's former manager, and Billy Madden, Martin's current manager, had been trying to call out Childs; Frank Childs, who held the title, had a different opinion.			
9. **Denver Ed Martin**	2/24/1902	Frank Childs	W6, Chicago, IL
Additional Notes: This was a media-recognized transfer of the WCHC. [See "Records of the Fighting Game Brought Up to the New Year," *Saint Paul Globe*, January 1, 1903, 5.]			
	7/25/1902	Bob Armstrong	W15, London, UK; TD
Additional Notes: Martin's title defense was acknowledged. The fight was originally scheduled for June 21 [*Waterbury Democrat*, June 11, 1902, 7].			
10. **Jack Johnson**	2/5/1903	Denver Ed Martin	W20, Los Angeles, CA
Additional Notes: This was a media-recognized transfer of the WCHC. Some sources list an incorrect date.			
	2/27/1903	Sam McVey	W20, Los Angeles, CA; TD
*On June 10, 1903, Bob Armstrong knocked out Denver Ed Martin in the third round of a fight held at the Tammany Club in Boston, and billed for the WCHC. No word from Jack Johnson.			
	10/27/1903	Sam McVey	W20, Los Angeles, CA; TD
	4/22/1904	Sam McVey	KO20, San Francisco, CA
Additional Notes: Both Johnson and McVey put on a pathetic performance. The battle certainly did not resemble a championship bout.			
	10/18/1904	Denver Ed Martin	KO2, Los Angeles, CA, TD
	2/19/1907	Peter Felix	KO1, Sydney, Australia; TD
Additional Notes: Peter Felix claimed the Australian heavyweight championship as early as 1897, if not before. [See *Watertown Republican*, January 13, 1897, 2.]			
*Jack Johnson defeated Tommy Burns, on December 26, 1908, in Sydney, Australia, to capture the Heavyweight Championship of the World (W14)—the decision, following police intervention, was awarded by the referee.			
*World Colored Heavyweight Championship title was obscured due to Johnson's reign as Heavyweight Championship of the World.			
11. **Sam McVey**	2/20/1909	Joe Jeannette	W20, Paris, France, RD

Champion	Date	Opponent	Results/Notes
Additional Notes: Jack Johnson was believed to have relinquished the WCHC title after he defeated Tommy Burns to win the Heavyweight Championship of the World. Sam McVey, who claimed the Heavyweight Championship of France in 1907, defeated Joe Jeannette and claimed the vacant WCHC. McVey defeated novice "Cyclone" Billy Warren, a Black pugilist, on April 9, 1909.			
12. **Joe Jeannette**	4/17/1909	Sam McVey	WT49, Paris, France
Additional Notes: Initial reports called it "the greatest fight witnessed in France since John L. Sullivan and Charley Mitchell fought in Chantilly in 1888."			
	12/11/1909	Sam McVey	D20, Paris, France, TD
*On May 24, 1909, Sam Langford defeated William "Iron" Hague in London and claimed the heavyweight championship of England (KO4). Hague did not believe in "drawing the Color Line."			
13. **Sam Langford**	9/6/1910	Joe Jeannette	
Additional Notes: In 1909, after Jack Johnson refused to give Sam Langford a title shot, the Boston boxer claimed the WCHC, and he clearly defended it against Jeannette. Afterwards, Langford focused all his efforts on Johnson and not the WCHC. The majority of the articles that appeared nationwide after the fight made no mention of the WCHC. By the end of May 1909, Langford had in his possession a championship belt from the National Sporting Club. [See "Hail Langford as Champion," *Washington Herald*, May 31, 1909, 8.]			
*On November 19, 1910, Sam McVey knocked out Battling Jim Johnson in the 21st round of a fight for the championship of Europe.			
	4/1/1911	Sam McVey	D20, Paris, France, TD
14. **Sam McVey**	12/26/1911	Sam Langford	W20, Sydney, Australia
Additional Notes: Viewed, at least by some, as an elimination contest for the right to challenge champion Jack Johnson—in-fighting was not allowed.			
15. **Sam Langford**	4/8/1912	Sam McVey	W20, Sydney, Australia
*On January 1, 1913, the White Heavyweight Champion of the World was crowned in Vernon, California, as "White Hope" Luther "Luck" McCarty disposed of Al Palzer in the 18th round.			
	9/9/1913	John Lester Johnson	KO1, New York, TD
	12/20/1913	Joe Jeannette	W20, Paris, France, TD
Additional Notes: This match was an arrangement by the Parisian Boxing Association, which stated that Johnson forfeited his right to the heavyweight championship by his failure to meet the aspirants.			
	5/1/1914	Harry Wills	ND10, New Orleans, LA, RD
Additional Notes: Both participants claimed victory and the title. Most sources viewed the fight as a draw.			
	11/26/14	Harry Wills	KO14, Vernon, CA
*Jack Johnson loses Heavyweight Championship of the World to Jess Willard (LT26), on April 5, 1915, in Havana, Cuba.			
16. **Joe Jeannette**	4/13/1915	Sam Langford	W12, Boston, MA
Additional Notes: There was no mention of a title transfer in the bulk of the media coverage.			
16.a. **Sam McVey**	6/29/1915	Sam Langford	W12, Boston, MA, RD

Champion	Date	Opponent	Results/Notes
Additional Notes: This fight took place in Boston, Langford's hometown; Although Langford disputed the results, some see this as a title exchange; Langford had now lost to both Jeannette and McVey in 1915.			
16.b. **Harry Wills**	9/7/1915	Sam McVey	W12, Boston, MA
Additional Notes: Prompted by Jack Johnson's loss to Jess Willard, on April 5, 1915, Harry Wills claimed the World Colored Heavyweight Championship from obscurity.			
	1/3/1916	Sam Langford	W20, New Orleans, LA, TD
Additional Notes: The headline in the *Tacoma Times* read "Wills Is Colored Champ." It was the first such headline to recognize the title in many a year.			
16.c. **Sam Langford**	2/11/1916	Harry Wills	KO19; Jeannette disputes claim
	2/17/16	Sam McVey	ND10; New York, NY, TD
Additional Notes: The bout was billed as a title fight [*Daily Gate City*, February 14, 1916, 6]. Most sources claim Langford was the victor.			
	4/7/1916	Sam McVey	ND10, Syracuse, NY
Additional Notes: Most sources claim Langford was the winner.			
	5/12/1916	Joe Jeannette	KO7, Syracuse, NY, TD, RD
Additional Notes: If Jeannette believed he had the title, he definitely lost it after this bout. Some sources state the location as Rochester, New York.			
	8/12/1916	Sam McVey	D20, Buenas Aires, Argentina, TD
Additional Notes: Most sources believe this fight was a draw.			
17. **Bill Tate**	1/25/1917	Sam Langford	W12, Kansas City, MO
18. **Sam Langford**	5/1/1917	Bill Tate	KO5, St. Louis, MO
Additional Notes: Sources vary: the *Sun*, *Ogden Standard*, *Tulsa Daily World*, *Albuquerque Morning Journal*, and *Bisbee Daily Review* claimed a KO5 on May 2, 1917. *Free Trader-Journal* claimed a KO6 on May 2, 1917, as does Langford's biographer, Clay Moyle; Langford was on the canvas for five minutes.			
19. **Harry Wills**	4/14/1918	Sam Langford	KO6, Panama City, Panama
*In August 1919, Tulsa boxing promoter Billy McClain conducted an elimination series for the Negro Heavyweight Championship of the World. The title included a belt valued at $1,500.			
	5/19/18	Sam Langford	WT7, Panama City, Panama, TD
*Following a 15-round draw against Jack Thompson, in Tulsa, Oklahoma, on October 20, 1919, Sam Langford claimed the WCHC. However, it remains difficult to find a scenario that would support such an action.			
	11/5/1919	Sam Langford	W15; Tulsa, OK, TD
Additional Notes: Harry Wills clearly held the WCHC following this engagement.			
	1/12/1920	Jack Thompson	W15; Tulsa, OK, TD

Appendix B.

Champion	Date	Opponent	Results/Notes
Additional Notes: Wills' fight with Thompson was billed as for the "World's Negro Heavyweight Championship" and "Colored Heavyweight Championship of the World." [See *Morning Tulsa Daily World*, January 11, 1920, Section B, 2.]			
Kid Norfolk	12/14/1920	Bill Tate	W10; New York, NY
Additional Notes: Norfolk took the 10-round Madison Square Garden victory along with Tate's claim to the Negro Heavyweight Championship. [See *Seattle Star*, December 15, 1920, 12.] Norfolk was viewed as a claimant [See *New York Tribune*, March 22, 1921, 13] by the press. Lee Anderson defeated Norfolk on May 30, 1921, by way of a tenth-round technical knockout—the event was advertised as for the Negro Heavyweight Championship [see *Omaha Daily Bee*, June 1, 1921, 9]. Lee Anderson would later bill himself as the Negro Light Heavyweight Champion [see *Arizona Republican*, June 27, 1921, 3].			
	1/17/1921	Bill Tate	KO2; Buffalo, NY; Wills retains title
*On July 16, 1921, Harry Wills openly opposed any claim made by Jack Johnson regarding the World Colored Heavyweight Championship. [See *East Oregonian*, July 16, 1921, 5.]			
*In September 1921, the Riverside Club of Covington, Kentucky, advertised an elimination tournament to determine the world's championship among Negro heavyweights. The winner received a diamond-studded belt emblematic of the title [see *South Bend News-Times*, September 18, 1921, 9.]			
*On November 18, 1921, Harry Wills defeats Denver Ed Martin by way of a first round knockout.			
	12/8/1921	Bill Tate	W13; Denver, CO; TD
20. **Bill Tate**	1/2/1922	Harry Wills	WF1, Milwaukie, OR
	1/6/1922	Harry Wills	D10; RD; Milwaukie, OR, both claim title
*On March 2, 1922, Harry Wills knocked out Kid Norfolk in the second round of their Madison Square Garden battle. With the victory, Wills believed he defended his WCHC. There was no word from Bill Tate.			
*The battle between Jack Johnson and "Tut" Jackson, scheduled for July 4, 1922, was ordered stopped by authorities. The fight was advertised as for the Negro Heavyweight Championship of the United States. [See *South Bend News-Times*, June 27, 1922, 9.]			
*On August 29, 1922, Harry Wills knocked out "Tut" Jackson in the third round of a scheduled 15-round battle at Ebbets Field. Chairman William Muldoon, of the New York State Athletic Commission, announced that due to Jackson's poor performance, there would be an investigation. Harry Wills believed he defended his claim to the World Colored Heavyweight Championship. [See *Richmond Planet*, September 9, 1922, 8.]			
21. **George Godfrey**	11/8/1926	Larry Gains	WT6, Buffalo, NY
Additional Notes: With Harry Wills' loss to Jack Sharkey (October 12, 1926), the WCHC was declared vacant. It wasn't clear if Wills vacated the title or it was deemed vacant upon the fighter's believed retirement. Regardless, George Godfrey defeated Larry Gains and claimed the title.			
	7/5/1927	Neil Clisby	KO7, Los Angeles, CA
22. **Larry Gains**	8/15/1928	George Godfrey	WF3, Toronto, Ontario, Canada
Additional Notes: The newspapers recognized this as a title transfer.			
	12/20/1928	Seal Harris	ND10, Indianapolis, IN, TD, RD

Champion	Date	Opponent	Results/Notes
Additional Notes: Larry Gains battled 10 rounds to a no-decision against Cecil "Seal" Harris, a rising star fighting out of Chicago. Many newspapers saw the fight in favor of Harris. Confident, strong and bold, Harris claimed the title. Not everyone saw the engagement as a title fight.			
*On August 18, 1930, "Long" Tom Hawkins took a newspaper decision over title claimant Seal Harris. The San Diego fighter then laid claim to the title, and, depending upon your perspective, may have successfully defended it until his retirement.			
*On December 19, 1930, George Godfrey drew "Bearcat" Wright in a bout claimed to be for the Black American Heavyweight Title.			
23. **George Godfrey**	8/24/1931	Seal Harris	KO2, Toronto, Ontario, Canada
Additional Notes: After Larry Gains relinquished the designation, George Godfrey defeated Seal Harris and claimed the vacant title.			
*On December 30, 1931, Billy Jones won a unanimous 10-round decision over Larry Johnson, at Chicago Stadium in Chicago. Although all cards were part of an NBA light heavyweight elimination tournament, Jones claimed the WCHC.			
	9/1/1932	Roy "Ace" Clark	KO3, Nuevo Laredo, Mexico, TD
	2/10/1933	"Bearcat" Wright	NC (stalling), Kansas City, TD, RD
*On September 6, 1933, Billy Jones, in his heavyweight debut, knocked out Larry Johnson, at Twin City Arena in Laurel, MD, in a bout billed as for the Colored Heavyweight Championship of the World.			
24. **Obie Walker**	10/9/1933	George Godfrey	W10, Philadelphia, PA
25. **Larry Gains**	7/20/1935	Obie Walker	W15, Leicester, England
*Joe Louis defeated James J. Braddock (KO8), on June 22, 1937, in Chicago, IL to win the Heavyweight Championship of the World.			
*Following Max Baer's victory over Pat Comiskey on September 26, 1940, at Roosevelt Stadium in Jersey City, New Jersey, Jack Kearns presented the fighter with a belt for the "White Heavyweight Championship."			

World Colored Heavyweight Champions & Associated Members of the International Boxing Hall of Fame

Inductee	Induction Year	Bouts	Won	Lost	Drew	KOs	ND	NC
Peter Jackson	1990	85	45	4	5	30	31	–
Jack Johnson	1990	123	77	13	14	48	19	–
Sam Langford	1990	293	167	38	37	117	48	3
Harry Wills	1992	130	65	8	2	47	25	3
Joe Jeannette	1997	157	79	9	6	66	62	1
Sam McVey	1999	97	63	12	7	48	13	2
George Godfrey	2007	120	97	20	3	80	–	–
(1897–1947) Associated Inductees								
James J. Corbett	1990	19	11	4	3	7	–	1
Jack Dempsey	1990	81	61	6	8	50	6	–
Bob Fitzsimmons	1990	115	74	8	3	67	30	–
James J. Jeffries	1990	21	18	1	2	15	–	–
Joe Louis	1990	71	68	3	0	54	–	–
Gene Tunney	1990	83	61	1	1	45	19	1
Max Schmeling	1992	70	56	10	4	39	–	–
Jack Sharkey	1994	55	38	13	3	14	1	–
Max Baer	1995	84	72	12	–	53	–	–
Tommy Burns	1996	60	46	5	8	37	1	–
James J. Braddock	2001	86	46	23	4	27	11	2
Jess Willard	2003	36	24	6	1	21	5	–
Kid Norfolk	2007	98	80	16	2	31	–	–

Also (Name, Induction year): *John L. Sullivan, 1990; Jack Blackburn, 1992; William Muldoon, 1996; Tom Molineaux, 1997; Jeff Dickson, 2000; Bill Richmond, 2005; Hugh McIntosh, 2012 (Source: International Boxing Hall of Fame)*

Chapter Notes

Chapter One

1. No offense to A. J. Liebling, who was often quick to note: On the floor of the Bardo National Museum in Tunis, Tunisia, there is a mosaic picture of a knockdown in a prizefight that took place in AD 200.

2. Sources note Figg's retirement anywhere from 1731 until his passing in 1734.

3. Mordaunt was the 3rd Earl of Peterborough and 1st Earl of Monmouth KG PC; in 1734, following Figg's death, Taylor took over the business.

4. This list is not intended to be comprehensive; a few Black fighters surfaced during this time period but much of the information surrounding their lives cannot be verified.

5. Percy was opposed to the government's policies on the American colonies and believed it would eventually lead to confrontation. This said, his loyalty to the crown was never at risk.

6. Percy was given command in Boston, along with the brevet rank of brigadier—above colonel but below major general.

7. Of the latter, it was a battle fought in New York on November 16, 1776, during the American Revolutionary War. More importantly, it was a British victory that gained the surrender of the remnant of the garrison of Fort Washington near the north end of Manhattan Island.

8. In July 1776, Percy, according to his notes, was in Staten Island. He sailed from Newport in early May 1777, and reached Falmouth, England on June 2, 1777.

9. For three decades, Charlton was rector of St. Andrews Episcopal Church in Richmondtown, New York; Charlton also owned Richmond's mother.

10. Charlton had a passion for Christianity and education; Percy may have observed Richmond defending himself during a pub melee. Impressed, Percy persuaded Charlton to sell the youngster.

11. It was common among British troops to place a wager on their favorite fighter, be it a single contest or a battle royal—the latter a fight involving many combatants that is fought until only one fighter remains standing. Some believe Percy initially encountered Richmond during one of these occasions. Also, some historians claim that on September 22, 1776, Richmond was one of the hangmen who executed Nathan Hale. Given a series of coincidences (published accounts, Percy's military maneuvers and artwork), it seems a reasonable enough piece of speculation. However, other sources contradict the possibility of Richmond's involvement. Granted, Richmond was only a teenager, but he was also Percy's valet.

12. The journalist Pierce Egan spoke to Richmond's athletic prowess, having witnessed a handful of battles. Richmond moved to London in 1795 and worked for Thomas Pitt, 2nd Baron of Camelford. Pitt was a boxing enthusiast.

13. Although embarrassing to the subject, it must be noted that Maddox, despite never being a champion, was an outstanding competitor. With regard to the Youssop bout: The crowd's anti-black sentiment was stronger than their anti-Semitism. The difficulty of Black fighters to attract wealthy White backing was often understated.

14. Richmond was a second in Tom Cribb's corner during the encounter; central to English pugilism at the time, not to mention an all-to-familiar venue to Richmond, was the Fives Court in London; Cribb would not allow the color of Richmond's skin to impact his relationship with the fighter.

15. Richmond had contributed greatly to the art of pugilism—his art of "hitting and not being hit" (self-defense) often recalled. Richmond attempted a comeback in the spring of 1808.

16. Richmond closed the "Horse and Dolphin" in 1818.

17. Craftsman included: Thomas Chippendale, who moved there in 1753; Vile and Cobb; and William Hallett, who were around the corner on Newport Street. Records indicate the fighter was forced to dispose of the pub in 1812.

18. Officially known as the Abolition of the Slave Trade Act.

19. The Davis engagement was part of the newly formed Pugilistic Club, a boxing league. Shelton was a disgruntled Richmond student; in 1818, Richmond also had an impromptu conflict with Lancashire Hero Jack Carter. The brief three-round battle ended when a bloodied and floored Carter was unable to continue.

20. The literate Richmond, who stood at five feet, nine inches, was the only Black person in attendance at the coronation.

21. Washington's father, Augustine, died in 1743

and willed his slaves and his farm of 280 acres near Fredericksburg, Virginia, to his son. The enslaved population at the time of his death included those he owned (less than half) and dower slaves from the Custis estate, George Washington's Mount Vernon. "10 Facts About Washington & Slavery." mountvernon.org https://www.mountvernon.org/george-washington/slavery/ten-facts-about-washington-slavery/

22. Lund Washington, "List of Runaways, April 1781," *The Writings of George Washington*, Vol. 22, 14n (accessed January 23, 2019).

23. Martha Washington (Dandridge) had first married Daniel Parke Custis, with whom she had four children, and was widowed by the age of 25.

24. Washington's plantation, wealth, and position in society depended on slaves. Servitude had the potential to destroy a fragile union or his life's work. In 1929, the Mount Vernon Ladies' Association placed a marker noting the location of the slave cemetery. Then, in 1983, Mount Vernon dedicated a new memorial designed by students at Howard University. Details regarding the identity and number of slaves (est. 100–150 people) buried in the cemetery are incomplete. In 2014, a multi-year archaeological survey began to provide additional information.

25. Excerpt from John Adams (1735–1826) to George Churchman and Jacob Lindley, 1801 (The Gilder Lehrman Institute of American History); as the second President of the United States, his term ran from March 4, 1797, until March 4, 1801.

26. Excerpt from James Monroe (1758–1831) to John Mason, August 1829; Monroe was the fifth President of the United States.

27. United States Census of 1830.

28. Tom Molineaux became close friends with the wealthy plantation owner's son, Algernon Molineaux; Sources have questioned Molineaux's origin, conversely believing he was part of a free Black population rather than a slave. His surname was also spelled Molyneaux according to the Virginia Historical Society. The *Sporting Magazine* noted him as "a Baltimore man of colour," while other references acknowledged his association with New York State; Pierce Egan, who penned *Boxiana*, has been a primary source for much of the information regarding Tom Molineaux.

29. The purse, which some believe was brokered by Davis, was believed to be in the range of $100, although the final sum of $500—which seems somewhat unbelievable for the period—has also appeared in some sources.

30. Molineaux, who may have traveled with Davis, according to some sources, may have spent a lengthy time in New York training prior to his European departure.

31. Richmond likely met Molineaux—some tales have him showing up at the famed pugilist's doorstep—that summer and took him under his wing.

32. It has also been said that Molineaux went as far as claiming the British heavyweight crown as a way to lure Cribb from retirement.

33. Under Broughton's rules, if a man went down and could not continue after a count of 30 seconds,

the fight was over. The mischievous act of prizefighting, its legality nearly constantly question, saw only a small percentage of battles actually interrupted by authorities.

34. Reports at this stage of the battle varied. Some claim Cribb was knocked out, or close to it. Cribb fans entered the ring to save their White fighter from the inevitable. The pretext of doctored gloves, or a foul, may also have been given. At this stage, some sources also believe Molineaux's finger may have been broken during the chaos.

35. "Tom Cribb's Final Triumph," *Salt Lake Tribune*, March 20, 1910, 38.

36. *Ibid.*

37. *Ibid.*

38. Had Richmond discontinued his relationship with Molineaux after the first battle, as some believe, it would be unlikely to find him in the fighter's corner during the rematch. Most believe the falling-out happened after this battle.

39. Captain Robert Barclay Allardice was the leading prizefighting trainer of the period. He was said to have won 10,000 pounds as a result of the match.

40. "Tom Cribb's Final Triumph," *Salt Lake Tribune*, March 20, 1910, 38.

41. For an American-born Black pugilist to enter a boxing ring against an English-born White champion the caliber of Cribb made an enormous socio-cultural statement; Captain Robert Barclay, commenting on the culinary delights of the pugilists, stated that just before the fight, Cribb, under his orders, had partaken of "only two boiled eggs, while the Negro had bolted a roast chicken, an apple pie, and a tankard of beer."

42. Turner received no formal burial; his headless remains were possibly buried in an unmarked grave.

Chapter Two

1. "Relations of the Races," *New York Herald*, September 11, 1874, 4; this was a quote from an article that originated out of Tuscumbia, Alabama, on September 5, 1874, and the opinion was reprinted in numerous newspapers.

2. Draw a bell curve, or a visual representation of normal distribution, and place the year 1876 to the far left and the year 1936 to the far right on the bottom or x-axis. Place the year 1899 underneath the pinnacle of the curve. What you have is a frequency distribution for the term "The Color Line" as it appeared in daily newspapers across the USA—the y-axis measures frequency. "The Color Line," an article penned by Frederick Douglass, was published in the *North American Review* in 1881. It took only 14 years for the use of that term to double (1895) since 1881. It took only 16 years for the use of that term to triple (1897) in frequency of use since 1881. In 1916, the frequency of use of "The Color Line" dropped to about the same level as 1896. Boxing drove the use of this term as its frequency mimicked major events within the sport. For example,

when Jess Willard defeated Jack Johnson, the use of the term was at its highest point for that particular decade (1910–1919).

3. There were only a few active fighters at the time.

4. London Prize Ring rules, adopted in 1838, stated: a knockdown ended the round, followed by a 30-second rest and an additional 8 seconds to regain the center of the ring. Butting, gouging, hitting below the waist, and kicking were banned.

5. Sources vary regarding the fighter's date of birth; facts surrounding his childhood and adolescence are scarce.

6. For those deprived of a right or privilege, some of these influences were restricted.

7. Smith was believed to have given up his occupation as a barber and boxing instructor to pursue prizefighting full-time.

8. Reilly would soon become familiar to some as a result of his alliance with John L. Sullivan.

9. "A Savage Glove Fight—The Negro Boxer Smith Knocked Out in Two Rounds," New Haven *Morning Journal and Courier*, August 17, 1883, 3; Stewart was seconded by Andy Hanly and Steve Taylor, while Smith was assisted by George Taylor and Charley Williams. "Smith was Black, short and heavy built with great knots of muscle," according to the report.

10. Smith defeated Charles Hadley as a result of a second-round foul on February 2, 1884.

11. "A Glove Fight," *St. Paul Globe*, March 11, 1884, 1; Thompson, seconded by Jack Stewart, scaled at 210, while Smith, assisted by Charles Hadley, tipped at 204. Smith had met Hadley in his previous two recorded battles.

12. "Pugilism," *Chicago Tribune*, April 4, 1867, 2; colored pugilists were often not mentioned by name in the newspapers.

13. In a testament to his ability, Goss, in his mid–40s, would fight 87 rounds in defeat to Paddy Ryan on May 30, 1880. He passed on March 24, 1885, in Boston, Massachusetts. As a hub fighter in his later years, there was little, if any, possibility of him ever fighting a colored pugilist.

14. According to the letter sent to the *Buffalo Courier*, Smith believed Reilly had been exploiting his name since 1883.

15. William A. Muldoon (May 25, 1852–June 3, 1933) was a Greco-Roman Wrestling Champion, physical culturist, and the first chairman of the New York State Athletic Commission. He also liked what he saw in Smith and took him under his wing. In 1889, Muldoon trained John L. Sullivan for his famous 75-round fight against Jake Kilrain for the world heavyweight bare-knuckle boxing championship. Smith called Port Huron, Michigan, his home by 1883.

16. "Maher Wins a Six-Round Bout," *San Francisco Call*, February 16, 1867, 5.

17. Other fighters would also use the popular moniker "Thunderbolt."

18. So few understand the depths of the plight of Black men and women in the South from the end of the American Civil War until the middle of the 20th century.

19. "Condensed Telegrams," Washington *Evening Star*, April 7, 1882, 1.

20. "Heavy-Weight Colored Boxer," Wilmington, Delaware *Daily Republican*, April 7, 1882, 4; the *National Police Gazette*, or *Police Gazette*, was a popular American magazine founded in 1845. Publisher Richard K. Fox transformed it into a men's lifestyle magazine by the use of gossip, sports, and pin-ups of beautiful women.

21. Throughout the 1860s and 1870s, Harry Hill was involved in virtually every major bare-knuckle boxing event of the era; Hadley was viewed by some as the Colored champion of Connecticut.

22. "The Ring," *Lancaster Daily Intelligencer*, December 8, 1882, 2.

23. *Ibid.;* sources vary regarding the details of the fight; the "n-word," an ethnic slur as repulsive as it is racist, will appear only in a few quotations, or examples, to illustrate the ignorance and insensitivity of the time. The *National Republican* reported on page 1 of their December 8, 1882 edition, "Grant was knocked out in the first round. A row ensued, in the course of which Charles Cooley, Grant's trainer, drew a revolver, and threatened to shoot Hadley."

24. "A Colored Boxer's Large Heart," New York *Sun*, February 19, 1883, 1.

25. In January 1882, it was reported by the *Morning Journal* that "Prof. C.W. Hadley is 29 years of age, 5 feet 10½ inches tall and weighs 170½ pounds."

26. "Hadley's Retirement," *St. Paul Daily Globe*, August 31, 1885, 2; McGlinchey, more of an instructor and sparring partner than pugilist, fought out of Bridgeport, Connecticut.

27. "Boxing Match," New Haven *Morning Journal and Courier*, January 14, 1882, 2.

28. "Mr. Grant Knocked Entirely Out," New York *Sun*, December 8, 1882, 3; it was also referred to as the Fox Colored Heavyweight Championship. Details and accounts of such early confrontations could vary.

29. "Hadley's Retirement," *St. Paul Daily Globe*, August 31, 1885, 2.

30. "A Slugging Match," *St. Paul Daily Globe*, February 24, 1883, 5.

31. Interesting, as many sources acknowledge far more conflicts. However, that was the way he saw it.

32. "Hadley and Taylor Fight a Stubborn Battle, Which Is Declared a Draw," *St. Paul Daily Globe*, January 1, 1887, 4.

33. *Ibid.*

34. Little information has surfaced regarding the final days of Charles Hadley. He died just before the turn of the century (1897) and believed buried in Fairmount Cemetery in Spokane, Washington.

35. His gravestone at the Woodlawn Cemetery, in Everett, Massachusetts, states 1852, which is believed incorrect. Charlottestown's West End was ravaged by poverty and minor crimes.

36. He likely arrived in Boston about 1870; he had some noted early boxing instruction.

37. "Boston Scandal," Carson City *Morning Appeal*, February 25, 1883, 2. This article also

appeared on the front page of the *Wheeling Daily Intelligencer* and the *Sacramento Daily-Record Union.* Many sources note the wrong date.

38. McHenry Johnson (1859–1889), the "Minneapolis Star," was an accomplished fighter who stood about six feet and weighed around 190 pounds. Early in his career, he fought out of New York City before heading to the Midwest, then on to Denver. Johnson battled Godfrey to a likely draw on May 10, 1884. On January 25, 1888, he was given a victory over Godfrey due to a foul. However, the decision was later overturned. Johnson claimed the title, or a similar version (Police Gazette Colored Heavyweight Championship), on numerous occasions. The fighters wore two-ounce gloves.

39. *Ibid.*

40. *Ibid.*

41. *Ibid.*

42. The fight with Lannon was a pre-arranged distance draw.

43. During his career, Cardiff won the Heavyweight Championship of the Northwest and Heavyweight Championship of Illinois.

44. Richard K. Fox, editor of the *Police Gazette,* detested Sullivan. So he recognized Kilrain as champion. Fox's relationship with Sullivan was contentious following a perceived slight at a saloon. His creation of the Colored Championship Tournament was an open challenge to John L. Sullivan to cross the color line. As a White supremacist, Sullivan wasn't going to risk the Holy Grail.

45. "Kilrain a Victor," *Rock Island Argus,* March 14, 1891, 2; the battle was so vicious Referee Hiram Cook preferred to call the fight from outside the 24-foot ring.

46. *Ibid.,* 4.

47. "The Black Man Wins," *Seattle Post-Intelligencer,* May 17, 1892, 2.

48. "A Vicious Prize Fight," *Helena Independent,* November 1, 1892, 1.

49. "Maher the Winner," Bradford, Vermont *United Opinion,* June 1, 1894, 2.

50. He was buried in the Laurel Hill Section in Woodlawn Cemetery; some sources state August 18, 1901.

51. It was Aristotle who quipped, "Those who know, do. Those that understand, teach." By teaching his trade, George Godfrey passed his wisdom to those who might follow—included in that scholarship was the history of the coveted title.

52. Too many boxing commentators have simply stated that a fighter drew the color line or gave their opinion without a period source. There is never an elaboration, or even a citation to prove it. By using this approach, you can hear it straight from the source and draw your own conclusion.

53. "Theory and Fact as to the Color Line," *Wheeling Register,* January 6, 1883, 2.

54. "The Color Line," *Salt Lake Herald,* January 4, 1885, 4.

55. "Sullivan Won't Notice a Coon," *St. Paul Daily Globe,* December 30, 1888, 7.

Chapter Three

1. "Death Calls Peter Jackson," *San Francisco Call,* August 9, 1901, 5.

2. Other sources, such as the International Boxing Hall of Fame, note July 3, 1861.

3. His travels likely took him to New York prior to his arrival in Australia.

4. Since 1832, the hotel has been located at the corner of Pacific Highway & Greengate Road in Killara.

5. Lees was the second reported person to hold the title Heavyweight Champion of Australia, from May 1885 to September 1886.

6. "Down the Line," Washington *Evening Star,* March 20, 1931, 48.

7. Sources vary regarding the date of the fight; some state December 27, 1888.

8. Jackson, who scaled at 204, dropped McAuliffe, who tipped at 219, in the 18th frame.

9. This was a skin-tight gloves bout; Jim Corbett was also on hand and rooting for Cardiff. The California Athletic Club tried and failed to match Jackson with Sullivan.

10. He sailed back to England on August 21, 1889.

11. "Jem Smith Beaten," *Salt Lake Herald,* November 12, 1889, 2.

12. *Ibid.;* This was a reprinted British account adding even more credence to Jackson's incomparable style.

13. "John Will Fight Pete," St. Paul *Appeal,* December 14, 1889, 1.

14. *Ibid.*

15. Using four-ounce gloves, Jackson dropped Smith—trained by Sullivan and Muldoon—three times in the first round.

16. On July 26, Jackson sailed for Australia.

17. "South Sea Islands, Peter Jackson Meets His Equal in Melbourne," *Los Angeles Herald,* November 23, 1890, 2.

18. *Ibid.*

19. In 1890, Slavin was crowned Heavyweight Champion of the World by the *National Police Gazette.* Although Sullivan was commonly regarded as the titleholder, the *Gazette* declared Slavin the world champion in light of Sullivan's reluctance to fight challengers.

20. "Great Fights Next Week," *Helena Independent,* May 15, 1891, 7.

21. The boxers wore five-ounce gloves.

22. "No Contest! All Bets Off!" *Salem Daily News,* May 22, 1891, 1. The fight ended as a no-contest; accordingly, each fighter was paid only $2,500 by the California Athletic Club. Both boxers were furious and castigated the club.

23. As both he and Jackson were insufficiently compensated for their battle, atonement, at least in his case, came in the form of opportunity.

24. "The Coon Victorious," *Caldwell Tribune,* June 4, 1892, 4. Reports of the fighter's weight varied.

25. The Mason-Dixon line was the boundary between Maryland and Pennsylvania, taken as the northern limit of the slave-owning states before the abolition of slavery.

26. "The Corbett-Jackson Duel at Long Range," *Fort Worth Gazette*, June 14, 1894, 4.

27. American copyright laws were inadequate, and there were no international copyright laws.

28. At the hands of a sadistic Simon Legree, Uncle Tom's death by flogging was a well-known part of the performance.

29. Parson Davies was also in the production. He played the Auctioneer; Joe Choynski played the role of George Shelby in later productions.

30. It has also been claimed that he gave up the World Colored heavyweight Championship this same year.

31. "With the Sporting Folks," *Times*, March 20, 1898, 5.

32. "Jackson Knocked Out," *Waterbury Evening Democrat*, March 23, 1898, 5. Referee Jim McDonald had little choice but to stop the fight as Jackson, supported only by a corner post, was barely cognizant.

33. "Death Calls Peter Jackson," *San Francisco Call*, August 9, 1901; reports stated that Jackson died of consumption and was penniless. He depended on the charity of friends to live.

34. "Record of the Late Peter Jackson, Pugilist," *St. Louis Republic*, August 26, 1901, 7.

35. *Ibid.*

36. Davies, as Jackson's voice, was the perfect spokesman—he kept critics off his fighter's back.

37. "The Color Line," *Appeal*, January 24, 1891, 1.

38. "The Color Line," *Watauga Democrat,* March 13, 1889, 1.

39. "No Color Line Is Drawn" *Omaha Daily Bee*, May 10, 1893, 8.

Chapter Four

1. Newspaper articles regarding Sullivan's wealth as champion appeared routinely in dailies across the country.

2. "Gentleman Jim" was no nobleman in Fitz's eyes as he doled out insults like firemen dispense water.

3. "Training Methods," *Philipsburg Mail*, August 29, 1895, 2; both Choynski and McCoy would have been sparring sessions at best. No source has been found for his contact with McCoy.

4. "Slavin's Career Wound Up," *Record-Union*, November 24, 1896, 1; The pair met, at catchweight, for a 20-round battle; The attendance at the event was estimated at 2,000.

5. *Ibid.*

6. Jackson's primary interest was in the Heavyweight Championship of the World. Relinquishing his claim to the Colored title the following year, Jackson likely saw Armstrong's claim as being a bit presumptuous.

7. "Fistic Events," *Evening Bulletin*, December 22, 1896, 1; Armstrong's claim to the title was far from front page news and didn't appear in the bulk of the coverage of the fight.

8. "With the Sluggers," *Salt Lake Herald*, December 22, 1896, 2.

9. Some sources report a fight with Frank Childs in Philadelphia on March 7, 1897, but newspaper reports contradict the possibility.

10. On April 23, Armstrong tossed four strong punches at the face of San Francisco fighter Sam Pruitt (Pruett). Fearing for his life when he saw blood, the local man quit in the first round.

11. Jeffries was in Nevada and didn't plan on getting serious about his ring record until spring 1898.

12. "Bob Armstrong Easily Bested," *San Francisco Call*, January 30, 1898, 2; this newspaper did not indicate a title transfer.

13. The warning sheds some light on the legitimacy of the contest. Childs, frustrated by his role as an understudy, clearly wanted to display his talent.

14. "General Sporting News," *Kansas City Journal*, February 5, 1898, 5; some believe the World Colored Heavyweight title may have been transferred.

15. Armstrong was in Syracuse doing some work for Tommy Ryan. Often such a circumstance lends itself to informal financial opportunities, in the form of exhibitions and bootleg battles.

16. "Jeffries Shatters His Left Arm," *Record-Union*, August 6, 1898, 8.

17. Armstrong was under Tom O'Rourke's managerial umbrella at this point.

18. While some view this as a title defense for Childs, others see it as an official title transfer.

19. Harry Rousela, listed here as a second, may have actually been Herman C. Roussellot.

20. "Childs Colored Champion," *Saint Paul Daily Globe*, March 5, 1899, 11.

21. "Knocked Over the Ropes," *Seattle Post-Intelligencer*, November 28, 1899, 6.

22. The Martin battles were under constant scrutiny due to the friendship between the fighter's managers (Charles E. "Parson" Davies and Billy Madden).

23. "Armstrong Picks Jeffries to Win," *Evening Times*, April 21, 1910, 3.

24. *Ibid.*

25. "Day of Great Ring Battles Are Past, Says Black Trainer," *Santa Fe New Mexican*, October 22, 1913, 4.

26. Armstrong's death date conflicts with some sources—they state July 6, 1933.

27. "If Not Why Not?" *Washington Bee,* November 14, 1896, 4.

28. "Fistic News," *Times*, September 20, 1897, 6.

Chapter Five

1. Known for his trademark "pivot punch," LaBlanche was more of a scrapper than a boxer. He was often recalled for his 1889 ring battle against "Nonpareil" Jack Dempsey.

2. "Peter Jackson on Exhibition," *Herald*, January 20, 1893, 5.

3. *Ibid.*

4. "Smith Put to Sleep," *Herald*, February 16, 1893, 1.

5. "On American Soil," *Comet*, April 5, 1894, 7.

6. "The Native and the Negro," *Pacific Commercial Advertiser*, October 16, 1897, 4.

7. "Hotel Men and the Color Line," *San Francisco Call*, September 29, 1897, 4.

8. *Ibid.*

9. "Program of Services," *Copper Country Evening News*, June 19, 1897, 8.

10. According to some sources, this was the fighter's professional debut. Haynes would become a formidable figure who always appeared one step from the championship level. The fight took place at the 2nd Regiment Armory.

11. The fight took place on February 26, 1898, and was stopped by the referee in the fourth round. It was part of a boxing carnival that included five limited bouts.

12. Depending upon your perspective, Childs may have defended his title. Certain was that he did not lose a fight—he met George Grant, Klondike, Billy Keough and Charley Strong prior to meeting George Byers on September 14, 1898.

13. "Byers Defeats Frank Childs," *Sun,* September 15, 1898, 5.

14. *Ibid.*

15. The fighter was believed to be one of eight children born to William Byers, III (c.1813–1890) and Charlotte Ellen Goodwin (c. 1828–c. 1877).

16. "Celebrated Boxers Travel Through Town," *Waterbury Evening Democrat*, December 8, 1897, 3; Byers had drawn Dan Murphy in Waterbury, Connecticut, during a 20-round affair on November 11, 1897. Waterbury, Connecticut, has the moniker "The Brass City."

17. "Colored Lads Fought Nobly," *Waterbury Evening Democrat*, December 10, 1897, 5. Some sources view this as a middleweight championship. Following the fight, Peppers sent an open letter to the *Waterbury Evening Democrat* that was printed on December 13, 1897, on page five. The fighter had lost use of his right hand in the third round.

18. The first Byers-Childs conflict was one of the best fights of the year at the Lenox A.C. according to *The Sun,* September 15, 1898, 5. Byers, who shredded his opponents face over 20 rounds, was clearly the winner. But was it a title transfer? By 1902, he was fighting mainly out of New England as his career began to fade. By 1910, he was focusing on training and working with Sam Langford for his bout with Jim Flynn.

19. Byers worked out of both the Atlas Athletic Club and the Criterion Club; Sam Langford praised him both as an instructor and friend. Byers spent years working for the Boston and Maine Railroad (later part of the Pan Am Railways).

20. Certainly one of the most gifted middleweights of his era, not to mention a Stanley Ketchel type of a fighter, Byers, aka "Budge," saw no opponent as too large. But he considered himself a middleweight and was billed as a member of that weight class. The fighter was married to Julia Byers.

21. "Childs Knocks Out Armstrong," *San Francisco Call*, March 5, 1899, 15; If—yes, that's an enormous "if"—Byers held the title, what was at stake?

22. "Working Up a Crowd," *Saint Paul Globe*, March 12, 1899, 9.

23. On August 11, Childs defeated "Klondike" in Chicago, at the Fort Dearborn Athletic Club. In a rematch on October 28, he sent the gold digger to the Promised Land in the third round.

24. Sam Summerfield was a bookmaker in the summer and a promoter of boxing in the winter. When he retired from the Fort Dearborn Athletic Club, Charles Essig filled the role of manager and matchmaker.

25. Some records vary regarding these dates.

26. "Wasn't a Fake," *Saint Paul Daily Globe*, December 16, 1900, 13.

27. "Byers Outclassed," *Saint Paul Globe,* March 17, 1901, 8.

28. "Colored Champion Won," *Indianapolis Journal*, January 19, 1902, 6.

29. In truth, the match had been argued for months.

30. "Hanrahan Is Put Out," *Saint Paul Globe*, February 4, 1902, 5.

31. "Martin Wins the Fight," *Salt Lake Herald*, February 25, 1902, 7. This newspaper did not acknowledge the fight as a championship contest, however the *Saint Paul Globe* did cite the title.

32. George Siler, despite a Hall of Fame career, has been criticized for appearing biased toward some fighters. Some feel he disliked Childs, therefore accounting for his customary long counts over the fighter's antagonists.

33. Childs, who did not fight in 1903, fought three times in 1904, and is believed to have fought once in 1911.

34. The *Indianapolis Journal* claimed he deliberately quit, but also stated that he had the edge during the first two rounds.

35. "Charity Profited," *Arizona Republican*, October 10, 1902, 1.

36. "Walcott Fakes Another Fight," *Evening World*, October 10, 1902, 10.

37. This was reported by the *Evening Times* on October 11, 1902, 6.

38. "Childs Throws Up the Sponge," *Topeka State Journal*, October 22, 1902, 2.

39. "Peter Maher's Defeat Marks the Elimination of a Veteran," *St. Louis Republic*, December 7, 1902, 5.

40. "M'Clelland, Johnson and Holly Win Three Fights," *Evening World*, June 3, 1904, 12.

41. *Ibid.*

42. "Hot Talk From Fitz," *Topeka State Journal*, January 24, 1899, 4.

43. "Color Line Is Drawn," *Topeka State Journal*, November 6, 1903, 2.

44. "Some Sensible Talk," *Ocala Evening Star*, February 14, 1902, 4; the opinion, as the newspaper points out, was "viewed from a Colored man's standpoint."

Chapter Six

1. Those who came were known as "Fifty-Niners," after the peak year of the rush—their motto became "Pike's Peak or Bust!" The location of the Pike's Peak

Gold Rush was actually centered 85 miles north of Pike's Peak (now spelled Pikes). The name Pike's Peak Gold Rush was used mainly because of how well-known and important Pike's Peak was at the time.

2. The explosion in European immigration created a population boom. New York City was forced to expand its boundaries into Queens and Staten Island, as neighborhoods drew ethnic lines as a source of comfort.

3. Interesting for fight historians was that Bellfield Walcott, Joe's brother, was also on the bill, fighting at 135 pounds.

4. "'Culled' Event at Coney," *Kansas City Journal*, July 25, 1899, 5.

5. The fight with Haynes was viewed by the press as a victory, the battle with Armstrong a draw.

6. "Yank Kenny Beaten," *Waterbury Evening Democrat*, September 1, 1900, 7. Although Kenny was a popular fighter, it still surprises many why the defeated White fighter grabbed the headline.

7. "Jeffries to Train at Baden," *Topeka State Journal*, December 21, 1900, 4.

8. "Sporting News," *Topeka State Journal*, January 1, 1901, 2.

9. An Edison studio film, called *Ruhlin Boxing with "Denver" Ed Smith*, documented the pair's sparring.

10. "Purcell and Denver Ed Martin," *Butte Inter Mountain*, July 8, 1901, 8.

11. "Madden's Ambition Is Now Realized," *Evening World*, October 3, 1901, 8.

12. "Gus Ruhlin the Akron Giant Exhibits Before Butte Sports," *Butte Inter Mountain*, July 18, 1901, 8.

13. "Denver Ed Beats Childs," *Omaha Daily Bee*, February 25, 1902, 4.

14. "Huge Jokes," *Albuquerque Daily Citizen*, June 21, 1902, 1.

15. The press claimed that the battle was a "fake." Remarks made by both managers, Charles E. "Parson" Davies and Billy Madden, quelled the concern. Naturally, Martin and company called out Jeffries—he kayoed Fitz in the eighth round.

16. "Wants Chance with Jeffries," *Saint Paul Globe*, August 25, 1902, 5; confusing were some reports, such as what appeared in the *Bisbee Daily Review*, that Martin's defeat of Ferguson garnered him the English Heavyweight Championship. Unclear was how Jack Scales, Ben Taylor, and Jack Palmer felt about the claim.

17. "Madden Returns from Old World," *Butte Inter Mountain*, September 26, 1902, 7.

18. "In the Prize Ring," *Minneapolis Journal*, December 11, 1902, 16.

19. "Johnson Whips 'Denver' Ed Martin," Washington *Evening Star*, February 7, 1903, 9; Martin, who was floored four times in the 11th round, managed to finish strong. Johnson just could not put Martin away.

20. The bout was delayed in the second round when Chelsea heavyweight Sandy Ferguson, prompted by being called "the stubborn child," decided to brawl with sportswriter Ben Benton.

21. "Oxnard Boxer Proves a Wonder," *San Francisco Call*, September 16, 1903, 8.

22. "Denver Ed Martin Defeats McVey," *San Fran-cisco Call*, August 13, 1904, 5; the battle was initially scheduled for 20 rounds.

23. "Fight Was Fast While It Lasted," *Salt Lake Herald*, October 19, 1904, 7.

24. "Johnson Almost Killed Ed Martin," *Washington Times*, October 19, 1904, 10.

25. "McCarey Driving Laundry Wagon When He Got Idea of Being Boxing Promoter," *Los Angeles Herald*, September 30, 1915, 12; McCarey joined hands with Jim Morley and Al Levy in a club.

26. "Thomas Jefferson McCarey, Successful Boxing Promoter," *Los Angeles Herald*, May 28, 1911, 6.

27. *Ibid.*

28. "Jeffries Will Not Fight a Negro," *Spokane Press*, November 18, 1904, 2. Jeffries performed exhibitions with Bob Armstrong and Hank Griffin in 1901, but discontinued the practice the following year. He refereed the Joe Gans v. George Memsic World Lightweight Championship bout at Los Angeles, California on September 27, 1907. Jeffries would perform exhibitions in 1910 with Bob Armstrong, who was assisting him in preparations for the Johnson fight on July 4, 1910.

29. "Champion's Story of Hardest Battle," *Spokane Press*, December 21, 1909, 12.

30. "Negro Foolishness," *Seattle Republican*, April 17, 1903, 3.

31. "England Draws Color Line," *Sedalia Weekly Conservator*, September 18, 1903, 1.

Chapter Seven

1. A Halberstamish line, as I call it, or salute if you will, to Mr. David Halberstam.

2. There is not enough space in a work such as this to make the reader understand just how difficult it had been for a Black person to register to vote, let alone to cast a ballot, in the South prior to 1957. The indignation felt by black southerners cannot be understated.

3. While in Chicago in 1899, Jack Johnson worked as a sparring partner for Frank Childs.

4. Johnson's first wife, although no record exists, was believed to be a Black girl from Galveston named Mary Austin.

5. "Choynski Knocks Out Johnson," *Daily Morning Journal and Courier*, February 26, 1901, 1.

6. It was rumored that Choynski was brought to Galveston to flatten an over-confident Johnson during an exhibition, but not a fight. Choynski's bag of dirty tricks was infamous, and he brought it with him.

7. From behind bars, Choynski passed the time by educating the youngster on the fine art of self-defense. The pair had a good laugh when they learned they spent more time in jail than a man who killed his wife.

8. This bout was on the undercard of the Abe Attell versus Young Cassidy fight; Johnson would receive far more media attention in Denver.

9. Both Denver and Southern California were strong boxing markets for both Black and White pugilists.

10. Some of Johnson's early battles in 1902 were not recorded. The word was that Hank Griffin backed out of this opportunity due to a disagreement over the purse.

11. "Jeffries' Brother Is Knocked Out in Five Rounds," *San Francisco Call*, May 17, 1902, 5.

12. On page three of Johnson's Petition for Pardon (July 12, 2004), it acknowledged Johnson's 1903 victory for the "Negro heavyweight championship." The document notes that the title was "a contrivance by California sportswriters, reflecting the fact that African American boxers, at least in the important weight classes, were not permitted to compete against White fighters in championship matches." The report also notes that myths about Blacks were used to rationalize the color line.

13. "Boxer Johnson Defeats Martin," *San Francisco Call*, February 6, 1903, 4; Martin was trained by Billy Madden, while Hank Griffin conditioned Johnson.

14. The lackluster event—partially attributed to a movement to end prizefighting—saw Johnson kayo McVey 20 seconds from the final bell.

15. In Philadelphia, laws stated that boxing matches, such as the one between Ferguson and Black Bill, could not exceed six rounds.

16. "Denver Ed Martin Is Knocked Out by Jack Johnson," *San Francisco Call*, October 19, 1904, 10; Johnson also picked up some extra cash by briefly playing baseball for the Philadelphia Giants, a Negro League team. His Texas friend, Andrew "Rube" Foster, was a star pitcher for the club. Recent work by the Society for American Baseball Research (SABR) suggests that William Edward White may have been the first African American to play major league baseball (June 21, 1879), predating the longer careers of Moses Fleetwood Walker and his brother Weldy Walker by five years, and Jackie Robinson by 68 years.

17. "Did Jack Johnson Fake?" *Los Angeles Herald*, February 15, 1904, 5.

18. "Jeff Refuses to Fight a Negro," *Los Angeles Herald*, November 19, 1904, 10.

19. "Hart Receives the Decisions," *Los Angeles Herald*, March 29, 1905, 10.

20. "Jeffries Is Willing to Meet Marvin Hart," *San Francisco Call*, March 30, 1905, 6.

21. Johnson was arrested for hitting Joe Jeannette too low in the second round. The *Washington Times* reported on November 27, 1905, "There was a hot mix-up, in which Johnson threw out his ponderous left at random. The blow was palpably low. Jeannette fell to the floor and the bout stopped, Johnson being disqualified." Although Johnson had been noted as holding the Colored designation in some pre-fight reports, there was no mention of this being a title fight. Later, he was mentioned by sources, such as the Washington *Evening Star*, as still holding the Colored designation.

22. Kerr ran off with a racehorse trainer named William Bryant, a friend (or so it was believed) of the fighter. Johnson tracked the couple down to Arizona and had Kerr arrested on burglary charges—when she left, she took everything she perceived as value.

Johnson and Kerr temporarily reconciled. On May 9, Johnson met both Joe Jeannette and Walter Johnson, each Black fighter for three rounds.

23. Fight sources vary; some list a battle against Jeannette in New York on December 9; however, according to reports, including the Washington *Evening Star*, Johnson arrived in Boston that morning. See "New York Sports Were Outwitted," *Evening Star*, December 11, 1906, 22.

24. Drawing too much attention to the World Colored Heavyweight Championship could, as Johnson believed, give a White champion the option of saying, "you got your title and I have mine." Johnson did not want this to happen.

25. This was Johnson's recollection, however those ringside recalled it differently.

26. Although the fight details vary, Langford was an experienced fighter by this point. He not only held his own against some great fighters, but beat legendary Joe Gans.

27. Tommy Burns defended his title: twice (Los Angeles) in 1906, three times (twice in Southern California, once in England) in 1907; and seven times (England, Ireland, twice in France, and three times in Australia) in 1908.

28. "Jack Johnson Makes Short Work of Felix," *San Francisco Call*, February 20, 1907, 7.

29. "Fitzsimmons Knocked Out in Second Round by Jack Johnson," *Nashville Globe*, July 19, 1907, 8. One can only imagine the personal satisfaction Johnson felt from breaking the jaw of the racist fireman with the winning punch.

30. "Flynn Tucked Away in 11th," *Salt Lake Herald*, November 3, 1907, 8.

31. A White woman, Alma "Lola" Toy, briefly distracted Johnson. The fighter was also determined to turn his back to Black women following his episodes with Kerr.

32. Johnson understood that Burns could relent at a moment's notice; consequently, proximity could be an obstacle to success. By immediately signing a contract, Johnson could prevent Burns from changing his mind.

33. Johnson also received $500 for the moving pictures plus three round-trip tickets from London.

34. Champion under the Marquess of Queensberry Rules.

35. "Jim Jeffries Says Tommy Burns Is a False Favorite in Betting," *Detroit Times*, December 23, 1908, 7; according to a report printed by the *Omaha Daily Bee* on December 25, 1908, James J. Jeffries cabled to Australia a challenge to meet the winner of the contest. The cable was sent to Hugh McIntosh.

36. "The Pugilists," *Waterbury Evening Democrat*, December 9, 1908, 11.

37. "I Will Uphold the White Supremacy, Cables Burns," *Evening World*, December 25, 1908, 4.

38. "Burns-Johnson Fight Tonight," *Salt Lake Herald*, December 25, 1908, 10; nationalism, or patriotic feeling, principles, or efforts, eclipses racism.

39. "Jack Johnson Defeats Burns," *Salt Lake Herald*, December 26, 1908, 8.

40. "Jeff Refuses to Bring Title Back to Whites," *Seattle Star*, December 26, 1908, 1.

41. *Ibid.*

42. "Jack Johnson Wins Heavyweight Championship of the World in Fourteen Fast Fighting Rounds," *Seattle Star,* December 26, 1908, 2.

43. Jack Johnson made a pilgrimage to the grave of Peter Jackson at Toowong Cemetery in February 1909.

44. Later, film revenue would fall under ancillary rights, or supplementary rights given to a fighter. Typically a boxer received a percentage of the profits derived from the sale, viewing, or distribution of the film. They would also be used as a bargaining chip during the contract negotiation process.

45. While some historians view this bout as Johnson's fourth title defense, others see it differently.

46. Both veterans received 60 percent of the gross receipts, of which Johnson got 65 percent and Ketchel 35 percent. Each boxer posted a forfeiture of $5,000 to go as a side bet.

47. Little would soon be replaced by Tom Flanagan. Johnson met Belle at an exclusive all–White bordello in Chicago called the Everleigh Club.

48. "P'izen? Say, Li'l Artha Has It All Over Czar Nick for Taking Precautions," *Seattle Star*, June 14, 1910, 2.

49. *Ibid.*

50. "Reno Draw Color Line," *Tacoma Times*, June 20, 1910, 2.

51. "Fight Aggressor Will Be Jeffries," Washington *Evening Star,* June 19, 1910, 55.

52. "All Pick Jeffries as the Winner," *Pacific Commercial Advertiser*, June 22, 1910, 3.

53. "Joe Gans Thinks That Jack Johnson Will Win," *Spokane Press*, June 22, 1910, 3.

54. "Jennette, Colored, Say Jeff Will Win, " *Spokane Press*, June 25, 1910, 3.

55. "Colored Men to Have Fight Special," *Spokane Press*, June 24, 1910, 9; a White train, the Hancock-Berry special, was scheduled to leave for Reno on July 1.

56. "Should Be No Color Prejudice," Ogden *Morning Examiner*, June 12, 1910, 3.

57. "Chicago Writer Discusses Topic," Grand Forks *Evening Times*, June 13, 1910, 3.

58. "Results of Riots Following Fight," *Salt Lake Tribune*, July 5, 1910, 9.

59. "In the Wake of Halley's Comet Come Ruin and Wild Rebellion," *Los Angeles Herald*, June 27, 1910, 8; the final line was a spin on the classic line by Joe Gans and an execrable racial slur.

60. "Was Like a Funeral," *Ogden Standard*, July 5, 1910, 1.

61. Adrenaline is a hormone secreted by the adrenal glands, especially in conditions of stress, increasing rates of blood circulation, breathing, and carbohydrate metabolism and preparing muscles for exertion. It often provides a euphoric sense of immortality.

62. "Jack Johnson Gets Big Money," *Tacoma Times*, January 1, 1912, 2; Johnson would have his price met.

63. "Fear of Deadly 'Hoodoo' Figures in Ring Careers of Most Famous Fighters," New York *Evening World*, January 3, 1920, 8; always certain to mask Johnson's intellect, the racist press always printed their own interpretation of his remarks.

64. "Johnson Indicted," Ogden *Evening Standard*, June 21, 1912, 10.

65. "Johnson Won in the Ninth," *Topeka State Journal*, July 4, 1912, 1.

66. "Cuspidors de Luxe at Jack Jonson's," *Fairmount West Virginian*, July 11, 1912, 3.

67. "Jack Johnson's White Wife Dies in Hospital After Shooting Herself," *Detroit Times*, September 12, 1912, 6; the *Devils Lake Weekly World,* on September 13, 1912, ran a subtitled article: "The Fact That the Man of Her Choice Was Colored, Responsible."

68. The Everleigh Club, owned and operated by Ada and Minna Everleigh, was a high-class brothel in Chicago, Illinois. It existed from February 1900 until October 1911.

69. "Miss Lucille Cameron side stepped her mother Mrs. Cameron-Falconet after she Emerged from Prison," *Broad Ax*, December 7, 1912, 1.

70. "Conviction of a Black Brute," *Jones County News*, May 22, 1913, 6.

71. The International Boxing Union (IBU) was created June 1911 in Paris. It was an attempt to create a unified international governing body for professional boxing.

72. Johnson claimed his left arm was broken in the third round; he used only his right hand following that term. There was medical confirmation of a slight fracture. The lack of engagement between the fighters led to enormous speculation, and some spectators demanded a refund.

73. "Johnson Knocked Out in Twenty-sixth Round," Clarksburg *Daily Telegram*, April 6, 1915, 3.

74. Editorial, *Ocala Evening Star*, April 6, 1915, 2.

75. "J. Johnson, Negro Pug, Is Jailed," *Rock Island Argus*, July 20, 1920, 1.

76. After his release from prison, he was denied boxing licenses in numerous states including Ohio, Pennsylvania, New York, and New Jersey.

77. Nobody, including Jack Johnson, is quite sure just when, or if, he surrendered the World Colored Heavyweight Championship.

78. President Donald J. Trump pardoned (Executive Grant of Clemency) Jack Johnson on May 24, 2018.

79. "Fitz Advises Against Drawing Color Line," *Los Angeles Herald*, September 11, 1905, 8.

80. "The Old-time Ring Figures," *Salt Lake Tribune*, March 18, 1906, 2.

81. "The Following of the Color Line," *Broad Ax*, May 11, 1907, 1.

82. "Draws the Color Line," *Topeka State Journal*, September 12, 1908, 11.

83. "Color Line Plea Is a Life Saver," *Evening Times*, March 30, 1910, 3.

Chapter Eight

1. "Jack London Describes the Fight and Jack Johnson's Golden Smile," *San Francisco Call*, December 27, 1908, 34.

2. "None but Negroes to Fight Dusky Winner of the Title," *Detroit Times*, December 28, 1908, 2.

3. A potter's field, pauper's grave, or common grave is an American expression for a place for the burial of unknown or indigent people; as Sam McVey appears on the fighter's gravestone, then that is the way it will appear in the text.

4. "Jack Johnson Lauds Old Ring Foe, Sam McVey, and Saves Him From Potter's Field," *Bridgeport Times and Evening Farmer*, December 28, 1921, 4.

5. *Ibid.*

6. McVey would be measured as tall as six feet (1905) and had an amazing 77-inch reach.

7. On his draft card and passport application, McVey listed his date of birth as February 24, 1884.

8. Located about 60 miles west of downtown Los Angeles, it would eventually be part of the greater Los Angeles area.

9. "Boxer Russell Defeated," *San Francisco Call*, November 3, 1902, 6.

10. "May Prove a Champion," *Minneapolis Journal*, December 13, 1902, 14.

11. For a short period of time, Hank Griffin and his wife operated a training camp for boxers in Monrovia, California, just northeast of Los Angeles (about 24 miles outside of the heart of the city).

12. Carter, who was a whirlwind barroom brawler, enjoyed keeping the Black fighters in line.

13. "Sam M'Vey Aspires to Heavyweight Honors," *Washington Times*, August 29, 1903, 4.

14. "Sam M'Vey Aspires for Ring Honors," *Los Angeles Herald*, June 16, 1906, 5.

15. "Martin Is Knocked Out," *Los Angeles Herald*, January 26, 1906, 2.

16. Turner's first name was also spelled as Mat.

17. In London, McVey participated in a boxing carnival at the National Sporting Club before heading to France. In Australia and England, boxers typically fought with two-ounce gloves, while in America they wore five- or even seven-ounce gloves.

18. "Colored Fighters Barred," *Salt Lake Herald*, October 27, 1907, 9.

19. "Burns Draw Color Line for All But Johnson," *Detroit Times*, January 10, 1908, 9.

20. *Ibid.*

21. "France Home of Easy Money for Fighters," *Los Angeles Herald*, April 13, 1908, 8.

22. "Unmuzzled and Unchained Sam McVey Drives With Dukes," *Detroit Times*, May 6, 1908, 2. The career of Willie Lewis spanned from 1901 to 1915. In early 1910, Lewis made an unsuccessful bid at the world middleweight title, losing to Billy Papke. Popular in France, his jealousy of McVey often translated into racial slurs.

23. "McVey Gets Decision," *Times Dispatch*, February 21, 1909, 5.

24. The dollar experienced an average inflation rate of 3.08 percent per year during this period. In other words, $100 in 1909 is equivalent in purchasing power to $2,814 in 2019. The 1909 inflation rate was −1.09%. Source: Bureau of Labor Statistics' Consumer Price Index (CPI).

25. "Jeannette Beats Sam McVey in 50 Rounds," *San Francisco Call*, April 18, 1909, 38.

26. *Ibid.*

27. Sources such as *The Encyclopedia of Boxing* by Gilbert Odd and *An Illustrated History of Boxing* by Nat Fleischer offer an alternative perspective on the battle; for a detailed summary see: Colleen Aycock and Mark Scott's book, *The First Black Boxing Champions*, published by McFarland in 2011.

28. See Colleen Aycock and Mark Scott's *The First Black Boxing Champions*, for a round-by-round analysis.

29. "Wants Another Chance," *Washington Herald*, April 24, 1908, 8. Oxygen use had come to the forefront of boxing in 1908, thanks to Sir Leonard Hill (1862–1952), of London Hospital who believed in its use to shorten recovery time.

30. "Black Heavies Draw," *Daily Missoulian*, December 12, 1909, 11.

31. "Jeannette Returns," Washington *Evening Star*, December 24, 1909, 12.

32. Johnson's counter was picked up by the newspapers, including the *Washington Post*.

33. According to some accounts, the event attracted 25,000 fans. The police interfered in the second round and barred kidney punches in clinches. Billing a fight as a right to challenge a fighter didn't mean that contest would ever take place; consequently, promoters understood the marketing advantage it contained and used it wisely.

34. Some newspaper reports regarding a title exchange between the two pugilists may refer to this designation.

35. "Blackpugs Contenders," *Honolulu Star-Bulletin*, May 7, 1913, 9.

36. "Negro Boxers Dropping Fast from Rungs," *Bridgeport Evening Farmer*, October 17, 1913, 12.

37. His fourth-round knockout of Pelkey was decisive and his last bout ever in Australia. Battling Wills on his home turf of New Orleans wasn't going to be easy, yet McVey pulled out the victory. R.L. "Snowy" Baker purchased Sydney Stadium from Hugh McIntosh in 1913 for $155,000 and converted it into a corporation. McVey was never a big fan of referee turned promoter Baker, which was likely why he soured on Sydney.

38. A connected boxer rarely loses a decision in his hometown.

39. "Aftermath of Havana Fight," *Washington Herald*, April 9, 1915, 9.

40. *Ibid.*; Runyon believed Johnson was just being, well, himself. And that the fight was legitimate.

41. McVey's final battle with Langford was interesting because American Sporting Club manager Joe Levine inaugurated a "no satisfaction, no pay" policy for the club. Boxers who appeared in the main event would not be paid until the following day. Only if, of course, the patrons were properly entertained. Refund coupons were given to each ticket holder.

42. "Sable Sams Are Last Notable Survivors of Race of Fighters," *Tacoma Times*, December 22, 1915, 2; sources may vary with regard to age and fight frequency.

43. McVey also squeezed in a no-decision against pool fighter Jack Thompson in St. Louis.

44. Wills was awarded a knockout (KO5) on February 17, 1918 and June 16, 1918 (KO6); Wills was being touted as a successor to Johnson at this point.

45. Johnson would eventually claim he faked the finish of the battle in lieu of a $30,000 payment. The black & white photograph of Johnson horizontal on the canvas—arms flung over his head to block the sun—provided the proof. The claim was never substantiated.

46. "All Eyes Are Turned to Turbulent Mexico for Willard-Johnson Fight," *Washington Herald*, February 28, 1915, 4.

47. "To Draw Color Line," Harrisburg *Star-Independent*, April 7, 1915, 8.

48. Due to the obscurity of the World Colored Heavyweight Title, nobody was absolutely certain when it changed hands.

49. *Ibid.* This section dates to the various title reigns of Sam McVey, Joe Jeannette, and Sam Langford. The latter will be dealt with in detail at the conclusion of Chapter Ten.

50. "Colored Boxers Strong for Coin," *Evening Statesman*, March 29, 1910, 3.

51. "They Draw Color Line," Ogden *Evening Standard*, December 14, 1912, 2; the name of the periodical was not given.

52. *Ibid.*

Chapter Nine

1. "Six Hot Rounds in Philadelphia," *Washington Times*, July 7, 1905, 9.

2. "Notes of the Boxers," Washington *Evening Star*, January 5, 1906, 9; the Johnson fight referenced happened in Philadelphia on November 25, 1905. Jeannette picked up a second-round victory as a result of a foul. It was the third time the pair had met.

3. Some sources indicate an additional battle with Johnson on December 9, 1906.

4. Right, meaning marketable White talent that didn't draw the color line.

5. "Heavyweights Not Good for Athletic Club Stags," New York *Evening World*, January 9, 1906, 10; Having already met Jack Johnson at least nine times polished Jeannette's skills but not his record.

6. *Ibid.*

7. "Boxing Outlook on the Far Coast," Washington *Evening Star*, September 1, 1907, 3.

8. Forced to battle each other for a paycheck, Black pugilists grew familiar with a rival's strengths and weaknesses. This was particularly true of the relationship between Jack Johnson and Joe Jeannette. While Johnson never lost control of their battles, once Jeannette showed some polish, "The Galveston Giant" was smart enough to no longer enter a ring against him. Their final official battle, a three-round draw, took place on January 3, 1908; Jeannette fought twice on January 13, 1908, against Joe Phillips (KO3) and Griff Jones (KO3). Fighting Sam Langford twice in 1908, Jeannette drew him over 12 rounds (March

3, 1908), then lost a close, six-round newspaper decision.

9. Douglass, Fredrick "We Have Decided to Stay," speech to American Slavery Society, May 9, 1848. http://www.wfu.edul-zulick/340/Douglass1848.

10. Jeannette's manager also handled Willie Lewis, so the Brooklyn welter also made the journey back to France.

11. "Fight Goes 50 Rounds," Newport News *Daily Press*, April 18, 1909, 1.

12. "Fifty-Round Fight at Paris," *Salt Lake Herald*, April 18, 1909, 6.

13. "Frenchmen Kiss a Negro on Winning," *Ogden Standard*, May 14, 1909, 1.

14. Likely there were times when Jeannette and Sandy Ferguson, a White Canadian-born pugilist, had a mutual understanding regarding engagements; Kubiak was another large White contender hailing from Michigan.

15. "Tip Wright's Column," *Detroit Times*, May 4, 1909, 7.

16. *Ibid.*

17. Some sources quote the Kubiak encounter as a five-round affair.

18. Some of the quoted purse figures varied, and the number of rounds fought is often misquoted at 20.

19. "Langford Wins After 15 Rounds," *Norwich Bulletin*, September 7, 1910, 3.

20. "Langford Gives Joe Jeannette a Beating," Washington *Evening Star*, September 7, 1910, 12.

21. Jeannette was knocked down in rounds one, four, and ten; the newspaper decisions favored Langford.

22. "Colored Men of the Ring," Grand Forks *Evening Times*, February 2, 1911, 3.

23. Of course there were incidents when newspaper decisions, or popular opinion, painted a different picture of an outcome. For example, when Joe Jeannette met Jeff Clark in Pittsburgh on September 2, 1912, the six-round fight, which most believe was won by Clark, entered the books as a mandated no-decision.

24. Reports of the fight, which were a bit confusing, claimed Tate was from Tennessee, which may have been the case at one point as the fighter's journey during this period is not well documented.

25. "The Decline of the Black Man in the Pugilistic Work Is Noticeable," *El Paso Herald*, September 21, 1912, 4; Jeannette's battle against Jeff Clark was held on September 2, 1912 and ended in a six-round no-decision.

26. "No More Mixing of Color in the Prize Ring; Whites to Fight Whites," *El Paso Herald*, November 5, 1912, 10; The Arizona Republic stated that Jeannette fought 25 times in 1912 and compiled a record of 20–0–0, with 5 no-decisions. It was also claimed that Jeannette was not a full-blooded Negro. His mother was believed to be part–German, and his father part–Arab (*Bridgeport Farmer*, June 18, 1913, 11.)

27. A spin on a classic Friedrich Nietzsche quote.

28. "Sam Langford Is Beaten in Points," *Rock Island Argus*, October 4, 1913, 3.

29. There was no indication of a title exchange.

30. "To Battle for Colored Heavyweight Championship in Paris December 20," Grand Forks *Evening Times*, December 17, 1913, 8.

31. Later, Langford would also be stripped of the same title.

32. The fight would enter the record books as a victory for Jeannette (DQ7).

33. There was no mention of a title transfer in the bulk of the media coverage.

34. "Jeannette Retires, Saying 'Color Line of Willard Will Help Game,'" New York *Sun*, September 3, 1915, 8.

35. Newspaper reports, along with fight conditions, cast doubt on the validity of the battle as a title exchange; this was the first registered—although Tommy Ryan and Charlie Huck debated it—career knockout of Joe Jeannette.

36. "Dempsey Hides Behind Color Line," *Norwich Bulletin*, November 20, 1918, 3.

37. A historical marker was dedicated at the corner of Summit Avenue and 27th Street in Union City on April 17, 2009, where Jeannette's former residence and gym once stood. It was Union City's first historical marker.

38. Once Jack Johnson captured the Heavyweight Championship of the World, the World Colored Heavyweight Championship, which was not sanctioned by a governing body, disappeared from the lips of many. But Johnson's loss to Jess Willard created a mild interest in resurrecting the World Colored Heavyweight Championship.

39. Due to the obscurity of the World Colored Heavyweight Title, nobody was absolutely certain when it changed hands.

40. "Negro Sams, Mighty Battlers, Have Only Each Other to Fight," *El Paso Herald*, November 26, 1915, 10.

41. *Ibid.*

42. *Ibid.*

Chapter Ten

1. Many sources, including the International Boxing Hall of Fame, quote his date of birth as March 4, 1883, but his biographer, Clay Moyle, and Canadian records claim he was three years younger.

2. As the sixth of seven children, his life became complicated after his mother passed in 1898.

3. Langford was recognized on page 30, in "Sporting Notes," which appeared in *Savannah Morning News* on February 11, 1903. This could be his earliest professional mention in what appears to be a filler piece.

4. "Joe Gans Whipped," *Evening Star*, December 9, 1903, 9.

5. "Jack Blackburn Whips Joe Gans Conqueror," *Washington Times*, December 24, 1903, 4.

6. "He Outpointed Walcott," *Waterbury Evening Democrat*, September 6, 1904, 9; the referee's name was also spelled Kenney. According to numerous sources, Langford outpointed Walcott.

7. Outweighed by 20 pounds, the Boston lad could not make the scheduled 20 rounds.

8. For the year 1905, Langford compiled a record of 9-2-3, and two no-contests; his only other loss was to Larry Temple on July 4.

9. Sailor Burke, scheduled to meet Langford after his fight with Jeannette, was believed the first of his would-be opponents to draw the color line.

10. Langford's defeat of Larry Temple, on August 27, 1907, was billed as for the Colored Middleweight Title (158 pounds), and his victory over Young Peter Jackson, on November 12, 1907, can be viewed as a successful defense of that crown.

11. Flynn, who outweighed Langford by about 15 pounds, was knocked out at the 2:14 mark of the first round. Carried to his corner, he needed five minutes to be revived.

12. When Langford's summer challenge to Jack Johnson was not met, he claimed the World Colored Heavyweight title.

13. Sources varied on the purse size. The *Daily Missoulian* reported (May 23, 1909, 9) a purse of $7,500 and a side bet of $500; the National Sporting Club heavyweight title spanned from 1891 until 1929.

14. By 1909, many boxers, including Willie Lewis, Joe Jeannette, Sam McVey, and Sam Langford, were taking advantage of the boxing season over in London and Paris.

15. "Locate Langford and Expect Favorable Reply During Today," *Los Angeles Herald*, January 5, 1910, 12.

16. "Johnson Drew Gun on Sam Langford," *Morning Examiner*, January 30, 1910, 2.

17. As a reminder: Newspaper decisions were made by a consensus of sportswriters attending a bout after it had ended inconclusively with a no-decision. As rendering a decision was made illegal in some states, a newspaper decision settled boxing bets. The opinions were subjective. For example: the *Los Angeles Herald* gave this fight to Flynn, while the *Los Angeles Times* believed Langford was the victor.

18. "Badly Aimed Blow Flynn's Undoing," *Evening Times*, March 18, 1910, 3.

19. "Langford Off Six Rounds," *Daily Arizona Silver Belt*, April 28, 1910, 1.

20. Possession of the title, Langford hoped, might call out Johnson.

21. Most of the press coverage made no mention of the title, nor was it used in marketing the fight.

22. "Langford Wins After 15 Rounds," *Norwich Bulletin*, September 7, 1910, 3; Jeannette fought at 190 pounds, while Langford tipped at 185.

23. A bulk of fight coverage made no mention of a title transfer; Langford simply dominated Jeannette.

24. Some view this battle as a successful title defense; Hugh McIntosh had far too much financial risk at stake to call the battle anything more than a draw.

25. "Sam Langford and Sam McVea Will Fight at Sydney, Australia," *Nashville Globe*, December 22, 1911, 8.

26. "Who Falls Heir to Championship," *El Paso Herald*, December 23, 1911, 18.

27. The fight attendance was estimated at 18,000; sources believe the World Colored Heavyweight Championship was exchanged even if the fight was not billed as such.

28. "Paris Fans Do Not Want Bout," *Tacoma Times*, January 29, 1912, 2; *United Press Leased Wire* reported that spectators believed both McVey and Langford laid down cold in a recent performance and that the referee, Eugene Corri, should have disqualified both fighters.

29. In-fighting was prohibited after the second round.

30. "Pertinent Comment on Happenings in Sportdum," Washington *Evening Star*, December 27, 1912, 14.

31. Standing six feet, four inches and tipping at 200 pounds, McCarty was a knockout artist who could deliver speedy combinations at a moment's notice.

32. "McCarty to Draw Line on Negroes," *Rock Island Argus*, January 3, 1913, 3.

33. "Luther McCarthy Acting Wisely in Declining to Challenge Johnson," *Washington Times*, January 8, 1913, 10; Note the spelling error.

34. Langford, who pocketed $10,000 for the engagement, needed only 30 seconds to deliver the knockout punch to Johnson. The only title mentioned in a majority of ring coverage was Johnson's South African heavyweight crown.

35. "Hagen, Newest White Hope, Loses Chance with Smith, New York *Evening World,* November 20, 1913, 16; Smith, in his next ring encounter, captured the White Heavyweight Championship of the World.

36. "Slattery's Spikes," *San Francisco Call*, November 19, 1913, 6.

37. In the pair's believed tenth meeting, Langford, who tipped at 185¾, took the decision easily over Jeannette, who weighed 188¼ pounds. The pairing was criticized for being "habitual." This was claimed to be for the French Boxing Federation's World Heavyweight Title that had been stripped from Jack Johnson. There was no mention of any other title in a majority of newspaper coverage.

38. Most press accounts did not acknowledge a title exchange, nor were they required to do so. Some dailies were so racist that they wouldn't acknowledge a Black fight, yet alone a title.

39. There was even an unconfirmed report of an actual belt exchange between the fighters. In Clay Moyle's *Sam Langford: Boxing's Greatest Uncrowned Champion*, on page 278, the author notes the World Colored Heavyweight Championship belt having been pawned by Langford.

40. "Langford Knocks Out Harry Wills," *Ogden Standard*, November 27, 1914, 2.

41. *Ibid.*

42. Most sources, including the International Boxing Hall of Fame, state this frequency range.

43. Sam Langford claimed at the beginning of the year that he had drawn the color line against Black fighters, calling them "tough as pig iron." This was according to an article published by *Richmond Palladium and Sun-Telegram*, January 2, 1915, 6.

44. "Joe Jeannette Trounces Langford," *Bridgeport Evening Farmer*, April 14, 1915, 8. On the same date, it was announced that Sam Langford had been reinstated at Philadelphia boxing clubs. He had been banished for four years.

45. "Sam McVey Defeats Langford in Twelve," *Washington Times*, June 30, 1915, 15.

46. "There's a Reason for These Stunts," *Rogue River Courier*, October 5, 1915, 3.

47. "Wills Wins Decision Over Langford Last Night in 20 Rounds," *Honolulu Star-Bulletin*, January 4, 1916, 10.

48. This was true even if Joe Jeannette likely still held the title.

49. "Pertinent Comment on Happenings in Sportdom," Washington *Evening Star*, January 13, 1916, 21.

50. "In the Prize Ring," *Daily Gate City*, February 17, 1916, 6; Langford tipped at 193 pounds, McVey at 212.

51. Langford biographer Clay Moyle notes that this bout took place in Syracuse, as does BoxRec.com, while other sources believe it may have taken place in Rochester. The author concurs with the former.

52. The Tate fight, held in Syracuse, New York, and the Devere bout, held in Montreal, were extremely close.

53. Perhaps Langford let his mind get sidetracked, as it was learned that he soon would open the Belmont Cafe at 3035 S. South State Street in Chicago. Langford always enjoyed Chicago, and the thought of making his home in the "Windy City" had crossed his mind on numerous occasions.

54. "Tham Langford Is Getting Old," *El Paso Herald*, June 9, 1917, 14.

55. Following his two fights with Harry Wills in Panama City, Panama, in 1918, Langford wouldn't leave the United States again until October 1921, when he met "Young" Peter Jackson in Toronto. In October 1922, he headed to Mexico for a pair of fights, and it proved to be a rebirth of sorts. Langford returned to Mexico in March 1923 and stayed there until the fall. During that time he picked up the Heavyweight Championship of Mexico and defended it numerous times before losing it to Clem Johnson on July 27, 1923.

56. "Shadows of the Past," Washington *Evening Star*, July 25, 1932, B-8.

57. *Ibid.*

58. Due to the obscurity of the World Colored Heavyweight Title, nobody was absolutely certain when it changed hands.

Chapter Eleven

1. Some sources differ regarding his date of birth.

2. The *El Paso Herald* noted his loss (ND 10) to Jeff Clarke in their June 27, 1913 issue, on page 13. The newspaper also noted his draw with Joe Jean-

nette on July 2, 1913, on page 10. Wills was a member of Joe Goldman's stable of fighters.

3. Newspaper accounts varied, with many seeing both battles as draws. The bout with Langford drew a $14,000 house.

4. "Langford and Wills Form Good Card," *El Paso Herald*, October 14, 1914, 7. This was just another example of the everpresent racism and subjectivity of the sport.

5. "Sam Langford Wins Battle," *Harrisburg Telegraph*, November 26, 1914, 13.

6. "McVey Too Much for Harry Wills," *Rock Island Argus*, December 21, 1914, 10.

7. "Harry Wills, Giant, Colored, Who Is Now the Sensation in Heavyweight Circles," *Evening Journal*, December 9, 1915, 11.

8. Not surprisingly, following this ring display Sam Langford was deluged with fight offers from aspiring White heavyweights—better late than never.

9. "Harry Wills Wins Decision Over Langford," *Evening World*, January 4, 1916, 16; The headline in the *Tacoma Times* read, "Wills Is Colored Champ," the first such headline in a long time recognizing the World Colored Heavyweight Champion. Referee Tommy Burns apologized to Langford for having to give the decision to Wills. That's how good the New Orleans fighter had become.

10. This was how one source put it, even though four knockdowns seldom equates to such.

11. Wills also grabbed two quick victories over Pittsburgh heavy George "Kid" Cotton and two easy victories over Jack Thompson. Some sources also claim a newspaper decision over Bill Tate; Harry Wills' fiancée, Miss Edna Jones, despondent over her current situation, committed suicide in 1916.

12. Some sources fail to note Wills' victory over Rough House Ware at the Clermont Sporting Club. Wills dropped Ware three times to a nine count.

13. From Wednesday, February 7, 1917, to but not including Monday, April 30, 1917.

14. The Langford engagement, with its "cream-puff blows," according to the *Pittsburgh Post*, appeared more like an exhibition.

15. During this period, the validity of a Wills versus Langford confrontation was always questioned; the status of the injury suffered by Wills must also be taken into consideration when evaluating the legitimacy of some of these events. Did Langford pull punches?

16. "Sport Snap Shots," *Richmond Palladium and Sun-Telegram*, November 5, 1917, 5.

17. Because ring records are incomplete, this bout has eluded some sources; Wills faced only Black opponents in 1917 and 1918.

18. Wills went 5–0–1 over the year—only his battle with McVey came into question.

19. Harry Wills finished out the year with a TKO of Jack Clark and two no-decision battles against Jack Thompson. Wills fought to a record of 4–0–0, with two no-decisions, in 1918; hey, Dempsey ink sold newspapers.

20. "Harry Wills Worthy Successor to Johnson," *Norwich Bulletin*, June 20, 1918, 3.

21. "Wills Issues Defi," *Washington Times*, September 12, 1918, 18.

22. "Negro Boxer Between Jack and the Title," *El Paso Herald*, October 1, 1918, 9.

23. *Ibid.*

24. "Harry Wills Takes Negro Heavy Title from Sam Langford," *News Scimitar*, November 6, 1919, 16. The review ran in other dailies including the *El Paso Herald* and the *Topeka State Journal.*

25. "Stalling Charged," *Butte Daily Bulletin*, January 2, 1920, 3.

26. Also on the card, and under the Mullins umbrella, was middleweight champion Mike O'Dowd.

27. "Harry Wills Frightens Bennett in 1st Round," *Bridgeport Times and Evening Farmer*, June 2, 1920, 4; results of the fight varied, however it is fair to say it was a no-contest.

28. "Fred Fulton Will Fight Harry Wills," *Washington Herald*, June 25, 1920, 10.

29. This was due to the club's inability to secure a suitable arena and properly define the new state boxing law.

30. "Dempsey Now Willing to Fight Negroes in Ring," *News Scimitar,* July 19, 1920, 9.

31. "Color Line Still Stands for Champ," *Washington Times*, July 25, 1920, 20.

32. A short right to the solar plexus, which broke three of Fulton's ribs, set up the finishing blow.

33. "Harry Wills Is Hunting Dempsey," *Seattle Star*, September 30, 1920, 12.

34. "Boxing Experiences Banner Year; Grid Teams Clash," *El Paso Herald*, January 1–2, 1921, 12; Wills is mentioned in a nearby article, on the same page, but only in reference to Fred Fulton.

35. That Thomas S. Andrews is in the International Boxing Hall of Fame, and individuals such as Tom McCarey and James F. Dougherty—to name only a few—are not, speaks to the hypocrisy of those involved with the selection process.

36. "No Color Line Dodge for Georges Carpentier," *Bridgeport Times and Evening Farmer*, March 24, 1921, 10.

37. Worth noting: Wills believed Carpentier didn't have a chance against Dempsey.

38. "No Color Line for Dempsey, Says Manager," *New York Tribune*, July 9, 1921, 9.

39. "Gunboat Smith Lasts 1 Minute," *Bisbee Daily Review*, October 11, 1921, 6.

40. Kearns knew the fight game inside and out, and he also knew which palms to grease.

41. "Heavyweight Champion Shows Wares He Used in Beating Frenchman," *Great Falls Tribune*, November 8, 1921, 8.

42. The World Colored Heavyweight title was not mentioned.

43. "Wills and Tate Ready for Big Fistic Mille," *Omaha Daily Bee*, January 2, 1922, 7.

44. "Negro Heavy Title in Dispute After Wills-Tate Draw," *Great Falls Tribune*, January 8, 1922, 8. By the end of January, New York columnist Robert Edgren was playing down demand for a Dempsey v. Wills match.

45. "Wills Pointed for Title Bout with Dempsey," Salem, Oregon *Capital Journal*, March 3, 1922, 10.

46. In a sign that both fighters, and New York City residents, felt economically sound: Harry Wills bought a four-story King model dwelling at 245 West 139th Street (Harlem), and Kid Norfolk bought a three-story dwelling at 191 Edgecombe Avenue (Harlem). The fighters residing only blocks apart; "Pugilist Buys Home," *New York Herald*, May 26, 1922, 24.

47. "Wills Manager Figure-head, Says Walsh," *Cordova Daily Times*, February 3, 1923, 7. The Dempsey v. Wills pairing came close a number of times—New York, Montreal, and Jersey City—but just could not overcome all the obstacles.

48. "Wills Offered $300,000 for Two Fights by Tex," Washington *Evening Star*, January 13, 1924, 59 (Part 4).

49. Firpo scaled at 224½ pounds, while Wills tipped at 217; Wills picked up a flat sum of $100,000 for the fight.

50. "Panther Tames Wild Bull in Battle for Supremacy Among Ring's Junglemen," *Evening Star*, September 12, 1924, 29. Bored, or so he claimed, Dempsey left in the eighth round.

51. "Tex Still Looking for Dempsey Rival," *Evening Star*, September 13, 1924, 9.

52. "Dempsey Plans to Fight Soon; May Meet Gibbons," *Evening Star*, January 5, 1925, 22.

53. Ironically, Jack Kearns was also at the pier when Wills set sail; consequently, he was likely the last person in the world Wills wanted to see.

54. "Wills Well Beaten Before Fouling," *Evening Star*, October 13, 1926, 35. The New York State licensing committee demanded that Dempsey fight Wills, so Rickard countered by moving the fight (Dempsey v. Tunney) to Philadelphia.

55. "Wills' Alibi of Illness Falling on Deaf Ears," *Evening Star*, October 19, 1926, 40; Wills felt he was on his game around 1921 and had fallen off by 1926. Let the speculation continue with regard to a winner.

56. Due to the obscurity of the World Colored Heavyweight Title, nobody was absolutely certain when it changed hands.

Chapter Twelve

1. This date appeared on his 1916 passport.

2. Some elements of Tate's early life were compiled by Nat Fleischer, Editor and Publisher of *The Ring*, the World's Leading Boxing Magazine.

3. "Jeannette Knocks Out Two Negro Opponents," *El Paso Herald*, August 21, 1912, 10.

4. "Tate Defeats Carlton," *Washington Herald*, November 29, 1912, 10.

5. "Many Bouts Staged in New York Rings," *Salt Lake Tribune*, December 9, 1912, 6.

6. Bill Tate likely participated in some bootleg and as yet undiscovered battles during this period.

7. "Langford Beats Tate," *Lake County Times*, May 2, 1917, 8.

8. "Smith Wins Over Tate," New York *Evening World*, August 11, 1917, 6.

9. "Jack Dempsey Is New One on Trail of Jess," *El Paso Herald*, January 21, 1918, 10.

10. "Jack Thompson Wins from Tate," Philadelphia *Evening Public Ledger*, April 30, 1918, 16.

11. The fight, as anticipated, entered record books as a ND6. Tate was handed a newspaper defeat.

12. Keep in mind that Tate's unofficial, not to mention unimpressive, record at this point in his career is believed to be 16–16–2.

13. Sources vary with regard to a fighter's measurements.

14. This is based on an informal survey of sports sections published during this period.

15. "The Sporting Spotlight," *News Scimitar*, March 12, 1920, 16; Tate would never battle Johnson inside a ring.

16. "Jack Dempsey Drops Miske in Third Round, Retaining World's Heavyweight Title," *Arizona Republican*, September 7, 1920, 1.

17. "Johnson, Federal Prisoner, Claims 'Colored Title,'" *Washington Herald*, December 26, 1920, 6.

18. "No Chance for Wills to Get Dempsey Bout," *Evening Star*, January 28, 1921, 28.

19. "Tate Gets Decision Over Kearns," *New York Herald*, February 4, 1921, 13.

20. "Wills Puts Out Tate," *Evening Star*, July 3, 1921, 16.

21. "Tate Wins on Foul in First Round of Match with Wills," *Bisbee Daily Review*, January 3, 1922, 3.

22. "Tate Beats Wills in Shady Bout," *Seattle Star*, January 3, 1922, 10.

23. "Frenchman Will Stay Abroad Where He Runs less Risk," *Evening World*, January 10, 1922, 22.

24. "Negro Heavyweights Will Finish Match," *Richmond Palladium and Sun-Telegram,* January 4, 1922, 11.

25. "Wills Held to Draw, but Retains His Title," *Washington Times*, January 7, 1922, 12.

26. The fight was a continuation and no admission was charged; a forfeit of $1,000 was posted against fouls in the second battle.

27. "Play Dempsey to Drop Wills Tate's Advice," *Washington Times,* January 15, 1922, 45; on April 5, Dempsey stated his willingness to meet Tate provided any promoter would offer acceptable terms.

28. Jack Dempsey, with Barbara Piattelli Dempsey, *Dempsey*. New York: Harper & Row, 1977, 150.

29. "Evening World Readers Write More on Color line," *Evening World*, December 6, 1918, 22. The names of the boxing fans commenting to the sporting editor of the newspaper were Eddie Reilly, Maurice Notkin, and H.H.M.

Chapter Thirteen

1. Williams' WWI Draft Registration Card indicated a date of birth as February 27, 1896, however his WWII Draft Card for Young Men indicated a date of birth as January 25, 1897. In an interview with the *New Britain Herald* Williams (Godfrey) claimed his date of birth as January 25, 1901.

2. Returning to Alabama, he spent his school years there.

3. With a majority of the fighting taking place on land in Europe, World War I (1914–1918) witnessed the balance shift in favor of the Allies (Britain and its dominions, France, Russia, and others) upon the United States' entrance in 1917.

4. Depending upon when you happened to catch up with Williams, some of the early facts surrounding his youth could vary.

5. Eddie Bransback was behind the promotion. The *News Scimitar*, on November 16, 1920, page 17, stated, "Whether or not he is taking a chance in Langford, one of the most clever and crafty mitt artists the game has produced, and Godfrey, who has never been known to do more than was required of him, remains to be seen."

6. "Dusky Heavyweights Fail to Flourish as Formerly," *Washington Times*, September 25, 1921, 23.

7. Dougherty bought out Godfrey's contract for $1,000. It was also reported that Godfrey worked as a sparring partner for Johnson but was simply too aggressive for the role. Another variation has Doc Kearns involved as well.

8. Godfrey left Chicago with the intent to make his home in the Philadelphia area.

9. "Money-Grabbing Policies Ruining the Fight Game," *Evening Star*, February 2, 1923, 30. Godfrey was also working in New York as a sparring partner for the promising Iowa heavyweight, Floyd Johnson.

10. Dougherty refereed fights in which Jack Dempsey (v. Levinsky, v. Miske), Joe Gans, George Dixon, Joe Goddard, Tim Callahan, and Harry Forbes were all principals. The talented manager also wrestled as a kid.

11. "Leonard Seems Afraid of New York Referees," *Evening Star*, March 4, 1923, 2; Kearns, who many thought managed Godfrey, often told Wills that Godfrey was the man he must defeat first before getting a shot at the heavyweight title.

12. Godfrey's battle—or performance, as some believed—against Tate was on the undercard of Jack Renault v. Floyd Johnson. Godfrey's impressive performance, at Billy Grupp's Gym in Harlem, was in front of Madison Square Garden matchmaker Leo P. Flynn, consequently appearing at the venue's matches.

13. In Nat Fleischer's book, *Black Dynamite, Volume V*, he claimed Flynn told Godfrey that the Ku Klux Klan had threatened the life of the fighter should he defeat Renault. This type of racist communication, or competitive fight strategy, was not uncommon to Colored fighters; Godfrey was defeating Owens before he committed a foul.

14. Godfrey, along with Dempsey's brother Johnny and Jack Burke, departed for Great Falls, Montana, on May 16.

15. Godfrey's battle with Renault was slow and marked by considerable clinching—it was a close fight. Godfrey was disqualified in the second round for hitting the floored veteran, Tom Cowler.

16. Speaking of biting, Dougherty's entire stable of fighters was bitten by a suspension in the fall, though the penalty had nothing to do with Godfrey.

17. In January, promoter Tex Rickard ranked Godfrey the eighth-best heavyweight.

18. "Negro's Home Attacked," *Evening Star*, October 10, 1925, 15.

19. If the title was vacated, as some sources stated, Godfrey was more than happy to claim it. Godfrey would never do battle with Wills, though he beat Tate twice (1920 and 1923).

20. Godfrey was also assisting in the creation of some boxing screenplays, including One Round Hogan; he would also act sporadically until 1937.

21. "Joe Anderson Is Touted as Middleweight Comer," Washington *Evening Star*, January 12, 1927, 29.

22. "Sharkey to Fight Only in New York," *Evening Star*, July 16, 1927, 24.

23. "Munn's Ring Hopes Jolted by Godfrey," *Evening Star*, September 15, 1927, 52.

24. "Kayoes Maloney," *New Britain Herald*, August 16, 1927, 12.

25. "Early September Bout Is Tex's Hope," *Evening Star*, December 30, 1927, 15.

26. The National Boxing Association ranked him the seventh-leading heavyweight on November 7, 1929. Ahead of him were: Otto Van Porat (6), Ernie Schaff (5), Max Schmeling (4), Tommy Loughran (3), and Jack Sharkey (2). The heavyweight championship was open.

27. "Demise of Boxing Seen as Hastened by Fouls," *Evening Star*, June 24, 1930, C-2, 28.

28. It was no secret that Godfrey made concessions, such as carrying opponents or fouling out, in order to meet quality fighters. His fight against Johnny Risko, on June 27, 1928, has often been cited as an example.

29. On December 19, 1930, Godfrey drew "Bearcat" Wright in a bout claimed to be for the Black American Heavyweight Title.

30. A majority of Godfrey's opponents had losing records, if any bouts at all.

31. It was pointed out that Godfrey liked the ladies but hated training, wasn't a drinker or gambler, and was generous to a fault. He delighted in the friendship he attained and wasn't hesitant to exhibit his generosity. Picking up large restaurant checks or paying for expensive theater tickets never bothered Godfrey. He also gave generously to the church. "The Baron" always noted that his friend was honest and good-natured.

32. Due to the obscurity of the World Colored Heavyweight Title, nobody was absolutely certain when it changed hands.

33. "Sport News," *Worcester Democrat and The Ledger-Enterprise*, April 17, 1926, 3.

34. "Tunney Hopes to Defend Title Twice Next Year," *New Britain Herald*, October 18, 1927, 14.

35. Staying in Florida: In July of 1935, while George Godfrey was in Belgium, Rubin Stacy (Reuben Stacey) was accused of attacking Marion Jones, a White woman in Ft. Lauderdale, Florida. A White mob, which many claim included the local sheriff, lynched Stacy. A photograph of the hanging was so disturbing that the NAACP used it in a campaign to call for anti-lynching legislation.

Chapter Fourteen

1. Gains would often state he was born in 1900.
2. "Chilean Wins Fight," Washington *Evening Star*, September 6, 1923, 30.
3. "Gains Whips Mahieu," *Evening Star*, December 6, 1923, 30.
4. Anastasie would conclude his relationship with Gains in 1924; Gains had other managers including: Otto Weichardt (1924–26), Herb Bee (1926), Dan Rogers (1926–29), and Harry Levine (1932–1939).
5. The fighter's European records are incomplete.
6. Schmeling, who was believed to have had fewer than 20 professional bouts, was given a standing count while using the ropes for support.
7. Gains dropped the Dixie Kid five times, while impressing everyone with his ring generalship. Dropping Gorman in the final round solidified his decision.
8. Stabenau was dropped twice (first and second rounds) before regaining his composure and dropping Gains four times in the fourth. However, Gains managed to take the decision.
9. "Gains Ring Title," *Evening Star*, March 1, 1927, 43; Jones was dropped twice in the third round and five times in the fifth before the fight was stopped. Gains would later defend the title against two extremely popular Canadian heavyweights, Jack Renault and Charlie Belanger.
10. This fight was rescheduled. The pair met in Toronto on November 11, 1927, and fought to a draw.
11. Gains made his Madison Square Garden debut on July 28, 1927. Unfortunately, he lost the ten-round decision to Martin Burke, a tough light heavyweight from New Orleans. Gains would defeat Burke in a rematch, in Toronto, on August 19, 1927.
12. A couple of periodicals, including the *Globe*, noted the dents in Gains' aluminum protection cup.
13. The *Indianapolis News, Indianapolis Star*, and Associated Press all believed Gains was the victor.
14. "After Sharkey and Schmeling—What?" *Sunday Star*, June 8, 1930, 10; The European record for Larry Gains is incomplete. For example, on March 10, "he decisively defeated Charlie Smith of Deptford." This information appeared in the *Richmond Planet* on April 5, 1930, 5.
15. His European record is believed incomplete.
16. That the fight was conducted surprised some, as the colored bar was still in place and wouldn't be formally lifted until the following year.
17. Gains' trainer and chief second, Jack Goodwin, collapsed in his fighter's corner and died at the end of the 13th round.
18. Taking nothing against the superb ring skills of Harvey, Gains was viewed as being out of condition.
19. His only loss came via a (Leicester, UK) rematch against South African heavy Ben Foord.
20. Gains tried without success—he took a 13th-round technical knockout loss—to vindicate his defeat of five years ago to Len Harvey, and he took a fifth-round loss, by way of technical knockout, to Tommy Farr.
21. "Would Not Draw Color Line in Olympic Games," *Evening Star*, April 8, 1923, 71.
22. "Wills Now in Line to Fight Champion," *Evening Star*, July 6, 1923, 21.

Chapter Fifteen

1. "Most Anything," *Tacoma Times*, September 19, 1911, 4.
2. By 1933, Walker would claim to have appeared in over 90 ring battles—bootleg battles, especially among Colored fighters, were as common as Georgia peaches.
3. Lew Burston managed Tarante and worked out of the Gaiety Theater building in New York. He also picked up the management of Obie Walker. Burston had a close relationship with Dickson, as the promoter fed him fighters like farmers feed chickens, or at least it felt that way.
4. This included Hans Schoenrath, a former German champion.
5. The Nuremberg Laws were enacted by the Reichstag on September 15, 1935.
6. The other fight stoppage of Braddock's career was a TKO due to a cut.

Chapter Sixteen

1. Naturally, such a surprising ending led to speculation. Gould was a friend of Owney Madden, the gangster who controlled Primo Carnera.
2. Mike Jacobs, the dominant boxing promoter of the 1930s and 1940s, controlled nearly all of New York City's boxing venues, including Madison Square Garden. He leased the venue under his banner of the Twentieth Century Sporting Club before signing an exclusive agreement.
3. Some sources claim a smaller amount.
4. The economics behind the Heavyweight Championship were astounding. In the end, Braddock, with a record of 51–25–7, received 50 percent of the receipts. Louis, with a record of 31–1–0, 17.5 percent. A crowd of only 55,000 attended the fight, well under estimates. The gross receipts were $715,400 (including $75,000 for radio and motion picture rights). After all the appropriate deductions, Braddock pocketed $262,000 and Louis about $110,000. The average wage per year was $1,780. By the way, Jacobs still had Schmeling under contract for one more fight.
5. Aware that NYSAC would never allow the fight to take place in New York, Jacobs turned to Chicago.
6. Roxborough and Black moved Louis and company from the Brewster Recreation Center in Detroit to Chicago's Trafton Gym this same year.
7. Roxborough, like many, witnessed the failures of Johnson and was hell-bent not to allow his fighter to take the same path. Blackburn, who knew the ropes as a gifted Black fighter, at first wanted no part in training a Black boxer, that is until he saw Louis. He still initially demanded a salary before agreeing to take a percentage.

8. Victories over Primo Carnera (June 25, 1935), King Levinsky (August 7, 1935), Max Baer (September 24, 1935), and Paulino Uzcudun (December 13, 1935), thrust Louis into the forefront of the heavyweight division. In preparation for Braddock, Louis worked with many fighters, including Cecil "Seal" Harris. In 1935, Mike Jacobs first saw Joe Louis in the ring during a February rematch against Lee Ramage.

9. Louis won NBA, NYSAC, *The Ring*, and lineal heavyweight titles.

10. The attendance at the event was 70,043. Net receipts were $803,113. Louis' share was $349,228, while Schmeling pocketed $175,622. The Nazis shunned Max Schmeling after his defeat by Joe Louis. The fighter was drafted, served in the *Luftwaffe,* and was trained as a paratrooper. Schmeling was wounded at the Battle of Crete. He did not consider himself a Nazi and never joined the Nazi Party. He detested their philosophy and actions.

Bibliography

Books

Aycock, Colleen, and Mark Scott. *The First Black Boxing Champions.* Jefferson, NC: McFarland, 2011.

Aycock, Colleen, with David W. Wallace. *The Magnificent Max Baer.* Jefferson, NC: McFarland, 2018.

Baker, Carlos, ed. *Ernest Hemingway: Selected Letters, 1917–1961.* New York: Charles Scribner's Sons, 1981.

Baker, Mark Allen. *Battling Nelson: The Durable Dane.* Jefferson, NC: McFarland, 2016.

_____. *Title Town USA: Boxing in Upstate New York.* Charleston: The History Press, 2010.

_____. *The Fighting Times of Abe Attell.* Jefferson, NC: McFarland, 2017.

Callis, Tracy, Chuck Hasson, and Mike Delisa. *Images of Sports: Philadelphia's Boxing Heritage 1876–1976.* Charleston, SC: Arcadia, 2002.

Calogero, Bill. *Tom Molineaux: From Bondage to Baddest Man on the Planet.* Sacramento, CA: JC Publications, 2015.

Carpentier, Georges. *Carpentier by Himself.* Translated by Edward Fitzgerald. London: Hutchinson, 1955.

Cavanaugh, Jack. *Tunney, Boxing's Brainiest Champ and His Upset of the Great Jack Dempsey.* New York: Ballantine, 2006.

Dempsey, Jack, with Barbara Piattelli Dempsey. *Dempsey.* New York: Harper & Row, 1977.

Du Bois, W.E.B. *The Souls of Black Folk.* New York: New American Library, 1903.

Egan, Pierce. *Boxiana.* Boston: Adamant Media, 2006.

Fleischer, Nat. *Black Dynamite: Story of the Negro in Boxing.* New York: Nat Fleischer, 1938.

_____. *50 Years at Ringside.* New York: Greenwood Press, 1969.

Fox, Richard K. *The Black Champions of the Prize Ring from Molineaux to Jackson.* New York: R.K. Fox, 1890.

Fraser, George MacDonald. *Black Ajax.* New York: Carroll & Graf, 1998.

Freedman, Lew. *Joe Louis: The Life of a Heavyweight.* Jefferson, NC: McFarland, 2013.

Goldman, Herbert G., ed. *Boxing: A Worldwide Record of Bouts and Boxers.* Jefferson, NC: McFarland, 2012.

_____. *The Ring Record Book and Boxing Encyclopedia.* New York: The Ring Publishing, 1985.

Hughes, Langston. *The Big Sea.* New York: Hill and Wang, 1993.

Kahn, Roger. *A Flame of Pure Fire: Jack Dempsey and the Roaring '20s.* New York: Harcourt, Brace, 1999.

Moore, Louis. *I Fight for a Living.* Urbana: University of Illinois Press, 2017.

Moyle, Clay. *Sam Langford: Boxing's Greatest Uncrowned Champion.* Seattle: Bennett & Hastings, 2006.

Pagano, Richard. *The Baron of Leiperville: The Life and Times of James F. Dougherty.* Aston, PA: Choice Marketing, 2014.

Roberts, Randy. *Jack Dempsey: The Manassa Mauler.* Chicago: University of Illinois Press, 2003.

Smith, Kevin R. *Black Genesis: The History of the Black Prizefighter 1760–1870.* Lincoln, NE: iUniverse, 2003.

Van Every, Edward. *Muldoon, the Solid Man of Sports.* New York: Frederick A. Stoles, 1928.

Ward, Geoffrey C. *Unforgivable Blackness: The Rise and Fall of Jack Johnson.* London: Yellow Jersey Press, 2015.

Williams, Luke. *Richmond Unchained: The Biography of the World's First Black Sporting Superstar.* Stroud, Gloucestershire: Amberley Publishing, 2015.

Archival Sources

Ernest Hemingway Collection at the John F. Kennedy Presidential Library and Museum: Boston, Massachusetts

Jim Crow Museum of Racist Memorabilia, Ferris State University, Big Rapids, Michigan

The Library of Congress

Articles

Buckner, Robert. "Who Is Obie Walker?" *Esquire,* August 1, 1935: 34–35, 170.

Internet Sites

badlefthook.com
boxing.com
boxrec.com
britannica.com
cyberboxingzone.com

espn.com
findagrave.com
ha.com
history.com
ibhof.com
imdb.com
josportsinc.com
mountvernon.org
PBS.org
thenegroinsports.blogspot.com
wikipedia.org
wikitree.com
youtube.com

Legal Documents

The White-Slave Traffic Act of 1910 (the "Mann Act"), 36 Stat. 825, codified as amended at 18 U.S.C. §§ 2421–2424.

Magazines

Boxing Monthly
Boxing News
Esquire
KO Magazine
Police Gazette
The Ring
Sporting News
Sports Illustrated
Weekly Boxing World

Newspapers

Albuquerque Daily Citizen
Appeal (St. Paul, Minnesota)
Arizona Republican (Phoenix)
Bisbee Daily Review
Bridgeport (Times and) Evening Farmer (Bridgeport, Connecticut)
Broad Ax (Salt Lake City)
Buffalo Courier
Butte Daily Bulletin
Butte Inter Mountain
Caldwell Tribune (Caldwell, Idaho)
Capital Journal (Salem, Oregon)
Chicago Tribune
Comet (Johnson City, Tennessee)
Copper Country Evening News (Calumet, Michigan)
Cordova Daily Times (Cordova, Alaska)
Daily Arizona Silver Belt (Globe, Arizona)
Daily Gate City and Constitution-Democrat (Keokuk, Iowa)
Daily Missoulian
Daily Morning Journal and Courier (New Haven, Connecticut)
Daily Press (Newport News, Virginia)
Daily Republican (Wilmington, Delaware)
Daily Telegram (Clarksburg, West Virginia)
Detroit Times
Devils Lake Weekly World (Devils Lake, North Dakota)
Duluth Evening Herald

East Oregonian (Pendleton)
El Paso Herald
Evening Bulletin (Honolulu)
Evening Public Ledger (Philadelphia)
Evening Standard (Ogden City, Utah)
Evening Star (Washington, D.C.)
Evening Statesman (Walla Walla, Washington)
Evening Times (Grand Forks, North Dakota)
Evening World (New York)
Fairmount West Virginian
Fort Worth Gazette
Globe & Mail (Toronto)
Great Falls Tribune
Harrisburg Telegraph (Harrisburg, Pennsylvania)
Helena Independent (Helena, Montana)
Herald (Los Angeles)
Honolulu Star-Bulletin
Independent (Elizabeth City, North Carolina)
Indianapolis Journal
Indianapolis News
Indianapolis Star
Irish Central (Dublin)
Irish Times (Dublin)
Jones County News (Ellisville, Mississippi)
Kansas City Journal
Lake County Times (Hammond, Indiana)
Lancaster Daily Intelligencer (Lancaster, Pennsylvania)
Los Angeles Herald
Minneapolis Journal
Montgomery Advertiser
Morning Appeal (Carson City, Nevada)
Morning Examiner (Ogden, Utah)
Morning Tulsa (Daily) World (Tulsa, Oklahoma)
Nashville Globe
New York Herald
New York Times
New York Tribune
News Scimitar (Memphis, Tennessee)
Norwich Bulletin (Norwich, Connecticut)
Ocala Evening Star (Ocala, Florida)
Ogden Standard (Ogden City, Utah)
Omaha Daily Bee
Pacific Commercial Advertiser (Honolulu, Hawaii)
Philipsburg Mail (Phillipsburg, Montana)
Record-Union (Sacramento, California)
Richmond Palladium and Sun-Telegram
Richmond Planet
Rock Island Argus (Rock Island, Illinois)
Rogue River Courier (Grants Pass, Oregon)
Sacramento Daily-Record Union
St. Louis Republic
Saint Paul (Daily) Globe
Salem Daily News (Salem, Ohio)
Salt Lake Herald
Salt Lake Tribune
San Diego Tribune
San Francisco Call
Santa Fe New Mexican
Scranton Tribune
Seattle Post-Intelligencer
Seattle Star
South Bend News-Times
Spokane Press

Star-Independent (Harrisburg, Pennsylvania)
Statesman (Denver, Colorado)
Sun (New York)
Tacoma Times
Times (Washington, D.C.)
Times Dispatch (Richmond, Virginia)
Topeka State Journal
Toronto Star
United Opinion (Bradford, Vermont)
Vineyard Gazette (Edgartown, Massachusetts)
Washington Bee
Washington Herald
Washington Post
Washington Times
Watauga Democrat (Boone, North Carolina)
Waterbury (Evening) Democrat (Waterbury, Connecticut)
Watertown Republican (Watertown, Wisconsin)
Wheeling Daily Intelligencer (Wheeling, West Virginia)
Wheeling Register (Wheeling, West Virginia)
Wilmington Daily Republican (Wilmington, Delaware)
Yorkshire Post and Leeds Intelligencer

Research and Press Organizations

Associated Press
Bureau of Labor Statistics' Consumer Price Index (CPI)
The Gilder Lehrman Institute of American History
International Boxing Hall of Fame
International Boxing Research Organization (IBRO)
The Smithsonian Institution
United States Census Bureau
United Press
University of Mary Washington
Virginia Historical Society

Index

Numbers in **bold italics** indicate pages with illustrations